W9-ALZ-685

FAVORITE BRAND NAME

Slow Cooker Casseroles & *More*

pil

Publications International, Ltd.

Favorite Brand Name Recipes at www.fbnr.com

Louis Weber, CEO
Publications International, Ltd.
7373 North Cicero Avenue
Lincolnwood, IL 60712

Some of the products listed in this publication may be in limited distribution.

Pictured on the front cover *(clockwise from top left):* Green Chile Chicken Enchilada *(page 90),* Turkey Vegetable Crescent Pie *(page 328),* Hearty One-Pot Chicken Stew *(page 246),* Broccoli and Beef Pasta *(page 20),* Barbara's Pork Chop Dinner *(page 36)* and Fiesta Black Bean Soup *(page 206).*

Pictured on the back cover *(top to bottom):* Jamaican Pork Skillet *(page 62),* 3-Cheese Chicken & Noodles *(page 94)* and Italian-Style Chicken and Rice *(page 89).*

ISBN: 0-7853-7742-5

Library of Congress Control Number: 2002100166

Manufactured in China.

8 7 6 5 4 3 2 1

Microwave Cooking: Microwave ovens vary in wattage. Use the cooking times as guidelines and check for doneness before adding more time.

Preparation/Cooking Times: Preparation times are based on the approximate amount of time required to assemble the recipe before cooking, baking, chilling or serving. These times include preparation steps such as measuring, chopping and mixing. The fact that some preparations and cooking can be done simultaneously is taken into account. Preparation of optional ingredients and serving suggestions is not included.

Slow Cooker, Casseroles, and One-Dish Meals

247

The Basics

Slow Cooker Basics

Slow cookers were introduced in the 1970's and found a renewed popularity in the mid 1990's that continues into the new century. Considering the hectic pace of today's lifestyles, it's no wonder so many people have rediscovered this time-saving kitchen helper. Spend a few minutes preparing the ingredients, turn on the slow cooker and relax. Low heat and long cooking times take the stress out of meal preparation. Leave for work or a day of leisure and come home four, eight or even ten hours later to a hot, delicious meal.

There are two types of slow cookers. The most common models have heat coils circling the crockery inset, allowing heat to surround the food and cook evenly. Two settings, LOW (about 200°F and HIGH (about 300°F regulate cooking temperatures. One hour on HIGH equals 2 to 2-1/2 hours on LOW. Less common models have heat coils on the bottom and have adjustable thermostats. If you own this type, consult your manufacturer's instructions for advice on converting the recipes in this publication.

The Benefits

- No need for constant attention or frequent stirring
- No worry about burning or overcooking
- No sink full of pots and pans to scrub at the end of a long day
- Great for parties and buffets
- Your kitchen stays cool because you don't turn on the oven
- Saves energy—cooking on the low setting uses less energy than most light bulbs

Tips and Techniques

Filling the Slow Cooker: Manufacturers recommend that slow cookers should be one-half to three-quarters full for best results.

Keep a Lid On It: A slow cooker can take as long as twenty minutes to regain heat lost when the cover is removed. If the recipe calls for stirring or checking the dish near the end of the cooking time, replace the cover as quickly as you can. Otherwise, resist the urge to remove the cover.

Cleaning Your Slow Cooker: To clean your slow cooker, follow the manufacturer's instructions. To make cleanup even easier, spray with nonstick cooking spray before adding food.

Tasting: Always taste the finished dish before serving to adjust seasonings to your preference. Consider adding a dash of the following: salt, freshly ground pepper, seasoned salt, seasoned herb blends, lemon juice, soy sauce, Worcestershire sauce, flavored vinegar or minced herbs.

Adapting Recipes: If you'd like to adapt your own favorite recipe to a slow cooker, you'll need to follow a few guidelines. First, try to find a similar slow cooker recipe in this publication or the manufacturer's guide. Note the cooking times, amount of liquid, and quantity and size of meat and vegetable pieces. Because the slow cooker captures moisture, you will want to reduce the amount of liquid, often by as much as half. Add dairy products toward the end of the cooking time so they do not curdle.

Follow this chart to estimate the cooking time you will need:

COOKING GUIDELINES		
Conventional Recipe	**Cook on Low**	**Cook on High**
30 to 45 minutes	6 to 10 hours	3 to 4 hours
50 minutes to 3 hours	8 to 15 hours	4 to 6 hours

Selecting the Right Meat: A good tip to keep in mind is that you can, and in fact should, use tougher, inexpensive cuts of meat. Top-quality cuts, such as loin chops or filet mignon, fall apart during long cooking periods and therefore are not good choices to use in the slow cooker. Keep those cuts for roasting, broiling or grilling, and save money when you use your slow cooker. You will

be amazed to find even the toughest cuts come out fork-tender and flavorful.

Reducing the Fat: The slow cooker can help you make lower-fat meals because you won't be cooking in fat as you do when you sauté and stir-fry. And tougher, inexpensive cuts of meat have less fat than prime cuts. Many recipes call for trimming excess fat from meat.

If you do use fatty cuts of meat, such as ribs, consider browning them first on top of the range to cook off excess fat before adding them to the slow cooker.

Chicken skin tends to shrivel and curl in the slow cooker, so most recipes call for skinless chicken. If you use skin-on pieces, brown them before adding them to the slow cooker.

You can also remove most of the fat from accumulated juices and soups. The simplest way is to refrigerate the liquid for several hours or overnight. The fat will float to the top and congeal for easy removal. If you plan to serve the liquid right away, ladle it into a bowl or measuring cup. Let it stand about 5 minutes so the fat can rise to the surface. Skim with a large spoon. You can also lightly pull a sheet of clean paper towel over the surface, letting it absorb the fat.

Cutting Your Vegetables: Vegetables often take longer to cook than meats. Cut vegetables into small, thin pieces and place them near the bottom or sides of the slow cooker. Pay careful attention to the recipe instructions in order to cut vegetables to the proper size so they will cook in the amount of time given.

Food Safety Tips: If you do any advance preparation, such as trimming meat or cutting vegetables, make sure to cover and refrigerate the food until you are ready to start cooking. Store uncooked meats and vegetables separately. If you are preparing meat, poultry or fish, remember to wash your cutting board, utensils and hands with hot, soapy water before touching other food.

Once the food is cooked, don't keep it in the slow cooker too long. Foods need to be kept cooler than 40°F or hotter than 140°F to avoid growth of harmful bacteria. Remove food to a clean container, cover and refrigerate as soon as possible. For large amounts of leftovers, it is best to divide them into several containers so they will cool faster. Do not reheat leftovers in the slow cooker. Use a microwave oven, the range top or the oven for reheating.

Foil to the Rescue: To easily lift a dish or a meatloaf out of the slow cooker, make foil handles according to the following directions.

Tear off three 18×3-inch strips of heavy-duty foil. Crisscross strips so they resemble the spokes of a wheel. Place the dish or food in the center of the strips.

Pull foil strips up and over and place them into the slow cooker. Leave them in while you cook so you can easily lift them out again when finished cooking.

By following these simple slow-cooker tips and techniques, you will soon be preparing some of the wonderful slow cooker recipes in this cookbook with the minimum of effort.

Casserole Basics

Casserole cookware comes in a variety of shapes, sizes and materials that fall into two general descriptions. They can be either deep, round containers with handles and tight-fitting lids or square and rectangular baking dishes. Casseroles are made of glass, ceramic or metal. When making a casserole, it's important to bake the casserole in the proper size dish so that the ingredients cook evenly in the time specified.

Size Unknown?

If the size of the casserole or baking dish isn't marked on the bottom of the dish, it can be measured to determine the size.

- Round and oval casseroles are generally measured by volume, not inches, and are listed by quart capacity. Fill a measuring cup with water and pour it into the empty casserole. Repeat until the casserole is filled with water, keeping track of the amount of water added. The amount of water is equivalent to the size of the dish.
- Square and rectangular baking dishes are usually measured in inches. If the dimensions are not marked on the bottom of a baking dish, use a ruler to measure on top from inside of one edge to the inside of the opposite edge. Repeat to determine the other dimension.

Prime-Time Beef

Beef and Vegetables in Rich Burgundy Sauce

Slow Cooker

- **1 package (8 ounces) sliced mushrooms**
- **1 package (8 ounces) baby carrots**
- **1 medium green bell pepper, cut into thin strips**
- **1 boneless chuck roast (2½ pounds)**
- **1 can (10½ ounces) golden mushroom soup**
- **¼ cup dry red wine or beef broth**
- **1 tablespoon Worcestershire sauce**
- **1 package (1 ounce) dried onion soup mix**
- **¼ teaspoon black pepper**
- **2 tablespoons water**
- **3 tablespoons cornstarch**
- **4 cups hot cooked noodles**
- **Chopped fresh parsley (optional)**

Slow Cooker Directions

1. Place mushrooms, carrots and bell pepper in slow cooker. Place roast on top of vegetables. Combine soup, wine, Worcestershire sauce, soup mix and black pepper in medium bowl; mix well. Pour soup mixture over roast. Cover and cook on LOW 8 to 10 hours.

2. Blend water into cornstarch in cup until smooth; set aside. Transfer roast to cutting board; cover with foil. Let stand 10 to 15 minutes before slicing.

3. Turn slow cooker to HIGH. Stir cornstarch mixture into vegetable mixture; cover and cook 10 minutes or until thickened. Serve over cooked noodles. Garnish with parsley, if desired. *Makes 6 to 8 servings*

Artichoke Casserole

- **¾ pound extra-lean (90% lean) ground beef**
- **½ cup sliced mushrooms**
- **¼ cup chopped onion**
- **1 clove garlic, minced**
- **1 can (14 ounces) artichoke hearts, drained, rinsed and chopped**
- **½ cup dry bread crumbs**
- **¼ cup (1 ounce) grated Parmesan cheese**
- **2 tablespoons chopped fresh rosemary *or* 1 teaspoon dried rosemary**
- **1½ teaspoons chopped fresh marjoram *or* ½ teaspoon dried marjoram**
- **Salt and black pepper**
- **3 egg whites**

Preheat oven to 400°F. Spray 1-quart casserole with nonstick cooking spray.

Brown ground beef in medium skillet. Drain off fat. Add mushrooms, onion and garlic; cook until tender.

Combine ground beef mixture, artichokes, bread crumbs, cheese, rosemary and marjoram; mix lightly. Season with salt and pepper to taste.

Beat egg whites until stiff peaks form; fold into ground beef mixture. Spoon into prepared casserole.

Bake 20 minutes or until lightly browned around edges.

Makes 4 servings

Beef and Vegetables in Rich Burgundy Sauce

Patchwork Casserole

- 2 pounds ground beef
- 2 cups chopped green bell peppers
- 1 cup chopped onion
- 2 pounds frozen Southern-style hash-brown potatoes, thawed
- 2 cans (8 ounces each) tomato sauce
- 1 cup water
- 1 can (6 ounces) tomato paste
- 1 teaspoon salt
- ½ teaspoon dried basil
- ¼ teaspoon black pepper
- 1 pound pasteurized process American cheese, thinly sliced

Preheat oven to 350°F.

Brown beef in large skillet over medium heat about 10 minutes; drain off fat.

Add bell peppers and onion; cook and stir until tender, about 4 minutes. Stir in potatoes, tomato sauce, water, tomato paste, salt, basil and black pepper.

Spoon half of mixture into 13×9×2-inch baking pan or 3-quart baking dish; top with half of cheese. Spoon remaining meat mixture evenly on top of cheese. Cover pan with foil. Bake 45 minutes.

Cut remaining cheese into decorative shapes; place on top of casserole. Let stand loosely covered until cheese melts, about 5 minutes.

Makes 8 to 10 servings

Baked Beef and Rice Marinara

- 1 pound lean ground beef
- ¾ cup sliced fresh mushrooms
- ½ cup chopped onion
- ½ cup chopped celery
- ½ cup diced green bell pepper
- 2 cups cooked rice
- 1 can (15 ounces) tomato sauce
- ¾ teaspoon ground oregano
- ½ teaspoon salt
- ½ teaspoon dried basil leaves
- ½ teaspoon garlic powder
- 3 slices American cheese

Microwave Directions

Combine crumbled beef and vegetables in plastic colander; place colander over 2-quart microwave-safe baking dish. Cook, uncovered, on HIGH (100% power) 4 minutes; stir after 2 minutes. Drain beef mixture; return mixture to baking dish. Stir in remaining ingredients except cheese. Cook on HIGH 2 minutes. Arrange cheese slices on top; cook on HIGH 2 minutes. Let stand 5 minutes.

Makes 4 servings

Conventional Oven Directions: Cook beef and vegetables over medium-high heat in large skillet until meat is no longer pink and vegetables are crisp-tender, stirring frequently; drain. Combine meat mixture with remaining ingredients except cheese in buttered 2-quart baking dish; arrange cheese slices on top. Bake at 350°F 20 to 25 minutes.

Favorite recipe from **USA Rice Federation**

Taco Pie

- 1 pound ground beef
- ½ cup chopped onion
- 1 teaspoon dried cilantro leaves
- ½ teaspoon salt
- ½ teaspoon ground cumin
- ½ teaspoon black pepper
- 1 can (4 ounces) chopped green chilies, drained
- 1 fresh jalapeño pepper,* minced
- 1 can (14½ ounces) FRANK'S® or SNOWFLOSS® Original Style Diced Tomatoes, drained slightly
- 1 can (15½ ounces) red kidney beans, rinsed and drained
- 1¼ cups milk
- 1 package (8½ ounces) corn bread mix
- 3 eggs
- 1 cup shredded Cheddar cheese
- Tortilla chips, any style
- Sour cream
- Shredded lettuce

**Jalapeño peppers can sting and irritate the skin; wear rubber gloves when handling peppers and do not touch eyes.*

1. Preheat oven to 400°F. Brown ground beef and onion. Drain grease. Stir in seasonings.

2. Spread meat mixture in well-greased shallow 10-inch baking dish.

3. Spread chilies, jalapeño pepper, diced tomatoes and kidney beans over meat.

4. Beat milk, corn bread mix and eggs 1 minute with mixer. Pour over ingredients in baking dish.

5. Bake 30 minutes. Top with cheese and bake 10 minutes. Serve with tortilla chips, sour cream and lettuce.

Makes 4 servings

Prep Time: 15 minutes
Cook Time: 40 minutes

Helpful Hints

Frozen hash-brown potatoes are the fuss-free way to add potatoes to a dish. Southern-style hash-brown potatoes are diced rather than shredded.

Patchwork Casserole

Beefy Tostada Pies

2 teaspoons olive oil
1½ cups chopped onions
2 pounds ground beef
1 teaspoon salt
1 teaspoon chili powder
1 teaspoon ground cumin
2 cloves garlic, minced
1 can (15 ounces) tomato sauce
1 cup sliced black olives
8 flour tortillas
4 cups shredded Cheddar cheese
Sour cream, salsa and chopped green onion (optional)

Slow Cooker Directions

Heat oil in large skillet over medium heat. Add onions and cook until tender. Add ground beef, salt, chili powder, cumin and garlic; cook until browned. Stir in tomato sauce; heat through. Stir in black olives.

Make foil handles using three 18×2-inch strips of heavy foil. Crisscross foil to form spoke design. Place in slow cooker. Lay one tortilla on foil strips. Spread with some of meat sauce and cheese. Top with another tortilla, meat sauce and cheese. Repeat layers with remaining tortillas, meat sauce and cheese, ending with cheese. Cover and cook on HIGH 1½ hours. To serve, lift out of slow cooker using foil handles and transfer to serving platter. Discard foil. Cut into wedges. Serve with sour cream, salsa and chopped green onion, if desired. *Makes 4 to 5 servings*

Main-Dish Pie

1 package (8 rolls) refrigerated crescent rolls
1 pound lean ground beef
1 medium onion, chopped
1 can (12 ounces) beef or mushroom gravy
1 box (10 ounces) BIRDS EYE® frozen Green Peas, thawed
½ cup shredded Swiss cheese
6 slices tomato

• Preheat oven to 350°F.

• Unroll dough and separate rolls. Spread to cover bottom of ungreased 9-inch pie pan. Press together to form lower crust. Bake 10 minutes.

• Meanwhile, in large skillet, brown beef and onion; drain excess fat.

• Stir in gravy and peas; cook until heated through.

• Pour mixture into partially baked crust. Sprinkle with cheese.

• Bake 10 to 15 minutes or until crust is brown and cheese is melted.

• Arrange tomato slices over pie; bake 2 minutes more.

Makes 6 servings

Prep Time: 10 minutes
Cook Time: 20 to 25 minutes

Chili Cornbread Casserole

1 pound ground beef
1 medium onion, chopped
1 jar (16 ounces) RAGÚ® Cheese Creations!® Double Cheddar Sauce
1 can (19 ounces) red kidney beans, rinsed and drained
1 can (8¾ ounces) whole kernel corn, drained
2 to 3 teaspoons chili powder
1 package (12 ounces) cornbread mix

1. Preheat oven to 400°F. In 12-inch skillet, brown ground beef and onion over medium-high heat; drain. Stir in Ragú Cheese Creations! Sauce, beans, corn and chili powder.

2. Meanwhile, prepare cornbread mix according to package directions. *Do not bake.*

3. In ungreased 2-quart baking dish, spread ground beef mixture. Top with cornbread mixture. Bake uncovered 20 minutes or until toothpick inserted in center of cornbread comes out clean and top is golden.

Makes 6 servings

Prep Time: 10 minutes
Cook Time: 20 minutes

Corned Beef and Cabbage

1 head cabbage (1½ pounds), cut into 6 wedges
4 ounces baby carrots
1 corned beef (3-pounds) with seasoning packet*
⅓ cup prepared mustard (optional)
⅓ cup honey (optional)

**If seasoning packet is not perforated, poke several small holes with tip of paring knife.*

Slow Cooker Directions

1. Place cabbage in slow cooker; top with carrots.

2. Place seasoning packet on top of vegetables. Place corned beef fat side up over seasoning packet and vegetables. Add 1 quart water. Cover and cook on LOW 10 hours.

3. Discard seasoning packet. Just before serving, combine mustard and honey in small bowl. Use as dipping sauce, if desired.

Makes 6 servings

Main-Dish Pie

Texas Ranch Chili Beans

1 pound lean ground beef
1 can (28 ounces) whole peeled tomatoes, undrained
2 cans (15½ ounces each) chili beans
1 cup chopped onions
1 cup water
1 package (1 ounce) HIDDEN VALLEY® Milk Recipe Original Ranch® salad dressing mix
1 teaspoon chili powder
1 bay leaf

In Dutch oven, brown beef over medium-high heat; drain off fat. Add tomatoes, breaking up with spoon. Stir in beans, onions, water, salad dressing mix, chili powder and bay leaf. Bring to boil; reduce heat and simmer, uncovered, 1 hour, stirring occasionally. Remove bay leaf just before serving.

Makes 8 servings

Beef with Cabbage and Carrots

¾ pound extra-lean (90% lean) ground beef
4 cups shredded cabbage
1½ cups shredded carrot (1 large carrot)
½ teaspoon caraway seeds
2 tablespoons seasoned rice vinegar
Salt and black pepper

Brown ground beef in large skillet. Drain. Reduce heat to low. Stir in cabbage, carrot and caraway seeds; cover. Cook 10 minutes or until vegetables are tender, stirring occasionally. Stir in vinegar. (Add 1 tablespoon water for extra moistness, if desired.) Season with salt and pepper to taste.

Makes 4 servings

Variation: Substitute 1 teaspoon sugar and 1 tablespoon white wine vinegar for 2 tablespoons seasoned rice vinegar.

Western Wagon Wheels

1 pound lean ground beef or ground turkey
2 cups wagon wheel pasta, uncooked
1 can (14½ ounces) stewed tomatoes
1½ cups water
1 box (10 ounces) BIRDS EYE® frozen Sweet Corn
½ cup barbecue sauce
Salt and pepper to taste

• In large skillet, cook beef over medium heat 5 minutes or until well browned.

• Stir in pasta, tomatoes, water, corn and barbecue sauce; bring to a boil.

• Reduce heat to low; cover and simmer 15 to 20 minutes or until pasta is tender, stirring occasionally. Season with salt and pepper.

Makes 4 servings

Serving Suggestion: Serve with corn bread or corn muffins.

Prep Time: 5 minutes
Cook Time: 25 minutes

Quick Beef Stroganoff

1 pound ground beef
1 package LIPTON® Noodles & Sauce—Butter
2¼ cups water
1 jar (4½ ounces) sliced mushrooms, drained
2 tablespoons finely chopped pimiento
⅛ teaspoon garlic powder
½ cup sour cream

In 10-inch skillet, brown ground beef; drain. Stir in remaining ingredients except sour cream. Bring to a boil, then simmer, stirring frequently, 7 minutes or until noodles are tender. Stir in sour cream; heat through but do not boil.

Makes about 2 servings

Skillet Spaghetti and Sausage

¼ pound mild or hot Italian sausage links, sliced
½ pound ground beef
¼ teaspoon dried oregano, crushed
4 ounces spaghetti, broken in half
1 can (14½ ounces) DEL MONTE® Diced Tomatoes with Basil, Garlic & Oregano
1 can (8 ounces) DEL MONTE® Tomato Sauce
1½ cups sliced fresh mushrooms
2 stalks celery, sliced

1. Brown sausage in large skillet over medium-high heat. Add beef and oregano; season to taste with salt and pepper, if desired.

2. Cook, stirring occasionally, until beef is browned; drain.

3. Add pasta, 1 cup water, undrained tomatoes, tomato sauce, mushrooms and celery. Bring to boil, stirring occasionally.

4. Reduce heat; cover and simmer 12 to 14 minutes or until spaghetti is tender. Garnish with grated Parmesan cheese and chopped parsley, if desired. Serve immediately.

Makes 4 to 6 servings

Prep Time: 5 minutes
Cook Time: 30 minutes

Classic Beef & Noodles

- **2 tablespoons oil**
- **2 pounds beef stew meat, trimmed and cut into cubes**
- **¼ pound mushrooms, sliced into halves**
- **2 tablespoons chopped onion**
- **2 cloves garlic, minced**
- **1 teaspoon salt**
- **1 teaspoon dried oregano leaves**
- **½ teaspoon black pepper**
- **¼ teaspoon dried marjoram leaves**
- **1 bay leaf**
- **1½ cups beef broth**
- **⅓ cup dry sherry**
- **1 (8-ounce) container sour cream**
- **½ cup all-purpose flour**
- **¼ cup water**
- **4 cups hot cooked noodles**

Slow Cooker Directions

Heat oil in large skillet. Brown beef on all sides. (Work in batches, if necessary.) Drain and discard fat.

Combine beef, mushrooms, onion, garlic, salt, oregano, pepper, marjoram and bay leaf in slow cooker. Pour in beef broth and sherry. Cover and cook on LOW 8 to 10 hours or on HIGH 4 to 5 hours. Remove and discard bay leaf.

If cooking on LOW, turn to HIGH. Stir together sour cream, flour and water in small bowl. Stir about 1 cup liquid from slow cooker into sour cream mixture. Stir mixture back into slow cooker. Cover and cook on HIGH 30 minutes or until thickened and bubbly. Serve over noodles.

Makes 8 servings

Sloppy Joes

- **1 pound lean ground beef**
- **½ cup chopped onion**
- **⅓ cup chopped green pepper**
- **1 bottle (12 ounces) HEINZ® Chili Sauce**
- **¼ cup water**
- **1 to 2 tablespoons brown sugar**
- **1 tablespoon HEINZ® Worcestershire Sauce**
- **¼ teaspoon salt**
- **⅛ teaspoon pepper**
- **Sandwich buns**

In large saucepan, cook beef, onion and green pepper until green pepper is tender; drain, if necessary. Stir in chili sauce, water, sugar, Worcestershire sauce, salt and pepper; simmer 10 minutes, stirring occasionally. Serve in sandwich buns.

Makes 6 to 8 servings

Classic Beef & Noodles

Beef Stroganoff Casserole

- 1 pound lean ground beef
- ¼ teaspoon salt
- ⅛ teaspoon black pepper
- 1 teaspoon vegetable oil
- 8 ounces sliced mushrooms
- 1 large onion, chopped
- 3 cloves garlic, minced
- ¼ cup dry white wine
- 1 can (10¾ ounces) condensed cream of mushroom soup, undiluted
- ½ cup sour cream
- 1 tablespoon Dijon mustard
- 4 cups cooked egg noodles
- Chopped fresh parsley (optional)

Preheat oven to 350°F. Spray 13×9-inch baking dish with nonstick cooking spray.

Place beef in large skillet; season with salt and pepper. Brown beef over medium-high heat until no longer pink, stirring to separate beef. Drain fat from skillet; set beef aside.

Heat oil in same skillet over medium-high heat until hot. Add mushrooms, onion and garlic; cook and stir 2 minutes or until onion is tender. Add wine. Reduce heat to medium-low and simmer 3 minutes. Remove from heat; stir in soup, sour cream and mustard until well combined. Return beef to skillet.

Place noodles in prepared dish. Pour beef mixture over noodles; stir until noodles are well coated.

Bake, uncovered, 30 minutes or until heated through. Sprinkle with parsley, if desired. *Makes 6 servings*

Corny Sloppy Joes

- 1 pound lean ground beef or ground turkey
- 1 small onion, chopped
- 1 can (15½ ounces) sloppy joe sauce
- 1 box (10 ounces) BIRDS EYE® frozen Sweet Corn
- 6 hamburger buns

• In large skillet, cook beef and onion over high heat until beef is well browned.

• Stir in sloppy joe sauce and corn; reduce heat to low and simmer 5 minutes or until heated through.

• Serve mixture in hamburger buns. *Makes 6 servings*

Serving Suggestion: Sprinkle with shredded Cheddar cheese.

Prep Time: 5 minutes
Cook Time: 15 minutes

French-American Walnut Rice

- ½ pound lean ground beef or ground turkey
- 1 box (10 ounces) BIRDS EYE® frozen White and Wild Rice
- 1½ teaspoons soy sauce
- ½ cup California walnuts

• In large skillet, cook beef over medium-high heat 5 minutes or until well browned.

• Stir in rice; cook 5 minutes more or until rice is tender, stirring occasionally.

• Stir in soy sauce and California walnuts; cook 1 minute or until heated. *Makes 4 servings*

Prep Time: 5 minutes
Cook Time: 10 to 12 minutes

Curry Beef

- 1 pound lean ground beef
- ½ cup beef broth
- 1 medium onion, thinly sliced
- 1 tablespoon curry powder
- 1 teaspoon ground cumin
- 2 cloves garlic, minced
- 1 cup (8 ounces) sour cream
- ¼ cup reduced-fat (2%) milk
- ½ cup raisins, divided
- 1 teaspoon sugar
- 12 ounces wide egg noodles *or* 1⅓ cups long-grain white rice
- ¼ cup chopped walnuts, almonds or pecans

Slow Cooker Directions

Heat large skillet over high heat. Add beef and cook until browned; pour off fat.

Add beef broth, onion, curry powder, cumin, garlic and cooked beef to slow cooker. Cover and cook on LOW 4 hours. Stir in sour cream, milk, ¼ cup raisins and sugar. Cover and cook 30 minutes or until thickened and heated through.

Cook noodles according to package directions; drain. Spoon beef curry over noodles. Sprinkle with remaining ¼ cup raisins and walnuts. *Makes 4 servings*

Serving Suggestion: Serve with sliced cucumber sprinkled with sugar and vinegar or plain yogurt topped with brown sugar, chopped bananas and green onions.

Beef Stroganoff Casserole

Biscuit-Topped Hearty Steak Pie

1½ pounds top round steak, cooked and cut into 1-inch cubes
1 package (9 ounces) frozen baby carrots
1 package (9 ounces) frozen peas and pearl onions
1 large baking potato, cooked and cut into ½-inch pieces
1 jar (18 ounces) home-style brown gravy
½ teaspoon dried thyme leaves
½ teaspoon black pepper
1 can (10 ounces) flaky buttermilk biscuits

Preheat oven to 375°F. Spray 2-quart casserole with nonstick cooking spray.

Combine steak, frozen vegetables and potato in prepared dish. Stir in gravy, thyme and pepper.

Bake, uncovered, 40 minutes. Remove from oven. *Increase oven temperature to 400°F.* Top with biscuits and bake 8 to 10 minutes or until biscuits are golden brown. *Makes 6 servings*

Hint: This casserole can be prepared with leftovers of almost any kind. Other steaks, roast beef, stew meat, pork, lamb or chicken can be substituted for round steak; adjust gravy flavor to complement meat. Red potatoes can be used in place of baking potato. Choose your favorite vegetable combination, such as broccoli, cauliflower and carrots or broccoli, corn and red peppers, as a substitute for the peas and carrots.

Chili Tamale Pie

1 pound ground beef
1 large onion, chopped
1 clove garlic, minced *or* ¼ teaspoon garlic powder
1 can (14½ ounces) stewed tomatoes, undrained
¼ cup *Frank's® RedHot®* Cayenne Pepper Sauce
2 tablespoons *plus* 1 teaspoon chili powder, divided
1 package (8½ ounces) corn muffin mix plus ingredients to prepare
1 green onion, thinly sliced

1. Preheat oven to 400°F. Cook beef, onion and garlic in large oven-safe* skillet 5 minutes or until meat is browned, stirring to separate meat. Drain fat. Stir in tomatoes, ***Frank's RedHot*** and 2 tablespoons chili powder. Heat to boiling. Reduce heat to medium-low. Cook 5 minutes, stirring occasionally.

2. Prepare corn muffin mix according to package directions. Stir in green onion and remaining *1 teaspoon* chili powder. Spoon batter over meat mixture, spreading evenly to edges. Bake 15 minutes or until toothpick inserted in corn bread comes out clean. Garnish with avocados, cheese or olives, if desired. Serve with a crisp green salad.
Makes 6 servings

*If handle of skillet is not oven-safe, wrap it with foil.

Prep Time: 10 minutes
Cook Time: 25 minutes

Glazed Corned Beef

1½ cups water
1 medium onion, sliced
3 strips fresh orange peel
2 whole cloves
3 to 4 pounds corned beef (round or rump cut)
Additonal whole cloves (optional)
Glaze (recipe follows)

Slow Cooker Directions
Combine water, onion, orange peel and 2 cloves in slow cooker. Add corned beef, fat side up, to slow cooker. Cover and cook on LOW 7 to 9 hours or until fork tender.

Remove corned beef from slow cooker. Score top of corned beef; insert additional cloves to decorate, if desired.

About 30 minutes before serving, place corned beef in ovenproof pan. Preheat oven to 375°F. Prepare Glaze; spoon over corned beef. Bake 20 to 30 minutes, basting occasionally with Glaze. *Makes 8 to 10 servings*

Glaze

3 tablespoons honey
2 tablespoons frozen orange juice concentrate, thawed
2 teaspoons prepared mustard

Combine all ingredients in large bowl.

Helpful Hints

Corned beef is usually beef brisket, round or rump that has been cured in a seasoned brine. The curing process preserves beef and imparts a distinctive flavor.

Biscuit-Topped Hearty Steak Pie

Broccoli and Beef Pasta

- **2 cups broccoli florets *or* 1 package (10 ounces) frozen broccoli, thawed**
- **1 onion, thinly sliced**
- **½ teaspoon dried basil leaves**
- **½ teaspoon dried oregano leaves**
- **½ teaspoon dried thyme leaves**
- **1 can (14½ ounces) Italian-style diced tomatoes, undrained**
- **¾ cup beef broth**
- **1 pound lean ground beef**
- **2 cloves garlic, minced**
- **2 tablespoons tomato paste**
- **2 cups cooked rotini pasta**
- **3 ounces shredded Cheddar cheese or grated Parmesan cheese**

Slow Cooker Directions
Layer broccoli, onion, basil, oregano, thyme, tomatoes and beef broth in slow cooker. Cover and cook on LOW 2½ hours.

Combine beef and garlic in large nonstick skillet; cook over high heat 6 to 8 minutes or until meat is no longer pink, breaking meat apart with wooden spoon. Pour off drippings. Add beef mixture to slow cooker. Cover and cook 2 hours.

Stir in tomato paste. Add pasta and cheese. Cover and cook 30 minutes or until cheese melts and mixture is heated through.

Makes 4 servings

Serving Suggestion: Serve with garlic bread.

Joe's Special

- **1 pound lean ground beef**
- **2 cups sliced mushrooms**
- **1 small onion, chopped**
- **2 teaspoons Worcestershire sauce**
- **1 teaspoon dried oregano leaves**
- **1 teaspoon ground nutmeg**
- **½ teaspoon garlic powder**
- **½ teaspoon salt**
- **1 package (10 ounces) frozen chopped spinach, thawed**
- **4 large eggs, lightly beaten**
- **⅓ cup grated Parmesan cheese**

1. Spray large skillet with nonstick cooking spray. Add ground beef, mushrooms and onion; cook over medium-high heat 6 to 8 minutes or until onion is tender, breaking beef apart with wooden spoon. Add Worcestershire, oregano, nutmeg, garlic powder and salt. Cook until meat is no longer pink.

2. Drain spinach (do not squeeze dry); stir into meat mixture. Push mixture to one side of pan. Reduce heat to medium. Pour eggs into other side of pan; cook, without stirring, 1 to 2 minutes or until set on bottom. Lift eggs to allow uncooked portion to flow underneath. Repeat until softly set. Gently stir into meat mixture and heat through. Stir in cheese.

Makes 4 to 6 servings

Serving Suggestion: Serve with salsa and toast.

Prep and Cook Time: 20 minutes

Reuben Casserole

- **1 cup FRANK'S® or SNOWFLOSS® Kraut, drained**
- **½ cup chopped onion**
- **2 tablespoons butter**
- **1 apple, peeled and chopped**
- **½ teaspoon caraway seeds**
- **1 cup cubed cooked corned beef**
- **¼ cup Thousand Island dressing**
- **1 cup cubed Swiss cheese**
- **2 slices rye bread, toasted and cubed**
- **2 tablespoons melted butter**
- **1 small jar red pimiento**
- **1 green bell pepper, sliced**

1. Preheat oven to 400°F. Sauté onion in 2 tablespoons butter until soft.

2. Add apple and sauté until soft.

3. Add caraway seeds, kraut and corned beef; sauté 1 minute to blend flavors. Place mixture in medium casserole dish.

4. Drizzle kraut mixture with Thousand Island dressing, top with Swiss cheese and toasted bread cubes.

5. Pour remaining 2 tablespoons melted butter over top, dot with pimiento and decorate with bell pepper.

6. Bake at 400°F for 20 minutes.

Makes 4 servings

Prep Time: 15 minutes
Bake Time: 20 minutes

Helpful Hints

To reduce the amount of fat in slow cooker recipes, choose leaner cuts of meat and remove the skin from poultry before cooking. Excess fat may be skimmed off the surface of food just before serving.

Broccoli and Beef Pasta

Western Skillet Noodles

- ½ pound ground beef
- 2 teaspoons chili powder
- 2⅓ cups water
- 1 can (11 ounces) whole kernel corn with sweet peppers, drained
- 1 tablespoon margarine or butter
- 1 package LIPTON® Noodles & Sauce—Beef Flavor
- ½ cup shredded Cheddar cheese (about 2 ounces), divided

Brown ground beef with chili powder in 12-inch nonstick skillet over medium-high heat; drain. Remove and set aside.

Add water, corn and margarine and bring to a boil. Stir in Noodles & Sauce—Beef Flavor and continue boiling over medium heat, stirring occasionally, 7 minutes or until noodles are tender.

Stir in beef mixture and ¼ cup cheese; heat through. Top with remaining ¼ cup cheese.

Makes about 2 servings

Texas-Style Deep-Dish Chili Pie

- 1 tablespoon vegetable oil
- 1 pound beef stew meat, cut into ½-inch cubes
- 2 cans (14½ ounces each) Mexican-style stewed tomatoes, undrained
- 1 medium green bell pepper, diced
- 1 package (1.0 ounce) LAWRY'S® Taco Spices & Seasonings
- 1 tablespoon yellow cornmeal
- 1 can (15¼ ounces) kidney beans, drained
- 1 package (15 ounces) flat refrigerated pie crusts
- ½ cup (2 ounces) shredded cheddar cheese, divided

In Dutch oven, heat oil. Add beef and cook over medium-high heat until browned; drain fat. Add stewed tomatoes, bell pepper, Taco Spices & Seasonings and cornmeal. Bring to a boil over medium-high heat; reduce heat to low and cook, uncovered, 20 minutes. Add kidney beans; mix well. In 10-inch pie plate, unfold 1 crust and fill with chili mixture and ¼ cup cheese. Top with remaining crust, fluting edges. Bake, uncovered, in 350°F oven 30 minutes. Sprinkle remaining cheese over crust; return to oven and bake 10 minutes longer.

Makes 6 servings

Serving Suggestion: Serve with an orange and red onion salad.

Steak San Marino

- ¼ cup all-purpose flour
- 1 teaspoon salt
- ½ teaspoon black pepper
- 4 beef round steaks, about 1 inch thick
- 1 can (8 ounces) tomato sauce
- 2 carrots, chopped
- ½ onion, chopped
- 1 rib celery, chopped
- 1 teaspoon dried Italian seasoning
- ½ teaspoon Worcestershire sauce
- 1 bay leaf
- Hot cooked rice

Slow Cooker Directions

Combine flour, salt and pepper in small bowl. Dredge each steak in flour mixture. Place in slow cooker. Combine tomato sauce, carrots, onion, celery, Italian seasoning, Worcestershire sauce and bay leaf in small bowl; pour into slow cooker. Cover and cook on LOW 8 to 10 hours or on HIGH 4 to 5 hours.

Remove and discard bay leaf. Serve steaks and sauce over rice.

Makes 4 servings

Spinach-Potato Bake

- 1 pound extra-lean (90% lean) ground beef
- ½ cup sliced fresh mushrooms
- 1 small onion, chopped
- 2 cloves garlic, minced
- 1 package (10 ounces) frozen chopped spinach, thawed, well drained
- ½ teaspoon ground nutmeg
- 1 pound russet potatoes, peeled, cooked, mashed
- ¼ cup light sour cream
- ¼ cup fat-free (skim) milk
- Salt and black pepper
- ½ cup (2 ounces) shredded Cheddar cheese

Preheat oven to 400°F. Spray deep 9-inch casserole dish with nonstick cooking spray.

Brown ground beef in large skillet. Drain. Add mushrooms, onion and garlic; cook until tender. Stir in spinach and nutmeg; cover. Heat thoroughly, stirring occasionally.

Combine potatoes, sour cream and milk. Add to ground beef mixture; season with salt and pepper to taste. Spoon into prepared casserole dish; sprinkle with cheese.

Bake 15 to 20 minutes or until slightly puffed and cheese is melted.

Makes 6 servings

Steak San Marino

Steaks with Peppers

2 tablespoons olive or vegetable oil
1½ pounds boneless beef chuck steaks, ½ inch thick (about 4 to 5)
2 medium red, green and/or yellow bell peppers, cut into thin strips
1 clove garlic, finely chopped (optional)
1 medium tomato, coarsely chopped
1 envelope LIPTON® RECIPE SECRETS® Onion or Onion-Mushroom Soup Mix
1 cup water

In 12-inch skillet, heat oil over medium-high heat and brown steaks. Remove steaks. Add peppers and garlic to skillet; cook over medium heat 5 minutes or until peppers are crisp-tender. Stir in tomato, then onion soup mix blended with water; bring to a boil over high heat. Reduce heat to low. Return steaks to skillet and simmer uncovered, stirring sauce occasionally, 25 minutes or until steaks and vegetables are tender.

Makes about 4 servings

Menu Suggestion: Serve with steak fries or baked potatoes.

Picadillo

1 pound ground beef
1 small onion, chopped
1 clove garlic, minced
1 can (16 ounces) diced tomatoes, undrained
¼ cup golden raisins
1 tablespoon chili powder
1 tablespoon cider vinegar
½ teaspoon ground cumin
½ teaspoon dried oregano leaves
½ teaspoon ground cinnamon
¼ teaspoon red pepper flakes
1 teaspoon salt
¼ cup slivered almonds (optional)

Slow Cooker Directions

Cook ground beef, onion and garlic in medium nonstick skillet over medium heat until beef is no longer pink; drain off fat. Place mixture in slow cooker. Add tomatoes, raisins, chili powder, vinegar, cumin, oregano, cinnamon and red pepper flakes to slow cooker. Cover and cook on LOW 6 to 7 hours. Stir in salt. Garnish with almonds, if desired.

Makes 4 servings

Creamy Beef and Vegetable Casserole

1 pound lean ground beef
1 small onion, chopped
1 bag (16 ounces) BIRDS EYE® frozen Farm Fresh Mixtures Broccoli, Corn & Red Peppers
1 can (10¾ ounces) cream of mushroom soup

• In medium skillet, brown beef and onion; drain excess fat.

• Meanwhile, in large saucepan, cook vegetables according to package directions; drain.

• Stir in beef mixture and soup. Cook over medium heat until heated through.

Makes 4 servings

Serving Suggestion: Serve over rice and sprinkle with ½ cup shredded Cheddar cheese.

Prep Time: 5 minutes
Cook Time: 10 to 15 minutes

Zesty Italian Stuffed Peppers

3 bell peppers (green, red or yellow)
1 pound ground beef
1 jar (14 ounces) spaghetti sauce
1⅓ cups *French's® Taste Toppers™* French Fried Onions, divided
2 tablespoons *Frank's® RedHot®* Cayenne Pepper Sauce
½ cup uncooked instant rice
¼ cup sliced ripe olives
1 cup (4 ounces) shredded mozzarella cheese

Preheat oven to 400°F. Cut bell peppers in half lengthwise through stems; discard seeds. Place pepper halves, cut side up, in 2-quart shallow baking dish; set aside.

Place beef in large microwavable bowl. Microwave on HIGH 5 minutes or until meat is browned, stirring once. Drain. Stir in spaghetti sauce, *⅔ cup **Taste Toppers***, ***Frank's RedHot***, rice and olives. Spoon evenly into bell pepper halves.

Cover; bake 35 minutes or until bell peppers are tender. Uncover; sprinkle with cheese and remaining *⅔ cup **Taste Toppers***. Bake 1 minute or until ***Taste Toppers*** are golden.

Makes 6 servings

Prep Time: 10 minutes
Cook Time: 36 minutes

Helpful Hints

Brown beef in a skillet to give it more flavor, then drain off the extra fat before adding the beef to the slow cooker.

Steaks with Peppers

Tacos in Pasta Shells

1 package (3 ounces) cream cheese with chives
18 jumbo pasta shells
1¼ pounds ground beef
1 teaspoon salt
1 teaspoon chili powder
2 tablespoons butter, melted
1 cup prepared taco sauce
1 cup (4 ounces) shredded Cheddar cheese
1 cup (4 ounces) shredded Monterey Jack cheese
1½ cups crushed tortilla chips
1 cup sour cream
3 green onions, chopped
Leaf lettuce, small pitted ripe olives and cherry tomatoes for garnish

1. Cut cream cheese into ½-inch cubes. Let stand at room temperature until softened. Cook pasta according to package directions. Place in colander and rinse under warm running water. Drain well. Return to saucepan.

2. Preheat oven to 350°F. Butter 13×9-inch baking pan.

3. Cook beef in large skillet over medium-high heat until brown, stirring to separate meat; drain drippings. Reduce heat to medium-low. Add cream cheese, salt and chili powder; simmer 5 minutes.

4. Toss shells with butter. Fill shells with beef mixture using spoon. Arrange shells in prepared pan. Pour taco sauce over each shell. Cover with foil.

5. Bake 15 minutes. Uncover; top with Cheddar cheese, Monterey Jack cheese and chips. Bake 15 minutes more or until bubbly. Top with sour cream and onions. Garnish, if desired. *Makes 4 to 6 servings*

Texas-Style Barbecued Brisket

Slow Cooker

1 beef brisket (3 to 4 pounds), cut into halves, if necessary, to fit slow cooker
3 tablespoons Worcestershire sauce
1 tablespoon chili powder
1 teaspoon celery salt
1 teaspoon black pepper
1 teaspoon liquid smoke
2 cloves garlic, minced
2 bay leaves
Barbecue Sauce (recipe follows)

Slow Cooker Directions
Trim excess fat from meat and discard. Place meat in resealable plastic food storage bag. Combine Worcestershire sauce, chili powder, celery salt, pepper, liquid smoke, garlic and bay leaves in small bowl. Spread mixture on all sides of meat; seal bag. Refrigerate 24 hours.

Place meat and marinade in slow cooker. Cover and cook on LOW 7 hours. Meanwhile, prepare Barbecue Sauce.

Remove meat from slow cooker and pour juices into 2-cup measure; let stand 5 minutes. Skim fat from juices. Remove and discard bay leaves. Stir 1 cup of defatted juices into Barbecue Sauce. Discard remaining juices. Return meat and Barbecue Sauce to slow cooker. Cover and cook on LOW 1 hour or until meat is fork-tender. Remove meat to cutting board. Cut across grain into ¼-inch-thick slices. Serve 2 to 3 tablespoons Barbecue Sauce over each serving.
Makes 10 to 12 servings

Barbecue Sauce

2 tablespoons vegetable oil
1 medium onion, chopped
2 cloves garlic, minced
1 cup ketchup
½ cup molasses
¼ cup cider vinegar
2 teaspoons chili powder
½ teaspoon dry mustard

Heat oil in medium saucepan over medium heat. Add onion and garlic; cook until onion is tender. Add remaining ingredients. Simmer 5 minutes.
Makes 2½ cups sauce

Stuffed Mexican Peppers

1 package LIPTON® Rice & Sauce—Beef Flavor
1¼ cups water, divided
½ pound ground beef
1 cup frozen corn, partially thawed
1 cup shredded Cheddar cheese (about 4 ounces), divided
1 medium tomato, chopped
1 tablespoon chopped green chilies
4 large green pepper cups

Preheat oven to 350°F.

In large bowl, combine rice & sauce—beef flavor with ¾ cup water; stir in ground beef, corn, ¾ cup cheese, tomato and chilies. Spoon into pepper cups; place upright in 8 or 9-inch baking pan filled with remaining ½ cup water. Cover tightly with aluminum foil and bake uncovered 45 minutes. Evenly top with remaining ¼ cup cheese and continue baking uncovered 10 minutes or until cheese melts.
Makes 4 servings

Tacos in Pasta Shells

Reuben Noodle Bake

- 8 ounces uncooked egg noodles
- 5 ounces thinly sliced deli-style corned beef
- 1 can (14½ ounces) sauerkraut with caraway seeds, drained
- 2 cups (8 ounces) shredded Swiss cheese
- ½ cup Thousand Island dressing
- ½ cup milk
- 1 tablespoon prepared mustard
- 2 slices pumpernickel bread
- 1 tablespoon margarine or butter, melted

Preheat oven to 350°F. Spray 13×9-inch baking dish with nonstick cooking spray.

Cook noodles according to package directions until al dente. Drain.

Meanwhile, cut corned beef into bite-size pieces. Combine noodles, corned beef, sauerkraut and cheese in large bowl. Spread in prepared dish.

Combine dressing, milk and mustard in small bowl. Spoon dressing mixture evenly over noodle mixture.

Tear bread into large pieces. Process in food processor or blender until crumbs form. Combine bread crumbs and margarine in small bowl; sprinkle evenly over casserole.

Bake, uncovered, 25 to 30 minutes or until heated through.

Makes 6 servings

Countdown Casserole

- 1 jar (8 ounces) pasteurized process cheese spread
- ¾ cup milk
- 2 cups (12 ounces) cubed cooked roast beef
- 1 bag (16 ounces) frozen vegetable combination (broccoli, corn, red pepper), thawed and drained
- 4 cups frozen hash brown potatoes, thawed
- 1⅓ cups *French's® Taste Toppers™* French Fried Onions, divided
- ½ teaspoon seasoned salt
- ¼ teaspoon freshly ground black pepper
- ½ cup (2 ounces) shredded Cheddar cheese

Reuben Noodle Bake

Preheat oven to 375°F. Spoon cheese spread into 12×8-inch baking dish; place in oven just until cheese melts, about 5 minutes. Using fork, stir milk into melted cheese until well blended. Stir in beef, vegetables, potatoes, ⅔ *cup* ***Taste Toppers*** and the seasonings. Bake, covered, at 375°F 30 minutes or until heated through. Top with Cheddar cheese; sprinkle remaining ⅔ *cup* ***Taste Toppers*** down center. Bake, uncovered, 3 minutes or until ***Taste Toppers*** are golden brown.

Makes 4 to 6 servings

Microwave Directions:
In 12×8-inch microwave-safe dish, combine cheese spread and milk. Cook, covered, on HIGH 3 minutes; stir. Add ingredients as directed. Cook, covered, 14 minutes or until heated through, stirring beef mixture halfway through cooking time. Top with Cheddar cheese and remaining ⅔ *cup* ***Taste Toppers*** as directed. Cook, uncovered, 1 minute or until cheese melts. Let stand 5 minutes.

Beef & Zucchini Quiche

1 unbaked 9-inch pie shell
½ pound lean ground beef
1 medium zucchini, shredded
3 green onions, sliced
¼ cup sliced mushrooms
1 tablespoon all-purpose flour
3 eggs, beaten
1 cup milk
¾ cup (3 ounces) shredded Swiss cheese
1½ teaspoons chopped fresh thyme *or* ½ teaspoon dried thyme leaves
½ teaspoon salt
Dash black pepper
Dash ground red pepper

Preheat oven to 475°F.

Line pie shell with foil; fill with dried beans or rice. Bake 8 minutes. Remove from oven; carefully remove foil and beans. Return pie shell to oven. Continue baking 4 minutes; set aside. *Reduce oven temperature to 375°F.*

Brown ground beef in medium skillet. Drain. Add zucchini, onions and mushrooms; cook, stirring occasionally, until vegetables are tender. Stir in flour; cook 2 minutes, stirring constantly. Remove from heat.

Combine eggs, milk, cheese and seasonings in medium bowl. Stir into ground beef mixture; pour into crust.

Bake 35 minutes or until knife inserted near center comes out clean.

Makes 6 servings

Old-Fashioned Beef Pot Pie

1 pound ground beef
1 can (11 ounces) condensed beef with vegetables and barley soup
½ cup water
1 package (10 ounces) frozen peas and carrots, thawed and drained
½ teaspoon seasoned salt
⅛ teaspoon garlic powder
⅛ teaspoon ground black pepper
1 cup (4 ounces) shredded Cheddar cheese, divided
1⅓ cups *French's® Taste Toppers™* French Fried Onions, divided
1 package (7.5 ounces) refrigerated biscuits

Preheat oven to 350°F. In large skillet, brown ground beef in large chunks; drain. Stir in soup, water, vegetables and seasonings; bring to a boil. Reduce heat and simmer, uncovered, 5 minutes. Remove from heat; stir in ½ cup cheese and ⅔ *cup* ***Taste Toppers***.

Pour mixture into 12×8-inch baking dish. Cut each biscuit in half; place, cut side down, around edge of casserole. Bake, uncovered, 15 to 20 minutes or until biscuits are done. Top with remaining cheese and ⅔ *cup* ***Taste Toppers***; bake, uncovered, 5 minutes or until ***Taste Toppers*** are golden brown.

Makes 4 to 6 servings

Rice-Stuffed Peppers

1 package LIPTON® Rice & Sauce—Cheddar Broccoli
2 cups water
1 tablespoon margarine or butter
1 pound ground beef
4 large red or green bell peppers, halved lengthwise and seeded

Preheat oven to 350°F.

Prepare rice & sauce—cheddar broccoli with water and margarine according to package directions.

Meanwhile, in 10-inch skillet, brown ground beef over medium-high heat; drain. Stir into rice & sauce. Fill each pepper half with rice mixture. In 13×9-inch baking dish, arrange stuffed peppers. Bake, covered, 20 minutes. Remove cover and continue baking 10 minutes or until peppers are tender. Sprinkle, if desired, with shredded Cheddar cheese.

Makes about 4 main-dish servings

Steak Fajitas Suprema

2 tablespoons vegetable oil, divided
1 medium-sized red bell pepper, thinly sliced
1 medium onion, very thinly sliced
1 pound beef sirloin steak, thinly sliced
1 package (1.27 ounces) LAWRY'S® Spices & Seasonings for Fajitas
¼ cup water
1 can (15 ounces) pinto beans, drained
6 medium flour or corn tortillas
1 cup (4 ounces) shredded cheddar cheese (optional)
Salsa (optional)
Dairy sour cream (optional)
Sliced peeled avocado (optional)

In large skillet, heat 1 tablespoon oil. Add bell pepper and onion and cook over medium-high heat until crisp-tender. Remove vegetables from skillet; set aside. In same skillet, heat remaining 1 tablespoon oil; add meat and cook 5 to 7 minutes or to desired doneness. Drain fat. Add Spices & Seasonings for Fajitas, water and pinto beans; mix well. Bring to a boil over medium-high heat; reduce heat to low. Simmer, uncovered, 3 to 5 minutes or until thoroughly heated, stirring occasionally. Return vegetables to skillet; heat 1 minute.

Makes 4 to 6 servings

Serving Suggestion: Serve in warm tortillas. If desired, add shredded cheddar cheese, salsa, sour cream and avocado for extra flavor.

Hint: Partially frozen meat is easier to slice thinly.

Easy Lasagna

1 pound lean ground beef
1 jar (28 ounces) meatless spaghetti sauce
16 ounces small curd cottage cheese
8 ounces sour cream
8 uncooked lasagna noodles
3 packages (6 ounces each) sliced mozzarella cheese (12 slices)
½ cup grated Parmesan cheese
1 cup water

1. For meat sauce, cook beef in large skillet over medium-high heat until meat is brown, stirring to separate meat; drain. Add spaghetti sauce. Reduce heat to low. Heat through, stirring occasionally; set aside.

2. Preheat oven to 350°F.

3. Combine cottage cheese and sour cream in medium bowl; blend well.

4. Spoon 1½ cups of meat sauce in bottom of 13×9-inch baking dish. Layer with 4 uncooked noodles, ½ of cottage cheese mixture, 4 slices mozzarella cheese, ½ of remaining meat sauce and ¼ cup Parmesan cheese. Repeat layers starting with uncooked noodles. Top with remaining 4 slices mozzarella cheese. Pour water around sides of dish. Cover tightly with foil.

5. Bake lasagna 1 hour. Uncover; bake 20 minutes more or until bubbly. Let stand 15 to 20 minutes before cutting. Garnish as desired. Serve immediately.

Makes 8 to 10 servings

Chili Spaghetti Casserole

8 ounces uncooked spaghetti
1 pound lean ground beef
1 medium onion, chopped
¼ teaspoon salt
⅛ teaspoon black pepper
1 can (15 ounces) vegetarian chili with beans
1 can (14½ ounces) Italian-style stewed tomatoes, undrained
1½ cups (6 ounces) shredded sharp Cheddar cheese, divided
½ cup reduced-fat sour cream
1½ teaspoons chili powder
¼ teaspoon garlic powder

Preheat oven to 350°F. Spray 13×9-inch baking dish with nonstick cooking spray.

Cook pasta according to package directions until al dente. Drain and place in prepared dish.

Meanwhile, place beef and onion in large skillet; season with salt and pepper. Brown beef over medium-high heat until beef is no longer pink, stirring to separate meat. Drain fat. Stir in chili, tomatoes with juice, 1 cup cheese, sour cream, chili powder and garlic powder.

Add chili mixture to pasta; stir until pasta is well coated. Sprinkle with remaining ½ cup cheese.

Cover tightly with foil and bake 30 minutes or until hot and bubbly. Let stand 5 minutes before serving.

Makes 8 servings

Chili Spaghetti Casserole

Beefy Bean Skillet

- 1 box (9 ounces) BIRDS EYE® frozen Cut Green Beans
- ½ pound lean ground beef
- ½ cup chopped onion
- 1 cup instant rice
- 1 can (10 ounces) au jus gravy*
- ¾ cup ketchup

Or, substitute 1 can (10 ounces) beef broth.

• In medium saucepan, cook green beans according to package directions; drain and set aside.

• Meanwhile, in large skillet, brown beef; drain excess fat. Add onion; cook and stir until onion is tender.

• Add rice, gravy and ketchup. Bring to boil over medium-high heat; cover and reduce heat to medium-low. Simmer 5 to 10 minutes or until rice is cooked, stirring occasionally.

• Stir in beans. Simmer until heated through. *Makes 4 servings*

Prep Time: 10 minutes
Cook Time: 20 minutes

Chili Wagon Wheel Casserole

- 8 ounces uncooked wagon wheel or other pasta
- Nonstick cooking spray
- 1 pound lean ground sirloin or ground turkey breast
- ¾ cup chopped green bell pepper
- ¾ cup chopped onion
- 1 can (14½ ounces) no-salt-added stewed tomatoes
- 1 can (8 ounces) no-salt-added tomato sauce
- ½ teaspoon black pepper
- ¼ teaspoon ground allspice
- ½ cup (2 ounces) shredded reduced-fat Cheddar cheese

1. Preheat oven to 350°F. Cook pasta according to package directions, omitting salt. Drain and rinse; set aside.

2. Spray large nonstick skillet with cooking spray. Add ground sirloin, bell pepper and onion; cook 5 minutes or until meat is no longer pink, stirring frequently. (Drain mixture if using ground sirloin.)

3. Stir in tomatoes, tomato sauce, black pepper and allspice; cook 2 minutes. Stir in pasta. Spoon mixture into 2½-quart casserole. Sprinkle with cheese.

4. Bake 20 to 25 minutes or until heated through.

Makes 6 servings

Zucchini Pasta Bake

- 1½ cups uncooked pasta tubes
- ½ pound ground beef
- ½ cup chopped onion
- 1 clove garlic, minced
- Salt and pepper
- 1 can (14½ ounces) DEL MONTE® Zucchini with Italian-Style Tomato Sauce
- 1 teaspoon dried basil, crushed
- 1 cup (4 ounces) shredded Monterey Jack cheese

1. Cook pasta according to package directions; drain.

2. Cook beef with onion and garlic in large skillet; drain. Season with salt and pepper.

3. Stir in zucchini with tomato sauce and basil. Place pasta in 8-inch square baking dish. Top with meat mixture.

4. Bake at 350°F for 15 minutes. Top with cheese. Bake 3 minutes or until cheese is melted.

Makes 4 servings

Prep and Cook Time: 33 minutes

Spanish Skillet Supper

- ½ pound ground beef
- 1 small onion, chopped
- 2¼ cups water
- 1 cup frozen whole kernel corn, partially thawed
- 1 tablespoon margarine or butter
- 1 package LIPTON® Rice & Sauce—Spanish
- ¼ cup shredded Cheddar cheese (about 1 ounce) (optional)

1. Brown ground beef and onion in 12-inch nonstick skillet over medium-high heat; drain. Remove and set aside.

2. Add water, corn, margarine and rice & sauce—Spanish and bring to a boil. Continue boiling over medium heat, stirring occasionally, 10 minutes or until rice is tender.

3. Stir in beef mixture; heat through. Sprinkle with cheese.

Makes about 2 servings

Prep Time: 5 minutes
Cook Time: 10 minutes

Helpful Hints

When cooking pasta for use in a casserole, cook it just until tender, but still firm to the bite. The pasta will continue to cook and absorb more liquid during the baking process.

Beefy Bean Skillet

Lasagna Beef 'n' Spinach Roll-Ups

- 1½ pounds ground beef
- 1 (28-ounce) jar spaghetti sauce
- ½ cup A.1.® Original or A.1.® BOLD & SPICY Steak Sauce
- ½ teaspoon dried basil leaves
- 1 (15-ounce) container ricotta cheese
- 1 (10-ounce) package frozen chopped spinach, thawed, well drained
- 2 cups shredded mozzarella cheese (8 ounces)
- ⅓ cup grated Parmesan cheese, divided
- 1 egg, beaten
- 12 lasagna noodles, cooked, drained
- 2 tablespoons chopped fresh parsley

Brown beef in large skillet over medium-high heat until no longer pink, stirring occasionally to break up beef; drain. Mix spaghetti sauce, steak sauce and basil in small bowl; stir 1 cup spaghetti sauce mixture into beef. Set aside remaining sauce mixture.

Mix ricotta cheese, spinach, mozzarella cheese, 3 tablespoons Parmesan cheese and egg in medium bowl. On each lasagna noodle, spread about ¼ cup ricotta mixture. Top with about ⅓ cup beef mixture. Roll up each noodle from short end; lay each roll, seam side down, in lightly greased 13×9×2-inch baking dish. Pour reserved spaghetti sauce mixture over noodles. Sprinkle with remaining Parmesan cheese and parsley.

Bake, covered, at 350°F 30 minutes. Uncover and bake 15 to 20 minutes more or until hot and bubbly. Serve with additional Parmesan cheese if desired. Garnish as desired.

Makes 6 servings

Yankee Pot Roast and Vegetables Slow Cooker

Slow Cooker

- 1 beef chuck pot roast (2½ pounds)
- Salt and black pepper
- 3 medium baking potatoes (about 1 pound), unpeeled and cut into quarters
- 2 large carrots, cut into ¾-inch slices
- 2 ribs celery, cut into ¾-inch slices
- 1 medium onion, sliced
- 1 large parsnip, cut into ¾-inch slices
- 2 bay leaves
- 1 teaspoon dried rosemary
- ½ teaspoon dried thyme leaves
- ½ cup reduced-sodium beef broth

Slow Cooker Directions

1. Trim excess fat from meat and discard. Cut meat into serving pieces; sprinkle with salt and pepper.

2. Combine vegetables, bay leaves, rosemary and thyme in slow cooker. Place beef over vegetables. Pour broth over beef. Cover and cook on LOW 8½ to 9 hours or until beef is fork-tender. Remove beef to serving platter. Arrange vegetables around beef. Remove and discard bay leaves. *Makes 10 to 12 servings*

Hint: To make gravy, ladle the juices into a 2-cup measure; let stand 5 minutes. Skim off and discard fat. Measure remaining juices and heat to a boil in small saucepan. For each cup of juice, mix 2 tablespoons of flour with ¼ cup of cold water until smooth. Stir mixture into boiling juices, stirring constantly 1 minute or until thickened.

Prep Time: 10 minutes
Cook Time: 8½ hours

Creamy Beef and Noodles

- 2 pounds beef stew meat, cut into 1-inch pieces
- 1 tablespoon vegetable oil
- 1 jar (4 ounces) sliced mushrooms, drained
- ½ cup thinly sliced carrot
- ¼ cup minced onion
- 3 cloves garlic, minced
- 1 teaspoon salt
- 1 teaspoon black pepper
- ⅛ teaspoon dried thyme
- 1 bay leaf
- 1 can (13¾ ounces) beef broth
- 1 carton (8 ounces) sour cream
- ½ cup all-purpose flour
- ¼ cup water
- 4 cups hot cooked noodles

Slow Cooker Directions

Brown beef in hot oil in large skillet. Drain off fat.

Combine beef, mushrooms, carrot, onion, garlic, salt, pepper, thyme and bay leaf in slow cooker. Pour in beef broth. Cover and cook on LOW 8 to 10 hours. Discard bay leaf.

Increase heat to HIGH. Combine sour cream, flour and water in small bowl. Stir about 1 cup of hot liquid into sour cream mixture. Return to slow cooker; stir. Cover and cook on HIGH 30 minutes or until thickened and bubbly. Serve over noodles.

Makes 6 to 8 servings

Lasagna Beef 'n' Spinach Roll-Ups

Irresistible Pork

Barbara's Pork Chop Dinner

- 1 tablespoon butter
- 1 tablespoon olive oil
- 6 bone-in pork loin chops
- 1 can (10¾ ounces) condensed cream of chicken soup, undiluted
- 1 can (4 ounces) mushrooms, drained and chopped
- ¼ cup Dijon mustard
- ¼ cup chicken broth
- 2 cloves garlic, minced
- ½ teaspoon salt
- ½ teaspoon dried basil leaves
- ¼ teaspoon black pepper
- 6 red potatoes, unpeeled, cut into thin slices
- 1 onion, sliced
- Chopped fresh parsley

Slow Cooker Directions

Heat butter and oil in large skillet. Brown pork chops on both sides. Set aside.

Combine soup, mushrooms, mustard, chicken broth, garlic, salt, basil and pepper in slow cooker. Add potatoes and onion, stirring to coat. Place pork chops on top of potato mixture. Cover and cook on LOW 8 to 10 hours or on HIGH 4 to 5 hours. Sprinkle with parsley.

Makes 6 servings

Orange Teriyaki Pork

- Nonstick cooking spray
- 1 pound lean pork stew meat, cut into 1-inch cubes
- 1 package (16 ounces) frozen pepper blend for stir-fry
- 4 ounces sliced water chestnuts
- ½ cup orange juice
- 2 tablespoons quick-cooking tapioca
- 2 tablespoons brown sugar
- 2 tablespoons teriyaki sauce
- ½ teaspoon ground ginger
- ½ teaspoon dry mustard
- 1⅓ cups hot cooked rice

Slow Cooker Directions

1. Spray large nonstick skillet with cooking spray; heat over medium heat until hot. Add pork; brown on all sides. Remove from heat; set aside.

2. Place peppers and water chestnuts in slow cooker. Top with browned pork. Mix orange juice, tapioca, brown sugar, teriyaki sauce, ginger and mustard in large bowl. Pour over pork mixture in slow cooker. Cover and cook on LOW 3 to 4 hours. Stir. Serve over rice.

Makes 4 servings

Cajun Sausage and Rice

- 8 ounces kielbasa sausage, cut in ¼-inch slices
- 1 can (14½ ounces) diced tomatoes, undrained
- 1 medium onion, diced
- 1 medium green bell pepper, diced
- 2 stalks celery, thinly sliced
- 1 tablespoon chicken bouillon granules
- 1 tablespoon steak sauce
- 3 bay leaves *or* 1 teaspoon dried thyme leaves
- 1 teaspoon sugar
- ¼ to ½ teaspoon hot pepper sauce
- 1 cup uncooked instant rice
- ½ cup chopped parsley (optional)

Slow Cooker Directions

1. Combine sausage, tomatoes, onion, bell pepper, celery, bouillon, steak sauce, bay leaves, sugar and hot pepper sauce in slow cooker. Cover and cook on LOW 8 hours or on HIGH 4 hours.

2. Remove bay leaves; stir in rice and ½ cup water. Cook an additional 25 minutes. Stir in parsley, if desired.

Makes 5 servings

Barbara's Pork Chop Dinner

Bayou-Style Pot Pie

- 1 tablespoon olive oil
- 1 large onion, chopped
- 1 green bell pepper, chopped
- 1½ teaspoons minced garlic
- 8 ounces boneless skinless chicken thighs, cut into 1-inch pieces
- 1 can (14½ ounces) stewed tomatoes, undrained
- 8 ounces fully cooked smoked sausage or kielbasa, thinly sliced
- ¾ teaspoon hot pepper sauce or to taste
- 2¼ cups buttermilk baking mix
- ¾ teaspoon dried thyme leaves
- ⅛ teaspoon black pepper
- ⅔ cup milk

1. Preheat oven to 450°F. Heat oil in medium ovenproof skillet over medium-high heat until hot. Add onion, bell pepper and garlic. Cook 3 minutes, stirring occasionally.

2. Add chicken and cook 1 minute. Add tomatoes with juice, sausage and hot pepper sauce. Cook, uncovered, over medium-low heat 5 minutes.

3. While chicken is cooking, combine baking mix, thyme and black pepper. Stir in milk. Drop batter by heaping tablespoonfuls in mounds over chicken mixture. Bake 14 minutes or until biscuits are golden brown and cooked through and chicken mixture is bubbly. *Makes 4 servings*

Note: You may use any of a variety of fully cooked sausages from your supermarket meat case. Andouille, a fairly spicy Louisiana-style sausage, is perfect for this dish.

Prep and Cook Time: 28 minutes

Spicy Black Bean & Sausage Stew

- 1 tablespoon olive oil
- ½ cup chopped onion
- ¼ cup chopped green bell pepper
- 4 ounces low-fat smoked sausage, cut into ¼-inch pieces
- 2 cloves garlic, minced
- 1 cup drained canned black beans, rinsed
- ¾ cup undrained no-salt-added stewed tomatoes
- 1½ teaspoons dried oregano leaves
- ¾ teaspoon ground cumin
- 2 tablespoons minced fresh parsley
- Hot pepper sauce
- Hot cooked rice (optional)

1. Heat oil in medium skillet over medium heat. Add onion, bell pepper and sausage. Cook and stir 3 to 4 minutes or until vegetables are tender. Add garlic; cook and stir 1 minute.

2. Stir in beans, tomatoes with juice, oregano and cumin, breaking up tomatoes into small chunks. Bring to a boil; reduce heat to low. Cover and simmer 20 minutes, stirring occasionally. Stir in parsley and pepper sauce to taste. Serve with hot cooked rice, if desired.

Makes 2 servings

Baked Rigatoni with Sausage

- ½ pound Italian sausage
- 2 cups milk
- 2 tablespoons all-purpose flour
- ½ pound rigatoni pasta, cooked and drained
- 2½ cups (10 ounces) shredded mozzarella cheese
- ¼ cup grated Parmesan cheese
- 1 teaspoon LAWRY'S® Garlic Salt
- ¾ teaspoon LAWRY'S® Seasoned Pepper
- 2 to 3 tablespoons dry bread crumbs *or* ¾ cup croutons

In large skillet, crumble Italian sausage. Cook over medium-high heat until browned, 5 minutes; drain fat. Add milk and flour. Bring to a boil over medium-high heat, stirring constantly. Stir in pasta, cheeses, Garlic Salt and Seasoned Pepper. Place in 1½-quart baking dish. Bake in 350°F oven 25 minutes. Sprinkle with bread crumbs; place under broiler to brown about 2 to 4 minutes.

Makes 6 servings

Serving Suggestion: Serve with green beans and crusty bread.

Hint: ¼ pound cooked, diced ham can replace sausage.

Helpful Hints

Kielbasa, also known as Polish sausage, is a smoked pork sausage that is usually precooked. Italian sausage is most commonly flavored with garlic and fennel seed. It is often sold in links and is available raw.

Spicy Black Bean & Sausage Stew

Cheesy Pork and Potatoes

- ½ pound ground pork, cooked and crumbled
- ½ cup finely crushed saltine crackers
- ⅓ cup barbecue sauce
- 1 egg
- 3 tablespoons margarine
- 1 tablespoon vegetable oil
- 4 potatoes, peeled and thinly sliced
- 1 onion, thinly sliced
- 1 cup grated mozzarella cheese
- ⅔ cup evaporated milk
- 1 teaspoon salt
- ¼ teaspoon paprika
- ⅛ teaspoon black pepper
- Chopped fresh parsley

Slow Cooker Directions

Combine pork, crackers, barbecue sauce and egg in large bowl; shape mixture into 6 patties. Heat margarine and oil in medium skillet. Sauté potatoes and onion until lightly browned. Drain and place in slow cooker.

Combine cheese, milk, salt, paprika and pepper in small bowl. Pour into slow cooker. Layer pork patties on top. Cover and cook on LOW 3 to 5 hours. Garnish with parsley.

Makes 6 servings

Hot Dog Macaroni

- 1 package (8 ounces) hot dogs
- 1 cup uncooked corkscrew pasta
- 1 cup shredded Cheddar cheese
- 1 box (10 ounces) BIRDS EYE® frozen Green Peas
- 1 cup 1% milk

• Slice hot dogs into bite-size pieces; set aside.

• In large saucepan, cook pasta according to package directions; drain and return to saucepan.

• Stir in hot dogs, cheese, peas and milk. Cook over medium heat 10 minutes or until cheese is melted, stirring occasionally.

Makes 4 servings

Prep Time: 10 minutes
Cook Time: 20 minutes

Ham & Barbecued Bean Skillet

- 1 tablespoon vegetable oil
- 1 cup chopped onion
- 1 teaspoon bottled minced garlic
- 1 can (15 ounces) red or pink kidney beans, rinsed and drained
- 1 can (15 ounces) cannellini or Great Northern beans, rinsed and drained
- 1 cup chopped green bell pepper
- ½ cup firmly packed light brown sugar
- ½ cup ketchup
- 2 tablespoons cider vinegar
- 2 teaspoons dry mustard
- 1 fully cooked smoked ham steak (about 12 ounces), cut ½ inch thick

1. Heat oil in large deep skillet over medium-high heat until hot. Add onion and garlic; cook 3 minutes, stirring occasionally.

2. Add kidney beans, cannellini beans, bell pepper, brown sugar, ketchup, vinegar and mustard; mix well.

3. Trim fat from ham; cut into ½-inch pieces. Add ham to bean mixture; simmer over medium heat 5 minutes or until sauce thickens and mixture is heated through, stirring occasionally. *Makes 4 servings*

Serving Suggestion: Serve with a Caesar salad and crisp breadsticks.

Prep and Cook Time: 20 minutes

Mediterranean Meatball Ratatouille

- 2 tablespoons olive oil, divided
- 1 pound mild Italian sausage, casings removed
- 1 package (8 ounces) sliced mushrooms
- 1 small eggplant, diced
- 1 zucchini, diced
- ½ cup chopped onion
- 1 clove garlic, minced
- 1 teaspoon dried oregano leaves, divided
- 1 teaspoon salt, divided
- ½ teaspoon black pepper, divided
- 1 tablespoon tomato paste
- 2 tomatoes, diced
- 2 tablespoons chopped fresh basil
- 1 teaspoon fresh lemon juice

Slow Cooker Directions

1. Pour 1 tablespoon olive oil into 5-quart slow cooker. Shape sausage into 1-inch balls. Place half the meatballs in slow cooker. Add half the mushrooms, eggplant and zucchini. Add onion, garlic, ½ teaspoon oregano, ½ teaspoon salt and ¼ teaspoon pepper.

2. Add remaining meatballs, mushrooms, eggplant and zucchini. Add remaining oregano, salt and pepper. Top with remaining olive oil. Cover and cook on LOW 6 to 7 hours.

3. Stir in tomato paste and diced tomatoes. Cover and cook on LOW 15 minutes. Stir in basil and lemon; serve.

Makes 6 (1⅔-cup) servings

Hot Dog Macaroni

Shredded Pork Wraps

1 cup salsa, divided
2 tablespoons cornstarch
1 bone-in pork sirloin roast (2 pounds)
6 (8-inch) flour tortillas
⅓ cup shredded reduced-fat Cheddar cheese
3 cups broccoli slaw mix

Slow Cooker Directions

1. Combine ¼ cup salsa and cornstarch in small bowl; stir until smooth. Pour mixture into slow cooker. Top with pork roast. Pour remaining ¾ cup salsa over roast.

2. Cover and cook on LOW 6 to 8 hours or until internal temperature reaches 165°F when tested with meat thermometer inserted into the thickest part of roast, not touching bone. Remove roast from slow cooker. Transfer roast to cutting board; cover with foil and let stand 10 to 15 minutes or until cool enough to handle before shredding. (Internal temperature will rise 5° to 10°F during stand time.) Trim and discard outer fat from pork. Using 2 forks, pull pork into coarse shreds.

3. Divide shredded meat evenly on each tortilla. Spoon about 2 tablespoons salsa mixture on top of meat in each tortilla. Top evenly with cheese and broccoli slaw mix. Fold bottom edge of tortilla over filling; fold in sides. Roll up completely to enclose filling. Repeat with remaining tortillas. Serve remaining salsa mixture as a dipping sauce.

Makes 6 servings

Shredded Pork Wrap

Italian Pork Skillet

1 pound pork tenderloin
1 small eggplant
1 medium summer squash
2 tablespoons olive oil, divided
1½ teaspoons salt, divided
⅛ teaspoon black pepper
1 clove garlic, minced
1 medium onion, thinly sliced
1 small red bell pepper, cut into thin strips
1 teaspoon Italian seasoning
⅓ cup water
1 teaspoon cornstarch

Partially freeze tenderloin. Cut pork diagonally into ¼-inch-thick slices; quarter slices. Cut eggplant in half. Cut halves into cubes. Cut squash lengthwise in half. Place on flat sides and cut crosswise into ¼-inch-thick slices. In skillet, brown half of pork in 1 tablespoon hot olive oil, stirring constantly; remove from pan. Add remaining pork; cook, stirring constantly, until pork is browned. Sprinkle ¾ teaspoon salt and pepper over pork. Place remaining 1 tablespoon olive oil, eggplant and minced garlic in skillet and cook over medium-high heat 3 minutes. Add squash, onion, bell pepper, Italian seasoning and remaining ¾ teaspoon salt; cook 7 minutes, stirring occasionally. Combine water and cornstarch; stir into vegetables. Return pork to skillet and cook 3 to 4 minutes or until thickened, stirring occasionally. *Makes 4 servings*

Preparation Time: 20 minutes

Favorite recipe from **National Pork Producers Council**

Mexican Sausage Pie

- ½ pound chorizo sausage
- 1 (1-pound) loaf frozen whole-wheat bread dough, thawed
- 1 (10-ounce) package frozen chopped broccoli, thawed, well drained
- 1 cup whole kernel corn, well drained
- ½ pound VELVEETA® Mexican Pasteurized Process Cheese Spread with Jalapeño Peppers, sliced
- 1 egg yolk
- 1 teaspoon cold water
- 1 tablespoon cornmeal

• Preheat oven to 375°F.

• Remove sausage from casing. Brown sausage; drain. Cool.

• Roll two-thirds of dough to 11-inch circle on lightly floured surface. Press onto bottom and up sides of greased 9-inch springform pan.

• Layer broccoli, corn, sausage and process cheese spread over dough in pan.

• Roll remaining dough to 10-inch circle; cut into eight wedges. Place over filling, overlapping edges and sealing ends to bottom crust. Brush with combined egg yolk and water. Sprinkle with cornmeal.

• Bake 35 to 40 minutes or until deep golden brown. Let stand 10 minutes. Garnish as desired.

Makes 10 servings

Microwave Tip: To cook sausage, remove sausage from casing. Crumble into 1-quart bowl. Microwave on HIGH 4 to 6 minutes or until sausage is cooked, stirring after 3 minutes; drain.

Prep Time: 20 minutes
Cooking Time: 40 minutes

Pork and Mushroom Ragoût

Slow Cooker

- Nonstick cooking spray
- 1 boneless pork loin roast (1¼ pounds)
- 1¼ cups canned crushed tomatoes, divided
- 2 tablespoons cornstarch
- 2 teaspoons dried savory leaves
- 3 sun-dried tomatoes, patted dry and chopped
- 1 package (8 ounces) sliced mushrooms
- 1 large onion, sliced
- 1 teaspoon black pepper
- 3 cups hot cooked noodles

Slow Cooker Directions

1. Spray large nonstick skillet with cooking spray; heat over medium heat until hot. Brown pork on all sides; set aside.

2. Combine ½ cup crushed tomatoes, cornstarch, savory and sun-dried tomatoes in large bowl. Pour mixture into slow cooker. Layer mushrooms, onion and pork over tomato mixture.

3. Pour remaining tomatoes over pork; sprinkle with pepper. Cover and cook on LOW 4 to 6 hours or until internal temperature reaches 165°F when tested with meat thermometer inserted into the thickest part of pork.

4. Remove pork from slow cooker. Transfer pork to cutting board; cover with foil. Let stand 10 to 15 minutes before slicing. (Internal temperature will continue to rise 5° to 10°F during stand time.) Serve pork and sauce over hot cooked noodles.

Makes 6 servings

Family-Style Frankfurters with Rice and Red Beans

- 1 tablespoon vegetable oil
- 1 medium onion, chopped
- ½ medium green bell pepper, chopped
- 2 cloves garlic, minced
- 1 can (14 ounces) red kidney beans, rinsed and drained
- 1 can (14 ounces) Great Northern beans, rinsed and drained
- ½ pound frankfurters, cut into ¼-inch-thick pieces
- 1 cup uncooked instant brown rice
- 1 cup vegetable broth
- ¼ cup packed brown sugar
- ¼ cup ketchup
- 3 tablespoons dark molasses
- 1 tablespoon Dijon mustard

Preheat oven to 350°F. Spray 13×9-inch baking dish with nonstick cooking spray.

Heat oil in Dutch oven over medium-high heat until hot. Add onion, pepper and garlic; cook and stir 2 minutes or until onion is tender.

Add beans, frankfurters, rice, broth, sugar, ketchup, molasses and mustard to vegetables; stir to combine. Pour into prepared dish.

Cover tightly with foil and bake 30 minutes or until rice is tender.

Makes 6 servings

Jambalaya

- 1 teaspoon vegetable oil
- ½ pound smoked deli ham, cubed
- ½ pound smoked sausage, cut into ¼-inch-thick slices
- 1 large onion, chopped
- 1 large green bell pepper, chopped (about 1½ cups)
- 3 ribs celery, chopped (about 1 cup)
- 3 cloves garlic, minced
- 1 can (28 ounces) diced tomatoes, undrained
- 1 can (10½ ounces) chicken broth
- 1 cup uncooked rice
- 1 tablespoon Worcestershire sauce
- 1 teaspoon salt
- 1 teaspoon dried thyme leaves
- ½ teaspoon black pepper
- ¼ teaspoon ground red pepper
- 1 package (12 ounces) frozen ready-to-cook shrimp, thawed
- Fresh chives (optional)

Preheat oven to 350°F. Spray 13×9-inch baking dish with nonstick cooking spray.

Heat oil in large skillet over medium-high heat until hot. Add ham and sausage. Cook and stir 5 minutes or until sausage is lightly browned on both sides. Remove from skillet and place in prepared dish. Place onion, bell pepper, celery and garlic in same skillet; cook and stir 3 minutes. Add to sausage mixture.

Combine tomatoes with juice, broth, rice, Worcestershire, salt, thyme and black and red peppers in same skillet; bring to a boil over high heat. Reduce heat to low and simmer 3 minutes. Pour over sausage mixture and stir until combined.

Cover tightly with foil and bake 45 minutes or until rice is almost tender. Remove from oven; place shrimp on top of rice mixture. Bake, uncovered, 10 minutes or until shrimp are pink and opaque. Garnish with thyme, if desired.

Makes 8 servings

Mexican Skillet Rice

- ¾ pound lean ground pork or lean ground beef
- 1 medium onion, chopped
- 1½ tablespoons chili powder
- 1 teaspoon ground cumin
- ½ teaspoon salt
- 3 cups cooked brown rice
- 1 can (16 ounces) pinto beans, drained
- 2 cans (4 ounces each) diced green chilies
- 1 medium tomato, seeded and chopped (optional)

Cook meat in large skillet over medium-high heat until brown, stirring to crumble; drain. Return meat to skillet. Add onion, chili powder, cumin and salt; cook until onion is soft but not brown. Stir in rice, beans, and chilies; heat through. Top with tomato, if desired. *Makes 6 servings*

Microwave Directions: Combine meat and onion in 2- to 3-quart microwavable baking dish, stirring well. Cover with waxed paper and cook on HIGH 4 to 5 minutes, stirring after 2 minutes, or until meat is no longer pink. Drain. Add chili powder, cumin, salt, rice, beans and chilies. Cook on HIGH 4 to 5 minutes, stirring after 2 minutes, or until thoroughly heated. Top with tomato, if desired.

Country Pork Skillet

- 4 boneless top loin pork chops, diced
- 1 (12-ounce) jar pork gravy
- 2 tablespoons ketchup
- 8 small red potatoes, diced
- 2 cups frozen mixed vegetables

In large skillet, brown pork cubes; stir in gravy, ketchup and potatoes; cover and simmer for 10 minutes. Stir in vegetables; cook for 10 to 15 minutes longer, until vegetables are tender.

Makes 4 servings

Favorite recipe from **National Pork Producers Council**

Ham and Potato Casserole

- 1½ pounds red potatoes, peeled and sliced
- 8 ounces thinly sliced ham
- 2 poblano chili peppers, cut into thin strips
- 2 tablespoons olive oil
- 1 tablespoon dried oregano leaves
- ¼ teaspoon salt
- 1 cup (4 ounces) shredded Monterey Jack cheese with or without hot peppers
- 2 tablespoons finely chopped cilantro leaves

Slow Cooker Directions

1. Combine all ingredients, except cheese and cilantro, in slow cooker; mix well. Cover and cook on LOW 7 hours or on HIGH 4 hours.

2. Transfer potato mixture to serving dish and sprinkle with cheese and cilantro. Let stand 3 minutes or until cheese melts.

Makes 6 to 7 servings

Polish Reuben Casserole

- **2 cans (10¾ ounces each) condensed cream of mushroom soup**
- **1⅓ cups milk**
- **½ cup chopped onion**
- **1 tablespoon prepared mustard**
- **2 cans (16 ounces each) sauerkraut, rinsed and drained**
- **1 package (8 ounces) uncooked medium-width noodles**
- **1½ pounds Polish sausage, cut into ½-inch pieces**
- **2 cups (8 ounces) shredded Swiss cheese**
- **¾ cup whole wheat bread crumbs**
- **2 tablespoons butter, melted**

Combine soup, milk, onion and mustard in medium bowl; blend well. Spread sauerkraut into greased 13×9-inch baking dish. Top with uncooked noodles. Spoon soup mixture evenly over noodles; cover with sausage. Top with cheese. Combine bread crumbs and butter in small bowl; sprinkle over cheese. Cover pan tightly with foil. Bake in preheated 350°F oven 1 hour or until noodles are tender. Garnish as desired. *Makes 8 to 10 servings*

Hash Brown Frittata

- **1 (10-ounce) package BOB EVANS® Skinless Link Sausage**
- **6 eggs**
- **1 (12-ounce) package frozen hash brown potatoes, thawed**
- **1 cup (4 ounces) shredded Cheddar cheese**
- **⅓ cup whipping cream**
- **¼ cup chopped green and/or red bell pepper**
- **¼ teaspoon salt**
- **Dash black pepper**

Preheat oven to 350°F. Cut sausage into bite-size pieces. Cook in small skillet over medium heat until lightly browned, stirring occasionally. Drain off any drippings. Whisk eggs in medium bowl; stir in sausage and remaining ingredients. Pour into greased 2-quart casserole dish. Bake, uncovered, 30 minutes or until eggs are almost set. Let stand 5 minutes before cutting into squares; serve hot. Refrigerate leftovers. *Makes 6 servings*

Helpful Hints

The noodles in Polish Rueben Casserole recipe are not precooked but are added uncooked to the baking dish. Be sure noodles are completely covered with soup mixture and sausage, before, covering with foil.

Jambalaya

Cheesy Pork Chops 'n' Potatoes

- 1 jar (8 ounces) pasteurized processed cheese spread
- 1 tablespoon vegetable oil
- 6 thin pork chops, ¼ to ½ inch thick
- Seasoned salt
- ½ cup milk
- 4 cups frozen cottage fries
- 1⅓ cups ***French's® Taste Toppers™*** **French Fried Onions, divided**
- 1 package (10 ounces) frozen broccoli spears,* thawed and drained

**1 small head fresh broccoli (about ½ pound) may be substituted for frozen spears. Divide into spears and cook 3 to 4 minutes before using.*

Preheat oven to 350°F. Spoon cheese spread into 12×8-inch baking dish; place in oven just about 5 minutes. Meanwhile, in large skillet, heat oil. Brown pork chops on both sides; drain. Sprinkle chops with seasoned salt; set aside. Using fork, stir milk into cheese until well blended. Stir cottage fries and *⅔ cup **Taste Toppers*** into cheese mixture. Divide broccoli spears into 6 small bunches. Arrange bunches of spears over potato mixture with flowerets around edges of dish. Arrange chops over broccoli *stalks*. Bake, covered, at 350°F for 35 to 40 minutes or until pork chops are no longer pink. Top chops with remaining *⅔ cup **Taste Toppers***; bake, uncovered, 5 minutes or until ***Taste Toppers*** are golden brown. *Makes 4 to 6 servings*

Microwave Directions: Omit oil. Reduce milk to ¼ cup. In 12×8-inch microwave-safe dish, place cheese spread and milk. Cook, covered, on HIGH 3 minutes; stir to blend. Stir in cottage fries and *⅔ cup **Taste Toppers***. Cook, covered, 5 minutes; stir. Top with broccoli spears as above. Arrange unbrowned pork chops over broccoli *stalks* with meatiest parts toward edges of dish. Cook, covered, on MEDIUM (50-60%) 24 to 30 minutes or until pork chops are no longer pink. Turn chops over, sprinkle with seasoned salt and rotate dish halfway through cooking time. Top with remaining *⅔ cup **Taste Toppers***; cook, uncovered, on HIGH 1 minute. Let stand 5 minutes.

Creamy Pasta Primavera

- 1 bag (16 ounces) BIRDS EYE® frozen Pasta Secrets Primavera
- ½ cup 1% milk
- 2 packages (3 ounces each) cream cheese, cubed
- 1 cup cubed ham
- ¼ cup grated Parmesan cheese

• In large skillet, heat Pasta Secrets in milk over medium heat to a simmer; cover and simmer 7 to 9 minutes or until vegetables are tender.

• Add cream cheese; reduce heat to low and cook until cream cheese is melted, stirring often.

• Stir in ham and Parmesan cheese; cover and cook 5 minutes more. *Makes 4 servings*

Prep Time: 10 minutes
Cook Time: 20 minutes

Pork and Peach Bake

- 1 (6-ounce) package stuffing mix
- ½ cup SMUCKER'S® Peach Preserves, divided
- 4 pork chops (½-inch thick)
- 2 tablespoons oil
- 1 (8-ounce) can sliced peaches, drained
- Parsley

Make stuffing mix according to package directions, decreasing water by ¼ cup; stir in ¼ cup preserves. Spoon stuffing into *ungreased* 1-quart casserole. Brown pork chops in oil over medium heat. Arrange pork chops and peaches over stuffing. Spoon remaining ¼ cup preserves over chops.

Cover and bake at 350°F for 45 minutes to 1 hour or until pork chops are tender. Garnish with parsley. *Makes 4 servings*

Sweet and Sour Spare Ribs

- 4 pounds spare ribs
- 2 cups dry sherry or chicken broth
- ½ cup pineapple, mango or guava juice
- ⅓ cup chicken broth
- 1 clove garlic, minced
- 2 tablespoons brown sugar
- 2 tablespoons cider vinegar
- 2 tablespoons soy sauce
- ½ teaspoon salt
- ¼ teaspoon black pepper
- ⅛ teaspoon red pepper flakes
- 1 tablespoon cornstarch

Slow Cooker Directions

1. Preheat oven to 400°F. Place ribs in foil-lined shallow roasting pan. Bake 30 minutes, turning over after 15 minutes. Remove from oven. Slice meat into 2-rib portions. Place ribs in 5-quart slow cooker. Add remaining ingredients, except cornstarch, to slow cooker.

2. Cover and cook on LOW 6 hours. Uncover and skim fat from liquid.

3. Combine cornstarch and ¼ cup liquid from slow cooker; stir until smooth. Pour mixture back into slow cooker; mix well. Cover and cook on HIGH 10 minutes or until slightly thickened. *Makes 4 servings*

Sweet and Sour Spare Ribs

Apple, Bean and Ham Casserole

- **1 pound boneless ham**
- **3 cans (15 ounces each) Great Northern beans, drained and rinsed**
- **1 small onion, diced**
- **1 medium Granny Smith apple, diced**
- **3 tablespoons dark molasses**
- **3 tablespoons packed brown sugar**
- **1 tablespoon Dijon mustard**
- **1 teaspoon ground allspice**
- **¼ cup thinly sliced green onions *or* 1 tablespoon chopped fresh parsley**

1. Preheat oven to 350°F. Cut ham into 1-inch cubes. Combine ham, beans, onion, apple, molasses, brown sugar, mustard and allspice in 3-quart casserole; mix well.

2. Cover; bake 45 minutes or until most liquid is absorbed. Sprinkle with green onions before serving.

Makes 6 servings

Potato and Pork Frittata

- **12 ounces (about 3 cups) frozen hash brown potatoes**
- **1 teaspoon Cajun seasoning**
- **4 egg whites**
- **2 whole eggs**
- **¼ cup low-fat (1%) milk**
- **1 teaspoon dry mustard**
- **¼ teaspoon black pepper**
- **10 ounces (about 3 cups) frozen stir-fry vegetables**
- **⅓ cup water**
- **¾ cup chopped cooked lean pork**
- **½ cup (2 ounces) shredded Cheddar cheese**

1. Preheat oven to 400°F. Spray baking sheet with nonstick cooking spray. Spread potatoes on baking sheet; sprinkle with Cajun seasoning. Bake 15 minutes or until hot. Remove from oven. *Reduce oven temperature to 350°F.*

2. Beat egg whites, eggs, milk, mustard and pepper in small bowl. Place vegetables and water in medium ovenproof nonstick skillet. Cook over medium heat 5 minutes or until vegetables are crisp-tender; drain.

3. Add pork and potatoes to vegetables in skillet; stir lightly. Add egg mixture. Sprinkle with cheese. Cook over medium-low heat 5 minutes. Place skillet in 350°F oven and bake 5 minutes or until egg mixture is set and cheese is melted.

Makes 4 servings

Prep and Cook Time: 30 minutes

Pizza Pasta

- **1 tablespoon vegetable oil**
- **1 medium green bell pepper, chopped**
- **1 medium onion, chopped**
- **1 cup sliced mushrooms**
- **½ teaspoon LAWRY'S® Garlic Powder with Parsley or Garlic Salt**
- **1 package (1.5 ounces) LAWRY'S® Original-Style Spaghetti Sauce Spices & Seasonings**
- **1¾ cups water**
- **1 can (6 ounces) tomato paste**
- **¼ cup sliced ripe olives**
- **10 ounces mostaccioli, cooked and drained**
- **3 ounces thinly sliced pepperoni**
- **¾ cup shredded mozzarella cheese**

In large skillet, heat oil. Add bell pepper, onion, mushrooms and Garlic Powder with Parsley and cook over medium-high heat. Stir in Spaghetti Sauce Spices & Seasonings, water, tomato paste and olives; mix well. Bring sauce to a boil over medium-high heat; reduce heat to low and simmer, uncovered, 10 minutes. Add cooked mostaccioli and sliced pepperoni; mix well. Pour in 12×8×2-inch baking dish; top with cheese. Bake at 350°F 15 minutes until cheese is melted.

Makes 6 servings

Serving Suggestion: Serve with warm rolls or bread since this pizza doesn't have any crust.

Helpful Hints

A frittata is an Italian omelet in which the eggs are combined with other ingredients before cooking. The egg mixture is poured into a heavy skillet and cooked over medium heat. Frittatas are often finished in the oven or under the broiler. To serve, cut the frittata into wedges.

Apple, Bean and Ham Casserole

Pork Chops and Stuffing Bake

6 (¾-inch-thick) boneless pork loin chops (about 1½ pounds)
¼ teaspoon salt
⅛ teaspoon black pepper
1 tablespoon vegetable oil
1 small onion, chopped
2 ribs celery, chopped
2 Granny Smith apples, peeled, cored and coarsely chopped (about 2 cups)
1 can (14½ ounces) reduced-sodium chicken broth
1 can (10¾ ounces) condensed cream of celery soup, undiluted
¼ cup dry white wine
6 cups herb-seasoned stuffing cubes

Preheat oven to 375°F. Spray 13×9-inch baking dish with nonstick cooking spray.

Season both sides of pork chops with salt and pepper. Heat oil in large deep skillet over medium-high heat until hot. Add chops and cook until browned on both sides, turning once. Remove chops from skillet; set aside.

Add onion and celery to same skillet. Cook and stir 3 minutes or until onion is tender. Add apples; cook and stir 1 minute. Add broth, soup and wine; mix well. Bring to a simmer; remove from heat. Stir in stuffing cubes until evenly moistened.

Spread stuffing mixture evenly in prepared dish. Place pork chops on top of stuffing; pour any accumulated juices over chops.

Cover tightly with foil and bake 30 to 40 minutes or until pork chops are juicy and barely pink in center.

Makes 6 servings

Ham & Potato Scallop

1 package (5 ounces) scalloped potatoes plus ingredients as package directs
1 bag (16 ounces) BIRDS EYE® frozen Broccoli Cuts
½ pound cooked ham, cut into ½-inch cubes
½ cup shredded Cheddar cheese (optional)

• Prepare potatoes according to package directions for stove top method, adding broccoli and ham when adding milk and butter.

• Stir in cheese just before serving.

Makes 4 servings

Serving Suggestion: Spoon mixture into shallow casserole dish. Sprinkle with cheese; broil until lightly browned.

Prep Time: 5 minutes
Cook Time: 25 minutes

Sweet and Savory Sausage Casserole

2 sweet potatoes, peeled and cut into 1-inch cubes
2 apples, peeled, cored and cut into 1-inch cubes
1 medium onion, cut into thin strips
2 tablespoons vegetable oil
2 teaspoons dried Italian seasoning
1 teaspoon garlic powder
½ teaspoon salt
½ teaspoon black pepper
1 pound cooked Italian sausage, cut into ½-inch pieces

Preheat oven to 400°F. Spray 13×9-inch baking pan with nonstick cooking spray.

Combine potatoes, apples, onion, oil, Italian seasoning, garlic powder, salt and pepper in large bowl. Toss to coat evenly. Place potato mixture into prepared pan. Bake, covered, 30 minutes. Add sausage to potato mixture; bake 5 to 10 minutes or until sausage is heated through and potatoes are tender.

Makes 4 to 6 servings

Macaroni and Cheese Dijon

1¼ cups milk
12 ounces pasteurized process Cheddar cheese spread, cubed
½ cup GREY POUPON® Dijon Mustard
⅓ cup sliced green onions
6 slices bacon, cooked and crumbled
⅛ teaspoon ground red pepper
12 ounces tri-color rotelle or spiral-shaped pasta, cooked and drained
1 (2.8-ounce) can French fried onion rings

Heat milk, cheese and mustard in medium saucepan over low heat until cheese melts and mixture is smooth. Stir in green onions, bacon and pepper; remove from heat.

Combine hot pasta and cheese mixture in large bowl tossing until well coated; spoon into greased 2-quart casserole. Cover; bake at 350°F for 15 to 20 minutes. Uncover and stir; top with onion rings. Bake, uncovered, for 5 minutes more. Let stand 10 minutes before serving. Garnish as desired.

Makes 6 servings

Pork Chop and Stuffing Bake

Hearty Potato and Sausage Bake

1 pound new potatoes, cut in halves or quarters
1 large onion, sliced
½ pound baby carrots
2 tablespoons melted butter
1 teaspoon salt
1 teaspoon garlic powder
½ teaspoon dried thyme leaves
½ teaspoon black pepper
1 pound pork sausage

Preheat oven to 400°F. Spray 13×9-inch baking pan with nonstick cooking spray.

Combine potatoes, onion, carrots, butter, salt, garlic powder, thyme and pepper in large bowl. Toss to coat evenly.

Place potato mixture into prepared pan; bake, uncovered, 30 minutes. Add sausage to potato mixture; mix well. Continue to bake 15 to 20 minutes or until potatoes are tender and golden brown.

Makes 4 to 6 servings

Pork Chops and Yams

4 pork chops (½ inch thick)
2 tablespoons oil
2 (16-ounce) cans yams or sweet potatoes, drained
¾ cup SMUCKER'S® Sweet Orange Marmalade or Apricot Preserves
½ large green bell pepper, cut into strips
2 tablespoons minced onion

Brown pork chops in oil over medium heat.

Place yams in 1½-quart casserole. Stir in marmalade, bell pepper and onion. Layer pork chops over yam mixture. Cover and bake at 350°F for 30 minutes or until pork chops are tender.

Makes 4 servings

Quick Bean Cassoulet

1½ cups diagonally cut carrot slices
3 cloves garlic, minced
2 tablespoons margarine, divided
2 (15½ ounce) cans Great Northern white beans, rinsed, drained
¾ pound smoked sausage slices, halved
1 cup dry white wine or chicken broth
¾ teaspoon rubbed sage
¾ pound VELVEETA® Pasteurized Prepared Cheese Product, cubed
1 large tomato, chopped
¼ cup chopped parsley
½ cup fresh bread crumbs

- Sauté carrots and garlic in 1 tablespoon margarine in Dutch oven 5 to 7 minutes or until carrots are crisp-tender.
- Stir in beans, sausage, wine and sage. Bring to boil. Reduce heat to low. Cover; simmer 5 minutes.
- Add prepared cheese product and tomato; stir until prepared cheese product is melted. Stir in 3 tablespoons parsley. Spoon into 2-quart casserole or serving bowl.
- Melt remaining margarine. Add to combined remaining parsley and bread crumbs; toss lightly. Sprinkle over cassoulet. Garnish with fresh sage.

Makes 6 (1¼-cup) servings

Microwave Directions: Microwave carrots, garlic and 1 tablespoon margarine in 3-quart casserole on HIGH 3 to 5 minutes or until carrots are crisp-tender. Add beans, sausage, wine and sage. Microwave 7 to 10 minutes or until thoroughly heated, stirring after 5 minutes. Stir in prepared cheese product and tomato. Microwave 4 to 6 minutes or until prepared cheese product is melted, stirring after 3 minutes. Stir in 3 tablespoons parsley. Prepare crumb topping as directed. Sprinkle over cassoulet. Garnish with fresh sage.

Prep Time: 30 minutes
Microwave Cooking Time: 21 minutes

Quick Cassoulet

2 slices bacon, cut into ½-inch pieces
¾ pound boneless pork chops, sliced crosswise ¼ inch thick
1 medium onion, chopped
1 clove garlic, minced
1 teaspoon dried thyme, crushed
1 can (14½ ounces) DEL MONTE® Original Recipe Stewed Tomatoes
½ cup dry white wine
1 can (15 ounces) white or pinto beans, drained

1. Cook bacon in large skillet over medium-high heat until almost crisp.

2. Stir in meat, onion, garlic and thyme. Season with salt and pepper, if desired.

3. Cook 4 minutes. Add undrained tomatoes and wine; bring to boil. Cook, uncovered, over medium-high heat 10 minutes or until thickened, adding beans during last 5 minutes.

Makes 4 servings

Prep and Cook Time: 30 minutes

Hearty Potato and Sausage Bake

Oven Jambalaya

- 1 pound sweet Italian sausage
- 2 stalks celery, sliced
- 1 green bell pepper, diced
- 1 medium onion, diced
- 2 cloves garlic, minced
- 1 (28-ounce) can crushed tomatoes
- 2 cups chicken broth
- 1 cup long-grain rice
- 2 teaspoons TABASCO® brand Pepper Sauce
- 1 teaspoon salt
- 1 pound large shrimp, peeled and deveined

Preheat oven to 400°F. Cook sausages in 12-inch skillet over medium-high heat until well browned on all sides, turning frequently. Remove sausages to plate; reserve drippings in skillet. When cool enough to handle, cut sausages into ½-inch slices. Add celery, green bell pepper, onion and garlic to same skillet; cook 3 minutes over medium heat, stirring occasionally.

Combine tomatoes, chicken broth, rice, TABASCO® Sauce, salt, sausages and vegetable mixture in 3-quart casserole. Bake 40 minutes. Stir in shrimp; cook 5 minutes or until rice is tender and shrimp are cooked.

Makes 8 servings

Sausage & Noodle Casserole

- 1 pound BOB EVANS® Original Recipe Roll Sausage
- 1 cup chopped onion
- ¼ cup chopped green bell pepper
- 1 (10-ounce) package frozen peas
- 1 (10¾-ounce) can condensed cream of chicken soup
- 1 (8-ounce) package egg noodles, cooked according to package directions and drained
- Salt and black pepper to taste
- 1 (2.8-ounce) can French fried onions, crushed

Preheat oven to 350°F. Crumble sausage into large skillet. Add onion and green pepper. Cook over medium heat until meat is browned and vegetables are tender, stirring occasionally. Drain off any drippings. Cook peas according to package directions. Drain, reserving liquid in 2-cup glass measuring cup; set aside. Add enough water to pea liquid to obtain 1⅓ cups liquid. Combine liquid and soup in large bowl; stir in sausage mixture, noodles, reserved peas, salt and black pepper. Mix well. Spoon mixture into greased 2½-quart baking dish. Sprinkle with onions. Bake 30 minutes or until bubbly. Serve hot. Refrigerate leftovers.

Makes 6 servings

That's Italian Meat Loaf

- 1 (8-ounce) can tomato sauce, divided
- 1 egg, lightly beaten
- ½ cup chopped onion
- ½ cup chopped green bell pepper
- ⅓ cup dry seasoned bread crumbs
- 2 tablespoons grated Parmesan cheese
- ½ teaspoon garlic powder
- ¼ teaspoon black pepper
- 1 pound ground beef
- ½ pound ground pork
- 1 cup shredded Asiago cheese

Slow Cooker Directions

Reserve ⅓ cup tomato sauce; set aside in refrigerator. Combine remaining tomato sauce and egg in large bowl. Stir in onion, bell pepper, bread crumbs, Parmesan cheese, garlic powder and black pepper. Add ground beef and pork; mix well and shape into loaf.

Place meat loaf on foil strips. Place in slow cooker. Cover and cook on LOW 8 to 10 hours or on HIGH 4 to 6 hours; internal temperature should read 170°F.

Spread meat loaf with reserved tomato sauce. Sprinkle with Asiago cheese. Cover and cook 15 minutes or until cheese is melted. Using foil strips, remove meat loaf from slow cooker.

Makes 8 servings

Helpful Hints

To easily lift a dish or a meat loaf out of a slow cooker, make foil handles. Tear off three 18×3-inch strips of heavy-duty foil. Crisscross strips and place the dish or meat loaf in the center of the strips. Pull strips up around dish and place it in the slow cooker. When the dish is finished cooking simply lift it out using foil strips.

Oven Jambalaya

Sausage Tetrazzini

- 1 pound BOB EVANS® Italian Roll Sausage
- 1 medium onion, chopped
- 1 red or green bell pepper, chopped
- ½ pound spaghetti, cooked according to package directions and drained
- 1 (10½-ounce) can condensed cream of mushroom soup
- 1 (10-ounce) can condensed tomato soup
- 1 (16-ounce) can stewed tomatoes, undrained
- ½ pound fresh mushrooms, chopped
- 1 teaspoon minced garlic
- ½ teaspoon black pepper
- Salt to taste
- 1½ cups (6 ounces) shredded Cheddar cheese

Preheat oven to 350°F. Crumble sausage into large skillet. Cook over medium heat until lightly browned, stirring occasionally. Remove sausage; set aside. Add onion and red pepper to drippings in skillet; cook and stir until tender. Place in large bowl. Stir in spaghetti, soups, tomatoes with juice, mushrooms, garlic, black pepper, salt and reserved sausage; place in 3-quart casserole dish. Sprinkle with cheese; bake, uncovered, 30 to 35 minutes or until heated through. Serve hot. Refrigerate leftovers.

Makes 6 to 8 servings

Savory Lentil Casserole

- 1¼ cups uncooked dried brown or green lentils, sorted and rinsed
- 2 tablespoons olive oil
- 1 large onion, chopped
- 3 cloves garlic, minced
- 8 ounces fresh shiitake or button mushrooms, sliced
- 2 tablespoons all-purpose flour
- 1½ cups beef broth
- 4 ounces Canadian bacon, minced
- 1 tablespoon Worcestershire sauce
- 1 tablespoon balsamic vinegar
- ½ teaspoon salt
- ½ teaspoon black pepper
- ½ cup grated Parmesan cheese
- 2 to 3 plum tomatoes, seeded and chopped

1. Preheat oven to 400°F. Place lentils in medium saucepan; cover with 1 inch water. Bring to a boil over high heat. Reduce heat to low. Simmer, covered, 20 to 25 minutes until lentils are barely tender; drain.

2. Meanwhile, heat oil in large skillet over medium heat. Add onion and garlic; cook and stir 10 minutes. Add mushrooms; cook and stir 10 minutes or until liquid is evaporated and mushrooms are tender. Sprinkle flour over mushroom mixture; stir well. Cook and stir 1 minute. Stir in beef broth, bacon, Worcestershire, vinegar, salt and pepper. Cook and stir until mixture is thick and bubbly.

3. Grease 1½-quart casserole. Stir lentils into mushroom mixture. Spread evenly into prepared casserole. Sprinkle with cheese. Bake 20 minutes.

4. Sprinkle tomatoes over casserole just before serving. Garnish with thyme and Italian parsley, if desired.

Makes 4 servings

Tuscan Pot Pie

- ¾ pound sweet or hot Italian sausage
- 1 jar (26 to 28 ounces) prepared chunky vegetable or mushroom spaghetti sauce
- 1 can (19 ounces) cannellini beans, rinsed and drained
- ½ teaspoon dried thyme leaves
- 1½ cups (6 ounces) shredded mozzarella cheese
- 1 package (8 ounces) refrigerated crescent dinner rolls

1. Preheat oven to 425°F. Remove sausage from casings. Brown sausage in medium ovenproof skillet, stirring to separate meat. Drain drippings.

2. Add spaghetti sauce, beans and thyme to skillet. Simmer uncovered over medium heat 5 minutes. Remove from heat; stir in cheese.

3. Unroll crescent dough; divide into triangles. Arrange in spiral with points of dough towards center, covering sausage mixture completely. Bake 12 minutes or until crust is golden brown and meat mixture is bubbly.

Makes 4 to 6 servings

Hint: To remove a sausage casing, use a pairing knife to slit the casing at one end. Be careful not to cut through the sausage. Grasp the cut edge and gently pull the casing away from the sausage.

Prep and Cook Time: 27 minutes

Savory Lentil Casserole

Fiesta Rice and Sausage

- **1 teaspoon vegetable oil**
- **2 pounds spicy Italian sausage, casing removed**
- **2 cloves garlic, minced**
- **2 teaspoons ground cumin**
- **4 onions, chopped**
- **4 green bell peppers, chopped**
- **3 jalapeño peppers,* seeded and minced**
- **4 cups beef broth**
- **2 packages (6¼ ounces each) long-grain and wild rice mix**

**Jalapeño peppers can sting and irritate the skin; wear rubber gloves when handling peppers and do not touch eyes. Wash hands after handling.*

Slow Cooker Directions
Heat oil in large skillet; add sausage. Break up sausage with back of spoon while cooking; cook until browned, about 5 minutes. Add garlic and cumin; cook 30 seconds. Add onions, bell peppers and jalapeño peppers. Sauté mixture until onions are tender, about 10 minutes. Pour mixture into slow cooker. Stir in beef broth and rice.

Cover and cook on HIGH 1 to 2 hours or on LOW 4 to 6 hours.

Makes 10 to 12 servings

Sausage Bake

- **1 cup uncooked egg noodles**
- **1 bag (16 ounces) BIRDS EYE® frozen Cut Green Beans**
- **1 pound smoked sausage links, fully cooked**
- **1 can (15 ounces) cream of celery soup**
- **½ teaspoon *each* sage, celery salt and garlic powder**

• In large saucepan, cook noodles according to package directions. Add green beans during last 10 minutes; drain and return to pan.

• Meanwhile, cut sausage into ½-inch pieces.

• Add all ingredients to noodles and beans; toss together.

• Cook over medium heat 3 to 5 minutes or until heated through. Add salt and pepper to taste.

Makes 4 servings

Prep Time: 2 minutes
Cook Time: 15 minutes

Vegetable-Stuffed Pork Chops

- **4 double pork loin chops, well trimmed**
- **Salt and black pepper**
- **1 can (15¼ ounces) kernel corn, drained**
- **1 green bell pepper, chopped**
- **1 cup Italian-style seasoned dry bread crumbs**
- **1 small onion, chopped**
- **½ cup uncooked long-grain converted rice**
- **1 can (8 ounces) tomato sauce**
- **Fresh salad (optional)**

Slow Cooker Directions
Cut pocket in each pork chop, cutting from edge nearest bone. Lightly season pockets with salt and pepper to taste. Combine corn, bell pepper, bread crumbs onion and rice in large bowl. Stuff pork chops with vegetable-rice mixture. Secure along fat side with wooden toothpicks.

Place any remaining vegetable-rice mixture into slow cooker. Add stuffed pork chops to slow cooker. Moisten top of each pork chop with tomato sauce. Pour any remaining tomato sauce over top. Cover and cook on LOW 8 to 10 hours or until done.

Remove pork chops to serving platter. Serve with vegetable-rice mixture and fresh salad, if desired.

Makes 4 servings

Smokehouse Red Bean and Sausage Casserole

- **3 slices bacon, chopped**
- **3 cups chopped onion**
- **1 medium-sized green bell pepper, chopped**
- **1 cup chopped fresh parsley**
- **1 pound smoked sausage, cut into ¼-inch slices**
- **2 cans (15¼ ounces each) kidney beans, undrained**
- **1 can (8 ounces) tomato sauce**
- **1 tablespoon Worcestershire sauce**
- **1 tablespoon LAWRY'S® Seasoned Salt**
- **¾ teaspoon hot pepper sauce**
- **½ teaspoon LAWRY'S® Garlic Powder with Parsley**
- **3 cups hot cooked white rice**

In Dutch oven or large saucepan, cook bacon and onion over medium-high heat until bacon is just crisp and onion is transparent; drain fat. Add remaining ingredients except rice; mix well. Bring to a boil over medium-high heat; reduce heat to low and simmer, uncovered, 20 minutes, stirring occasionally.

Makes 8 servings

Serving Suggestion: Serve over rice. This is perfect with a green salad and crusty bread.

Hint: Use 1 bag (12 ounces) frozen chopped onion instead of fresh onion.

Fiesta Rice and Sausage

Pork Chops with Jalapeño-Pecan Cornbread Stuffing

Slow Cooker

- 6 boneless loin pork chops, 1 inch thick (1½ pounds)
- Nonstick cooking spray
- ¾ cup chopped onion
- ¾ cup chopped celery
- ½ cup coarsely chopped pecans
- ½ medium jalapeño pepper,* seeded and chopped
- 1 teaspoon rubbed sage
- ½ teaspoon dried rosemary
- ⅛ teaspoon black pepper
- 4 cups unseasoned cornbread stuffing mix
- 1¼ cups reduced-sodium chicken broth
- 1 egg, slightly beaten

**Jalapeño peppers can sting and irritate the skin; wear rubber gloves when handling peppers and do not touch eyes. Wash hands after handling.*

Slow Cooker Directions

Trim excess fat from pork and discard. Spray large skillet with nonstick cooking spray; heat over medium heat. Add pork; cook 10 minutes or until browned on all sides. Remove; set aside. Add onion, celery, pecans, jalapeño pepper, sage, rosemary and pepper to skillet. Cook 5 minutes or until tender; set aside.

Combine cornbread stuffing mix, vegetable mixture and broth in medium bowl. Stir in egg. Spoon stuffing mixture into slow cooker. Arrange pork on top. Cover and cook on LOW about 5 hours or until pork is tender and barely pink in center. Serve with vegetable salad, if desired. *Makes 6 servings*

Note: If you prefer a more moist stuffing, increase the chicken broth to 1½ cups.

Spareribs Simmered in Orange Sauce

Slow Cooker

- 4 pounds country-style pork spareribs
- 2 tablespoons vegetable oil
- 2 medium white onions, cut into ¼-inch slices
- 1 to 2 tablespoons dried ancho chilies, seeded and finely chopped
- ½ teaspoon ground cinnamon
- ¼ teaspoon ground cloves
- 1 can (16 ounces) tomatoes, undrained
- 2 cloves garlic
- ½ cup orange juice
- ⅓ cup dry white wine
- ⅓ cup packed brown sugar
- 1 teaspoon shredded orange peel
- ½ teaspoon salt
- 1 to 2 tablespoons cider vinegar
- Orange wedges (optional)

Slow Cooker Directions

Trim excess fat from ribs. Cut into individual riblets. Heat oil in large skillet over medium heat. Add ribs; cook 10 minutes or until browned on all sides. Remove to plate. Remove and discard all but 2 tablespoons drippings from skillet. Add onions, chilies, cinnamon and cloves. Cook and stir 4 minutes or until softened. Transfer onion mixture to slow cooker.

Process tomatoes with juice and garlic in food processor or blender until smooth.

Combine tomato mixture, orange juice, wine, sugar, orange peel and salt in slow cooker. Add ribs; stir to coat. Cover and cook on LOW 5 hours or until ribs are fork-tender. Remove ribs to plates. Ladle out liquid to medium bowl. Let stand 5 minutes. Skim and discard fat. Stir in vinegar; serve over ribs. Garnish with orange wedges, if desired.

Makes 4 to 6 servings

Smoked Sausage and Sauerkraut Casserole

- 6 fully-cooked smoked sausage links, such as German or Polish sausage (about 1½ pounds)
- ⅓ cup water
- ¼ cup packed brown sugar
- 2 tablespoons country-style Dijon mustard, Dijon mustard or German-style mustard
- 1 teaspoon caraway seed
- ½ teaspoon dill weed
- 1 jar (32 ounces) sauerkraut, drained
- 1 small green bell pepper, stemmed, seeded and diced
- ½ cup (2 ounces) shredded Swiss cheese

1. Place sausage in large skillet with water. Cover; bring to a boil over medium heat. Reduce heat to low; simmer, covered, 10 minutes. Uncover and simmer until water evaporates and sausage browns lightly.

2. While sausage is cooking, combine sugar, mustard, caraway and dill in medium saucepan; stir until blended. Add sauerkraut and bell pepper; stir until well mixed. Cook, covered, over medium heat 10 minutes or until very hot.

3. Spoon sauerkraut into microwavable 2- to 3-quart casserole; sprinkle with cheese. Place sausage into sauerkraut; cover. Microwave at HIGH 30 seconds or until cheese melts. *Makes 6 servings*

Prep and Cook Time: 20 minutes

Pork Chop with Jalapeño-Pecan Cornbread Stuffing

Jamaican Pork Skillet

1 tablespoon vegetable oil
4 well-trimmed center cut pork chops, cut ½ inch thick
¾ teaspoon blackened or Cajun seasoning mix
¼ teaspoon ground allspice
1 cup chunky salsa, divided
1 can (15 ounces) black beans, drained and rinsed
1 can (about 8 ounces) whole kernel corn, drained or 1 cup thawed frozen whole kernel corn
1 tablespoon fresh lime juice

1. Heat oil in large deep skillet over medium-high heat until hot. Sprinkle both sides of pork chops with blackened seasoning mix and allspice; cook 2 minutes per side or until browned.

2. Pour ½ cup salsa over pork chops; reduce heat to medium. Cover and simmer about 12 minutes or until pork is no longer pink.

3. While pork chops are simmering, combine beans, corn, remaining ½ cup salsa and lime juice in medium bowl; mix well. Serve bean mixture with pork chops.

Makes 4 servings

Note: For a special touch, add chopped fresh cilantro to the bean mixture.

Prep and Cook Time: 20 minutes

Spicy-Sweet Pineapple Pork

¾ cup LAWRY'S® Hawaiian Marinade with Tropical Fruit Juices
1 tablespoon minced fresh ginger
1 pound pork loin, cut into ½-inch strips or cubes
1 cup salsa
3 tablespoons brown sugar
2 tablespoons cornstarch
2 cans (8 ounces each) pineapple chunks, undrained, divided
2 tablespoons vegetable oil, divided
1 green bell pepper, cut into chunks
3 green onions, diagonally sliced into 1-inch pieces
½ cup whole cashews

In large resealable plastic food storage bag, combine Hawaiian Marinade with Tropical Fruit Juices and ginger. Add pork; seal bag. Marinate in refrigerator at least 1 hour. In small bowl, combine salsa, brown sugar, cornstarch and juice from 1 can pineapple; set aside. In hot large skillet or wok, heat 1 tablespoon oil. Stir-fry pepper and onions until onions are transparent; remove and set aside. Remove pork; discard used marinade. Add remaining 1 tablespoon oil and pork to skillet; stir-fry 5 minutes or until just browned. Return pepper and onions to skillet. Stir salsa mixture; add to skillet. Cook until thickened, stirring constantly. Drain remaining 1 can pineapple. Add pineapple chunks from both cans and cashews; simmer 5 minutes.

Makes 6 servings

Serving Suggestion: Serve over steamed white rice and top with crunchy chow mein noodles.

Sweet and Sour Pork

¾ pound boneless pork
1 teaspoon vegetable oil
1 bag (16 ounces) BIRDS EYE® frozen Farm Fresh Mixtures Pepper Stir Fry vegetables
1 tablespoon water
1 jar (14 ounces) sweet and sour sauce
1 can (8 ounces) pineapple chunks, drained

• Cut pork into thin strips.

• In large skillet, heat oil over medium-high heat.

• Add pork; stir-fry until pork is browned.

• Add vegetables and water; cover and cook over medium heat 5 to 7 minutes or until vegetables are crisp-tender.

• Uncover; stir in sweet and sour sauce and pineapple. Cook until heated through.

Makes 4 servings

Serving Suggestion: Serve over hot cooked rice.

Prep Time: 5 minutes
Cook Time: 15 to 18 minutes

Jamaican Pork Skillet

New Orleans Rice and Sausage

½ pound smoked sausage,* cut into slices
1 can (14½ ounces) stewed tomatoes, Cajun- or Italian-style
¾ cup water
1¾ cups uncooked instant rice
Dash TABASCO® Pepper Sauce or to taste
1 bag (16 ounces) BIRDS EYE® frozen Farm Fresh Mixtures Broccoli, Corn and Red Peppers

**For a spicy dish, use andouille sausage. Any type of kielbasa or turkey kielbasa can also be used.*

Heat sausage in large skillet 2 to 3 minutes.

Add tomatoes, water, rice and TABASCO® Pepper Sauce; mix well.

Add vegetables; mix well. Cover and cook over medium heat 5 to 7 minutes or until rice is tender and vegetables are heated through.

Makes 6 servings

Prep Time: 5 minutes
Cook Time: 10 minutes

Chinese Pork & Vegetable Stir-Fry

2 tablespoons vegetable oil, divided
1 pound pork tenderloin or boneless beef sirloin, cut into ¼-inch slices
6 cups assorted fresh vegetables*
1 can (8 ounces) sliced water chestnuts, drained
1 envelope LIPTON® Recipe Secrets® Onion Soup Mix
¾ cup water
½ cup orange juice
1 tablespoon soy sauce
¼ teaspoon garlic powder

**Use any of the following to equal 6 cups: broccoli florets, snow peas, thinly sliced red or green bell peppers, or thinly sliced carrots.*

In 12-inch skillet, heat 1 tablespoon oil over medium-high heat; brown pork. Remove and set aside.

In same skillet, heat remaining 1 tablespoon oil and cook assorted fresh vegetables, stirring occasionally, 5 minutes. Stir in water chestnuts and onion soup mix blended with water, orange juice, soy sauce and garlic powder. Bring to a boil over high heat. Reduce heat to low and simmer, uncovered, 3 minutes. Return pork to skillet and cook 1 minute or until heated through.

Makes about 4 servings

Tip: Pick up pre-sliced vegetables from your local salad bar.

Ivory, Rubies and Jade

¾ pound lean pork, cut into thin 2-inch strips
2 tablespoons LA CHOY® Soy Sauce
1 teaspoon minced fresh garlic
4 tablespoons WESSON® Oil, divided
1½ cups diagonally sliced celery
1 cup chopped red bell pepper
1 can (8 ounces) LA CHOY® Sliced Water Chestnuts, drained
1 package (6 ounces) frozen pea pods, thawed and drained
1 jar (10 ounces) LA CHOY® Sweet & Sour Sauce
3 green onions, diagonally cut into 1-inch pieces
⅛ teaspoon cayenne pepper
1 can (5 ounces) LA CHOY® Chow Mein Noodles

In medium bowl, combine pork, soy sauce and garlic; cover and marinate 30 minutes in refrigerator. Drain. In large nonstick skillet or wok, heat 3 tablespoons oil. Add pork mixture; stir-fry until pork is no longer pink in center. Remove pork from skillet; set aside. Heat remaining 1 tablespoon oil in same skillet. Add celery and bell pepper; stir-fry until crisp-tender. Return pork to skillet with all remaining ingredients except noodles; heat thoroughly, stirring occasionally. Serve over noodles.

Makes 4 servings

Skillet Red Beans & Rice

1 tablespoon vegetable oil
1 medium onion, finely chopped
1 green bell pepper, finely chopped
1 rib celery, finely chopped
3 cloves garlic, minced
2½ cups water
1 can (about 15 ounces) kidney beans, rinsed and drained
1 cup uncooked converted white rice
¼ pound Canadian bacon, finely chopped
1 bay leaf
1 teaspoon dried thyme leaves
½ teaspoon black pepper

1. Heat oil in nonstick skillet over medium-high heat until hot. Add onion, bell pepper, celery and garlic; cook and stir 5 minutes or until vegetables are tender.

2. Add water, beans, rice, bacon, bay leaf, thyme and black pepper to skillet. Cover. Cook over medium heat 15 to 20 minutes or until liquid is absorbed and rice is tender. Remove bay leaf; discard. Garnish with sprigs of thyme, if desired.

Makes 6 servings

New Orleans Rice and Sausage

Best-Loved Chicken

Forty-Clove Chicken

1 frying chicken (3 pounds), cut into serving pieces
Salt and black pepper
1 to 2 tablespoons olive oil
¼ cup dry white wine
⅛ cup dry vermouth
2 tablespoons chopped fresh parsley *or* 2 teaspoons dried parsley leaves
2 teaspoons dried basil leaves
1 teaspoon dried oregano leaves
Pinch of red pepper flakes
40 cloves garlic (about 3 heads*), peeled
4 ribs celery, sliced
Juice and peel of 1 lemon
Fresh herbs (optional)

**The whole garlic bulb is called a head.*

Slow Cooker Directions
Remove skin from chicken, if desired. Sprinkle with salt and pepper. Heat oil in large skillet over medium heat. Add chicken; cook 10 minutes or until browned on all sides. Remove to platter.

Combine wine, vermouth, parsley, basil, oregano and red pepper flakes in large bowl. Add garlic and celery; coat well. Transfer garlic and celery to slow cooker with slotted spoon. Add chicken to remaining herb mixture; coat well. Place chicken on top of celery in slow cooker. Sprinkle with lemon juice and peel; add remaining herb mixture. Cover and cook on LOW 6 hours or until chicken is no longer pink in center. Garnish with fresh herbs, if desired.

Makes 4 to 6 servings

Chicken & Biscuits

¼ cup butter or margarine
4 boneless skinless chicken breast halves (about 1¼ pounds), cut into ½-inch pieces
½ cup chopped onion
½ teaspoon dried thyme leaves
½ teaspoon paprika
¼ teaspoon black pepper
1 can (about 14 ounces) chicken broth, divided
⅓ cup all-purpose flour
1 package (10 ounces) frozen peas and carrots
1 can (12 ounces) refrigerated biscuits

Preheat oven to 375°F. Melt butter in large skillet over medium heat. Add chicken, onion, thyme, paprika and pepper. Cook 5 minutes or until chicken is browned.

Combine ¼ cup chicken broth with flour; stir until smooth. Set aside.

Add remaining chicken broth to skillet; bring to a boil. Gradually add flour mixture; stirring constantly to prevent lumps from forming. Simmer 5 minutes. Add peas and carrots; continue cooking 2 minutes.

Transfer to 1½-quart casserole; top with biscuits. Bake 25 to 30 minutes or until biscuits are golden brown.

Makes 4 to 6 servings

Hint: Use an ovenproof skillet to cook chicken in and omit the 1½-quart casserole. Place biscuits directly on chicken and vegetable mixture and bake as directed.

Forty-Clove Chicken

Roasted Chicken and Vegetables over Wild Rice

- 3½ pounds chicken pieces
- ¾ cup olive oil vinaigrette dressing, divided
- 1 tablespoon margarine or butter, melted
- 1 package (6 ounces) long-grain and wild rice mix
- 1 can (about 14 ounces) reduced-sodium chicken broth
- 1 small eggplant, cut into 1-inch pieces
- 2 medium red potatoes, cut into 1-inch pieces
- 1 medium yellow squash, cut into 1-inch pieces
- 1 medium zucchini, cut into 1-inch pieces
- 1 medium red onion, cut into wedges
- 1 package (4 ounces) crumbled feta cheese with basil
- Chopped fresh cilantro (optional)
- Fresh thyme sprig (optional)

Remove skin from chicken; discard. Combine chicken and ½ cup dressing in large resealable plastic food storage bag. Seal bag and turn to coat. Refrigerate 30 minutes or overnight.

Preheat oven to 375°F. Coat bottom of 13×9-inch baking dish with margarine.

Add rice and seasoning packet to prepared dish; stir in broth. Combine eggplant, potatoes, squash, zucchini and onion in large bowl. Place on top of rice mixture.

Remove chicken from bag and place on top of vegetables; discard marinade. Pour remaining ¼ cup dressing over chicken.

Bake, uncovered, 45 minutes. Remove from oven and sprinkle with cheese. Bake 5 to 10 minutes or until chicken is no longer pink in centers, juices run clear and cheese is melted. Sprinkle with cilantro, if desired. Garnish with thyme, if desired.

Makes 4 to 6 servings

90's-Style Slow Cooker Coq Au Vin

- 2 packages BUTTERBALL® Boneless Skinless Chicken Breast Fillets
- 1 pound fresh mushrooms, sliced thick
- 1 jar (15 ounces) pearl onions, drained
- ½ cup dry white wine
- 1 teaspoon thyme leaves
- 1 bay leaf
- 1 cup chicken broth
- ⅓ cup flour
- ½ cup chopped fresh parsley

Slow Cooker Directions

Place chicken, mushrooms, onions, wine, thyme and bay leaf into slow cooker. Combine chicken broth and flour; pour into slow cooker. Cover and cook 5 hours on LOW setting. Add parsley. Serve over wild rice pilaf, if desired.

Makes 8 servings

Preparation Time: 30 minutes plus cooking time

Apple Curry Chicken

- 4 boneless skinless chicken breasts
- 1 cup apple juice, divided
- ¼ teaspoon salt
- Dash black pepper
- 1½ cups plain croutons
- 1 medium apple, chopped
- 1 medium onion, chopped
- ¼ cup raisins
- 2 teaspoons brown sugar
- 1 teaspoon curry powder
- ¾ teaspoon poultry seasoning
- ⅛ teaspoon garlic powder
- 2 apple slices and fresh thyme sprigs for garnish

1. Preheat oven to 350°F. Lightly grease 1-quart round baking dish.

2. Arrange chicken breasts in single layer in prepared dish.

3. Combine ¼ cup apple juice, salt and pepper in small bowl. Brush juice mixture over chicken.

4. Combine croutons, apple, onion, raisins, brown sugar, curry, poultry seasoning and garlic powder in large bowl. Toss with remaining ¾ cup apple juice.

5. Spread crouton mixture over chicken. Cover with foil; bake 45 minutes or until chicken is tender. Garnish, if desired.

Makes 4 servings

Helpful Hints

Long cooking in a slow cooker allows wine to mellow and blend with other ingredients. If you wish to avoid alcohol, replace the wine with chicken broth.

Roasted Chicken and Vegetables over Wild Rice

Homestyle Chicken Pot Pie

- **2 tablespoons margarine or butter, divided**
- **1 pound boneless skinless chicken breasts, cut into 1-inch pieces**
- **½ teaspoon salt**
- **½ teaspoon dried thyme leaves**
- **¼ teaspoon black pepper**
- **1 package (16 ounces) frozen mixed vegetables, such as potatoes, peas and carrots, thawed and drained**
- **1 can (10¾ ounces) condensed cream of chicken or mushroom soup, undiluted**
- **⅓ cup dry white wine or milk**
- **1 refrigerated ready rolled pie crust, at room temperature**

1. Preheat oven to 425°F. Melt 1 tablespoon margarine in medium broilerproof skillet over medium-high heat. Add chicken; sprinkle with salt, thyme and pepper. Cook 1 minute, stirring frequently.

2. Reduce heat to medium-low. Stir in vegetables, soup and wine; simmer 5 minutes.

3. While soup mixture is simmering, unwrap pie crust. Using small cookie cutter, make decorative cut-outs from pastry to allow steam to escape.

4. Remove chicken mixture from heat; top with pie crust. Melt remaining tablespoon margarine. Brush pie crust with 2 teaspoons melted margarine. Arrange cut-outs attractively over crust, if desired. Brush cut-outs with remaining 1 teaspoon melted margarine. Bake 12 minutes. Turn oven to broil; broil 4 to 5 inches from heat source 2 minutes or until crust is golden brown and chicken mixture is bubbly.

Makes 4 to 5 servings

Broccoli, Chicken and Rice Casserole

- **1 box UNCLE BEN'S® COUNTRY INN® Broccoli Rice Au Gratin**
- **4 TYSON® Individually Fresh Frozen® Boneless, Skinless Chicken Breasts**
- **2 cups boiling water**
- **¼ teaspoon garlic powder**
- **2 cups frozen broccoli**
- **1 cup shredded Cheddar cheese**

COOK: Preheat oven to 425°F. In 13×9-inch baking pan, combine rice and contents of seasoning packet. Add boiling water; mix well. CLEAN: Wash hands. Add chicken, sprinkle with garlic powder, cover and bake 30 minutes. Add broccoli and cheese; bake, covered, 8 to 10 minutes or until internal juices of chicken run clear. (Or insert instant-read meat thermometer in thickest part of chicken. Temperature should read 170°F.)

SERVE: Serve hot out of the oven with yeast rolls, if desired.

CHILL: Refrigerate leftovers immediately. *Makes 4 servings*

Prep Time: none
Cook Time: 40 minutes

Tip: If you skin and debone your own chicken breasts, be sure to reserve both the bones and skin. Let these scraps collect in a plastic bag in your freezer and soon you'll have enough to make flavorful homemade chicken stock.

Prep Time: 5 minutes
Cook Time: 25 minutes

Chicken Dijon & Pasta

- **1 (3- to 4-pound) chicken, cut-up, and skinned, if desired**
- **⅓ cup *FRENCH'S®* Dijon Mustard**
- **⅓ cup Italian salad dressing**
- **1 can (10¾ ounces) condensed cream of chicken soup**
- **4 cups hot cooked rotini pasta (8 ounces uncooked)**
- **1⅓ cups *French's® Taste Toppers™* French Fried Onions, divided**
- **1 cup diced tomatoes**
- **1 cup diced zucchini**
- **2 tablespoons minced parsley or basil leaves (optional)**

1. Preheat oven to 400°F. Place chicken in shallow roasting pan. Mix mustard and dressing. Spoon half of mixture over chicken. Bake, uncovered, 40 minutes.

2. Combine soup, *½ cup water* and remaining mustard mixture. Toss pasta with sauce, *⅔ cup* ***Taste Toppers,*** tomatoes, zucchini and parsley, if desired. Spoon mixture around chicken.

3. Bake, uncovered, 15 minutes or until chicken is no longer pink in center. Sprinkle with remaining *⅔ cup* ***Taste Toppers.*** Bake 1 minute or until ***Taste Toppers*** are golden.

Makes 6 servings

Prep Time: 15 minutes
Cook Time: about 1 hour

Homestyle Chicken Pot Pie

Pineapple Chicken and Sweet Potatoes

Slow Cooker

- ⅔ cup plus 3 tablespoons all-purpose flour, divided
- 1 teaspoon salt
- 1 teaspoon ground nutmeg
- ½ teaspoon ground cinnamon
- ⅛ teaspoon onion powder
- ⅛ teaspoon black pepper
- 6 chicken breasts
- 3 sweet potatoes, peeled and sliced
- 1 can (10¾ ounces) condensed cream of chicken soup, undiluted
- ½ cup pineapple juice
- ¼ pound mushrooms, sliced
- 2 teaspoons brown sugar
- ½ teaspoon grated orange peel
- Hot cooked rice

Slow Cooker Directions

Combine ⅔ cup flour, salt, nutmeg, cinnamon, onion powder and black pepper in large bowl. Thoroughly coat chicken in flour mixture. Place sweet potatoes on bottom of slow cooker. Top with chicken.

Combine soup, juice, mushrooms, remaining 3 tablespoons flour, sugar and orange peel in small bowl; stir well. Pour soup mixture into slow cooker. Cover and cook on LOW 8 to 10 hours or on HIGH 3 to 4 hours. Serve chicken and sauce over rice.

Make 6 servings

Chicken Teriyaki

- 1 pound boneless skinless chicken tenders
- 1 can (6 ounces) pineapple juice
- ¼ cup soy sauce
- 1 tablespoon sugar
- 1 tablespoon minced fresh ginger
- 1 tablespoon minced garlic
- 1 tablespoon vegetable oil
- 1 tablespoon molasses
- 24 cherry tomatoes (optional)
- 2 cups hot cooked rice

Slow Cooker Directions

Combine all ingredients, except rice, in slow cooker. Cover and cook on LOW 2 hours. Serve chicken and sauce over rice.

Makes 4 servings

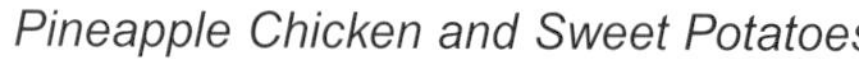

Pineapple Chicken and Sweet Potatoes

Brown Rice Chicken Bake

Vegetable cooking spray
3 cups cooked brown rice
1 package (10 ounces) frozen green peas
2 cups chopped cooked chicken breasts
½ cup cholesterol free, reduced calorie mayonnaise
⅓ cup slivered almonds, toasted (optional)
2 teaspoons soy sauce
¼ teaspoon ground black pepper
¼ teaspoon garlic powder
¼ teaspoon dried tarragon leaves

Spray 3-quart baking casserole with vegetable cooking spray. Combine rice, peas, chicken, mayonnaise, almonds, soy sauce, and seasonings in large bowl; mix well. Spoon into prepared casserole; cover. Bake at 350°F for 15 to 20 minutes or until heated through.

Makes 6 servings

Favorite recipe from **USA Rice Federation**

Cajun Chicken Bayou

1 box UNCLE BEN'S CHEF'S RECIPE™ Traditional Red Beans & Rice
3 TYSON® Individually Fresh Frozen® Boneless, Skinless Chicken Breasts
2 cups water
1 can (10 ounces) diced tomatoes and green chilies, undrained

COOK: CLEAN: Wash hands. In large skillet, combine water, tomatoes, beans and rice, and contents of seasoning packet; mix well. Add chicken. Bring to a boil. Cover, reduce heat; simmer 30 to 35 minutes or until internal juices of chicken run clear. (Or insert instant-read meat thermometer in thickest part of chicken. Temperature should read 170°F.)

SERVE: Serve with sliced avocados and whole wheat rolls, if desired.

CHILL: Refrigerate leftovers immediately. *Makes 3 servings*

Prep Time: none
Cook Time: 35 minutes

Cheesy Broccoli & Rice with Chicken

1½ pounds boneless skinless chicken, cut into strips
1 package (4.4 ounces) chicken flavor rice & sauce mix
1⅓ cups *French's® Taste Toppers™* French Fried Onions, divided
1 cup *each* chopped broccoli and red bell pepper
1 cup cubed pasteurized process cheese

1. Heat *1 tablespoon oil* in large skillet or wok until hot. Stir-fry chicken 5 minutes or until browned. Add rice mix and *2 cups water;* heat to boiling.

2. Stir in *⅔ cup* ***Taste Toppers,*** vegetables and cheese. Simmer, uncovered, 10 minutes or until rice is tender, stirring.

3. Sprinkle remaining *⅔ cup* ***Taste Toppers*** over rice just before serving.

Makes 6 servings

Prep Time: 10 minutes
Cook Time: 15 minutes

Chicken Enchiladas

2 cups chopped cooked chicken
2 cups shredded Wisconsin Cheddar cheese, divided
2 cups shredded Wisconsin Monterey Jack cheese, divided
1 cup Wisconsin dairy sour cream
1 teaspoon chili powder
¼ teaspoon salt
⅛ teaspoon ground red pepper
10 (6-inch) flour tortillas
1½ cups enchilada sauce
½ cup sliced black olives
¼ cup minced green onion

Combine chicken, 1 cup Cheddar cheese, 1 cup Monterey Jack cheese, sour cream and seasonings; mix well. Spread ¼ cup chicken mixture on each tortilla; roll up tightly. Pour ½ cup sauce on bottom of 12×8-inch baking dish. Place tortillas in baking dish, seam side down; top with remaining sauce. Sprinkle with remaining 1 cup Cheddar cheese and 1 cup Monterey Jack cheese. Bake at 350°F, 20 minutes or until thoroughly heated. Top with olives and green onion.

Makes 5 servings

Favorite recipe from **Wisconsin Milk Marketing Board**

Sweet & Sour Chicken and Rice

- 1 pound chicken tenders
- 1 can (8 ounces) pineapple chunks, drained and juice reserved
- 1 cup uncooked rice
- 2 carrots, thinly sliced
- 1 green bell pepper, cut into 1-inch pieces
- 1 large onion, chopped
- 3 cloves garlic, minced
- 1 can (14½ ounces) reduced-sodium chicken broth
- ⅓ cup soy sauce
- 3 tablespoons sugar
- 3 tablespoons apple cider vinegar
- 1 tablespoon sesame oil
- 1½ teaspoons ground ginger
- ¼ cup chopped peanuts (optional)
- Chopped fresh cilantro (optional)

Preheat oven to 350°F. Spray 13×9-inch baking dish with nonstick cooking spray.

Combine chicken, pineapple, rice, carrots, pepper, onion and garlic in prepared dish.

Place broth, reserved pineapple juice, soy sauce, sugar, vinegar, sesame oil and ginger in small saucepan; bring to a boil over high heat. Remove from heat and pour over chicken mixture.

Cover tightly with foil and bake 40 to 50 minutes or until chicken is no longer pink in centers and rice is tender. Sprinkle with peanuts and cilantro, if desired.

Makes 6 servings

Chicken Fajita Casserole

- 8 TYSON® Fresh Chicken Breast Tenders or Individually Fresh Frozen® Boneless, Skinless Chicken Tenderloins
- 1 box UNCLE BEN'S CHEF'S RECIPE™ Traditional Red Beans & Rice
- 1 can (4 ounces) sliced black olives, drained
- 1 can (4 ounces) diced green chilies, drained
- 2 cups boiling water
- 1 can (15 ounces) diced tomatoes
- 1 cup (4 ounces) shredded Monterey Jack cheese
- 1 cup crushed tortilla chips

PREP: Preheat oven to 350°F. CLEAN: Wash hands. Remove protective ice glaze from frozen chicken by holding under cool running water 1 to 2 minutes. Place red beans and rice (do not include seasoning packet) in 13×9-inch baking dish; top with olives and chilies. Place chicken in baking dish. CLEAN: Wash hands. In medium bowl, combine boiling water, tomatoes and contents of rice seasoning packet. Pour over chicken mixture.

COOK: Cover and bake 45 minutes. Remove cover; sprinkle with cheese and tortilla chips. Bake 5 minutes or until rice is cooked and internal juices of chicken run clear. (Or insert instant-read meat thermometer in thickest part of chicken. Temperature should read 170°F.)

SERVE: Serve with a tossed salad and lemon sherbet, if desired.

CHILL: Refrigerate leftovers immediately. *Makes 4 servings*

Prep Time: 10 minutes
Cook Time: 50 minutes

Chicken in French Onion Sauce

- 1 package (10 ounces) frozen baby carrots, thawed and drained *or* 4 medium carrots, cut into strips (about 2 cups)
- 2 cups sliced mushrooms
- ½ cup thinly sliced celery
- 1⅓ cups *French's® Taste Toppers™* French Fried Onions, divided
- 4 chicken breast halves, skinned and boned
- ½ cup white wine
- ¾ cup prepared chicken bouillon
- ½ teaspoon garlic salt
- ½ teaspoon pepper
- Paprika

Preheat oven to 375°F. In 12×8-inch baking dish, combine vegetables and *⅔ cup* ***Taste Toppers.*** Arrange chicken breasts on vegetables. In small bowl, combine wine, bouillon, garlic salt and pepper; pour over chicken and vegetables. Sprinkle chicken with paprika. Bake, covered, at 375°F for 35 minutes or until chicken is done. Baste chicken with wine sauce and top with remaining *⅔ cup* ***Taste Toppers;*** bake, uncovered, 3 minutes or until ***Taste Toppers*** are golden brown.

Makes 4 servings

Microwave Directions: In 12×8-inch microwave-safe dish, combine vegetables and *⅔ cup* ***Taste Toppers***. Arrange chicken breasts, skinned side down, along sides of dish. Prepare wine mixture as above, except reduce bouillon to ⅓ cup; pour over chicken and vegetables. Cook, covered, on HIGH 6 minutes. Turn chicken breasts over and sprinkle with paprika. Stir vegetables and rotate dish. Cook, covered, 7 to 9 minutes or until chicken is done. Baste chicken with wine sauce and top with remaining *⅔ cup* ***Taste Toppers;*** cook, uncovered, 1 minute. Let stand 5 minutes.

Sweet & Sour Chicken and Rice

Creamy Chicken and Pasta with Spinach

6 ounces uncooked egg noodles
1 tablespoon olive oil
¼ cup chopped onion
¼ cup chopped red bell pepper
1 package (10 ounces) frozen spinach, thawed and drained
2 boneless skinless chicken breast halves (¾ pound), cooked and cut into 1-inch pieces
1 can (4 ounces) sliced mushrooms, drained
2 cups (8 ounces) shredded Swiss cheese
1 container (8 ounces) sour cream
¾ cup half-and-half
2 eggs, slightly beaten
½ teaspoon salt
Red onion and fresh spinach for garnish

Preheat oven to 350°F. Prepare egg noodles according to package directions; set aside.

Heat oil in large skillet over medium-high heat. Add onion and bell pepper; cook and stir 2 minutes or until onion is tender. Add spinach, chicken, mushrooms and cooked noodles; stir to combine.

Combine cheese, sour cream, half-and-half, eggs and salt in medium bowl; blend well.

Add cheese mixture to chicken mixture; stir to combine. Pour into 13×9-inch baking dish coated with nonstick cooking spray. Bake, covered, 30 to 35 minutes or until heated through. Garnish with red onion and fresh spinach, if desired
Makes 8 servings

Serving Suggestion: Serve with orange slices sprinkled with coconut.

Chicken Pot Pie

2 teaspoons margarine
½ cup plus 2 tablespoons fat-free reduced-sodium chicken broth, divided
2 cups sliced mushrooms
1 cup diced red bell pepper
½ cup chopped onion
½ cup chopped celery
2 tablespoons all-purpose flour
½ cup fat-free half-and-half
2 cups cubed cooked chicken breasts
1 teaspoon minced fresh dill
½ teaspoon salt
¼ teaspoon black pepper
2 reduced-fat refrigerated crescent rolls

1. Heat margarine and 2 tablespoons chicken broth in medium saucepan until margarine is melted. Add mushrooms, bell pepper, onion and celery. Cook 7 to 10 minutes or until vegetables are tender, stirring frequently.

2. Stir in flour; cook 1 minute. Stir in remaining ½ cup chicken broth; cook and stir until liquid thickens. Stir in half-and-half. Add chicken, dill, salt and pepper.

3. Preheat oven to 375°F. Spoon mixture into 1-quart casserole. Roll out crescent rolls and place on top of chicken mixture.

4. Bake pot pie 20 minutes or until topping is golden and filling is bubbly.
Makes 4 (1-cup) servings

Note: For 2 cups cooked chicken breast, gently simmer 3 small chicken breast halves in 2 cups fat-free reduced-sodium chicken broth about 20 minutes or until meat is no longer pink in center. If desired, reserve chicken broth for pot pie.

Chicken Tetrazzini

1 can (10¾ ounces) condensed cream of mushroom soup
1⅓ cups *French's® Taste Toppers™* French Fried Onions, divided
1¼ cups milk
1 cup (4 ounces) shredded Monterey Jack cheese, divided
2 tablespoons minced parsley
¼ teaspoon dried oregano leaves
¼ teaspoon garlic powder
4 cups cooked spaghetti (8 ounces uncooked)
2 cups (10 ounces) finely cubed cooked chicken
1 package (10 ounces) frozen peas and carrots, thawed

1. Preheat oven to 350°F. In large bowl, combine soup, *⅔ cup* ***Taste Toppers,*** milk, *½ cup* cheese, parsley, oregano and garlic powder. Stir in spaghetti, chicken and vegetables. Pour into lightly greased 2-quart baking dish.

2. Bake, uncovered, 30 minutes or until heated through. Stir. Top with remaining *⅔ cup* ***Taste Toppers*** and *½ cup* cheese. Bake 5 minutes or until ***Taste Toppers*** are golden.
Makes 6 servings

Prep Time: 5 minutes
Cook Time: 35 minutes

Creamy Chicken and Pasta with Spinach

Chicken Caesar Tetrazzini

- 8 ounces uncooked spaghetti
- 2 cups shredded or cubed cooked chicken
- 1 cup chicken broth
- 1 cup HIDDEN VALLEY® Caesar Dressing
- 1 jar (4½ ounces) sliced mushrooms, drained
- ½ cup grated Parmesan cheese
- 2 tablespoons dry bread crumbs

Cook spaghetti according to package directions. Drain and combine with chicken, broth, dressing and mushrooms in a large mixing bowl. Place mixture in a 2-quart casserole. Mix together cheese and bread crumbs; sprinkle over spaghetti mixture. Bake at 350°F. for 25 minutes or until casserole is hot and bubbly.
Makes 4 servings

Chilaquiles

- 1 can (10¾ ounces) condensed cream of chicken soup
- ½ cup mild green chili salsa
- 1 can (4 ounces) diced green chilies, undrained
- 8 cups taco chips
- 2 to 3 cups shredded cooked chicken or turkey
- 2 cups (8 ounces) shredded Cheddar cheese
- Sliced pitted black olives for garnish
- Cilantro sprigs for garnish

Preheat oven to 350°F. Combine soup and salsa in medium bowl; stir in green chilies. Place ⅓ of chips in 2- to 2½-quart casserole; top with ⅓ of chicken. Spread ⅓ of soup mixture over chicken; sprinkle with ⅓ of cheese. Repeat layering. Bake, uncovered, 15 minutes or until casserole is heated through and cheese is melted. Garnish with olives and cilantro.
Makes 6 servings

Classic Chicken Biscuit Pie

- 12 TYSON® Individually Fresh Frozen® Boneless, Skinless Chicken Tenderloins
- 2 boxes UNCLE BEN'S® COUNTRY INN® Chicken Flavored Rice
- 4 cups water
- 1 can (10¾ ounces) condensed cream of chicken soup
- 1 bag (16 ounces) frozen mixed vegetables
- 1 container (12 ounces) refrigerated buttermilk biscuits

PREP: Preheat oven to 400°F. CLEAN: Wash hands. Remove protective ice glaze from frozen chicken by holding under cool running water 1 to 2 minutes. Cut chicken into 1-inch pieces. CLEAN: Wash hands.

COOK: In large saucepan, combine chicken, rice, contents of seasoning packets, water, soup and mixed vegetables; mix well. Bring to a boil. Cover, reduce heat; simmer 10 minutes or until internal juices of chicken run clear. (Or insert instant-read meat thermometer in thickest part of chicken. Temperature should read 170°F.) Place in 13×9-inch baking pan; top with biscuits. Bake 10 to 12 minutes or until biscuits are deep golden brown.

SERVE: Serve immediately.

CHILL: Refrigerate leftovers immediately.
Makes 8 servings

Prep Time: 10 minutes
Cook Time: 30 minutes

Country Captain Chicken

- 4 chicken thighs
- 2 tablespoons all-purpose flour
- 2 tablespoons vegetable oil, divided
- 1 cup chopped green bell pepper
- 1 large onion, chopped
- 1 stalk celery, chopped
- 1 clove garlic, minced
- ¼ cup chicken broth
- 2 cups canned or fresh crushed tomatoes
- ½ cup golden raisins
- 1½ teaspoons curry powder
- 1 teaspoon salt
- ¼ teaspoon paprika
- ¼ teaspoon black pepper
- 2 cups hot cooked rice

Slow Cooker Directions

1. Coat chicken with flour; set aside. Heat 1 tablespoon oil in large skillet over medium-high heat until hot. Add bell pepper, onion, celery and garlic. Cook and stir 5 minutes or until vegetables are tender. Place vegetables in slow cooker.

2. Heat remaining 1 tablespoon oil in same skillet over medium-high heat. Add chicken and cook 5 minutes per side. Place chicken in slow cooker.

3. Pour broth into skillet. Heat over medium-high heat, stirring frequently and scraping up any browned bits from bottom of skillet. Pour liquid into slow cooker. Add tomatoes, raisins, curry powder, salt, paprika and pepper. Cover and cook on LOW 3 hours. Serve chicken with sauce over rice.
Makes 4 servings

Chicken Caesar Tetrazzini

Chicken Tetrazzini

8 ounces uncooked vermicelli, broken in half
1 can (10¾ ounces) condensed cream of mushroom soup, undiluted
¼ cup half-and-half
3 tablespoons dry sherry
½ teaspoon salt
⅛ to ¼ teaspoon red pepper flakes
2 cups chopped cooked chicken breasts (about ¾ pound)
1 cup frozen peas
½ cup grated Parmesan cheese
1 cup fresh coarse bread crumbs
2 tablespoons margarine or butter, melted
Chopped fresh basil (optional)

Preheat oven to 375°F. Spray 8-inch square baking dish with nonstick cooking spray.

Cook pasta according to package directions until al dente. Drain and set aside.

Meanwhile, combine soup, half-and-half, sherry, salt and pepper flakes in large bowl. Stir in chicken, peas and cheese. Add pasta to chicken mixture; stir until pasta is well coated. Pour into prepared dish.

Combine bread crumbs and margarine in small bowl. Sprinkle evenly over casserole.

Bake, uncovered, 25 to 30 minutes or until heated through and crumbs are golden brown. Sprinkle with basil, if desired. *Makes 4 servings*

Hint: Serve with Caesar salad. Have rotisserie chicken from your local supermarket for dinner one night and use 2 cups leftover chicken to make Tetrazzini the next night.

Chicken Ricotta Enchiladas

⅛ teaspoon black pepper
⅛ teaspoon garlic powder
1 pound chicken tenders
Nonstick cooking spray
1 cup low-fat ricotta cheese
2 tablespoons finely chopped green onion
8 (6-inch) corn tortillas
¼ cup fat-free reduced-sodium chicken broth
1 large tomato, chopped
½ cup chipotle salsa or other salsa
½ cup (2 ounces) shredded reduced-fat mozzarella cheese

1. Preheat oven to 450°F. Combine pepper and garlic powder in small bowl; sprinkle evenly over chicken. Spray large nonstick skillet with cooking spray; heat over medium-high heat. Add chicken; cook without stirring 4 minutes or until golden. Turn chicken; cook 4 minutes more or until no longer pink in center. Cool; coarsely chop chicken.

2. Combine ricotta and green onion in small bowl; mix well. Spray 13×9×2-inch baking dish with cooking spray; set aside.

3. Spray large skillet with cooking spray; heat over medium heat. Heat tortillas one at a time just until soft, about 15 seconds per side.

4. Spread ricotta mixture across middle of warm tortillas; place chicken on top. Roll up tortillas; place seam-side down in prepared baking dish. Drizzle chicken broth evenly over top.

5. Combine tomato and salsa. Spoon over enchiladas; top with cheese. Cover with foil; bake 15 minutes or until enchiladas are heated through and cheese is melted. Garnish with parsley or cilantro, if desired.
Makes 4 servings

Fiesta Chicken and Rice

1 tablespoon vegetable oil
¾ cup chopped onion
4 boneless skinless chicken breast halves (about 1 pound), cut into 2-inch strips
1 can (14½ ounces) chicken broth
1 cup sliced fresh mushrooms
¾ cup uncooked long-grain rice
½ cup dry white wine
1 teaspoon LAWRY'S® Garlic Powder with Parsley
½ teaspoon LAWRY'S® Seasoned Pepper
⅛ teaspoon ground saffron or turmeric
1 bag (16 ounces) frozen mixed vegetables, thawed and drained
1 jar (2 ounces) sliced pimiento, drained
Grated Parmesan cheese

In large skillet heat oil. Add onion and cook over medium-high heat 5 minutes. Add chicken and cook over medium-high heat 5 minutes or just until chicken is browned on all sides. Stir in broth, mushrooms, rice, wine, Garlic Powder with Parsley, Seasoned Pepper and saffron. Bring to a boil over medium-high heat. Reduce heat to low; simmer covered 20 minutes or until rice is tender and liquid is absorbed. Stir in mixed vegetables and pimiento; heat through, about 5 minutes.
Makes 4 servings

Serving Suggestion: For added color, sprinkle finished dish with grated Parmesan cheese and chopped fresh parsley, if desired.

Chicken Tetrazzini

Crunchy Topped Chicken Pot Pie

1 sheet frozen puff pastry (½ of a 17-ounce package), thawed according to package directions
½ cup (2 ounces) shredded Swiss cheese
1⅓ cups *French's® Taste Toppers™* French Fried Onions, divided
1 can (10¾ ounces) condensed cream of chicken soup
1 cup milk or half-and-half
2 cups (12 ounces) cooked chicken, cut into ½-inch cubes
1 bag (16 ounces) frozen vegetable combination, thawed

1. Preheat oven to 400°F. Unfold pastry and place on floured board. Invert 9-inch plate on top of pastry. With sharp knife, cut pastry into 9-inch circle. Remove plate. Cut pastry into 6 equal triangles. Place pastry triangles on *ungreased* baking sheet.

2. Bake pastry 15 minutes or until puffed and golden. Sprinkle pastry with cheese and *⅔ cup* ***Taste Toppers.*** Bake 1 minute or until ***Taste Toppers*** are golden. Set aside.

3. Combine soup and milk in large saucepan. Stir in chicken, vegetables and remaining *⅔ cup* ***Taste Toppers.*** Heat to boiling. Reduce heat to medium-low. Cook 5 minutes or until vegetables are tender and mixture is hot. To serve, spoon filling into bowls. Top each serving with pastry triangle.
Makes 6 servings

Prep Time: 10 minutes
Cook Time: about 15 minutes

Oven Chicken & Rice

1 can (10¾ ounces) condensed cream of mushroom soup, undiluted
1⅓ cups water
1 cup long-grain or converted rice
1 teaspoon dried dill weed, divided
¼ teaspoon black pepper
1 chicken (3 pounds), cut up and skinned
½ cup crushed multi-grain crackers
1 teaspoon paprika
2 tablespoons butter or margarine, melted
Fresh dill sprigs for garnish

Preheat oven to 375°F. Combine soup, water, rice, ¾ teaspoon dill weed and pepper in 13×9-inch baking dish. Arrange chicken pieces on top of rice mixture. Cover tightly with foil. Bake 45 minutes.

Sprinkle chicken pieces with crackers, paprika and remaining ¼ teaspoon dill. Drizzle with butter. Bake 5 to 10 minutes or until chicken is tender. Season to taste with salt and pepper. Garnish with dill sprigs, if desired. *Makes 4 to 5 servings*

Enchiladas

1 package (10 ounces) fully cooked carved chicken breast*
1 cup cooked rice
2 jars (12 ounces *each*) salsa, divided
1 can (15 to 19 ounces) black beans, rinsed and drained
1⅓ cups *French's® Taste Toppers™* French Fried Onions, divided
1 cup (4 ounces) shredded Cheddar cheese, divided
12 (8-inch) flour tortillas

**You may substitute 2 cups shredded cooked chicken.*

1. Preheat oven to 350°F. Combine chicken, rice, *1 cup* salsa, beans, *⅔ cup* ***Taste Toppers*** and *½ cup* cheese in large bowl. Spread about ½ cup mixture down center of each tortilla. Roll up tortillas enclosing filling. Place seam-side down in greased 15×10-inch baking pan.

2. Pour remaining salsa on top of tortillas. Cover dish. Bake 30 minutes or until heated through.

3. Top with remaining *½ cup* cheese and *⅔ cup* ***Taste Toppers.*** Bake 5 minutes or until ***Taste Toppers*** are golden. *Makes 6 servings*

Prep Time: 10 minutes
Cook Time: 35 minutes

Helpful Hints

Always cook boneless pieces of chicken until they are no longer pink in the center or 170°F on an instant read thermometer. Bone-in chicken should be cooked until its juices run clear.

Oven Chicken & Rice

Chicken-Asparagus Casserole

- **2 teaspoons vegetable oil**
- **1 cup seeded and chopped green and/or red bell peppers**
- **1 medium onion, chopped**
- **2 cloves garlic, minced**
- **1 can (10¾ ounces) condensed cream of asparagus soup, undiluted**
- **2 eggs**
- **1 container (8 ounces) ricotta cheese**
- **2 cups (8 ounces) shredded Cheddar cheese, divided**
- **1½ cups chopped cooked chicken**
- **1 package (10 ounces) frozen chopped asparagus,* thawed and drained**
- **8 ounces egg noodles, cooked**
- **Black pepper (optional)**

**Or, substitute ½ pound fresh asparagus cut into ½-inch pieces. Bring 6 cups water to a boil over high heat in large saucepan. Add fresh asparagus. Reduce heat to medium. Cover and cook 5 to 8 minutes or until crisp-tender. Drain.*

1. Preheat oven to 350°F. Grease 13×9-inch casserole; set aside.

2. Heat oil in small skillet over medium heat. Add bell peppers, onion and garlic; cook and stir until vegetables are crisp-tender.

3. Mix soup, eggs, ricotta cheese and 1 cup Cheddar cheese in large bowl until well blended. Add onion mixture, chicken, asparagus and noodles; mix well. Season with pepper, if desired.

4. Spread mixture evenly in prepared casserole. Top with remaining 1 cup Cheddar cheese.

5. Bake 30 minutes or until center is set and cheese is bubbly. Let stand 5 minutes before serving. Garnish as desired. *Makes 12 servings*

Country Chicken Pot Pie

- **2 tablespoons margarine or butter**
- **¾ pound boneless skinless chicken breasts, cut into 1-inch pieces**
- **¾ teaspoon salt**
- **8 ounces fresh green beans, cut into 1-inch pieces (2 cups)**
- **½ cup chopped red bell pepper**
- **½ cup thinly sliced celery**
- **3 tablespoons all-purpose flour**
- **½ cup chicken broth**
- **½ cup half-and-half**
- **1 teaspoon dried thyme leaves**
- **½ teaspoon rubbed sage**
- **1 cup frozen pearl onions**
- **½ cup frozen corn**
- **Pastry for single-crust 10-inch pie**

Preheat oven to 425°F. Spray 10-inch deep-dish pie plate with nonstick cooking spray.

Melt margarine in large deep skillet over medium-high heat. Add chicken; cook and stir 3 minutes or until no longer pink in center. Sprinkle with salt. Add beans, bell pepper and celery; cook and stir 3 minutes.

Sprinkle flour evenly over chicken and vegetables; cook and stir 1 minute. Stir in broth, half-and-half, thyme and sage; bring to a boil over high heat. Reduce heat to low and simmer 3 minutes or until sauce is very thick. Stir in onions and corn. Return to a simmer; cook and stir 1 minute.

Transfer mixture to prepared pie plate. Place pie crust over chicken mixture; turn edge under and crimp to seal. Cut 4 slits in pie crust to allow steam to escape.

Bake 20 minutes or until crust is light golden brown and mixture is hot and bubbly. Let stand 5 minutes before serving. *Makes 6 servings*

Chicken Fajitas with Cowpoke Barbecue Sauce

Sauce

- **1 can (8 ounces) tomato sauce**
- **⅓ cup chopped green onions**
- **¼ cup ketchup**
- **2 tablespoons water**
- **2 tablespoons orange juice**
- **1 tablespoon cider vinegar**
- **1 tablespoon chili sauce**
- **2 cloves garlic, finely chopped**
- **Dash Worcestershire sauce**

Fajitas

- **Nonstick cooking spray**
- **10 ounces boneless skinless chicken breasts, cut lengthwise into 1×½-inch pieces**
- **2 green or red bell peppers, thinly sliced**
- **1 cup sliced onion**
- **2 cups tomato wedges**
- **4 (6-inch) warm flour tortillas**

Slow Cooker Directions

Combine all sauce ingredients in slow cooker. Cover and cook on HIGH 1½ hours.

Spray large nonstick skillet with nonstick cooking spray. Add chicken and cook over medium heat until browned. Reduce slow cooker heat to LOW. Add cooked chicken, bell peppers and onion to slow cooker. Stir until well coated. Cover and cook 3 to 4 hours or until chicken is no longer pink and vegetables are tender.

Add tomatoes; cover and cook 30 to 45 minutes or until heated through. Serve with warm tortillas.

Makes 4 servings

Chicken-Asparagus Casserole

Mile-High Enchilada Pie

Slow Cooker

8 (6-inch) corn tortillas
1 jar (12 ounces) prepared salsa
1 can (15½ ounces) kidney beans, rinsed and drained
1 cup shredded cooked chicken
1 cup shredded Monterey Jack cheese with jalapeño peppers

Slow Cooker Directions
Prepare foil handles for slow cooker (see below); place in slow cooker. Place 1 tortilla on bottom of slow cooker. Top with small amount of salsa, beans, chicken and cheese. Continue layering using remaining ingredients, ending with cheese. Cover and cook on LOW 6 to 8 hours or on HIGH 3 to 4 hours. Pull out by foil handles.

Makes 4 to 6 servings

Foil Handles: Tear off three 18×2-inch strips of heavy foil or use regular foil folded to double thickness. Crisscross foil strips in spoke design and place in slow cooker to make lifting of tortilla stack easier.

Hearty Chicken Bake

3 cups hot mashed potatoes
1 cup (4 ounces) shredded Cheddar cheese, divided
1⅓ cups *French's® Taste Toppers™* French Fried Onions, divided
1½ cups (7 ounces) cubed cooked chicken
1 package (10 ounces) frozen mixed vegetables, thawed and drained
1 can (10¾ ounces) condensed cream of chicken soup
¼ cup milk
½ teaspoon ground mustard
¼ teaspoon garlic powder
¼ teaspoon black pepper

Preheat oven to 375°F. In medium bowl, combine mashed potatoes, *½ cup* cheese and *⅔ cup **Taste Toppers***; mix thoroughly. Spoon potato mixture into greased 1½-quart casserole. Using back of spoon, spread potatoes across bottom and up sides of dish to form a shell. In large bowl, combine chicken, mixed vegetables, soup, milk and seasonings; pour into potato shell. Bake, uncovered, at 375°F for 30 minutes or until heated through. Top with remaining cheese and *⅔ cup **Taste Toppers***; bake, uncovered, 3 minutes or until ***Taste Toppers*** are golden brown. Let stand 5 minutes before serving.

Makes 4 to 6 servings

Home-Style Chicken 'n' Biscuits

5 slices bacon, fried crisp and crumbled
1½ cups (7 ounces) cubed cooked chicken
1 package (10 ounces) frozen mixed vegetables, thawed and drained
1½ cups (6 ounces) shredded Cheddar cheese
2 medium tomatoes, chopped (about 1 cup)
1 can (10¾ ounces) condensed cream of chicken soup
¾ cup milk
1½ cups biscuit baking mix
⅔ cup milk
1⅓ cups *French's® Taste Toppers™* French Fried Onions, divided

Preheat oven to 400°F. In large bowl, combine bacon, chicken, mixed vegetables, *1 cup* cheese, tomatoes, soup and ¾ cup milk. Pour chicken mixture into greased 12×8-inch baking dish. Bake, covered, at 400°F for 15 minutes. Meanwhile, in medium bowl, combine baking mix, ⅔ cup milk and *⅔ cup **Taste Toppers*** to form soft dough. Spoon biscuit dough in 6 mounds around edges of casserole. Bake, uncovered, 15 to 20 minutes or until biscuits are golden brown. Top biscuits with remaining cheese and *⅔ cup **Taste Toppers***; bake 1 to 3 minutes or until ***Taste Toppers*** are golden brown.

Makes 6 servings

Microwave Directions: Prepare chicken mixture as directed, except reduce ¾ cup milk to ½ cup; pour into 12×8-inch microwave-safe dish. Cook, covered, on HIGH 10 minutes or until heated through. Stir chicken mixture halfway through cooking time. Prepare biscuit dough as directed. Stir casserole and spoon biscuit dough over hot chicken mixture as directed. Cook, uncovered, 7 to 8 minutes or until biscuits are done. Rotate dish halfway through cooking time. Top biscuits with remaining cheese and *⅔ cup **Taste Toppers***; cook, uncovered, 1 minute or until cheese melts. Let stand 5 minutes.

Lemony Roasted Chicken

Slow Cooker

1 fryer or roasting chicken (3 to 4 pounds)
½ cup chopped onion
2 tablespoons butter
Juice of one lemon
1 tablespoon fresh parsley
2 teaspoons grated lemon peel
¼ teaspoon salt
¼ teaspoon dried thyme leaves

Slow Cooker Directions
Rinse chicken and pat dry with paper towels. Remove and discard any excess fat. Place onion in chicken cavity and rub skin with butter. Place chicken in slow cooker. Pour lemon juice over chicken. Sprinkle with grated lemon peel, salt and thyme. Cover and cook on LOW 6 to 8 hours.

Makes 6 servings

Mile-High Enchilada Pie

Mexican Chicken Bake

- 1 pound boneless skinless chicken thighs, cut into strips
- 2 cans (8 ounces *each*) tomato sauce
- 1 can (11 ounces) Mexican-style corn kernels, drained
- 1⅓ cups *French's® Taste Toppers™* French Fried Onions, divided
- 2 tablespoons *Frank's® RedHot®* Cayenne Pepper Sauce
- ½ teaspoon dried oregano leaves
- ½ teaspoon ground cumin
- ¼ teaspoon garlic powder

1. Preheat oven to 350°F. Combine chicken, tomato sauce, corn, *⅔ cup* ***Taste Toppers, Frank's RedHot*** and seasonings in lightly greased 2-quart baking dish. Stir until chicken is well coated.

2. Bake, uncovered, 30 minutes or until chicken is no longer pink and sauce is hot. Stir. Top with remaining *⅔ cup* ***Taste Toppers.*** Bake 5 minutes or until ***Taste Toppers*** are golden. Serve with hot cooked rice, if desired. *Makes 4 servings*

Prep Time: 10 minutes
Cook Time: 35 minutes

Jambalaya

- ¼ cup CRISCO® Oil,* divided
- 1 large onion, peeled and diced
- 1 green or red bell pepper, seeds and ribs removed, cut into 1-inch squares
- 2 teaspoons jarred minced garlic *or* 1 large garlic clove, peeled and minced
- 1 boneless, skinless chicken breast, cut into 1-inch cubes
- ⅓ pound smoked sausage (such as kielbasa or turkey kielbasa), cut into ¼-inch slices
- 1 package (5 ounces) yellow rice or white rice
- 1 can (14½ ounces) chicken stock or broth
- ½ teaspoon salt
- ½ teaspoon Italian seasoning
- ½ teaspoon freshly ground black pepper
- 1 cup fresh or frozen green peas
- ½ pound peeled and deveined shrimp

**Use your favorite Crisco Oil product.*

1. Heat oven to 375°F.

2. Heat 2 tablespoons oil in large ovenproof skillet on medium-high heat. Add onion, bell pepper and garlic. Sauté 3 minutes or until onion is translucent. Remove vegetables from skillet.

3. Rinse chicken. Pat dry. Heat remaining 2 tablespoons oil in skillet on medium-high heat. Add chicken and sausage. Sauté 3 minutes or until sausage is lightly browned. Add rice. Stir 1 minute. Return vegetables to skillet. Add stock, salt, Italian seasoning and pepper. Bring to a boil. Cover skillet.

4. Bake at 375°F for 15 minutes. Remove from oven. Stir in peas and shrimp. Recover. Return to oven for 15 minutes, or until shrimp are pink and cooked through and liquid is absorbed. Serve immediately. *Makes 4 servings*

Note: The jambalaya can be prepared up to two days in advance and refrigerated, tightly covered. Reheat at 350°F for 15 minutes or until hot, stirring occasionally. For a spicier dish, use Cajun andouille sausage in place of kielbasa. If using shell-on shrimp, increase preparation time by 10 minutes.

Preparation Time: 25 minutes
Total Time: 1 hour

Lemon Pepper Pasta with Chicken and Dijon Teriyaki Sauce

- 1 package (12 ounces) PASTA LABELLA™ Lemon Pepper Penne Rigate
- ¼ cup olive oil
- 9 ounces boneless skinless chicken breasts, cut into 1-inch cubes
- 1½ cups broccoli florets
- 1 cup sliced mushrooms
- ½ cup sliced red onion
- 1 tablespoon chopped garlic
- 1½ teaspoon ground ginger
- ¼ teaspoon salt
- ¼ teaspoon black pepper
- 1½ cups chicken broth
- 5 tablespoons Dijon mustard
- ¼ cup teriyaki sauce
- ¼ cup minced green onions

Cook pasta according to package directions. Meanwhile, heat olive oil in large skillet or saucepan over medium heat; sauté chicken for 5 minutes. Add broccoli, mushrooms, onion, garlic, ginger, salt and pepper. Continue to cook for 8 minutes. Add chicken broth; bring mixture to a simmer. Whisk in mustard and teriyaki sauce. Cook until sauce is of medium-thin consistency. Add hot pasta; mix well and heat thoroughly. Serve sprinkled with green onions. *Makes 4 servings*

Quick Chicken Pot Pie

- **1 pound boneless skinless chicken thighs**
- **1 can (about 14 ounces) chicken broth**
- **3 tablespoons all-purpose flour**
- **2 tablespoons butter, softened**
- **1 package (10 ounces) frozen mixed vegetables, thawed**
- **1 can (about 4 ounces) button mushrooms, drained**
- **¼ teaspoon dried basil leaves**
- **¼ teaspoon dried oregano leaves**
- **¼ teaspoon dried thyme leaves**
- **1 cup biscuit baking mix**
- **6 tablespoons milk**

1. Cut chicken into 1-inch cubes. Place chicken and broth in skillet; cover and bring to a boil over high heat. Reduce heat to medium; simmer, uncovered, 5 minutes or until chicken is tender.

2. While chicken is cooking, mix flour and butter; set aside. Combine mixed vegetables, mushrooms, basil, oregano and thyme in 2-quart casserole.

3. Add flour mixture to chicken and broth in skillet; stir with wire whisk until smooth. Cook and stir until thickened. Add to vegetable mixture; mix well.

4. Preheat oven to 450°F. Blend biscuit mix and milk in medium bowl until smooth. Drop 4 scoops batter onto chicken mixture.

5. Bake 18 to 20 minutes or until biscuits are browned and casserole is hot and bubbly.

Makes 4 servings

Tip: This dish can be prepared through step 3 and refrigerated up to 24 hours, if desired. Bake as directed for 20 to 25 minutes.

Italian-Style Chicken and Rice

- **1 tablespoon vegetable oil**
- **4 boneless skinless chicken breast halves (about 1 pound)**
- **2 cups low-fat reduced-sodium chicken broth**
- **1 box (about 6 ounces) chicken-flavored rice mix**
- **½ cup chopped red bell pepper**
- **½ cup frozen peas, thawed**
- **¼ cup Romano cheese**

1. Heat oil in large skillet. Add chicken; cook over medium-high heat 10 to 15 minutes or until lightly browned on both sides.

2. Add broth, rice mix, bell pepper and peas; mix well. Bring to a boil. Cover; reduce heat and simmer 10 minutes or until chicken is no longer pink in center. Remove from heat. Sprinkle with cheese; let stand covered 5 minutes or until liquid is absorbed.

Makes 4 servings

Quick Chicken Pot Pie

Green Chile Chicken Enchiladas

- **2 cups shredded cooked chicken**
- **1½ cups (6 ounces) shredded Mexican cheese blend or Cheddar cheese, divided**
- **½ cup HIDDEN VALLEY® Original Ranch® Dressing**
- **¼ cup sour cream**
- **2 tablespoons canned diced green chiles, rinsed and drained**
- **4 (9 to 10-inch) flour tortillas, warmed**

Mix together chicken, ¾ cup cheese, dressing, sour cream and green chiles in a medium bowl. Divide evenly down center of each tortilla. Roll up tortillas and place, seam side down, in a 9-inch baking dish. Top with remaining ¾ cup cheese. Bake at 350°F for 20 minutes or until cheese is melted and lightly browned.

Makes 4 servings

Note: Purchase rotisserie chicken at your favorite store to add great taste and save preparation time.

Pizza Chicken Bake

- **3½ cups uncooked bow tie pasta**
- **1 tablespoon vegetable oil**
- **1 cup sliced mushrooms**
- **1 jar (26 ounces) herb-flavored spaghetti sauce**
- **1 teaspoon pizza seasoning blend**
- **3 boneless skinless chicken breast halves (about ¾ pound), quartered**
- **1 cup (4 ounces) shredded mozzarella cheese**

Preheat oven to 350°F. Spray 2-quart round casserole with nonstick cooking spray.

Cook pasta according to package directions until al dente. Drain and place in prepared dish.

Meanwhile, heat oil in large skillet over medium-high heat until hot. Add mushrooms; cook and stir 2 minutes. Remove from heat. Stir in spaghetti sauce and pizza seasoning.

Pour half of spaghetti sauce mixture into casserole; stir until pasta is well coated. Arrange chicken on top of pasta. Pour remaining spaghetti sauce mixture evenly over chicken.

Bake, covered, 50 minutes or until chicken is no longer pink in centers. Remove from oven; sprinkle with cheese. Cover and let stand 5 minutes before serving.

Makes 4 servings

Old World Chicken and Vegetables

- **1 tablespoon dried oregano leaves**
- **1 teaspoon salt, divided**
- **1 teaspoon paprika**
- **½ teaspoon garlic powder**
- **¼ teaspoon black pepper**
- **2 medium green bell peppers, cut into thin strips**
- **1 small yellow onion, thinly sliced**
- **1 cut-up whole chicken (3 pounds)**
- **⅓ cup ketchup**
- **6 ounces dried uncooked egg noodles**

Slow Cooker Directions

1. In small bowl, combine oregano, ½ teaspoon salt, paprika, garlic powder and pepper; mix well.

2. Place bell peppers and onions in slow cooker. Top with chicken thighs and legs, sprinkle with half of oregano mixture, top with chicken breasts. Sprinkle chicken with remaining oregano mixture. Cover and cook on LOW 8 hours or on HIGH 4 hours. Stir in ketchup and remaining ½ teaspoon salt. Just before serving, cook noodles according to package directions; drain. Serve chicken pieces and vegetables over noodles.

Makes 4 servings

Mom's Best Chicken Tetrazzini

- **8 ounces uncooked vermicelli or other thin noodle**
- **2 tablespoons butter**
- **8 ounces fresh mushrooms, sliced**
- **¼ cup chopped green onions**
- **1 can (about 14½ ounces) chicken broth**
- **1 cup half-and-half, divided**
- **2 tablespoons dry sherry**
- **¼ cup all-purpose flour**
- **½ teaspoon salt**
- **¼ teaspoon ground nutmeg**
- **⅛ teaspoon white pepper**
- **2 ounces chopped pimiento, drained**
- **½ cup (4 ounces) grated Parmesan cheese, divided**
- **½ cup sour cream**
- **2 cups cooked skinless chicken, cut into bite-sized pieces**

1. Preheat oven to 350°F. Cook noodles according to package directions. Drain; set aside.

2. Melt butter in large nonstick skillet over medium-high heat. Add mushrooms and onions; cook and stir until onions are tender. Add chicken broth, ½ cup half-and-half and sherry to onion mixture. Pour remaining ½ cup half-and-half into small jar with tight-fitting lid; add flour, salt, nutmeg and pepper. Shake well. Slowly stir flour mixture into skillet. Bring to a boil; cook 1 minute. Reduce heat; stir in pimiento and ¼ cup Parmesan cheese. Stir in sour cream; blend well. Add chicken and noodles; mix well

3. Spread mixture into greased 1½-quart casserole. Sprinkle with remaining ¼ cup Parmesan cheese. Bake 30 to 35 minutes until hot. Let cool slightly before serving.

Makes 6 servings

Green Chile Chicken Enchilada

Mexican Chicken Casserole

- **8 ounces uncooked elbow noodles or small shell pasta**
- **2 teaspoons olive oil**
- **1 large carrot, grated**
- **1 medium green bell pepper, finely chopped**
- **1 tablespoon minced garlic**
- **¾ pound chicken tenders, cut in ¾-inch pieces**
- **2 teaspoons ground cumin**
- **1½ teaspoons dried oregano leaves**
- **½ teaspoon salt**
- **¼ teaspoon ground red pepper**
- **8 ounces (2 cups) shredded Monterey Jack cheese, divided**
- **1 bottle (16 ounces) tomato salsa, divided**

1. Cook pasta according to package directions. While pasta is cooking, heat oil in large nonstick skillet over medium heat. Add carrot, bell pepper and garlic; cook and stir 3 minutes until vegetables are tender. Add chicken, increase heat to medium-high; cook and stir 3 to 4 minutes or until chicken is no longer pink in center. Add cumin, oregano, salt and ground red pepper; cook and stir 1 minute. Remove from heat; set aside.

2. Grease 13×9-inch microwavable dish. Drain and rinse pasta under cold running water; place in large bowl. Add chicken mixture, 1 cup cheese and 1 cup salsa. Mix well; pour into prepared dish. Top with remaining 1 cup salsa and 1 cup cheese. Cover with plastic wrap; microwave at HIGH 4 to 6 minutes, turning dish halfway through cooking time. Serve immediately.

Makes 4 to 6 servings

Prep and Cook Time: 20 minutes

Snappy Pea and Chicken Pot Pie

- **2½ cups chicken broth**
- **1 medium-size baking potato, peeled and cut into ½-inch chunks**
- **1½ cups sliced carrots (½-inch slices)**
- **1 cup frozen pearl onions**
- **½ teaspoon dried rosemary**
- **½ teaspoon TABASCO® brand Pepper Sauce**
- **¼ teaspoon salt**
- **1 medium red bell pepper, coarsely diced**
- **4 ounces (about 1 cup) sugar-snap peas, trimmed and halved lengthwise**
- **3 tablespoons butter *or* margarine**
- **¼ cup flour**
- **8 ounces cooked chicken-breast meat, cut in 3×1-inch strips**
- **1 sheet frozen puff pastry**
- **1 egg, beaten with 1 teaspoon water**

In large heavy saucepan bring chicken broth to a boil over high heat. Add potato, carrots, pearl onions, rosemary, TABASCO® Sauce and salt. Reduce heat to medium; cover and simmer 8 to 10 minutes, until vegetables are tender. Add bell pepper and sugar-snap peas; boil 30 seconds, just until peas turn bright green. Drain vegetables, reserving chicken broth; set aside.

Melt butter in saucepan over low heat. Stir in flour and cook 3 to 4 minutes, stirring constantly. Pour in 2 cups of the reserved chicken broth and whisk until smooth. Bring to a boil over medium heat, stirring constantly. Reduce heat to low and simmer 5 minutes, stirring frequently, until thickened and bubbly.

Put chicken strips in bottoms of four lightly buttered ramekins or soufflé dishes. Top chicken with vegetables and sauce. Heat oven to 475°F.

Thaw pastry and unfold on floured surface according to package directions. Cut pastry into four rectangles. Brush outside rims of ramekins with some of the beaten egg mixture. Place pastry rectangle over each ramekin and press firmly around edges to seal. Trim dough and flute edges. Brush tops with remaining beaten egg mixture.

Place ramekins on baking sheet and bake 10 to 12 minutes, until pastry is puffed and well browned. Serve at once.

Makes 4 servings

Spicy Chicken & Rice Bake

- **4 boneless, skinless chicken breast halves (about 1 pound)**
- **1 jar (26 to 28 ounces) RAGÚ® Robusto! Pasta Sauce**
- **2 cups water**
- **⅔ cup uncooked white rice**
- **½ cup sliced pitted ripe olives**
- **1 tablespoon capers, drained and chopped**
- **1 teaspoon salt**
- **½ teaspoon ground black pepper**
- **¼ teaspoon dried oregano leaves, crushed**
- **⅛ teaspoon crushed red pepper flakes**

Preheat oven to 375°F. In 13×9-inch casserole, combine all ingredients. Bake uncovered 40 minutes or until rice is tender and chicken is no longer pink.

Makes 4 servings

Mexican Chicken Casserole

3-Cheese Chicken & Noodles

Slow Cooker

- 3 cups chopped cooked chicken
- 1½ cups cottage cheese
- 1 can (10¾ ounces) condensed cream of chicken soup, undiluted
- 1 (8-ounce) package wide egg noodles, cooked and drained
- 1 cup grated Monterey Jack cheese
- ½ cup chicken broth
- ½ cup diced celery
- ½ cup diced onion
- ½ cup diced green bell pepper
- ½ cup diced red bell pepper
- ½ cup grated Parmesan cheese
- 1 can (4 ounces) sliced mushrooms, drained
- 2 tablespoons butter, melted
- ½ teaspoon dried thyme leaves

Slow Cooker Directions

Combine all ingredients in slow cooker. Stir to coat evenly. Cover and cook on LOW 6 to 10 hours or on HIGH 3 to 4 hours.

Makes 6 servings

Tortilla Chicken Bake

- 1 can (14½ ounces) DEL MONTE® Mexican Recipe Stewed Tomatoes
- ½ cup chopped onion
- 2 cloves garlic, crushed
- ½ teaspoon dried oregano, crushed
- ½ teaspoon chili powder
- ½ pound boneless chicken, skinned and cut into strips
- 4 cups tortilla chips
- ¾ cup shredded Monterey Jack cheese with jalapeño peppers or Cheddar cheese

1. Preheat oven to 375°F. Drain tomatoes, reserving liquid; chop tomatoes.

2. Combine reserved liquid, onion, garlic, oregano and chili powder in large skillet; boil 5 minutes, stirring occasionally.

3. Stir in tomatoes and chicken; cook over medium heat until chicken is no longer pink, about 3 minutes. Layer half of chips, chicken mixture and cheese in shallow 2-quart baking dish; repeat layers ending with cheese.

4. Cover and bake 15 minutes or until heated through. Serve with sour cream, if desired.

Makes 4 servings

Prep Time: 3 minutes
Cook Time: 25 minutes

3-Cheese Chicken & Noodles

Spinach Quiche

1 medium leek
¼ cup butter or margarine
2 cups finely chopped cooked chicken
½ package (10 ounces) frozen chopped spinach or broccoli, cooked and drained
1 unbaked ready-to-use pie crust (10 inches in diameter)
1 tablespoon all-purpose flour
1½ cups (6 ounces) shredded Swiss cheese
4 eggs
1½ cups half-and-half or evaporated milk
2 tablespoons brandy
½ teaspoon salt
¼ teaspoon black pepper
¼ teaspoon ground nutmeg

Preheat oven to 375°F. Cut leek in half lengthwise; wash and trim, leaving 2 to 3 inches of green tops intact. Cut leek halves crosswise into thin slices. Place in small saucepan; add enough water to cover. Bring to a boil over high heat; reduce heat and simmer 5 minutes. Drain; reserve leek.

Melt butter in large skillet over medium heat. Add chicken; cook until chicken is golden, about 5 minutes. Add spinach and leek to chicken mixture; cook 1 to 2 minutes longer. Remove from heat.

Spoon chicken mixture into pie crust. Sprinkle flour and cheese over chicken mixture. Combine eggs, half-and-half, brandy, salt, pepper and nutmeg in medium bowl. Pour egg mixture over cheese.

Bake 35 to 40 minutes or until knife inserted into center comes out clean. Let stand 5 minutes before serving. Serve hot or cold.

Makes 6 servings

Spanish Braised Chicken with Green Olives and Rice

2 pounds bone-in skinless chicken thighs
1 teaspoon paprika
Nonstick cooking spray
¾ cup dry sherry
1 can (about 14 ounces) fat-free reduced-sodium chicken broth plus water to measure 2¼ cups
¾ cup sliced pimiento-stuffed green olives
1½ teaspoons dried sage leaves
1½ cups long-grain white rice

1. Sprinkle chicken thighs with paprika. Spray large nonstick skillet with cooking spray; heat over medium-high heat. Add thighs; cook without stirring 3 to 4 minutes or until golden. Turn chicken; cook 3 to 4 minutes.

2. Add sherry to skillet. Slide metal spatula under chicken and scrape cooked bits from bottom of skillet. Add chicken broth mixture, olives and sage; bring to a boil. Reduce heat to low; cover and simmer 10 minutes. Pour rice into liquid around chicken; gently stir to distribute evenly in skillet. Return to a boil; cover and simmer 18 minutes or until liquid is absorbed and rice is tender.

Makes 6 servings

"Wildly" Delicious Casserole

1 package (14 ounces) ground chicken
1 package (14 ounces) frozen broccoli with red peppers
2 cups cooked wild rice
1 can (10¾ ounces) condensed cream of chicken soup, undiluted
½ cup mayonnaise
½ cup plain yogurt
1 teaspoon lemon juice
½ teaspoon curry powder
¼ cup dry bread crumbs
3 to 4 slices process American cheese, cut in half diagonally

Preheat oven to 375°F. Grease 8-inch square casserole; set aside. In large skillet, cook chicken until no longer pink. Drain; set aside. Cook broccoli and peppers according to package directions; set aside. In large bowl, combine rice, soup, mayonnaise, yogurt, lemon juice and curry. Stir in chicken and broccoli and peppers. Pour into prepared casserole; sprinkle with bread crumbs. Bake 45 to 55 minutes. During last 5 minutes of baking, arrange cheese slices on top of casserole. Remove from oven; let stand 5 minutes.

Makes 6 to 8 servings

Favorite recipe from **Minnesota Cultivated Wild Rice Council**

Helpful Hints

To remove skin from chicken pieces, using a paper towel, grasp the edge of the skin and pull it away from the chicken.

Northwoods Mushroom Swiss Melt

4 TYSON® Individually Fresh Frozen® Boneless, Skinless Chicken Breasts
2 boxes UNCLE BEN'S® Long Grain & Wild Rice Original Recipe
3¾ cups water
½ cup chopped green bell pepper
½ cup chopped red bell pepper
1 cup sliced mushrooms
4 slices Swiss cheese

COOK: CLEAN: Wash hands. Remove protective ice glaze from frozen chicken by holding under cool running water 1 to 2 minutes. Spray large skillet with nonstick cooking spray. Add chicken; cook over medium-high heat 5 to 7 minutes or until light brown. Add water, rice and contents of seasoning packets. Bring to a boil. Cover, reduce heat; simmer 20 minutes. Stir in bell peppers; sprinkle mushrooms over chicken. Cook, covered, 5 to 8 minutes or until internal juices of chicken run clear. (Or insert instant-read meat thermometer in thickest part of chicken. Temperature should read 170°F.) Place cheese over chicken; remove from heat. Let stand, covered, 5 minutes or until cheese is melted.

SERVE: Serve chicken while still hot with rolls and mixed vegetables, if desired.

CHILL: Refrigerate leftovers immediately. *Makes 4 servings*

Prep Time: none
Cook Time: 40 minutes

Spanish Rice & Chicken Skillet

1 tablespoon oil
4 chicken drumsticks (about 1 pound)
1 onion, chopped
½ green bell pepper, chopped
½ red bell pepper, chopped
1 package (about 4 ounces) Spanish rice mix
1 can (14½ ounces) diced tomatoes, undrained
1¼ cups chicken broth

1. Heat oil in medium skillet over high heat until hot. Add chicken; cook 5 minutes or until lightly browned on all sides. Add onion and bell peppers; cook and stir 2 minutes.

2. Stir in rice mix, tomatoes with juice and broth. Bring to a boil. Cover and simmer over low heat 15 minutes or until rice is tender and liquid is absorbed. Remove from heat and let stand, covered, 5 minutes.
Makes 4 servings

Teriyaki Chicken Medley

2 cups cooked white rice (about ¾ cup uncooked)
2 cups (10 ounces) cooked chicken, cut into strips
1⅓ cups *French's® Taste Toppers™* French Fried Onions, divided
1 package (12 ounces) frozen bell pepper strips, thawed and drained*
1 jar (12 ounces) chicken gravy
3 tablespoons teriyaki sauce

**Or, substitute 2 cups sliced bell peppers for frozen pepper strips.*

Preheat oven to 400°F. Grease 2-quart rectangular baking dish. Press rice into bottom of prepared dish.

Combine chicken, *⅔ cup* ***Taste Toppers***, bell pepper strips, gravy and teriyaki sauce in large bowl; mix well. Pour mixture over rice layer. Cover; bake 30 minutes or until heated through. Top with remaining *⅔ cup* ***Taste Toppers.*** Bake 1 minute or until ***Taste Toppers*** are golden.
Makes 4 to 6 servings

Prep Time: 10 minutes
Cook Time: 31 minutes

Zesty Chicken Succotash

1 (3- to 4-pound) chicken, cut up, and skinned, if desired
1 onion, chopped
1 rib celery, sliced
¼ cup *Frank's® RedHot®* Cayenne Pepper Sauce
1 package (10 ounces) frozen lima beans
1 package (10 ounces) frozen whole kernel corn
2 tomatoes, coarsely chopped

1. Heat *1 tablespoon oil* in large skillet until hot. Add chicken; cook 10 minutes or until browned on both sides. Drain off all but 1 tablespoon fat. Add onion and celery; cook and stir 3 minutes or until tender.

2. Stir in *¾ cup water,* ***Frank's RedHot*** and remaining ingredients. Heat to boiling. Reduce heat to medium-low. Cook, covered, 20 to 25 minutes or until chicken is no longer pink near bone. Sprinkle with chopped parsley, if desired.
Makes 6 servings

Prep Time: 10 minutes
Cook Time: 35 minutes

Northwoods Mushroom Swiss Melt

Chicken and Linguine in Creamy Tomato Sauce

1 tablespoon olive or vegetable oil
1 pound boneless, skinless chicken breasts, cut into ½-inch strips
1 jar (26 to 28 ounces) RAGÚ® Old World Style® Pasta Sauce
2 cups water
8 ounces uncooked linguine or spaghetti
½ cup whipping or heavy cream
1 tablespoon fresh basil leaves, chopped *or* ½ teaspoon dried basil leaves, crushed

1. In 12-inch skillet, heat oil over medium heat and brown chicken. Remove chicken and set aside.

2. In same skillet, stir in Ragú Pasta Sauce and water. Bring to a boil over high heat. Stir in uncooked linguine and return to a boil. Reduce heat to low and simmer covered, stirring occasionally, 15 minutes or until linguine is tender.

3. Stir in cream and basil. Return chicken to skillet and cook 5 minutes or until chicken is no longer pink.

Makes 4 servings

Prep Time: 10 minutes
Cook Time: 30 minutes

Stir-Fry Pita Sandwiches

12 ounces chicken tenders
1 onion, thinly sliced
1 red bell pepper, cut into strips
½ cup zesty Italian dressing
¼ teaspoon red pepper flakes
4 pita bread rounds
8 leaves leaf lettuce
4 tablespoons crumbled feta cheese

1. Cut chicken tenders in half lengthwise and crosswise. Coat large nonstick skillet with nonstick cooking spray. Cook and stir chicken over medium heat 3 minutes. Add onion and bell pepper; cook and stir 2 minutes. Add Italian dressing and red pepper flakes; cover and cook 3 minutes. Remove from heat; uncover and let cool 5 minutes.

2. While chicken mixture is cooling, cut pita breads in half to form pockets. Line each pocket with lettuce leaf. Spoon chicken filling into pockets; sprinkle with feta cheese.

Makes 4 servings

Note: Salad dressings offer a surprising amount of convenience in the kitchen. Their basic components of oil, vinegar, herbs and spices provide a ready-made marinade or seasoned oil for cooking meats and poultry.

Prep and Cook Time: 17 minutes

Sautéed Chicken with Brown Rice

2 bags SUCCESS® Brown Rice
Vegetable cooking spray
¼ cup flour
½ teaspoon paprika
¼ teaspoon black pepper
2 cups chopped cooked chicken
1 medium onion, sliced
1 green bell pepper, chopped
1 jar (14 ounces) sliced mushrooms, drained
¼ cup apple juice
2 tablespoons packed brown sugar

Prepare rice according to package directions. Spray 13×9-inch baking dish with cooking spray.

Preheat oven to 425°F.

Combine flour, paprika and black pepper in shallow dish. Add chicken; coat with flour mixture. Place chicken in prepared baking dish; cover. Bake 30 minutes.

Remove chicken from baking dish; drain drippings from dish. Place rice in baking dish. Add onion, green pepper and mushrooms to baking dish. Top with chicken. Combine apple juice and brown sugar; pour over chicken. Cover. Bake until chicken is no longer pink in center, 20 to 30 minutes.

Makes 8 servings

Helpful Hints

Skillet meals like Chicken and Linguine in Creamy Tomato Sauce are easy to prepare—all you need is a skillet. Since everything is cooked in one skillet, cleanup is simple, too.

Chicken and Linguine in Creamy Tomato Sauce

Indian-Spiced Chicken with Wild Rice

½ teaspoon salt
½ teaspoon ground cumin
½ teaspoon black pepper
¼ teaspoon ground cinnamon
¼ teaspoon ground turmeric
4 boneless skinless chicken breast halves (about 1 pound)
2 tablespoons olive oil
2 carrots, sliced
1 red bell pepper, chopped
1 rib celery, chopped
2 cloves garlic, minced
1 package (6 ounces) long grain and wild rice mix
2 cups reduced-sodium chicken broth
1 cup raisins
¼ cup sliced almonds

Combine salt, cumin, black pepper, cinnamon and turmeric in small bowl. Rub spice mixture on both sides of chicken. Place chicken on plate; cover and refrigerate 30 minutes.

Preheat oven to 350°F. Spray 13×9-inch baking dish with nonstick cooking spray.

Heat oil in large skillet over medium-high heat until hot. Add chicken; cook 2 minutes per side or until browned. Remove chicken; set aside.

Place carrots, bell pepper, celery and garlic in same skillet. Cook and stir 2 minutes. Add rice; cook 5 minutes, stirring frequently. Add seasoning packet from rice mix and broth; bring to a boil over high heat. Remove from heat; stir in raisins. Pour into prepared dish; place chicken on rice mixture. Sprinkle with almonds.

Cover tightly with foil and bake 35 minutes or until chicken is no longer pink in center and rice is tender. *Makes 4 servings*

Sour Cream Chicken Quiche

CRUST
Classic Crisco® Single Crust (recipe follows)

Filling
2 tablespoons CRISCO® Stick or 2 tablespoons CRISCO® all-vegetable shortening
2 tablespoons chopped green bell pepper
2 tablespoons chopped onion
1 cup cubed cooked chicken
1 tablespoon all-purpose flour
¼ teaspoon salt
Dash nutmeg
Dash black pepper
½ cup shredded sharp Cheddar cheese
¼ cup shredded Swiss cheese
2 eggs, lightly beaten
¾ cup milk
¾ cup dairy sour cream

1. For crust, prepare as directed. Press into 9-inch pie pan. *Do not bake.* Heat oven to 400°F.

2. For filling, melt Crisco in small skillet. Add green pepper and onion. Cook on medium-high heat 3 minutes, stirring frequently. Add chicken and flour. Cook and stir 2 minutes. Spread in bottom of unbaked pie crust. Sprinkle with salt, nutmeg and pepper. Top with Cheddar cheese and Swiss cheese.

3. Combine eggs, milk and sour cream in medium bowl. Stir until smooth. Pour carefully over cheese.

4. Bake at 400°F for 20 minutes. *Reduce oven temperature to 350°F.* Bake 30 to 35 minutes or until knife inserted near center comes out clean. *Do not overbake.* Cool 10 minutes before cutting and serving. Refrigerate leftover pie.
Makes 1 (9-inch) pie

Classic Crisco® Single Crust

1⅓ cups all-purpose flour
½ teaspoon salt
½ CRISCO® Stick or ½ cup CRISCO® all-vegetable shortening
3 tablespoons cold water

1. Spoon flour into measuring cup and level. Combine flour and salt in medium bowl.

2. Cut in shortening using pastry blender or 2 knives until all flour is blended to form pea-size chunks.

3. Sprinkle with water, 1 tablespoon at a time. Toss lightly with fork until dough forms a ball.

4. Press dough between hands to form 5- to 6-inch "pancake." Flour rolling surface and rolling pin lightly. Roll dough into circle. Trim circle 1 inch larger than upside-down pie plate. Carefully remove trimmed dough. Set aside to reroll and use for pastry cutout garnish, if desired.

5. Fold dough into quarters. Unfold and press into pie plate. Fold edge under. Flute.

6. For recipes using a baked pie crust, heat oven to 425°F. Prick bottom and side thoroughly with fork (50 times) to prevent shrinkage. Bake at 425°F for 10 to 15 minutes or until lightly browned.

7. For recipes using an unbaked pie crust, follow directions given for that recipe.
Makes 1 (9-inch) single crust

Indian-Spiced Chicken with Wild Rice

Chicken Tetrazzini

8 ounces uncooked spaghetti
2 teaspoons margarine
8 ounces mushrooms, sliced
½ cup chopped onion
½ cup diced red bell pepper
1 can (about 14 ounces) fat-free reduced-sodium chicken broth
1 cup low-fat (1%) milk, divided
¼ cup all-purpose flour
¼ teaspoon salt
⅛ teaspoon black pepper
Dash paprika
4 tablespoons (2 ounces) grated Parmesan cheese, divided
½ cup reduced-fat sour cream
2 cups cooked boneless skinless chicken breasts, cut into chunks

1. Preheat oven to 350°F. Cook spaghetti according to package directions, omitting salt. Drain; set aside.

2. Melt margarine in large nonstick skillet over medium-high heat. Add mushrooms, onions and bell pepper; cook and stir until onions are tender. Add chicken broth, ½ cup milk and sherry to onion mixture. Pour remaining ½ cup milk into small jar with tight-fitting lid; add flour, salt, black pepper and paprika. Shake well. Slowly stir flour mixture into skillet. Bring to a boil; cook 1 minute. Reduce heat; stir in 2 tablespoons Parmesan cheese. Stir in sour cream; blend well. Add chicken and noodles; mix well.

3. Lightly coat 1½-quart casserole with nonstick cooking spray. Spread mixture evenly into prepared casserole. Sprinkle with remaining 2 tablespoons Parmesan cheese. Bake 30 to 35 minutes until hot. Let cool slightly before serving.

Makes 6 servings

Artichoke-Olive Chicken Bake

1½ cups uncooked rotini pasta
1 tablespoon olive oil
1 medium onion, chopped
½ green bell pepper, chopped
2 cups shredded cooked chicken
1 can (14½ ounces) diced tomatoes with Italian-style herbs, undrained
1 can (14 ounces) artichoke hearts, drained and quartered
1 can (6 ounces) sliced black olives, drained
1 teaspoon dried Italian seasoning
2 cups (8 ounces) shredded mozzarella cheese

Preheat oven to 350°F. Spray 2-quart casserole with nonstick cooking spray.

Cook pasta according to package directions until al dente. Drain and set aside.

Meanwhile, heat oil in large deep skillet over medium heat until hot. Add onion and pepper; cook and stir 1 minute. Add chicken, tomatoes with juice, pasta, artichokes, olives and Italian seasoning; mix until combined.

Place half of chicken mixture in prepared dish; sprinkle with half of cheese. Top with remaining chicken mixture and cheese.

Bake, covered, 35 minutes or until hot and bubbly. *Makes 8 servings*

Sausage & Chicken-Stuffed Pita Sandwiches

¾ pound Italian sausage links, sliced
¾ pound boneless, skinless chicken breasts, cut into ¾-inch cubes
1 clove garlic, finely chopped
1½ cups RAGÚ® Old World Style® Pasta Sauce
1 cup shredded mozzarella cheese (about 4 ounces)
6 large pita breads, heated

Preheat oven to 350°F. In 12-inch nonstick skillet, cook sausage over medium-high heat, stirring occasionally, 5 minutes. Add chicken and garlic and cook, stirring occasionally, 5 minutes. Stir in Ragú® Old World Style Pasta Sauce and simmer uncovered 5 minutes or until sausage is done and chicken is no longer pink. Remove from heat; stir in cheese. To serve, generously stuff pita bread with sausage mixture. Garnish, if desired, with grated Parmesan cheese.

Makes 6 servings

Tip: The quickest way to peel garlic is to press each clove with the flat side of a knife until the paper-like skin breaks; the skin slips off easily.

Helpful Hints

Canned artichokes are available unseasoned and marinated in seasoned oil. Be sure to choose the correct product for your recipe.

Artichoke-Olive Chicken Bake

Chicken & Three-Cheese Rice Wraps

- **1 package (1 pound) TYSON® Fresh Ground Chicken**
- **1 box UNCLE BEN'S® COUNTRY INN® Three Cheese Rice**
- **1¾ cups water**
- **3 tablespoons chopped green chilies**
- **½ cup chopped tomato**
- **12 (8- or 10-inch) flour tortillas**

COOK: CLEAN: Wash hands. Heat large nonstick skillet over medium-high heat. Add chicken; cook, stirring frequently, 6 to 9 minutes or until chicken is no longer pink. **CLEAN:** Wash hands. Add rice, contents of seasoning packet, water and chilies; mix well. Bring to a boil. Reduce heat; cover. Simmer 10 to 15 minutes or until rice is tender and liquid is absorbed. Stir in tomato; let stand 5 minutes. Meanwhile, heat tortillas according to package directions. Spoon chicken mixture evenly down center of tortillas. Wrap or roll to enclose chicken mixture.

SERVE: Serve wraps with sour cream and salsa, if desired.

CHILL: Refrigerate leftovers immediately. *Makes 6 servings*

Prep Time: none
Cook Time: 20 minutes

Fettuccine with Chicken Breasts

- **12 ounces uncooked fettuccine or egg noodles**
- **1 cup HIDDEN VALLEY® Original Ranch® Dressing**
- **⅓ cup Dijon mustard**
- **8 boneless, skinless chicken breast halves, pounded thin**
- **½ cup butter**
- **⅓ cup dry white wine**

Cook fettuccine according to package directions; drain. Preheat oven to 425°F. Stir together dressing and mustard; set aside. Pour fettuccine into oiled baking dish. Sauté chicken in butter in a large skillet until no longer pink in center. Transfer cooked chicken to the bed of fettuccine. Add wine to the skillet; cook until reduced to desired consistency. Drizzle over chicken. Pour reserved dressing mixture over chicken. Bake at 425°F. about 10 minutes, or until dressing forms a golden brown crust.

Makes 8 servings

Creamy Chicken & Rice Bake

- **6 boneless, skinless chicken thighs (about 1½ pounds)**
- **1 jar (16 ounces) RAGÚ® Cheese Creations!® Classic Alfredo Sauce**
- **1 can (14½ ounces) chicken broth**
- **1½ cups uncooked converted rice**
- **1 medium tomato, coarsely chopped**
- **2 tablespoons grated Parmesan cheese**

1. Preheat oven to 400°F. Season chicken, if desired, with salt and pepper.

2. In 13×9-inch baking dish, thoroughly combine Ragú Cheese Creations! Sauce, broth, uncooked rice and tomato. Arrange chicken on rice mixture.

3. Cover with aluminum foil and bake 35 minutes. Remove foil and sprinkle chicken with cheese. Bake an additional 10 minutes or until chicken is no longer pink.

Makes 6 servings

Tip: Substitute boneless, skinless chicken breasts for chicken thighs, if desired.

Prep Time: 5 minutes
Cook Time: 45 minutes

Easy Chicken & Stuffing Skillet

- **4 tablespoons butter or margarine, divided**
- **4 small boneless skinless chicken breast halves (about 1 pound)**
- **1 package (6 ounces) STOVE TOP® Lower Sodium Stuffing Mix for Chicken**
- **1⅓ cups water**

MELT 2 tablespoons butter in large nonstick skillet on medium-high heat. Add chicken; cover. Cook 4 minutes on each side or until cooked through. Remove from skillet.

ADD contents of Vegetable/Seasoning packet, water and remaining 2 tablespoons butter to skillet; bring to boil. Reduce heat to low; cover and simmer 5 minutes. Stir in Stuffing Crumbs just to moisten. Top with chicken; cover. Cook on low heat 5 minutes.

Makes 4 servings

Prep Time: 5 minutes
Cook Time: 20 minutes

Chicken & Three-Cheese Rice Wraps

Turkey and Macaroni

1 teaspoon vegetable oil
1½ pounds ground turkey
2 cans (10¾ ounces each) condensed tomato soup, undiluted
2 cups uncooked macaroni, cooked and drained
1 can (16 ounces) corn, drained
½ cup chopped onion
1 can (4 ounces) sliced mushrooms, drained
2 tablespoons ketchup
1 tablespoon mustard
Salt and black pepper to taste

Slow Cooker Directions

Heat oil in medium skillet; cook turkey until browned. Transfer mixture to slow cooker. Add remaining ingredients to slow cooker. Stir to blend. Cover and cook on LOW 7 to 9 hours or on HIGH 3 to 4 hours.

Makes 4 to 6 servings

Red Beans with Sausage

1 pound lite turkey smoked sausage or smoked pork turkey
2 tablespoons CRISCO® Oil*
2 stalks celery, chopped
1 large onion, peeled and diced
1 large green bell pepper, seeds and ribs removed, and chopped
2 teaspoons jarred minced garlic *or* 1 large clove garlic, peeled and minced
2 cans (16 ounces each) kidney beans, drained and rinsed
2 cups water
2 bay leaves
1 teaspoon Italian seasoning
½ to 1 teaspoon hot red pepper sauce
½ teaspoon salt

1. Heat 3-quart saucepan on medium-high heat. Add sausage. Cook 3 minutes or until lightly brown. Remove sausage from pan with slotted spoon. Discard drippings from pan.

2. Reduce heat to medium. Add oil to pan, along with celery, onion, green pepper and garlic. Sauté 3 minutes, or until onions are translucent. Add beans, water, bay leaves, Italian seasoning, hot red pepper sauce and salt to pan. Return sausage to pan. Bring to boil.

3. Simmer mixture 30 to 45 minutes, or until thick. Stir occasionally. Discard bay leaves. Serve immediately over rice.

Makes 4 servings

Preparation Time: 25 minutes
Total Time: 60 to 70 minutes

**Use your favorite Crisco Oil product.*

Helpful Hints

If you want to reduce the fat in a recipe using ground turkey, be sure to choose ground turkey breast meat. Ground turkey dark meat and skin will be higher in fat.

Turkey and Macaroni

Turkey and Stuffing Bake

- 1 jar (4½ ounces) sliced mushrooms
- ¼ cup butter or margarine
- ½ cup diced celery
- ½ cup chopped onion
- 1¼ cups HIDDEN VALLEY® Original Ranch® Dressing, divided
- ⅔ cup water
- 3 cups seasoned stuffing mix
- ⅓ cup sweetened dried cranberries
- 3 cups coarsely shredded cooked turkey (about 1 pound)

Drain mushrooms, reserving liquid; set aside. Melt butter over medium-high heat in a large skillet. Add celery and onion; sauté for 4 minutes or until soft. Remove from heat and stir in ½ cup dressing, water and reserved mushroom liquid. Stir in stuffing mix and cranberries until thoroughly moistened. Combine turkey, mushrooms and remaining ¾ cup dressing in a separate bowl; spread evenly in a greased 8-inch baking dish. Top with stuffing mixture. Bake at 350°F. for 40 minutes or until bubbly and brown.

Makes 4 to 6 servings

Cheesy Turkey Veg•All® Bake

- 1 package (5½ ounces) au gratin potato mix
- 2⅔ cups boiling water
- 1 can (15 ounces) VEG•ALL® Original Mixed Vegetables, drained
- 1 cup cubed cooked turkey
- 2 tablespoons butter

Preheat oven to 350°F. Place au gratin potato mix and sauce packet into large mixing bowl. Add water, Veg•All®, turkey and butter; mix well. Pour into greased 2-quart casserole. Bake for 20 minutes or until top is golden brown. Cool 5 minutes before serving.

Makes 6 servings

Easy Tex-Mex Bake

- 8 ounces uncooked thin mostaccioli
- Nonstick cooking spray
- 1 pound ground turkey breast
- ⅔ cup bottled medium or mild salsa
- 1 package (10 ounces) frozen corn, thawed and drained
- 1 container (16 ounces) low-fat cottage cheese
- 1 egg
- 1 tablespoon minced fresh cilantro
- ½ teaspoon white pepper
- ¼ teaspoon ground cumin
- ½ cup (2 ounces) shredded Monterey Jack cheese

1. Cook pasta according to package directions, omitting salt. Drain and rinse well; set aside.

2. Spray large nonstick skillet with nonstick cooking spray. Add turkey; cook until no longer pink, about 5 minutes. Stir in salsa and corn. Remove from heat.

3. Preheat oven to 350°F. Combine cottage cheese, egg, cilantro, white pepper and cumin in small bowl.

4. Spoon ½ turkey mixture in bottom of 11×7-inch baking dish. Top with pasta. Spoon cottage cheese mixture over pasta. Top with remaining turkey mixture. Sprinkle Monterey Jack cheese over casserole.

5. Bake 25 to 30 minutes or until heated through.

Makes 6 servings

Green Bean & Turkey Bake

- 1 can (10¾ ounces) condensed cream of mushroom soup
- ¾ cup milk
- ⅛ teaspoon pepper
- 2 packages (9 ounces *each*) frozen cut green beans, thawed
- 2 cups (12 ounces) cubed cooked turkey or chicken
- 1⅓ cups *French's® Taste Toppers™* French Fried Onions, divided
- 1½ cups (6 ounces) shredded Cheddar cheese, divided
- 3 cups hot mashed potatoes

1. Preheat oven to 375°F. In 3-quart casserole, combine soup, milk and pepper; mix well. Stir in beans, turkey, *⅔ cup* ***Taste Toppers*** and *1 cup* cheese. Spoon mashed potatoes on top.

2. Bake, uncovered, 45 minutes or until hot. Sprinkle with remaining *½ cup* cheese and *⅔ cup* ***Taste Toppers*** Bake 3 minutes or until ***Taste Toppers*** are golden.

Makes 6 servings

Microwave Directions: Prepare mixture as above except do not top with potatoes. Cover casserole with vented plastic wrap. Microwave on HIGH 15 minutes or until heated through, stirring halfway. Uncover. Top with mashed potatoes, remaining cheese and ***Taste Toppers***. Microwave on HIGH 2 to 4 minutes. Let stand 5 minutes.

Tip: Two (14½-ounce) cans cut green beans (drained) may be used instead of frozen beans. You may substitute instant mashed potatoes prepared according to package directions for 6 servings.

Prep Time: 10 minutes
Cook Time: 50 minutes

Turkey and Stuffing Bake

Tex-Mex Turkey

1 can (10¾ ounces) reduced-fat condensed tomato soup
½ cup nonfat sour cream
Nonstick cooking spray
1 cup sliced green onions
½ cup diced green chilies
½ cup frozen corn
½ cup chopped red bell pepper
¼ cup sliced ripe olives (optional)
2 cloves garlic, minced
1 teaspoon chili powder
1 pound turkey tenderloins, cut into thin strips
½ teaspoon salt
Hot cooked rice (optional)

Combine soup and sour cream in small bowl; mix well. Set aside. Spray large nonstick skillet with cooking spray. Add onions, chilies, corn, bell pepper, olives, if desired, garlic and chili powder; cook and stir over medium-high heat until onions and pepper are tender.

Add turkey to skillet; brown evenly. Add soup mixture and salt; bring to a boil. Reduce heat to low; cover and simmer 5 minutes. Serve with rice, if desired. *Makes 4 servings*

Mexican Rice and Turkey Bake

1 bag SUCCESS® Rice
Vegetable cooking spray
3 cups chopped cooked turkey
1 can (10 ounces) tomatoes with chilies, undrained*
1 can (12 ounces) Mexican-style corn with sweet peppers, drained
1 cup fat-free sour cream
½ cup (2 ounces) shredded low-fat Cheddar cheese

**Or, use 1 can (14½ ounces) stewed tomatoes. Add 1 can (4 ounces) drained chopped mild green chilies.*

Prepare rice according to package directions.

Spray 1½-quart microwavesafe casserole with cooking spray; set aside. Combine rice, turkey, tomatoes and corn in large bowl; mix well. Spoon into prepared casserole. Microwave on HIGH until hot and bubbly, 8 to 10 minutes, stirring after 5 minutes. Top with sour cream and cheese. *Makes 6 servings*

Conventional Oven: Assemble casserole as directed. Spoon into ovenproof 1½-quart casserole sprayed with vegetable cooking spray. Bake at 350°F until thoroughly heated, 15 to 20 minutes.

Creamy Turkey & Broccoli

1 package (6 ounces) stuffing mix, plus ingredients to prepare mix*
1⅓ cups *French's® Taste Toppers™* French Fried Onions, divided
1 package (10 ounces) frozen broccoli spears, thawed and drained
1 package (about 1⅛ ounces) cheese sauce mix
1¼ cups milk
½ cup sour cream
2 cups (10 ounces) cubed cooked turkey or chicken

**3 cups leftover stuffing may be substituted for stuffing mix. If stuffing is dry, stir in water, 1 tablespoon at a time, until moist but not wet.*

Preheat oven to 350°F. In medium saucepan, prepare stuffing mix according to package directions; stir in *⅔ cup **Taste Toppers***. Spread stuffing over bottom of greased 9-inch round baking dish. Arrange broccoli spears over stuffing with flowerets around edge of dish. In medium saucepan, prepare cheese sauce mix according to package directions using 1¼ cups milk. Remove from heat; stir in sour cream and turkey. Pour turkey mixture over broccoli stalks. Bake, covered, at 350°F for 30 minutes or until heated through. Sprinkle remaining *⅔ cup* ***Taste Toppers*** over turkey; bake, uncovered, 5 minutes or until ***Taste Toppers*** are golden brown.
Makes 4 to 6 servings

Microwave Directions: In 9-inch round microwave-safe dish, prepare stuffing mix according to package microwave directions; stir in *⅔ cup* ***Taste Toppers***. Arrange stuffing and broccoli spears in dish as above; set aside. In medium microwave-safe bowl, prepare cheese sauce mix according to package microwave directions using 1¼ cups milk. Add turkey and cook, covered, 5 to 6 minutes, stirring turkey halfway through cooking time. Stir in sour cream. Pour turkey mixture over broccoli stalks. Cook, covered, 8 to 10 minutes or until heated through. Rotate dish halfway through cooking time. Top turkey with remaining *⅔ cup* ***Taste Toppers***; cook, uncovered, 1 minute. Let stand 5 minutes.

Helpful Hints

Try turkey tenderloins for a change of pace. Tenderloins come from the lean breast of the turkey, are boneless and quick cooking.

Tex-Mex Turkey

Fusilli Pizzaiola with Turkey Meatballs

- 2 cans (14½ ounces each) no-salt-added tomatoes, undrained
- 1 can (8 ounces) no-salt-added tomato sauce
- ¼ cup chopped onion
- ¼ cup grated carrot
- 2 tablespoons no-salt-added tomato paste
- 2 tablespoons chopped fresh basil
- 1 clove garlic, minced
- ½ teaspoon dried thyme leaves
- ¼ teaspoon sugar
- ¼ teaspoon black pepper, divided
- 1 bay leaf
- 1 pound ground turkey breast
- 1 egg, lightly beaten
- 1 tablespoon fat-free (skim) milk
- ¼ cup Italian-seasoned dry bread crumbs
- 2 tablespoons chopped fresh parsley
- 8 ounces uncooked fusilli or other spiral-shaped pasta

Slow Cooker Directions
Combine tomatoes with juice, tomato sauce, onion, carrot, tomato paste, basil, garlic, thyme, sugar, ⅛ teaspoon black pepper and bay leaf in slow cooker. Break up tomatoes gently with wooden spoon. Cover and cook on LOW 4½ to 5 hours.

About 45 minutes before end of cooking, prepare meatballs. Preheat oven to 350°F. Combine turkey, egg and milk; blend in bread crumbs, parsley and remaining ⅛ teaspoon black pepper. With wet hands, shape mixture into small balls. Spray baking sheet with nonstick cooking spray. Arrange meatballs on baking sheet. Bake 25 minutes or until no longer pink in center.

Add meatballs to slow cooker. Cover and cook 45 minutes to 1 hour or until meatballs are heated through. Discard bay leaf. Prepare pasta according to package directions. Drain. Place in serving bowl; top with meatballs and sauce.

Makes 4 servings

Sausage & Mushroom Pasta

- 1 can (10¾ ounces) reduced-fat condensed tomato soup
- ¼ cup fat-free (skim) milk
- ½ cup chopped onion
- ½ cup chopped green bell pepper
- 2 cloves garlic, minced
- 1 teaspoon dried Italian seasoning
- 1 cup sliced mushrooms
- ½ teaspoon salt (optional)
- 1 (7-ounce package) reduced-fat smoked turkey sausage, cut into ⅛-inch slices
- 4 cups cooked bow tie pasta

Combine soup and milk in small bowl; mix well and set aside. Spray large nonstick skillet with nonstick cooking spray; heat over medium-high heat until hot. Add onion, pepper, garlic and Italian seasoning; cook and stir until onion and pepper are tender. Add mushrooms and salt, if desired; cook and stir 2 to 3 minutes. Add sausage; mix well. Reduce heat; cover and simmer an additional 2 minutes. Add pasta; toss until coated with sauce.

Makes 6 servings

Microwave Turkey Enchiladas

- 1 cup chopped LOUIS RICH® Breast of Turkey
- 1 package (8 ounces) PHILADELPHIA® Cream Cheese, softened
- ¼ cup sliced green onions
- Corn tortillas
- Oil
- ¾ pound (12 ounces) VELVEETA® Mild Mexican Pasteurized Process Cheese Spread with Jalapeño Peppers, cut up
- 1 cup chopped tomato, divided
- ¼ cup milk

MIX turkey, cream cheese and onions until well blended.

BRUSH tortillas lightly with oil. Stack 4 tortillas on a microwavable plate. Microwave on HIGH 30 seconds or until soft. Repeat with remaining tortillas.

FILL each tortilla with ¼ cup turkey mixture. Roll up; place, seam-side down, in 12×8-inch microwavable baking dish. Stir Velveeta, ½ cup tomatoes and milk in glass bowl. Microwave on HIGH 2 to 4 minutes or until Velveeta is melted, stirring after each minute. Pour sauce over tortillas; top with remaining tomatoes.

MICROWAVE on HIGH 12 to 14 minutes, or until thoroughly heated, turning dish after 6 minutes.

Makes 4 servings

Prep Time: 15 minutes

Sausage & Mushroom Pasta

Rice Lasagna

- 1 bag SUCCESS® Rice
- Vegetable cooking spray
- 2 tablespoons reduced-calorie margarine
- 1 pound ground turkey
- 1 cup chopped onion
- 1 cup sliced fresh mushrooms
- 1 clove garlic, minced
- 2 cans (8 ounces each) no-salt-added tomato sauce
- 1 can (6 ounces) no-salt-added tomato paste
- 1 teaspoon dried oregano leaves, crushed
- 1 carton (15 ounces) low-fat cottage cheese
- ½ cup (2 ounces) grated Parmesan cheese
- 2 cups (8 ounces) shredded mozzarella cheese
- 1 tablespoon dried parsley flakes

Prepare rice according to package directions.

Preheat oven to 350°F.

Spray 13×9-inch baking dish with cooking spray; set aside. Melt margarine in large skillet over medium heat. Add ground turkey, onion, mushrooms and garlic; cook until turkey is no longer pink and vegetables are tender, stirring occasionally to separate turkey. Drain. Stir in tomato sauce, tomato paste and oregano; simmer 15 minutes, stirring occasionally. Layer half each of rice, turkey mixture, cottage cheese, Parmesan cheese and mozzarella cheese in prepared baking dish; repeat layers. Sprinkle with parsley; cover. Bake 30 minutes. Uncover; continue baking 15 minutes.

Makes 8 servings

Mexican Stuffed Peppers

- Nonstick cooking spray
- 6 ounces breakfast bulk turkey sausage
- 1 cup frozen corn
- 4 ounces uncooked orzo pasta or small shell pasta
- 1 cup canned black beans, rinsed and drained
- Salsa Cruda (recipe follows) or 1¾ cups mild picante sauce, divided
- ½ cup water
- ¼ cup cornmeal
- 1 tablespoon chili powder
- ½ teaspoon ground cumin
- 4 medium green bell peppers, halved lengthwise with stems and seeds removed
- ½ cup (2 ounces) shredded reduced-fat sharp Cheddar cheese
- ½ cup nonfat sour cream
- ¼ cup chopped fresh cilantro leaves or finely chopped green onions

1. Preheat oven to 350°F. Spray large nonstick skillet with cooking spray. Heat over high heat until hot. Brown turkey over medium-high heat 6 to 8 minutes or until no longer pink, stirring to separate turkey; drain fat. Add corn, pasta, beans, 1¼ cups Salsa Cruda, water, cornmeal, chili powder and cumin. Bring to a boil; remove from heat.

2. Place pepper halves in 13×9-inch baking pan. Fill each pepper half with equal amounts of sausage mixture; cover tightly with foil. Bake 1 hour and 15 minutes. Remove from oven; top each pepper half with ⅛ of remaining Salsa Cruda. Sprinkle cheese over peppers. Top each half with 1 tablespoon sour cream; sprinkle with cilantro.

Makes 4 servings

Salsa Cruda

- 2 cups chopped tomato
- ¼ cup minced onion
- ¼ cup minced fresh cilantro (optional)
- ¼ cup lime juice
- 1 jalapeño pepper,* seeded, minced
- 2 cloves garlic, minced

**Jalapeño peppers can sting and irritate the skin; wear rubber gloves when handling peppers and do not touch eyes. Wash hands after handling.*

1. Combine tomato, onion, cilantro, lime juice, jalapeño and garlic in small bowl. Stir to combine.

Turkey Broccoli Bake

- 1 bag (16 ounces) frozen broccoli cuts, thawed, drained
- 2 cups cubed cooked turkey or chicken
- 2 cups soft bread cubes
- 8 ounces sliced American cheese, divided
- 1 jar (12 ounces) HEINZ® HomeStyle Turkey or Chicken Gravy
- ½ cup undiluted evaporated milk
- Dash pepper

In buttered 9-inch square baking dish, layer broccoli, turkey, bread cubes and cheese. Combine gravy, milk and pepper; pour over cheese. Bake in 375°F oven, 40 minutes. Let stand 5 minutes.

Makes 6 servings

Rice Lasagna

Turkey and Rice Quiche

- **3 cups cooked rice, cooled to room temperature**
- **1½ cups chopped cooked turkey**
- **1 medium tomato, seeded and finely diced**
- **¼ cup sliced green onions**
- **¼ cup finely diced green bell pepper**
- **1 tablespoon chopped fresh basil *or* 1 teaspoon dried basil leaves**
- **½ teaspoon seasoned salt**
- **⅛ to ¼ teaspoon ground red pepper**
- **½ cup skim milk**
- **3 eggs, beaten**
- **Vegetable cooking spray**
- **½ cup (2 ounces) shredded Cheddar cheese**
- **½ cup (2 ounces) shredded mozzarella cheese**

Combine rice, turkey, tomato, onions, bell pepper, basil, salt, red pepper, milk and eggs in 13×9×2-inch pan coated with cooking spray. Top with cheeses. Bake at 375°F for 20 minutes or until knife inserted near center comes out clean. To serve, cut quiche into 8 squares; cut each square diagonally into 2 triangles.

Makes 8 servings (2 triangles each)

Favorite recipe from **USA Rice Federation**

Southwestern Turkey in Chilies and Cream

Slow Cooker

- **1 boneless skinless turkey breast, cut into 1-inch pieces**
- **2 tablespoons plus 2 teaspoons flour, divided**
- **1 can (15 ounces) corn, well drained**
- **1 can (4 ounces) diced green chilies, well drained**
- **1 tablespoon butter**
- **½ cup chicken broth**
- **1 clove garlic, minced**
- **1 teaspoon salt**
- **½ teaspoon paprika**
- **¼ teaspoon dried oregano leaves**
- **¼ teaspoon black pepper**
- **½ cup heavy cream**
- **2 tablespoons chopped cilantro**
- **3 cups hot cooked rice or pasta**

Slow Cooker Directions

1. Coat turkey pieces with 2 tablespoons flour; set aside. Place corn and green chilies in slow cooker.

2. Melt butter in large nonstick skillet over medium heat. Add turkey pieces; cook and stir 5 minutes or until lightly browned. Place turkey in slow cooker. Add broth, garlic, salt, paprika, oregano and pepper. Cover and cook on LOW 2 hours.

3. Stir cream and remaining 2 teaspoons flour in small bowl until smooth. Pour mixture into slow cooker. Cover and cook on HIGH 10 minutes or until slightly thickened. Stir in cilantro. Serve over rice.

Makes 6 (11⁄2-cups) servings

Turkey Breast with Barley-Cranberry Stuffing

Slow Cooker

- **2 cups fat-free reduced-sodium chicken broth**
- **1 cup quick-cooking barley**
- **½ cup chopped onion**
- **½ cup dried cranberries**
- **2 tablespoons slivered almonds, toasted**
- **½ teaspoon rubbed sage**
- **½ teaspoon garlic-pepper seasoning**
- **Nonstick cooking spray**
- **1 fresh or frozen bone-in turkey breast half (1¾- to 2-pounds), thawed and skinned**
- **⅓ cup finely chopped parsley**

Slow Cooker Directions

1. Combine broth, barley, onion, cranberries, almonds, sage and garlic-pepper seasoning in slow cooker.

2. Spray large nonstick skillet with cooking spray. Heat over medium heat until hot. Brown turkey breast on all sides; add to slow cooker. Cover and cook on LOW 3 to 4 hours or until internal temperature reaches 170°F when tested with meat thermometer inserted into the thickest part of breast, not touching bone.

3. Transfer turkey to cutting board; cover with foil and let stand 10 to 15 minutes before carving. (Internal temperature will rise 5° to 10°F during stand time.) Stir parsley into sauce mixture in slow cooker. Spoon sauce over turkey.

Makes 6 servings

Helpful Hints

Store white rice in an airtight container in a cool, dry place. It will keep indefinitely. Brown rice is subject to rancidity because the bran is intact. It can be stored for only six months.

Turkey and Rice Quiche

Lasagna Verdi

SAUCE

- **¼ cup (½ stick) butter *or* margarine**
- **3 tablespoons flour**
- **1 (14½-ounce) can chicken broth**
- **1 cup milk**
- **2 tablespoons TABASCO® brand Green Pepper Sauce**

FILLING

- **2 tablespoons vegetable oil**
- **1 pound ground turkey**
- **1 medium onion, diced**
- **1 tablespoon TABASCO® brand Green Pepper Sauce**
- **1 teaspoon salt**
- **1 (15-ounce) container ricotta cheese**
- **1 egg**
- **2 tablespoons chopped fresh parsley**
- **12 no-boil lasagna noodles**
- **1 (8-ounce) package mozzarella cheese, shredded**
- **¼ cup grated Parmesan cheese**

For sauce, melt butter in 2-quart saucepan over medium heat; stir in flour until well blended and smooth. Gradually add chicken broth, milk and TABASCO® Green Pepper Sauce; cook over high heat until mixture boils and thickens, stirring frequently.

Preheat oven to 375°F. For filling, heat oil in 12-inch skillet over medium-high heat. Add turkey and onion; cook until meat is well browned, stirring frequently. Stir in TABASCO® Green Pepper Sauce and salt. Mix ricotta cheese, egg and parsley in small bowl.

Grease 12×8-inch baking dish. Spread 1 cup sauce on bottom of baking dish. Layer 3 lasagna noodles in baking dish. Spread ⅓ of turkey mixture, ⅓ of ricotta mixture, ¼ of mozzarella cheese and ¼ of remaining sauce over noodles. Repeat layers two more times. Top with remaining 3 lasagna noodles. Spread remaining sauce over noodles; sprinkle with remaining mozzarella cheese and Parmesan cheese.

Cover with foil and bake 30 minutes. Uncover and bake 10 minutes or until lasagna is hot and bubbly. Let stand 5 minutes before serving.

Makes 8 servings

Turkey and Biscuits

- **2 cans (10¾ ounces each) condensed cream of chicken soup, undiluted**
- **¼ cup dry white wine**
- **¼ teaspoon poultry seasoning**
- **2 packages (8 ounces each) frozen cut asparagus, thawed**
- **3 cups cubed cooked turkey or chicken**
- **Paprika (optional)**
- **1 can (11 ounces) refrigerated flaky biscuits**

Preheat oven to 350°F. Spray 13×9-inch baking dish with nonstick cooking spray.

Combine soup, wine and poultry seasoning in medium bowl.

Arrange asparagus in single layer in prepared dish. Place turkey evenly over asparagus. Spread soup mixture over turkey. Sprinkle lightly with paprika, if desired.

Cover tightly with foil and bake 20 minutes. Remove from oven. *Increase oven temperature to 425°F.* Top with biscuits and bake, uncovered, 8 to 10 minutes or until biscuits are golden brown.

Makes 6 servings

Turkey Jambalaya

- **1 teaspoon vegetable oil**
- **1 cup chopped onion**
- **1 green bell pepper, chopped**
- **½ cup chopped celery**
- **3 cloves garlic, finely chopped**
- **1¾ cups fat-free reduced-sodium chicken broth**
- **1 cup chopped seeded tomato**
- **¼ pound cooked ground turkey breast**
- **¼ pound cooked turkey sausage**
- **3 tablespoons tomato paste**
- **1 bay leaf**
- **1 teaspoon dried basil leaves**
- **¼ teaspoon ground red pepper**
- **1 cup uncooked white rice**
- **¼ cup chopped fresh parsley**

1. Heat oil in large nonstick skillet over medium-high heat until hot. Add onion, bell pepper, celery and garlic. Cook and stir 5 minutes or until vegetables are tender.

2. Add chicken broth, tomato, turkey, turkey sausage, tomato paste, bay leaf, basil and red pepper. Stir in rice. Bring to a boil over high heat, stirring occasionally. Reduce heat to medium-low. Simmer, covered, 20 minutes or until rice is tender.

3. Remove skillet from heat. Remove and discard bay leaf. Top servings evenly with parsley. Serve immediately.

Makes 4 servings

Turkey and Biscuit

Chipotle Tamale Pie

¾ pound ground turkey breast or lean ground beef
1 cup chopped onion
¾ cup diced green bell pepper
¾ cup diced red bell pepper
4 cloves garlic, minced
2 teaspoons ground cumin
1 can (15 ounces) pinto or red beans, rinsed and drained
1 can (8 ounces) no-salt-added stewed tomatoes, undrained
2 canned chipotle chilies in adobo sauce, minced (about 1 tablespoon)
1 to 2 teaspoons adobo sauce from canned chilies (optional)
1 cup (4 ounces) low-sodium reduced-fat shredded Cheddar cheese
½ cup chopped fresh cilantro
1 package (8½ ounces) corn bread mix
⅓ cup low-fat (1%) milk
1 egg white

1. Preheat oven to 400°F.

2. Cook turkey, onion, bell peppers and garlic in large nonstick skillet over medium-high heat 8 minutes or until turkey is no longer pink, stirring occasionally. Drain fat; sprinkle mixture with cumin.

3. Add beans, tomatoes, chilies and adobo sauce; bring to a boil over high heat. Reduce heat to medium; simmer, uncovered, 5 minutes. Remove from heat; stir in cheese and cilantro.

4. Spray 8-inch square baking dish with nonstick cooking spray. Spoon turkey mixture evenly into prepared dish, pressing down to compact mixture. Combine corn bread mix, milk and egg white in medium bowl; mix just until dry ingredients are moistened. Spoon batter evenly over turkey mixture to cover completely.

5. Bake 20 to 22 minutes or until corn bread is golden brown. Let stand 5 minutes before serving.

Makes 6 servings

Turkey 'n' Stuffing Pie

1¼ cups water*
¼ cup butter or margarine*
3½ cups seasoned stuffing crumbs*
1⅓ cups *French's® Taste Toppers™* French Fried Onions, divided
1 can (10¾ ounces) condensed cream of celery soup
¾ cup milk
1½ cups (7 ounces) cubed cooked turkey
1 package (10 ounces) frozen peas, thawed and drained

**3 cups leftover stuffing may be substituted for water, butter and stuffing crumbs. If stuffing is dry, stir in water, 1 tablespoon at a time, until moist but not wet.*

Preheat oven to 350°F. In medium saucepan, heat water and butter; stir until butter melts. Remove from heat. Stir in seasoned stuffing crumbs and *⅔ cup* ***Taste Toppers***. Spoon stuffing mixture into 9-inch round or fluted baking dish. Press stuffing evenly across bottom and up sides of dish to form a shell. In medium bowl, combine soup, milk, turkey and peas; pour into stuffing shell. Bake, covered, at 350°F for 30 minutes or until heated through. Top with remaining *⅔ cup* ***Taste Toppers***; bake, uncovered, 5 minutes or until ***Taste Toppers*** are golden brown.

Makes 4 to 6 servings

Microwave Directions: In 9-inch round or fluted microwave-safe dish, place water and butter. Cook, covered, on HIGH 3 minutes or until butter melts. Stir in stuffing crumbs and *⅔ cup* ***Taste Toppers***. Press stuffing mixture into dish as above. Reduce milk to ½ cup. In large microwave-safe bowl, combine soup, milk, turkey and peas; cook, covered, 8 minutes. Stir turkey mixture halfway through cooking time. Pour turkey mixture into stuffing shell. Cook, uncovered, 4 to 6 minutes or until heated through. Rotate dish halfway through cooking time. Top with remaining *⅔ cup* ***Taste Toppers***; cook, uncovered, 1 minute. Let stand 5 minutes.

Turkey Olé

½ cup minced onions
2 tablespoons butter or margarine
1 tablespoon all-purpose flour
1½ cups cubed cooked turkey
1½ cups prepared HIDDEN VALLEY® Original Ranch® Salad Dressing
3 ounces rotini (spiral macaroni), plain or spinach, cooked
½ (10-ounce) package frozen peas, thawed
⅓ cup canned diced green chiles, drained
⅛ to ¼ teaspoon black pepper (optional)
1 teaspoon dried oregano, crushed
3 tablespoons dry bread crumbs
1 tablespoon butter or margarine, melted
Tomato wedges

Preheat oven to 350°F. In skillet, sauté onions in 2 tablespoons butter until tender. Stir in flour and cook until smooth and bubbly; remove from heat. In 1½-quart casserole, combine turkey, salad dressing, rotini, peas, chiles, pepper and oregano; stir in onions. In small bowl, combine bread crumbs with melted butter; sprinkle over casserole. Bake until heated through and bread crumbs are browned, 15 to 20 minutes. Garnish with tomato wedges.

Makes 6 servings

Chipotle Tamale Pie

Turkey & Zucchini Enchiladas with Tomatillo-Green Chili Sauce

1¼ pound turkey leg
1 tablespoon olive oil
1 small onion, thinly sliced
1 tablespoon minced garlic
1 pound zucchini, quartered lengthwise and sliced thinly crosswise
1½ teaspoons ground cumin
½ teaspoon dried oregano leaves
¾ cup (3 ounces) shredded reduced-fat Monterey Jack cheese
12 (6-inch) corn tortillas
Tomatillo-Green Chilie Sauce (recipe follows)
½ cup crumbled feta cheese
6 sprigs fresh cilantro for garnish

1. Place turkey in large saucepan; cover with water. Bring to a boil over high heat. Reduce heat to medium-low. Cover and simmer 1½ to 2 hours or until meat pulls apart easily when tested with fork. Drain; discard skin and bone. Cut meat into small pieces. Place in medium bowl; set aside.

2. Preheat oven to 350°F.

3. Heat oil over medium-high heat in large skillet. Add onion; cook and stir 3 to 4 minutes or until tender. Reduce heat to medium. Add garlic; cook and stir 3 to 4 minutes or until onion is golden. Add zucchini, 2 tablespoons water, cumin and oregano. Cover; cook and stir over medium heat 10 minutes or until zucchini is tender. Add to turkey. Stir in Monterey Jack cheese.

4. Heat large nonstick skillet over medium-high heat. Place 1 inch water in medium bowl. Dip 1 tortilla in water; shake off excess. Place in hot skillet. Cook 10 to 15 seconds on each side or until tortilla is hot and pliable. Repeat with remaining tortillas.

5. Spray bottom of 13×9-inch baking pan with nonstick cooking spray. Spoon ¼ cup filling in center of each tortilla; fold sides over to enclose. Place seam side down in pan. Brush tops with ½ cup Tomatillo-Green Chili Sauce. Cover; bake 30 to 40 minutes or until heated through. Top enchiladas with remaining Tomatillo-Green Chili Sauce and feta cheese. Garnish with cilantro.

Makes 6 servings

Cook's Tip: Herbs are a good way to add flavor to foods without adding calories, sodium or fat. This recipe combines oregano, cumin and fresh cilantro to pack it full of flavor.

Tomatillo-Green Chili Sauce

¾ pound fresh tomatillos *or* 2 cans (18 ounces each) whole tomatillos, drained
1 can (4 ounces) diced mild green chilies, drained
½ cup chicken broth
½ teaspoon ground cumin
1 teaspoon dried oregano leaves, crushed
2 tablespoons chopped fresh cilantro (optional)

1. Place tomatillos in large saucepan; cover with water. Bring to a boil over high heat. Reduce heat to medium-high and simmer gently 20 to 30 minutes or until tomatillos are tender.

2. Place tomatillos, chilies, broth (omit if using canned tomatillos), cumin and oregano in food processor or blender; process until smooth. Return mixture to pan. Cover; heat over medium heat until bubbling. Stir in cilantro, if desired.

Makes about 3 cups

Turkey Tamale Pie with Cornbread

2 tablespoons vegetable oil
1 small onion, chopped
1 small green bell pepper, chopped
1¼ pounds turkey cutlets, chopped
1 can (15¼ ounces) whole kernel corn, drained
1 can (15 ounces) kidney beans, drained
1 can (14½ ounces) stewed tomatoes
1 can (6 ounces) tomato paste
½ cup water
1 package (1.0 ounces) LAWRY'S® Taco Spices & Seasonings
1 can (4 ounces) chopped green chiles, drained
1 package (16 ounces) cornbread mix plus ingredients to prepare

In large skillet, heat oil. Add onion and bell pepper and cook 5 minutes. Add turkey and cook over medium-high heat 7 to 10 minutes or until no longer pink in center, stirring occasionally; reduce heat to low. Stir in corn, beans, stewed tomatoes, tomato paste, water, Taco Spices & Seasonings and green chiles. Cook over low heat 10 minutes, stirring occasionally. Pour mixture into lightly greased 13×9-inch baking pan. In medium bowl, prepare cornbread batter according to package directions. Spoon dollops of batter over turkey mixture. Spoon remaining batter into lightly greased muffin tins. Bake in 375°F oven 25 minutes for casserole (15 to 20 minutes for muffins) or until toothpick inserted into cornbread comes out clean.

Makes 8 to 10 servings

Serving Suggestion: Serve with a tossed green salad and your favorite cool beverage.

Hint: Cool muffins completely. Wrap tightly and freeze for later use, if desired.

One-Dish Meal

2 bags SUCCESS® Rice
Vegetable cooking spray
1 cup cubed cooked turkey-ham*
1 cup (4 ounces) shredded low-fat Cheddar cheese
1 cup peas

**Or, use cooked turkey, ham or turkey franks.*

Prepare rice according to package directions.

Spray 1-quart microwave-safe dish with cooking spray; set aside. Place rice in medium bowl. Add ham, cheese and peas; mix lightly. Spoon into prepared dish; smooth into even layer with spoon. Microwave on HIGH 1 minute; stir. Microwave 30 seconds or until thoroughly heated.

Makes 4 servings

Conventional Oven Directions: Assemble casserole as directed. Spoon into ovenproof 1-quart baking dish sprayed with vegetable cooking spray. Bake at 350°F until thoroughly heated, about 15 to 20 minutes

Spinach & Turkey Skillet

6 ounces turkey breast tenderloin
1/8 teaspoon salt
2 teaspoons olive oil
1/4 cup chopped onion
2 cloves garlic, minced
1/3 cup uncooked rice
3/4 teaspoon dried Italian seasoning
1/4 teaspoon black pepper
1 cup fat-free reduced-sodium chicken broth, divided
2 cups torn fresh spinach
2/3 cup diced plum tomatoes
3 tablespoons freshly grated Parmesan cheese

1. Cut turkey tenderloins into bite-size slices; sprinkle with salt. Heat oil in medium skillet over medium-high heat.

2. Add turkey slices; cook and stir until lightly browned. Remove from skillet. Reduce heat to low. Add onion and garlic; cook and stir until tender. Return turkey to skillet. Stir in rice, Italian seasoning and pepper.

3. Reserve 2 tablespoons chicken broth. Stir remaining broth into mixture in skillet. Bring to a boil. Reduce heat. Simmer, covered, 14 minutes. Stir in spinach and reserved broth. Cover and cook 2 to 3 minutes more or until liquid is absorbed and spinach is wilted. Stir in tomatoes. Heat through. Serve with Parmesan cheese.

Makes 2 servings

Spinach & Turkey Skillet

Tuscan Turkey Cutlets

- 1 pound turkey cutlets
- ¾ teaspoon salt, divided
- ¾ teaspoon black pepper, divided
- 1 tablespoon olive oil, divided
- 2 cups onions, coarsely chopped
- 1 cup carrot, coarsely chopped
- 3 to 4 cloves garlic, minced
- ½ teaspoon dried oregano
- ½ teaspoon dried thyme
- 1 (10-ounce) bag fresh spinach leaves, stems removed
- 1 (14½-ounce) can diced tomatoes, undrained
- 1 (19-ounce) can cannellini beans, drained and rinsed
- ¼ cup Parmesan cheese, divided

1. Place cutlets on cutting board and sprinkle with ¼ teaspoon each, salt and pepper. Slice cutlets into ½-inch strips.

2. In 12-inch or larger non-stick skillet over medium-high heat, sauté turkey strips in ½ tablespoon oil, 4 to 5 minutes or until no longer pink (165°F). Remove from skillet; set aside.

3. Add remaining ½ tablespoon oil to skillet. Sauté onions, carrots, garlic, oregano and thyme 5 minutes or until vegetables are tender. Gradually add spinach and stir an additional 2 minutes or until spinach is wilted, but not quite done. Add tomatoes and remaining ½ teaspoon salt and ½ teaspoon pepper; cook 2 minutes.

4. Stir in turkey strips and beans. Cook until heated through.

5. Serve topped with Parmesan cheese. *Makes 4 servings*

Serving Suggestion: Serve over orzo, noodles or a whole grain such as quinoa.

Favorite recipe from **National Turkey Federation**

Turkey-Spinach Manicotti

- 1 package (1.5 ounces) LAWRY'S® Original Style Spaghetti Sauce Spices & Seasoning
- 1 can (28 ounces) whole tomatoes, cut up
- 1 can (8 ounces) tomato sauce
- ¼ cup chopped green onions
- 1 cup ricotta cheese
- 2 cups chopped fresh spinach
- 2 cups cooked, minced turkey or chicken
- 2 tablespoons milk
- 1 teaspoon LAWRY'S® Seasoned Pepper
- ½ teaspoon LAWRY'S® Garlic Powder with Parsley
- 8 manicotti shells, cooked and drained
- ⅓ cup grated Parmesan cheese

In medium saucepan, combine Spaghetti Sauce Spices & Seasoning, tomatoes, tomato sauce and onions. Bring to a boil over medium-high heat; reduce heat to low and cook, covered, 20 minutes, stirring occasionally. In medium bowl, combine ricotta cheese, spinach, turkey, milk, Seasoned Pepper and Garlic Powder with Parsley; mix well. Carefully spoon mixture into manicotti shells. Pour ½ of sauce in bottom of 12×8×2-inch baking dish. Place stuffed shells on top of sauce; pour remaining sauce over shells. Cover and bake in 375°F oven 30 minutes or until heated through. Sprinkle with Parmesan cheese.

Makes 4 to 8 servings

Serving Suggestion: Sprinkle with chopped parsley. Garnish with fresh basil leaves. Serve with garlic bread.

Hint: 1 package (10 ounces) frozen chopped spinach, thawed and drained, can be substituted for the fresh spinach.

Washington Apple Turkey Gyros

- 1 cup thinly sliced onion wedges
- 1 cup thinly sliced red bell pepper
- 1 cup thinly sliced green bell pepper
- 2 tablespoons lemon juice
- 1 tablespoon vegetable oil
- ½ pound cooked turkey breast, cut into thin strips
- 1 medium Washington Golden Delicious or Winesap apple, cored and thinly sliced
- 8 pita rounds, lightly toasted
- ½ cup plain low-fat yogurt

Cook and stir onion, bell peppers and lemon juice in oil in nonstick skillet until crisp-tender; stir in turkey and cook until heated through. Remove from heat; stir in apple. Fold pita in half and fill with apple mixture; drizzle with yogurt. Repeat with remaining ingredients. Serve warm.

Makes 6 servings

Favorite recipe from **Washington Apple Commission**

Helpful Hints

Turkey breasts are sold whole or as halves. The breasts may be boneless, or with bone in. Prepare them by roasting or grilling.

Tuscan Turkey Cutlets

Turkey-Tortilla Bake

- **9 (6-inch) corn tortillas**
- **½ pound 93% fat-free ground turkey**
- **½ cup chopped onion**
- **¾ cup mild or medium taco sauce**
- **1 can (4 ounces) chopped green chilies, drained**
- **½ cup frozen corn, thawed**
- **½ cup (2 ounces) shredded reduced-fat Cheddar cheese**

1. Preheat oven to 400°F. Place tortillas on large baking sheet, overlapping tortillas as little as possible. Bake 4 minutes; turn tortillas. Continue baking 2 minutes or until crisp. Cool completely on wire rack.

2. Heat medium nonstick skillet over medium heat until hot. Add turkey and onion. Cook and stir 5 minutes or until turkey is browned and onion is tender. Add taco sauce, chilies and corn. Reduce heat and simmer 5 minutes.

3. Break 3 tortillas and arrange over bottom of 1½-quart casserole. Spoon half the turkey mixture over tortillas; sprinkle with half the cheese. Repeat layers. Bake 10 minutes or until cheese is melted and casserole is heated through. Break remaining tortillas and sprinkle over casserole. Garnish with sour cream, if desired.

Makes 4 servings

Prep and Cook Time: 30 minutes

Turkey Pot Pie

- **1 (1-pound) package frozen vegetables for stew, cooked according to package directions**
- **1 cup frozen peas, cooked according to package directions**
- **2 cups Cooked TURKEY from a TURKEY ROAST, cut into ½-inch cubes (cook roast according to package directions)***
- **1 (12-ounce) jar non-fat turkey gravy**
- **1 tablespoon dried parsley**
- **1 teaspoon dried thyme**
- **1 teaspoon dried rosemary**
- **½ teaspoon salt**
- **¼ teaspoon black pepper**
- **1 refrigerated pie crust (brought to room temperature)**

**Leftover cooked turkey may be substituted for the pre-packaged turkey roast.*

1. Drain any cooking liquid from stew vegetables and peas.

2. Add turkey cubes, gravy, parsley, thyme, rosemary, salt and pepper to vegetables in oven-safe, 2-quart cooking dish.

3. Unfold pie crust and place on top of dish, trimming edges to approximately 1 inch and securing edges to dish. Make several 1-inch slits on crust to allow steam to escape.

4. Bake in preheated 400°F oven for 25 to 30 minutes or until crust is brown and mixture is hot and bubbly.

Makes 5 servings

Favorite recipe from **National Turkey Federation**

Turkey Wild Rice Chili

- **1 tablespoon oil**
- **1 medium onion, chopped**
- **1 clove garlic, minced**
- **1¼ pounds turkey breast slices, cut into ½-inch pieces**
- **2 cups cooked wild rice**
- **1 can (15 ounces) great Northern beans, drained**
- **1 can (11 ounces) white corn**
- **2 cans (4 ounces each) diced green chilies**
- **1 can (14½ ounces) low-sodium chicken broth**
- **1 teaspoon ground cumin**
- **Hot pepper sauce (optional)**
- **4 ounces low-fat Monterey Jack Cheese, shredded**
- **Parsley (optional)**

Heat oil in large skillet over medium heat; add onion and garlic. Cook and stir until onion is tender. Add turkey, wild rice, beans, corn, chilies, broth and cumin. Cover and simmer over low heat 30 minutes or until turkey is tender. Stir in hot pepper sauce to taste. Serve with shredded cheese. Garnish with parsley, if desired.

Makes 8 servings

Favorite recipe from **Minnesota Cultivated Wild Rice Council**

Helpful Hints

The next time you make a casserole, assemble and bake two. Allow one to cool completely, then wrap it in heavy-duty foil and freeze it. To reheat a frozen 2-quart casserole, unwrap it and microwave it, covered, at HIGH for 20 to 30 minutes, stirring once or twice during cooking.

Turkey-Tortilla Bake

Turnip Shepherd's Pie

1 pound small turnips,* peeled and cut into ½-inch cubes
1 pound lean ground turkey
⅓ cup dry bread crumbs
¼ cup chopped onion
¼ cup ketchup
1 egg
½ teaspoon salt
½ teaspoon pepper
½ teaspoon beau monde seasoning
⅓ cup half-and-half
1 tablespoon butter or margarine
Additional salt and black pepper
1 tablespoon chopped fresh parsley
¼ cup shredded sharp Cheddar cheese

**For Rutabaga Shepherd's Pie, use 1 pound rutabagas in place of turnips.*

Preheat oven to 400°F. Place turnips in large saucepan; cover with water. Cover and bring to a boil; reduce heat to medium-low. Simmer 20 minutes or until fork-tender.

Mix turkey, crumbs, onion, ketchup, egg, salt, pepper and seasoning. Pat on bottom and side of 9-inch pie pan. Bake 20 to 30 minutes until turkey is no longer pink. Blot with paper towel to remove any drippings.

Drain cooked turnips. Mash turnips with electric mixer until smooth, blending in half-and-half and butter. Season to taste with additional salt and pepper to taste. Fill meat shell with turnip mixture; sprinkle with parsley, then cheese. Return to oven until cheese melts. Garnish as desired. *Makes 4 servings*

Pizza Rice Casserole

1 bag SUCCESS® Rice
1 pound ground turkey or lean ground beef
½ cup chopped green bell pepper
½ cup chopped onion
1 jar (15½ ounces) pizza sauce
1 cup water
1 can (4 ounces) mushroom pieces, drained
¼ cup flour
½ cup chopped turkey ham
½ teaspoon garlic salt
1 cup (4 ounces) shredded mozzarella cheese

Prepare rice according to package directions.

Brown ground turkey with green pepper and onion in large skillet or saucepan, stirring occasionally to separate turkey. Add rice, pizza sauce, water, mushrooms, flour, ham and garlic salt; heat thoroughly, stirring occasionally. Sprinkle with cheese. *Makes 4 servings*

Turkey with Mustard Sauce

1 tablespoon butter or margarine
1 pound turkey cutlets
1 cup BIRDS EYE® frozen Mixed Vegetables
1 box (9 ounces) BIRDS EYE® frozen Pearl Onions in Cream Sauce
1 teaspoon spicy brown mustard

• In large nonstick skillet, melt butter over medium-high heat. Add turkey; cook until browned on both sides.

• Add mixed vegetables, onions with cream sauce and mustard; bring to boil. Reduce heat to medium-low; cover and simmer 6 to 8 minutes or until vegetables are tender and turkey is no longer pink in center. *Makes 4 servings*

Serving Suggestion: Serve with a fresh garden salad.

Prep Time: 5 minutes
Cook Time: 15 minutes

Turkey Fajitas

½ cup sliced green onions
½ cup lemon juice
½ cup honey
½ cup warm water
3 tablespoons vegetable oil
1 clove garlic, minced
1 (1-pound) package turkey breast slices, cut into 2×¾-inch strips
1 medium yellow or green bell pepper, cut into strips
1 medium tomato, chopped
½ cup chopped fresh cilantro
4 (8-inch) flour tortillas
Picante sauce

Combine green onions, lemon juice, honey and water in small bowl; set aside. Heat oil and garlic in large skillet over medium-high heat. Add turkey; cook and stir for 2 minutes. Add pepper strips and lemon juice mixture; continue to cook and stir until liquid evaporates and turkey is golden brown. Stir in tomato and cilantro. Spoon mixture onto tortillas. Fold in half or roll up. Serve with picante sauce. *Makes 4 servings*

Turnip Shepherd's Pie

Turkey Meatball & Olive Casserole

2 cups uncooked rotini pasta
½ pound ground turkey
¼ cup dry bread crumbs
1 egg, slightly beaten
2 teaspoons dried minced onion
2 teaspoons white wine Worcestershire sauce
½ teaspoon dried Italian seasoning
½ teaspoon salt
⅛ teaspoon black pepper
1 tablespoon vegetable oil
1 can (10¾ ounces) condensed cream of celery soup, undiluted
½ cup low-fat plain yogurt
¾ cup pimiento-stuffed green olives, sliced
3 tablespoons Italian-style bread crumbs
1 tablespoon margarine or butter, melted
Paprika (optional)

Preheat oven to 350°F. Spray 2-quart round casserole with nonstick cooking spray.

Cook pasta according to package directions until al dente. Drain and set aside.

Meanwhile, combine turkey, bread crumbs, egg, onion, Worcestershire, Italian seasoning, salt and pepper in medium bowl. Shape mixture into ½-inch meatballs.

Heat oil in medium skillet over high heat until hot. Add meatballs in single layer; cook until lightly browned on all sides and still pink in centers, turning frequently. Do not overcook. Remove from skillet; drain on paper towels.

Mix soup and yogurt in large bowl. Add pasta, meatballs and olives; stir gently to combine. Transfer to prepared dish.

Combine bread crumbs and margarine in small bowl; sprinkle evenly over casserole. Sprinkle lightly with paprika, if desired.

Bake, covered, 30 minutes. Uncover and bake 12 minutes or until meatballs are no longer pink in centers and casserole is hot and bubbly. *Makes 6 to 8 servings*

Rice and Turkey Skillet Curry

2 cups water
1 cup UNCLE BEN'S® ORIGINAL CONVERTED® Brand Rice
¾ cup (6 ounces) pineapple juice
⅓ cup diced dried apricots
¼ cup dried cranberries
1 teaspoon curry powder
1½ cups (8 ounces) cooked turkey

1. In large skillet, bring 2 cups water, rice, pineapple juice, apricots, cranberries and curry powder to a boil. Cover; reduce heat and simmer 15 minutes or until rice is tender and liquid is absorbed.

2. Add turkey to rice. Cover and cook over low heat 5 minutes or until turkey is hot. *Makes 4 servings*

Lighter Stuffed Peppers

1 can (10¾ ounces) reduced-fat condensed tomato soup, divided
¼ cup water
8 ounces extra-lean ground turkey
1 cup cooked rice
¾ cup frozen corn, thawed
¼ cup sliced celery
¼ cup chopped red bell pepper
1 teaspoon dried Italian seasoning
½ teaspoon hot pepper sauce
2 green, yellow or red bell peppers, cut in half lengthwise, seeds removed

Blend ¼ cup soup and water in small bowl. Pour into 8×8-inch baking dish; set aside. Brown turkey in large skillet over medium-high heat; drain well. Combine remaining soup with cooked turkey, rice, corn, celery, chopped pepper, Italian seasoning and hot pepper sauce in large bowl; mix well.

Fill pepper halves equally with turkey mixture. Place stuffed peppers on top of soup mixture in baking dish. Cover and bake at 350°F 35 to 40 minutes. Place peppers on serving dish and spoon remaining sauce from baking dish over peppers.
Makes 4 servings

Pasta and Spinach with Sun-Dried Tomatoes

⅓ pound BUTTERBALL® Oven Roasted Deli Turkey Breast, sliced thin and cut into strips
¼ cup sun-dried tomatoes, packed in oil, drained and chopped, reserve oil
1 clove garlic, minced
5 ounces fresh spinach, rinsed
2 ounces bow tie pasta, cooked and drained
¼ cup Italian salad dressing
3 tablespoons feta cheese, divided

Pour 1 teaspoon reserved sun-dried tomato oil in nonstick skillet. Add turkey, tomatoes and garlic. Cook and stir over medium heat 2 minutes. Add spinach, pasta, dressing and 2 tablespoons cheese; toss to coat. Cover; warm over low heat for about 1 minute. Sprinkle with remaining 1 tablespoon cheese.
Makes 2 servings

Prep Time: 20 minutes

Turkey Meatball & Olive Casserole

Southwest Stir-Fry

- 1 bag SUCCESS® Rice
- 1 pound ground turkey
- 1 medium onion, chopped
- 1 package (1.7 ounces) taco seasoning mix
- 1 can (15¼ ounces) kidney beans, drained
- 1 can (8 ounces) Mexican-style corn, drained
- ½ cup fat-free sour cream

Prepare rice according to package directions.

Brown ground turkey with onion in large skillet, stirring occasionally to separate turkey; drain. Stir in taco seasoning. Add rice, beans and corn; heat thoroughly, stirring occasionally. Stir in sour cream.

Makes 4 servings

Chili Turkey Loaf

- 2 pounds ground turkey
- 1 cup chopped onion
- ⅔ cup Italian-style seasoned dry bread crumbs
- ½ cup chopped green bell pepper
- ½ cup chili sauce
- 4 cloves garlic, minced
- 2 eggs, slightly beaten
- 2 tablespoons horseradish mustard
- 1 teaspoon salt
- ½ teaspoon Italian seasoning
- ¼ teaspoon black pepper
- Prepared salsa (optional)

Slow Cooker Directions

Make foil handles for loaf using technique described below. Mix all ingredients except salsa in large bowl. Shape into round loaf and place on top of foil strips. Transfer to bottom of slow cooker using foil handles. Cover and cook on LOW 4½ to 5 hours or until juices run clear and temperature is 170°F. Remove loaf from slow cooker using foil handles. Place on serving plate. Let stand 5 minutes before serving. Cut into wedges and top with salsa, if desired. Serve with steamed carrots, if desired.

Makes 8 servings

Foil Handles: Tear off three 18×2-inch strips of heavy foil or use regular foil folded to double thickness. Crisscross foil strips in spoke design and place in slow cooker to allow for easy removal of Turkey Loaf.

Spicy Lasagna Roll-Ups

- 1 pound ground turkey breast or extra-lean ground beef
- ½ cup chopped onion
- 2 cloves garlic, minced
- 1 teaspoon dried Italian seasoning
- ¼ teaspoon red pepper flakes
- 1 can (10¾ ounces) reduced-fat condensed tomato soup
- 1 cup chopped zucchini
- ¾ cup water
- 1 (15-ounce) container fat-free ricotta cheese
- ½ cup shredded part-skim mozzarella cheese
- 1 egg
- 4 cooked lasagna noodles

Preheat oven to 350°F. Spray large nonstick skillet with nonstick cooking spray; heat over medium heat until hot. Add turkey, onion, garlic, Italian seasoning and red pepper flakes; cook and stir until turkey is no longer pink and onion is tender. Add soup, zucchini and water; simmer 5 minutes. Pour soup mixture into shallow 2-quart baking dish.

Combine ricotta and mozzarella cheeses and egg in medium bowl; mix well. Lay lasagna noodles on flat surface; spread ½ cup cheese mixture on each noodle. Roll up noodles, enclosing filling; place rolls seam sides down over soup mixture.

Cover and bake 30 minutes; uncover and continue baking an additional 10 minutes or until sauce is bubbly. Place lasagna rolls on serving dish; spoon remaining sauce over rolls.

Makes 4 servings

Turkey & Green Bean Casserole

- ¼ cup slivered almonds
- 1 package (7 ounces) herb-seasoned stuffing cubes
- ¾ cup reduced-sodium chicken broth
- 1 can (10¾ ounces) condensed cream of mushroom soup, undiluted
- ¼ cup milk or half-and-half
- ¼ teaspoon black pepper
- 1 package (10 ounces) frozen French-style green beans, thawed and drained
- 2 cups (½-inch-thick) deli turkey breast cubes or cooked turkey or chicken

Preheat oven to 350°F. Spray 11×7-inch baking dish with nonstick cooking spray.

Spread almonds in single layer on baking sheet. Bake 5 minutes or until golden brown, stirring frequently. Set aside.

Arrange stuffing cubes in prepared dish; drizzle with broth. Stir to coat bread cubes with broth.

Combine soup, milk and pepper in large bowl. Add green beans and turkey; stir until combined. Spoon over stuffing cubes; top with almonds.

Bake, uncovered, 30 to 35 minutes or until heated through.

Makes 4 servings

Chili Turkey Loaf

Fabulous Fish

Baked Fish with Potatoes and Onions

- 1 pound baking potatoes, very thinly sliced
- 1 large onion, very thinly sliced
- 1 small red or green bell pepper, thinly sliced
- Salt
- Black pepper
- ½ teaspoon dried oregano leaves, divided
- 1 pound lean fish fillets, cut 1 inch thick
- ¼ cup butter or margarine
- ¼ cup all-purpose flour
- 2 cups milk
- ¾ cup (3 ounces) shredded Cheddar cheese

Preheat oven to 375°F.

Arrange half of potatoes in buttered 3-quart casserole. Top with half of onion and half of bell pepper. Season with salt and black pepper. Sprinkle with ¼ teaspoon oregano. Arrange fish in one layer over vegetables. Arrange remaining potatoes, onion and bell pepper over fish. Season with salt, black pepper and remaining ¼ teaspoon oregano.

Melt butter in medium saucepan over medium heat. Stir in flour; cook until bubbly, stirring constantly. Gradually stir in milk. Cook until thickened, stirring constantly. Pour white sauce over casserole. Cover and bake at 375°F 40 minutes or until potatoes are tender. Sprinkle with cheese. Bake, uncovered, about 5 minutes more or until cheese is melted.

Makes 4 servings

Mediterranean Cod

- 1 bag (16 ounces) BIRDS EYE® frozen Farm Fresh Mixtures Broccoli, Green Beans, Pearl Onions and Red Peppers
- 1 can (14½ ounces) stewed tomatoes
- ½ teaspoon dried basil leaves
- 1 pound cod fillets, cut into serving pieces
- ½ cup orange juice, divided
- 2 tablespoons all-purpose flour
- ¼ cup sliced black olives (optional)

• Combine vegetables, tomatoes and basil in large skillet. Bring to a boil over medium-high heat.

• Place cod on vegetables. Pour ¼ cup orange juice over fish. Cover and cook 5 to 7 minutes or until fish is tender and flakes with fork.

• Remove cod and keep warm. Blend flour with remaining ¼ cup orange juice; stir into skillet. Cook until liquid is thickened and vegetables are coated.

• Serve fish with vegetables; sprinkle with olives.

Makes about 4 servings

Serving Suggestion: Serve with rice or couscous.

Prep Time: 5 minutes
Cook Time: 15 minutes

Helpful Hints

When buying fish fillets and steaks, look for those with moist flesh and shiny skin. They should have a mild, slightly oceanlike odor rather than a fishy or sour smell. Store fresh fish in the coldest part of the refrigerator.

Mediterranean Cod

Angel Hair Pasta with Seafood Sauce

- **½ pound firm whitefish, such as sea bass, monkfish or grouper**
- **2 teaspoons olive oil**
- **½ cup chopped onion**
- **2 cloves garlic, minced**
- **3 pounds fresh plum tomatoes, seeded and chopped**
- **¼ cup chopped fresh basil**
- **2 tablespoons chopped fresh oregano**
- **1 teaspoon red pepper flakes**
- **½ teaspoon sugar**
- **2 bay leaves**
- **½ pound fresh bay scallops or shucked oysters**
- **8 ounces uncooked angel hair pasta**
- **2 tablespoons chopped fresh parsley**

1. Cut whitefish into ¾-inch pieces. Set aside.

2. Heat oil in large nonstick skillet over medium heat; add onion and garlic. Cook and stir 3 minutes or until onion is tender. Reduce heat to low; add tomatoes, basil, oregano, red pepper, sugar and bay leaves. Cook, uncovered, 15 minutes, stirring occasionally.

3. Add whitefish and scallops. Cook, uncovered, 3 to 4 minutes or until fish flakes easily when tested with fork and scallops are opaque. Remove bay leaves; discard. Set seafood sauce aside.

4. Cook pasta according to package directions, omitting salt. Drain well.

5. Combine pasta with seafood sauce in large serving bowl. Mix well. Sprinkle with parsley. Serve immediately. *Makes 6 servings*

Herb-Baked Fish & Rice

- **1½ cups hot chicken bouillon**
- **½ cup uncooked regular rice**
- **¼ teaspoon Italian seasoning**
- **¼ teaspoon garlic powder**
- **1 package (10 ounces) frozen chopped broccoli, thawed and drained**
- **1⅓ cups *French's® Taste Toppers™* French Fried Onions, divided**
- **1 tablespoon grated Parmesan cheese**
- **1 pound unbreaded fish fillets, thawed if frozen**
- **Paprika (optional)**
- **½ cup (2 ounces) shredded Cheddar cheese**

Preheat oven to 375°F. In 12×8-inch baking dish, combine hot bouillon, uncooked rice and seasonings. Bake, covered, at 375°F for 10 minutes. Top with broccoli, ⅔ *cup* ***Taste Toppers*** and Parmesan cheese. Place fish fillets diagonally down center of dish; sprinkle fish lightly with paprika. Bake, covered, at 375°F for 20 to 25 minutes or until fish flakes easily with fork. Stir rice. Top fish with Cheddar cheese and remaining ⅔ *cup* ***Taste Toppers***; bake, uncovered, 3 minutes or until ***Taste Toppers*** are golden brown. *Makes 3 to 4 servings*

Microwave Directions: In 12×8-inch microwave-safe dish, prepare rice mixture as above, except reduce bouillon to 1¼ cups. Cook, covered, on HIGH 5 minutes, stirring halfway through cooking time. Stir in broccoli, ⅔ *cup* ***Taste Toppers*** and Parmesan cheese. Arrange fish fillets in single layer on top of rice mixture; sprinkle fish lightly with paprika. Cook, covered, on MEDIUM (50-60%) 18 to 20 minutes or until fish flakes easily with fork and rice is done. Rotate dish halfway through cooking time. Top fish with Cheddar cheese and remaining ⅔ *cup* ***Taste Toppers***; cook, uncovered, on HIGH 1 minute or until cheese melts. Let stand 5 minutes.

By-the-Sea Casserole

- **1 bag (16 ounces) BIRDS EYE® frozen Mixed Vegetables**
- **2 cans (6 ounces each) tuna in water, drained**
- **1 cup uncooked instant rice**
- **1 can (10¾ ounces) cream of celery soup**
- **1 cup 1% milk**
- **1 cup cheese-flavored fish-shaped crackers**

- In medium bowl, combine vegetables and tuna.
- Stir in rice, soup and milk.
- Place tuna mixture in 1½-quart microwave-safe casserole dish; cover and microwave on HIGH 6 minutes. Stir; microwave, covered, 6 to 8 minutes more or until rice is tender.
- Stir casserole and sprinkle with crackers. *Makes 6 servings*

Prep Time: 10 minutes
Cook Time: 15 minutes

Helpful Hints

Choose solid white tuna or chunk tuna for By-the-Sea Casserole. Solid white tuna is firm; break up any large pieces with a fork. Chunk tuna is not as firm and pieces are generally smaller than those of solid white tuna.

By-the-Sea Casserole

Tuna Pot Pie

1 tablespoon margarine or butter
1 small onion, chopped
1 can (10¾ ounces) condensed cream of potato soup, undiluted
¼ cup milk
½ teaspoon dried thyme leaves
¼ teaspoon salt
⅛ teaspoon black pepper
2 cans (6 ounces each) albacore tuna in water, drained
1 package (16 ounces) frozen vegetable medley, such as broccoli, green beans, carrots and red peppers, thawed
2 tablespoons chopped fresh parsley
1 can (8 ounces) refrigerated crescent roll dough

Preheat oven to 350°F. Spray 11×7-inch baking dish with nonstick cooking spray.

Melt margarine in large skillet over medium heat. Add onion; cook and stir 2 minutes or until onion is tender. Add soup, milk, thyme, salt and pepper; cook and stir 3 to 4 minutes or until thick and bubbly. Stir in tuna, vegetables and parsley. Pour mixture into prepared dish.

Unroll crescent roll dough and divide into triangles. Place triangles over tuna filling without overlapping dough.

Bake, uncovered, 20 minutes or until triangles are golden brown. Let stand 5 minutes before serving.

Makes 6 servings

Broccoli-Salmon Quiche

1 (9-inch) Pastry Shell (recipe follows)
1 tablespoon vegetable oil
1½ cups chopped broccoli
⅓ cup chopped onion
⅓ cup chopped red bell pepper
½ cup (2 ounces) shredded Swiss cheese
1 cup flaked canned or cooked salmon (about 5 ounces)
3 eggs, beaten
1¼ cups milk
1 teaspoon dried tarragon leaves
¼ teaspoon salt
⅛ teaspoon black pepper

1. Preheat oven to 425°F.

2. Place piece of foil inside pastry shell; partially fill with uncooked beans or rice. Bake 10 minutes. Remove foil and beans; continue baking pastry shell 5 minutes or until lightly browned. Let cool.

3. *Reduce oven temperature to 375°F.*

4. Heat oil in medium skillet over medium heat. Add broccoli, onion and bell pepper; cook and stir 3 to 4 minutes or until crisp-tender. Set aside to cool.

5. Sprinkle cheese over bottom of pastry shell. Arrange salmon and vegetables over cheese.

6. Combine eggs, milk, tarragon, salt and black pepper in medium bowl. Pour over salmon and vegetables.

7. Bake 35 to 40 minutes or until filling is puffed and knife inserted into center comes out clean. Let stand 10 minutes before cutting.

Makes 6 servings

Pastry Shell

1½ cups all-purpose flour
¼ teaspoon salt
¼ cup butter or margarine, chilled
¼ cup shortening
4 to 5 tablespoons cold water

1. Combine flour and salt in large bowl. With pastry blender or 2 knives, cut in butter and shortening until mixture resembles cornmeal.

2. Add water, 1 tablespoon at a time; stir just until mixture holds together. Knead lightly with hands to form ball. Wrap in plastic wrap and refrigerate 30 minutes.

3. Roll out dough on lightly floured surface to 12-inch circle. Gently press into 9-inch quiche dish or pie pan. Trim edges and flute.

Potato Tuna au Gratin

1 package (5 or 6 ounces) Cheddar cheese au gratin potatoes
1 can (12 ounces) STARKIST® Solid White or Chunk Light Tuna, drained and chunked
¼ cup chopped onion
1 package (16 ounces) frozen broccoli cuts, cooked and drained
¾ cup shredded Cheddar cheese
¼ cup bread crumbs

Prepare potatoes according to package directions. While potatoes are standing, stir in tuna and onion. Arrange cooked broccoli in bottom of lightly greased 11×7-inch baking dish. Pour tuna-potato mixture over broccoli; top with cheese. Broil 3 to 4 minutes or until cheese is bubbly. Sprinkle bread crumbs over top.

Makes 6 servings

Prep Time: 35 minutes

Tuna Pot Pie

Lemony Dill Salmon and Shell Casserole

Nonstick cooking spray
1½ cups sliced mushrooms
⅓ cup sliced green onions
1 clove garlic, minced
2 cups fat-free (skim) milk
3 tablespoons all-purpose flour
1 tablespoon grated lemon peel
¾ teaspoon dried dill weed
¼ teaspoon salt
⅛ teaspoon black pepper
1½ cups frozen green peas
6 ounces uncooked medium shell pasta, cooked, rinsed and drained
1 can (7½ ounces) salmon, drained and flaked

1. Preheat oven to 350°F.

2. Spray medium nonstick saucepan with cooking spray; heat over medium heat until hot. Add mushrooms, onions and garlic; cook and stir 5 minutes or until vegetables are tender.

3. Combine milk and flour in medium bowl until smooth. Stir in lemon peel, dill weed, salt and pepper. Stir into saucepan; heat over medium-high heat 5 to 8 minutes or until thickened, stirring constantly. Remove saucepan from heat. Stir in peas, pasta and salmon. Pour pasta mixture into 2-quart casserole.

4. Bake, covered, 35 to 40 minutes. Serve immediately. Garnish as desired. *Makes 6 servings*

Lemony Dill Salmon and Shell Casserole

Mediterranean-Style Tuna Noodle Casserole

1 tablespoon Lucini Premium Select Extra Virgin Olive Oil
4 cloves garlic, minced
2 large onions, chopped (1½ cups)
12 ounces mushrooms, chopped (4 cups)
2 large tomatoes, chopped
1 red bell pepper, diced (1 cup)
1 green bell pepper, diced (1 cup)
1 cup chopped fresh cilantro leaves *or* ¼ cup dried oregano leaves
2 tablespoons dried marjoram or oregano leaves
1 to 2 teaspoons ground red pepper
1 pound JARLSBERG LITE™ cheese, shredded (4 cups)
1 (16-ounce) can black-eyed peas, rinsed and drained
2 (7-ounce) cans tuna, drained and flaked
6 ounces cooked pasta (tricolor rotelle, bows or macaroni)

Preheat oven to 350°F. Heat oil in large skillet; sauté garlic until golden. Add onions; sauté until transparent, about 2 minutes on medium-high heat.

Add mushrooms, tomatoes and bell peppers, stirring 3 to 5 minutes or until mushrooms begin to brown. Add cilantro, marjoram and ground red pepper.

Toss with cheese, peas, tuna and pasta. Pour into greased baking dish. Bake, covered, 45 minutes or until cooked through.
Makes 6 to 8 servings

Serving Suggestion: Serve with crusty bread and homemade coleslaw.

Rice-Stuffed Fish Fillets with Mushroom Sauce

3 cups cooked rice
¼ cup diced pimientos
2 tablespoons snipped parsley
1 teaspoon grated lemon peel
¼ teaspoon salt
¼ teaspoon ground white pepper
1 pound white fish fillets*
Vegetable cooking spray
2 teaspoons margarine, melted
½ teaspoon seasoned salt
¼ teaspoon paprika
Lemon slices for garnish
Mushroom Sauce (recipe follows)

**Haddock, orange roughy, sole, or turbot may be used.*

Combine rice, pimientos, parsley, lemon peel, salt, and pepper in large bowl. Place fillets in shallow baking dish coated with cooking spray. Spoon rice mixture on lower portion of each fillet. Fold over to enclose rice mixture; fasten with wooden toothpicks soaked in water. Brush fillets with margarine; sprinkle with seasoned salt and paprika. Bake at 400°F for 10 to 15 minutes or until fish flakes easily with fork. Prepare Mushroom Sauce while fillets are baking. Transfer fillets to serving platter; garnish platter with lemon slices. Serve fillets with Mushroom Sauce. *Makes 4 servings*

Favorite recipe from **USA Rice Federation**

Mushroom Sauce

2 cups (about 8 ounces) sliced fresh mushrooms
½ cup sliced green onions
1 teaspoon margarine
½ cup water
⅓ cup white wine
1 tablespoon white wine Worcestershire sauce
½ cup cholesterol-free, reduced-calorie mayonnaise

Cook mushrooms and onions in margarine in large skillet until tender. Add water, wine and Worcestershire sauce; bring to a boil. Reduce sauce slightly. Stir in mayonnaise; keep warm.

Starkist® Swiss Potato Pie

1 cup milk
4 large eggs, beaten
4 cups frozen shredded hash brown potatoes, thawed
2 cups shredded Swiss cheese
½ to 1 cup chopped green onions, including tops
½ cup sour cream
½ cup chopped green bell pepper (optional)
½ teaspoon garlic powder
1 (3-ounce) pouch STARKIST® Solid White Tuna, drained and flaked

In large bowl, combine all ingredients. Pour into lightly greased deep 10-inch pie plate. Bake in 350°F oven 1 hour and 20 minutes or until golden and crusty. Let stand a few minutes before slicing into serving portions. *Makes 6 servings*

Prep/Cook Time: 90 minutes

Kid's Favorite Tuna Casserole

¾ pound VELVEETA® Pasteurized Prepared Cheese Product, cubed
⅔ cup milk
1 package (3 ounces) PHILADELPHIA® Cream Cheese, cubed
3 cups (6 ounces) medium noodles, cooked, drained
1 package (10 ounces) frozen peas, thawed, drained
1 can (6 ounces) tuna, drained, flaked
1 cup crushed potato chips

• Preheat oven to 350°F.

• Stir together prepared cheese product, milk and cream cheese in saucepan over low heat until prepared cheese product is melted.

• Stir in noodles, peas and tuna. Spoon into 2-quart casserole. Top with chips.

• Bake 20 to 25 minutes or until thoroughly heated.
Makes 4 to 6 servings

MICROWAVE DIRECTIONS: Reduce milk to 3 tablespoons. Microwave prepared cheese product, milk and cream cheese in 2-quart casserole on HIGH 3 to 4 minutes or until prepared cheese product is melted, stirring after 2 minutes. Stir in noodles, peas and tuna. Microwave 3 to 4 minutes or until thoroughly heated, stirring after 2 minutes. Top with chips.

Prep Time: 15 minutes
Cooking Time: 25 minutes
Microwave Cooking Time: 8 minutes

Flounder Fillets over Zesty Lemon Rice

- **¼ cup margarine or butter**
- **3 tablespoons fresh lemon juice**
- **2 teaspoons chicken bouillon granules**
- **½ teaspoon black pepper**
- **1 cup cooked rice**
- **1 package (10 ounces) frozen chopped broccoli, thawed**
- **1 cup (4 ounces) shredded sharp Cheddar cheese**
- **1 pound flounder fillets**
- **½ teaspoon paprika**

Preheat oven to 375°F. Spray 2-quart square casserole with nonstick cooking spray.

Melt margarine in small saucepan over medium heat. Add lemon juice, bouillon and pepper; cook and stir 2 minutes or until bouillon dissolves.

Combine rice, broccoli, cheese and ¼ cup lemon sauce in medium bowl; spread on bottom of prepared dish. Place fillets over rice mixture. Pour remaining lemon sauce over fillets.

Bake, uncovered, 20 minutes or until fish flakes easily when tested with fork. Sprinkle evenly with paprika.

Makes 6 servings

Old-Fashioned Tuna Noodle Casserole

- **¼ cup plain dry bread crumbs**
- **3 tablespoons margarine or butter, melted and divided**
- **1 tablespoon finely chopped parsley**
- **½ cup chopped onion**
- **½ cup chopped celery**
- **1 cup water**
- **1 cup milk**
- **1 package LIPTON® Noodles & Sauce—Butter**
- **2 cans (6½ ounces each) tuna, drained and flaked**

In small bowl, thoroughly combine bread crumbs, 1 tablespoon margarine and parsley; set aside.

In medium saucepan, melt remaining 2 tablespoons margarine over medium heat and cook onion and celery, stirring occasionally, 2 minutes or until onion is tender. Add water and milk; bring to the boiling point. Stir in Noodles & Sauce—Butter. Continue boiling over medium heat, stirring occasionally, 8 minutes or until noodles are tender. Stir in tuna. Turn into greased 1-quart casserole, then top with bread crumb mixture. Broil until bread crumbs are golden.

Makes about 4 servings

Pasta with Salmon and Dill

- **6 ounces uncooked mafalda pasta**
- **1 tablespoon olive oil**
- **2 ribs celery, sliced**
- **1 small red onion, chopped**
- **1 can (10¾ ounces) condensed cream of celery soup, undiluted**
- **¼ cup reduced-fat mayonnaise**
- **¼ cup dry white wine**
- **3 tablespoons chopped fresh parsley**
- **1 teaspoon dried dill weed**
- **1 can (7½ ounces) pink salmon, drained**
- **½ cup dry bread crumbs**
- **1 tablespoon margarine or butter, melted**
- **Fresh dill sprigs (optional)**

Preheat oven to 350°F. Spray 1-quart square baking dish with nonstick cooking spray.

Cook pasta according to package directions until al dente; drain and set aside.

Meanwhile, heat oil in medium skillet over medium-high heat until hot. Add celery and onion; cook and stir 2 minutes or until vegetables are tender. Set aside.

Combine soup, mayonnaise, wine, parsley and dill weed in large bowl. Stir in pasta, vegetables and salmon until pasta is well coated. Pour salmon mixture into prepared dish.

Combine bread crumbs and margarine in small bowl; sprinkle evenly over casserole. Bake, uncovered, 25 minutes or until hot and bubbly. Garnish with dill sprigs, if desired.

Makes 4 servings

Biscuit-Topped Tuna Bake

- **2 tablespoons vegetable oil**
- **½ cup chopped onion**
- **½ cup chopped celery**
- **1 can (12 ounces) STARKIST® Solid White or Chunk Light Tuna, drained and chunked**
- **1 can (10¾ ounces) condensed cream of potato soup**
- **1 package (10 ounces) frozen peas and carrots, thawed**
- **¾ cup milk**
- **¼ teaspoon ground black pepper**
- **¼ teaspoon garlic powder**
- **1 can (7½ ounces) refrigerator flaky biscuits**

In large skillet, heat oil over medium-high heat; sauté onion and celery until onion is soft. Add remaining ingredients except biscuits; heat thoroughly. Transfer mixture to 1½-quart casserole. Arrange biscuits around top edge of dish; bake in 400°F oven 10 to 15 minutes or until biscuits are golden brown.

Makes 4 to 6 servings

Prep and Cook Time: 25 minutes

Flounder Fillets over Zesty Lemon Rice

Tuna and Pasta Frittata

1 tablespoon olive oil
2 cups cooked spaghetti
4 large eggs
¼ cup prepared pesto sauce
2 tablespoons milk
1 (3-ounce) pouch STARKIST® Solid White or Chunk Light Tuna, drained and flaked
½ cup shredded mozzarella cheese

Preheat broiler. In medium ovenproof skillet, heat oil over medium-high heat; sauté spaghetti. In bowl, combine eggs, pesto sauce and milk; blend well. Add tuna; pour mixture over hot spaghetti. Cook over medium-low heat, stirring occasionally until eggs are almost completely set. Sprinkle cheese over cooked eggs; place under broiler until cheese is bubbly and golden. Serve hot or at room temperature.
Makes 2 to 4 servings

Prep Time: 8 minutes

Tempting Tuna Parmesano

2 large cloves garlic
1 package (9 ounces) refrigerated fresh angel hair pasta
¼ cup butter or margarine
1 cup whipping cream
1 cup frozen peas
¼ teaspoon salt
1 can (6 ounces) white tuna in water, drained
¼ cup grated Parmesan cheese, plus additional cheese for serving
Black pepper

1. Fill large deep skillet ¾ full with water. Cover and bring to a boil over high heat. Meanwhile, peel and mince garlic.

2. Add pasta to skillet; boil 1 to 2 minutes or until pasta is al dente. Do not overcook. Drain; set aside.

3. Add butter and garlic to skillet; cook over medium-high heat until butter is melted and sizzling. Stir in cream, peas and salt; bring to a boil.

4. Break tuna into chunks and stir into skillet with ¼ cup cheese. Return pasta to skillet; cook until heated through; toss gently. Serve with additional cheese and pepper to taste. *Makes 2 to 3 servings*

Easy Tuna & Pasta Pot Pie

1 tablespoon margarine or butter
1 large onion, chopped
1½ cups cooked small shell pasta or elbow macaroni
1 can (10¾ ounces) condensed cream of celery or mushroom soup, undiluted
1 cup frozen peas, thawed
1 can (6 ounces) tuna in water, drained and flaked into pieces
½ cup sour cream
½ teaspoon dried dill weed
¼ teaspoon salt
1 package (7½ ounces) buttermilk or country biscuits

1. Preheat oven to 400°F. Melt margarine in medium ovenproof skillet over medium heat. Add onion; cook 5 minutes, stirring occasionally.

2. Stir in pasta, soup, peas, tuna, sour cream, dill and salt; mix well. Cook 3 minutes or until hot. Press mixture down in skillet to form even layer.

3. Unwrap biscuit dough; arrange individual biscuits over tuna mixture. Bake 15 minutes or until biscuits are golden brown and tuna mixture is bubbly. *Makes 5 servings*

Prep and Cook Time: 28 minutes

Crustless Salmon & Broccoli Quiche

¾ cup cholesterol-free egg substitute
¼ cup plain nonfat yogurt
¼ cup chopped green onions with tops
2 teaspoons all-purpose flour
1 teaspoon dried basil leaves
⅛ teaspoon salt
⅛ teaspoon black pepper
¾ cup frozen broccoli florets, thawed and drained
⅓ cup (3 ounces) drained and flaked water-packed boneless skinless canned salmon
2 tablespoons grated Parmesan cheese
1 plum tomato, thinly sliced
¼ cup fresh bread crumbs

1. Preheat oven to 375°F. Spray 6-cup rectangular casserole or 9-inch pie plate with nonstick cooking spray.

2. Combine egg substitute, yogurt, green onions, flour, basil, salt and pepper in medium bowl until well blended. Stir in broccoli, salmon and Parmesan cheese. Spread evenly in prepared casserole. Top with tomato slices. Sprinkle bread crumbs over top.

3. Bake 20 to 25 minutes or until knife inserted into center comes out clean. Let stand 5 minutes before serving.
Makes 2 servings

Tempting Tuna Parmesano

Mom's Tuna Casserole

2 cans (12 ounces each) tuna, drained and flaked
3 cups diced celery
3 cups crushed potato chips, divided
6 hard-cooked eggs, chopped
1 can (10¾ ounces) condensed cream of mushroom soup, undiluted
1 can (10¾ ounces) condensed cream of celery soup, undiluted
1 cup mayonnaise
1 teaspoon dried tarragon leaves
1 teaspoon black pepper

Slow Cooker Directions
Combine all ingredients, except ½ cup potato chips, in slow cooker; stir well. Top mixture with remaining ½ cup potato chips. Cover and cook on LOW 5 to 8 hours.

Makes 8 servings

Fish Burritos

WESSON® No-Stick Cooking Spray
1 cup diced onion
1 pound orange roughy fillets or any white fish fillets
3 limes
1 (16-ounce) can ROSARITA® No Fat Traditional Refried Beans
8 burrito-size fat-free flour tortillas
2 cups cooked white rice
1½ cups shredded cabbage
¾ cup reduced-fat shredded sharp Cheddar cheese
¾ cup diced tomatoes
ROSARITA® Traditional Mild Salsa

1. Spray large no-stick skillet with Wesson Cooking Spray. Sauté onion until tender.

2. Add fish and juice from 1 lime. Cook until fish becomes flakey; shred with fork. Remove from heat. Set aside.

3. Evenly divide Rosarita Beans among *each* tortilla; spread beans down center of tortillas. Top beans with even amounts of fish, rice, cabbage, cheese and tomatoes.

4. Roll burrito-style, folding in edges. Serve with Rosarita Salsa and lime wedges.

Makes 8 burritos

Spicy Tuna and Linguine with Garlic and Pine Nuts

2 tablespoons olive oil
4 cloves garlic, minced
2 cups sliced mushrooms
½ cup chopped onion
½ teaspoon crushed red pepper
2½ cups chopped plum tomatoes
1 can (14½ ounces) chicken broth plus water to equal 2 cups
½ teaspoon salt
¼ teaspoon coarsely ground black pepper
1 package (9 ounces) uncooked fresh linguine
1 can (12 ounces) STARKIST® Solid White Tuna, drained and chunked
⅓ cup chopped fresh cilantro
⅓ cup toasted pine nuts or almonds

In 12-inch skillet, heat olive oil over medium-high heat; sauté garlic, mushrooms, onion and red pepper until golden brown. Add tomatoes, chicken broth mixture, salt and black pepper; bring to a boil.

Separate uncooked linguine into strands; place in skillet and spoon sauce over. Reduce heat to simmer; cook, covered, 4 more minutes or until cooked through. Toss gently; add tuna and cilantro and toss again. Sprinkle with pine nuts.

Makes 4 to 6 servings

Spicy Snapper & Black Beans

1½ pounds fresh red snapper fillets, cut into 4 portions (6 ounces each)
Juice of 1 lime
½ teaspoon coarsely ground black pepper
Nonstick cooking spray
1 cup GUILTLESS GOURMET® Spicy Black Bean Dip
½ cup water
½ cup (about 35) crushed GUILTLESS GOURMET® Baked Tortilla Chips (yellow or white corn)
1 cup GUILTLESS GOURMET® Roasted Red Pepper Salsa

Wash fish thoroughly; pat dry with paper towels. Place fish in 13×9-inch glass baking dish. Pour juice over top; sprinkle with pepper. Cover and refrigerate 1 hour.

Preheat oven to 350°F. Coat 11×7-inch glass baking dish with cooking spray. Combine bean dip and water in small bowl; spread 1 cup bean mixture in bottom of prepared baking dish. Place fish over bean mixture, discarding juice. Spread remaining bean mixture over top of fish; sprinkle with crushed chips.

Bake about 20 minutes or until chips are lightly browned and fish turns opaque and flakes easily when tested with fork. To serve, divide fish among 4 serving plates; spoon ¼ cup salsa over top of each serving.

Makes 4 servings

Note: This recipe can be made with 4 boneless skinless chicken breast halves in place of red snapper fillets. Prepare as directed and bake about 40 minutes or until chicken is no longer pink in center. Serve as directed.

Mom's Tuna Casserole

Broccoli-Fish Roll-Ups

1 can (10¾ ounces) cream of broccoli soup
½ cup fat-free (skim) milk
2 cups seasoned stuffing crumbs
¾ pound flounder (4 medium pieces)
1 box (10 ounces) frozen broccoli spears, thawed
Paprika

1. Preheat oven to 375°F. Grease 9×9-inch baking pan. Combine soup and milk in medium bowl. Set aside ½ cup soup mixture.

2. Combine stuffing crumbs and remaining soup mixture. Pat into prepared pan.

3. Place fish on clean work surface. Arrange 1 broccoli spear across narrow end of fish. Starting at narrow end, gently roll up fish. Place over stuffing mixture, seam side down. Repeat with remaining fish and broccoli.

4. Arrange any remaining broccoli spears over stuffing mixture. Spoon reserved ½ cup soup mixture over broccoli-fish roll-ups. Sprinkle with paprika.

5. Bake 20 minutes or until fish flakes easily when tested with fork.
Makes 4 servings

Variation: Asparagus spears and cream of asparagus soup may be substituted for broccoli spears and cream of broccoli soup.

Prep and Cook Time: 30 minutes

Pasta With Tuna

1 pound uncooked pasta, such as spaghetti or penne
¼ cup CRISCO® Oil,* divided
1 medium red onion, peeled and diced
2 teaspoons jarred minced garlic *or* 1 large clove garlic, peeled and minced
1½ teaspoons Italian seasoning
½ to 1 teaspoon dried red pepper flakes, depending on taste
½ teaspoon salt
2 cans (8 ounces each) tomato sauce
2 cans (6 ounces each) white tuna packed in water, drained and broken into chunks
3 tablespoons chopped fresh parsley
¼ cup sliced black or green olives (optional)
Freshly grated Parmesan cheese (optional)

**Use your favorite Crisco Oil product.*

1. Bring large pot of salted water to a boil. Add pasta and 2 tablespoons oil. Cook pasta according to package directions until al dente. Drain pasta. Keep warm.

2. While pasta is boiling, heat remaining 2 tablespoons oil in large skillet on medium-high heat. Add onion and garlic. Sauté 3 minutes, or until onion is translucent. Add Italian seasoning, pepper flakes and salt. Cook 1 minute. Add tomato sauce. Bring to a boil. Reduce heat to low. Simmer 5 minutes.

3. Add tuna, parsley and olives, if used, to sauce. Simmer 2 minutes. Toss sauce with cooked pasta and Parmesan cheese, if used. Serve immediately.
Makes 4 servings

Note: The sauce can be prepared one day in advance and refrigerated, tightly covered. Reheat in pan used to cook pasta while pasta drains.

Preparation Time: 15 minutes
Total Time: 30 minutes

Homestyle Tuna Pot Pie

1 package (15 ounces) refrigerated pie crusts
1 can (12 ounces) STARKIST® Solid White or Chunk Light Tuna, drained and chunked
1 can (10¾ ounces) cream of potato or cream of mushroom soup
1 package (10 ounces) frozen peas and carrots, thawed and drained
½ cup chopped onion
⅓ cup milk
½ teaspoon poultry seasoning or dried thyme
Salt and pepper to taste

Line 9-inch pie pan with one crust; set aside. Reserve second crust. In medium bowl, combine remaining ingredients; mix well. Pour tuna mixture into pie shell; top with second crust. Crimp edges to seal. Cut slits in top crust to vent. Bake in 375°F oven 45 to 50 minutes or until golden brown.
Makes 6 servings

Prep and Cook Time: 55 to 60 minutes

Broccoli-Fish Roll-Ups

Tuna and Broccoli Bake

- 1 package (16 ounces) frozen broccoli cuts, thawed and well drained
- 2 slices bread, cut in ½-inch cubes
- 1 can (12 ounces) STARKIST® Solid White or Chunk Light Tuna, drained and chunked
- 3 eggs
- 2 cups cottage cheese
- 1 cup shredded Cheddar cheese
- ¼ teaspoon ground black pepper

Place broccoli on bottom of 2-quart baking dish. Top with bread cubes and tuna. In medium bowl, combine eggs, cottage cheese, Cheddar cheese and pepper. Spread evenly over tuna mixture. Bake in 400°F oven 30 minutes or until golden brown and puffed. *Makes 4 servings*

Prep Time: 35 minutes

Rice Pilaf with Fish Fillets

- 1 cup UNCLE BEN'S® ORIGINAL CONVERTED® Brand Rice
- 1 can (14½ ounces) fat-free reduced-sodium chicken broth
- 1 cup sliced green onions
- 2 cups sugar snap peas or snow peas
- 12 ounces Dover sole fillets
- ¼ cup reduced-fat Caesar salad dressing
- 2 tomatoes, cut into wedges
- ¼ cup chopped parsley

1. In large skillet, combine rice, chicken broth and ½ cup water. Bring to a boil. Cover; reduce heat and simmer 12 minutes.

2. Add green onions and peas to rice pilaf. Season to taste with salt and pepper. Place fish fillets on pilaf. Spoon salad dressing onto fillets. Cover and cook over low heat 8 minutes or until fish flakes when tested with a fork and rice is tender.

3. Garnish with tomatoes and parsley. *Makes 4 servings*

Variation: Orange roughy fillets or swordfish steaks can be substituted for sole fillets.

Tuna Noodle Casserole

- 1 can (10¾ ounces) condensed cream of mushroom soup
- 1 cup milk
- 3 cups hot cooked rotini pasta (2 cups uncooked)
- 1 can (12 ounces) tuna packed in water, drained and flaked
- 1⅓ cups ***French's® Taste Toppers™*** French Fried Onions, divided
- 1 package (10 ounces) frozen peas and carrots
- ½ cup (2 ounces) shredded Cheddar or grated Parmesan cheese

Combine soup and milk in 2-quart microwavable shallow casserole. Stir in pasta, tuna, *⅔ cup **Taste Toppers***, vegetables and cheese. Cover; microwave on HIGH 10 minutes* or until heated through, stirring halfway through cooking time. Top with remaining *⅔ cup **Taste Toppers***. Microwave 1 minute or until ***Taste Toppers*** are golden. *Makes 6 servings*

*Or, bake, covered, in 350°F oven 25 to 30 minutes.

Tip: Garnish with chopped pimiento and parsley sprigs, if desired.

Prep Time: 10 minutes
Cook Time: 11 minutes

Veggie Mac and Tuna

- 1½ cups (6 ounces) elbow macaroni
- 3 tablespoons butter or margarine
- 1 small onion, chopped
- ½ medium red bell pepper, chopped
- ½ medium green bell pepper, chopped
- ¼ cup all-purpose flour
- 1¾ cups milk
- 8 ounces cubed light pasteurized process cheese product
- ½ teaspoon dried marjoram leaves
- 1 package (10 ounces) frozen peas
- 1 can (9 ounces) tuna in water, drained

Slow Cooker Directions

Cook macaroni according to package directions until just tender; drain. Melt butter in medium saucepan over medium heat. Add onion and bell peppers. Cook and stir 5 minutes or until tender. Add flour. Stir constantly over medium heat 2 minutes. Stir in milk and bring to a boil. Boil, stirring constantly, until thickened. Reduce heat to low; add cheese and marjoram. Stir until cheese is melted.

Combine macaroni, cheese sauce, peas and tuna in slow cooker. Cover and cook on LOW 2½ hours or until bubbly at edge. *Makes 6 servings*

Tuna and Broccoli Bake

Tuna & Shrimp Fajitas

- **1 large red onion, cut in half and thinly sliced**
- **1 red bell pepper, cut into bite-sized strips**
- **1 large green bell pepper, cut into bite-sized strips**
- **2 tablespoons vegetable oil**
- **1 jar (12 ounce) salsa**
- **1 (3-ounce) pouch STARKIST® Tuna, drained and broken into chunks**
- **½ pound frozen cooked bay shrimp, thawed**
- **8 (8-inch) flour tortillas, warmed if desired**
- **Diced avocado, shredded low-fat Cheddar or Monterey Jack cheese, sliced pitted ripe olives and bottled salsa for toppings**

In large skillet or wok, stir-fry onion and bell peppers in oil for 3 minutes over high heat. Add ¼ cup salsa, tuna and shrimp; stir-fry 2 minutes more, or until heated through.

To assemble fajitas, spoon some of tuna mixture in center of each tortilla, then add desired toppings and serve immediately. *Makes 4 servings*

Prep Time: 10 minutes

Veggie Tuna Pasta

- **1 package (16 ounces) medium pasta shells**
- **1 bag (16 ounces) BIRDS EYE® frozen Farm Fresh Mixtures Broccoli, Corn & Red Peppers**
- **1 can (10 ounces) chunky light tuna, packed in water**
- **1 can (10¾ ounces) reduced-fat cream of mushroom soup**

• In large saucepan, cook pasta according to package directions. Add vegetables during last 10 minutes; drain and return to saucepan.

• Stir in tuna and soup. Add salt and pepper to taste. Cook over medium heat until heated through. *Makes 4 servings*

Variation: Stir in 1 can (4 to 6 ounces) chopped ripe olives with tuna.

Serving Suggestion: For a creamier dish, add a few tablespoons water; blend well.

Prep Time: 2 minutes
Cook Time: 12 to 15 minutes

Cheesy Tuna Mac

- **8 ounces uncooked elbow macaroni**
- **2 tablespoons margarine or butter**
- **2 tablespoons all-purpose flour**
- **1 teaspoon paprika**
- **¼ teaspoon salt**
- **1 cup canned reduced-sodium chicken broth**
- **6 ounces reduced-fat reduced-sodium cheese spread, cut into cubes**
- **1 can (6 ounces) tuna packed in water, drained and flaked**

1. Cook macaroni according to package directions, omitting salt. Drain; set aside.

2. Melt margarine in medium saucepan over medium heat. Add flour, paprika and salt; cook and stir 1 minute. Add broth; bring to a simmer for 2 minutes or until sauce thickens.

3. Add cheese spread; cook and stir until cheese melts. Combine tuna and pasta in medium bowl; pour sauce mixture over tuna mixture; toss to coat. Garnish with additional paprika, if desired. *Makes 4 servings*

Linguini with Tuna Antipasto

- **1 package (9 ounces) uncooked refrigerated flavored linguini, such as tomato and herb**
- **1 jar (6½ ounces) marinated artichoke hearts, coarsely chopped and liquid reserved**
- **1 can (6 ounces) tuna in water, drained and broken into pieces**
- **½ cup roasted red peppers, drained and coarsely chopped**
- **⅓ cup olive oil**
- **¼ cup coarsely chopped black olives**
- **½ teaspoon minced garlic**
- **¼ teaspoon salt**
- **¼ teaspoon red pepper flakes**
- **⅛ teaspoon black pepper**
- **½ cup grated Parmesan cheese**

1. Cook linguini according to package directions.

2. While linguini is cooking, combine remaining ingredients except cheese in large microwavable bowl. Mix well; cover with vented plastic wrap. Microwave at HIGH 2 to 3 minutes or until heated through.

3. Drain linguini; add to bowl. Toss well; arrange on 4 plates. Sprinkle with cheese; garnish as desired. *Makes 4 servings*

Prep and Cook Time: 18 minutes

Linguini with Tuna Antipasto

Sensational Shellfish

Zesty Shrimp and Pasta

1 pound large shrimp, cleaned
1 cup prepared GOOD SEASONS® Italian Salad Dressing for Fat Free Dressing, divided
2 cups sliced fresh mushrooms
1 small onion, thinly sliced
1 can (14 ounces) artichoke hearts, drained, cut into halves
1 tablespoon chopped fresh parsley
1 package (9 ounces) DIGIORNO® Pasta, any variety, cooked as directed on package, drained
¼ cup KRAFT® 100% Grated Parmesan Cheese

COOK and stir shrimp in ½ cup of the dressing in large skillet on medium-high heat 2 minutes.

ADD mushrooms, onion, artichoke hearts and parsley. Continue cooking until shrimp are pink and vegetables are tender.

TOSS with hot cooked pasta and remaining ½ cup dressing. Sprinkle with cheese. *Makes 6 servings*

Variation: Prepare as directed, substituting scallops for shrimp.

Variation: Prepare as directed, substituting hot cooked MINUTE® White Rice for pasta.

Prep Time: 10 minutes
Cook Time: 15 minutes

Chicken and Shrimp Jambalaya

1 package (7 ounces) wild pecan aromatic rice *or* 1 cup basmati rice
2½ to 3 cups fat-free reduced-sodium chicken broth, divided
¾ teaspoon salt
⅛ teaspoon black pepper
⅛ teaspoon ground red pepper
½ pound boneless skinless chicken breast, cut into ½-inch pieces
1 tablespoon vegetable oil
1 large onion, chopped
2 cups chopped red, yellow and green bell peppers
2 cloves garlic, minced
6 ounces peeled and deveined medium shrimp
1 large ripe tomato, chopped
2 tablespoons chopped fresh parsley

1. Cook rice according to package directions, substituting 2 cups chicken broth for water and omitting salt.

2. Meanwhile, combine salt, black pepper and red pepper in small bowl; sprinkle half over chicken. Heat oil in large nonstick skillet over medium heat. Add chicken; cook without stirring 2 minutes or until golden. Turn chicken; cook 2 minutes more. Remove chicken; set aside.

3. Add onion and bell peppers to same skillet; cook and stir 2 to 3 minutes or until onion is translucent. Add garlic; cook 1 minute longer. Stir in chicken, shrimp, tomato, remaining pepper mixture and ½ cup chicken broth; bring to a boil. Reduce heat; simmer 5 minutes or until shrimp are opaque.

4. Stir in parsley and rice. Add additional chicken broth if needed to moisten rice. Cook 3 minutes longer or until liquid is absorbed and jambalaya is hot.

Makes 4 servings

Zesty Shrimp and Pasta

Shrimp Primavera Pot Pie

1 can (10¾ ounces) condensed cream of shrimp soup, undiluted
1 package (12 ounces) frozen peeled uncooked medium shrimp
2 packages (1 pound each) frozen mixed vegetables, such as green beans, potatoes, onions and red peppers, thawed and drained
1 teaspoon dried dill weed
¼ teaspoon salt
¼ teaspoon black pepper
1 can (11 ounces) refrigerated breadstick dough

1. Preheat oven to 400°F. Heat soup in medium ovenproof skillet over medium-high heat 1 minute. Add shrimp; cook and stir 3 minutes or until shrimp begin to thaw. Stir in vegetables, dill, salt and pepper; mix well. Reduce heat to medium-low; cook and stir 3 minutes.

2. Unwrap breadstick dough; separate into 8 strips. Twist strips, cutting to fit skillet. Arrange attractively over shrimp mixture. Press ends of dough lightly to edges of skillet to secure. Bake 18 minutes or until crust is golden brown and shrimp mixture is bubbly.

Makes 4 to 6 servings

Prep and Cook Time: 30 minutes

Creamy Alfredo Seafood Lasagna

1 jar (16 ounces) RAGÚ® Cheese Creations!® Classic Alfredo Sauce
1 container (15 ounces) ricotta cheese
1 pound imitation crabmeat, separated into bite-size pieces
1 green onion, chopped (optional)
¼ teaspoon ground white pepper
⅛ teaspoon ground nutmeg (optional)
9 lasagna noodles, cooked and drained
2 cups shredded mozzarella cheese (about 8 ounces)
2 tablespoons grated Parmesan cheese

1. Preheat oven to 350°F. In medium bowl, combine ½ cup Ragú Cheese Creations! Sauce, ricotta cheese, crabmeat, green onion, pepper and nutmeg; set aside.

2. In 13×9-inch baking dish, spread ½ cup Ragú Cheese Creations! Sauce. Arrange 3 lasagna noodles lengthwise over sauce. Spread ½ of the ricotta mixture over noodles; evenly top with ¾ cup mozzarella cheese. Repeat layers, ending with noodles. Top with remaining ½ cup sauce, then sprinkle with remaining ½ cup mozzarella cheese and Parmesan cheese.

3. Cover with aluminum foil and bake 40 minutes. Remove foil and continue baking 10 minutes or until cheese is melted and lightly golden. Let stand 10 minutes before serving. Garnish, if desired, with additional chopped green onions. *Makes 8 servings*

Prep Time: 20 minutes
Cook Time: 50 minutes

Roasted Red Pepper Pasta with Shrimp

1 jar (7 ounces) roasted red peppers packed in oil, undrained
2 tablespoons finely chopped fresh basil leaves,* divided
2 teaspoons finely chopped garlic, divided
2 tablespoons olive or vegetable oil
1 pound uncooked medium shrimp, cleaned
2 tablespoons dry white wine
1½ cups water
½ cup milk
1 package LIPTON® Noodles & Sauce—Alfredo
Ground black pepper to taste

**Substitution: Use 1 teaspoon dried basil leaves, crushed.*

In food processor or blender, process red peppers, 1 tablespoon basil and 1 teaspoon garlic until smooth; set aside.

In 12-inch skillet, heat oil over medium-high heat and cook remaining 1 teaspoon garlic with shrimp, stirring constantly, until shrimp turn pink; remove and set aside.

In same skillet, add wine and cook 1 minute. Add water and milk; bring to the boiling point. Stir in noodles & sauce—Alfredo, then simmer, stirring occasionally, 8 minutes or until noodles are tender. Stir in red pepper purée and black pepper; heat through. To serve, arrange shrimp over noodles, then sprinkle with remaining 1 tablespoon basil. Garnish, if desired, with fresh basil.

Makes about 4 servings

Shrimp Primavera Pot Pie

Spicy Shrimp Puttanesca

- 8 ounces uncooked linguine, capellini or spaghetti
- 1 tablespoon olive oil
- 12 ounces medium shrimp, peeled and deveined
- 4 cloves garlic, minced
- ¾ teaspoon red pepper flakes
- 1 cup finely chopped onion
- 1 can (14½ ounces) no-salt-added stewed tomatoes, undrained
- 2 tablespoons tomato paste
- 2 tablespoons chopped pitted kalamata or black olives
- 1 tablespoon drained capers
- ¼ cup chopped fresh basil or parsley

1. Cook linguine according to package directions, omitting salt. Drain; set aside.

2. Meanwhile, heat oil in large nonstick skillet over medium high heat. Add shrimp, garlic and red pepper flakes; cook and stir 3 to 4 minutes or until shrimp are opaque. Transfer shrimp mixture to bowl with slotted spoon; set aside.

3. Add onion to same skillet; cook over medium heat 5 minutes, stirring occasionally. Add tomatoes with juice, tomato paste, olives and capers; simmer, uncovered, 5 minutes.

4. Return shrimp mixture to skillet; simmer 1 minute. Stir in basil; simmer 1 minute. Place linguine in large serving bowl; top with shrimp mixture.

Makes 4 servings

Creamy Alfredo Seafood Newburg

French Quarter Shrimp Creole

- ½ cup *each* chopped onion, celery and green bell pepper
- 1 clove garlic, minced
- 1 can (14½ ounces) stewed tomatoes, undrained
- ¼ cup ***Frank's® RedHot®*** Cayenne Pepper Sauce
- 1 pound medium shrimp, peeled and deveined
- Hot cooked rice

1. Melt *2 tablespoons butter* in medium skillet; blend in *2 tablespoons flour.* Add onion, celery, bell pepper and garlic; cook and stir over medium-high heat 5 minutes or until vegetables are tender and flour mixture is lightly golden.

2. Stir in tomatoes and ***Frank's RedHot***. Heat to boiling. Reduce heat to medium-low. Cook, uncovered, 5 minutes or until slightly thickened. Stir occasionally. Add shrimp. Cook 5 minutes or just until shrimp are pink. Serve over rice.

Makes 4 servings

Prep Time: 10 minutes
Cook Time: 15 minutes

Creamy Alfredo Seafood Newburg

- 2 tablespoons margarine or butter
- ¼ cup finely chopped onion
- 1 pound uncooked medium shrimp, peeled, deveined and coarsely chopped
- 1 jar (16 ounces) RAGÚ® Cheese Creations!® Classic Alfredo Sauce
- ¼ teaspoon ground white pepper
- 4 croissants or crescent rolls

1. In 12-inch nonstick skillet, melt margarine over medium-high heat and cook onion, stirring occasionally, 2 minutes or until tender.

2. Stir in shrimp and cook, stirring constantly, 2 minutes or until shrimp are almost pink. Stir in Ragú Cheese Creations! Sauce and pepper. Bring to a boil over high heat.

3. Reduce heat to low and simmer uncovered, stirring occasionally, 5 minutes or until shrimp turn pink. To serve, spoon shrimp mixture onto bottom of croissants and sprinkle, if desired, with chopped fresh parsley. Top with remaining croissant halves.

Makes 4 servings

Variation: For a light dish, substitute Ragú Cheese Creations! Light Parmesan Alfredo Sauce

Tip: Substitute 1 pound imitation crabmeat for shrimp.

Prep Time: 5 minutes
Cook Time: 15 minutes

Ginger Shrimp and Green Beans

1 pound cleaned uncooked shrimp
½ pound green beans, cut into 2-inch pieces
1 tablespoon minced peeled gingerroot
2 teaspoons grated lemon peel
1 to 2 red chili peppers, seeded, finely chopped
2 tablespoons butter or margarine
½ pound (8 ounces) VELVEETA® Pasteurized Prepared Cheese Product, cut up
2 tablespoons milk
6 ounces angel hair pasta, cooked, drained

Sauté shrimp, beans, gingerroot, lemon peel and peppers in margarine over medium heat 3 to 5 minutes or until shrimp are pink. Reduce heat to low. Add prepared cheese product and milk; stir until prepared cheese product is melted. Serve over hot pasta.

Makes 4 servings

Prep Time: 25 minutes

Shanghai Shrimp Stir-Fry

2 tablespoons cornstarch, divided
3 tablespoons KIKKOMAN® Soy Sauce, divided
1 tablespoon minced fresh gingerroot
½ teaspoon sugar
½ pound medium-size raw shrimp, peeled and deveined
1¼ cups water
¼ teaspoon fennel seed, crushed
⅛ teaspoon ground cloves
⅛ teaspoon pepper
1 pound fresh broccoli
3 tablespoons vegetable oil, divided
1 onion, chunked and separated

Combine 1 tablespoon *each* cornstarch and soy sauce with ginger and sugar in small bowl; stir in shrimp. Let stand 10 minutes. Meanwhile, combine water, remaining 1 tablespoon cornstarch and 2 tablespoons soy sauce, fennel, cloves and pepper; set aside. Remove flowerets from broccoli; cut into bite-size pieces. Peel stalks; cut into thin slices. Heat 1 tablespoon oil in hot wok or large skillet over high heat. Add shrimp and stir-fry 1 minute; remove. Heat remaining 2 tablespoons oil in same pan. Add broccoli; stir-fry 2 minutes. Add onion; stir-fry 3 minutes longer. Stir in shrimp and soy sauce mixture; cook and stir until sauce boils and thickens.

Makes 4 servings

Shrimp Omelets

3 to 5 tablespoons vegetable oil, divided
8 fresh medium mushrooms, finely chopped
4 teaspoons cornstarch
1 cup water
2 teaspoons soy sauce
2 teaspoons instant chicken bouillon granules
1 teaspoon sugar
8 eggs
½ teaspoon salt
⅛ teaspoon black pepper
8 ounces bean sprouts
8 ounces shrimp, peeled, deveined and finely chopped
4 green onions with tops, finely chopped
1 stalk celery, finely chopped
Cooked whole shrimp and slivered green onions for garnish

1. Heat 1 tablespoon oil in small skillet. Add mushrooms; cook 1 minute. Remove from skillet; set aside.

2. Combine cornstarch, water, soy sauce, bouillon granules and sugar in small saucepan. Cook and stir over medium heat until mixture boils and thickens, about 5 minutes. Keep warm.

3. Combine eggs, salt and pepper in large bowl. Beat until frothy. Add sprouts, shrimp, chopped onions, celery and mushrooms; mix well.

4. For each omelet, heat ½ tablespoon oil in 7-inch omelet pan or skillet. Pour ½ cup egg mixture into pan. Cook until lightly browned, 2 to 3 minutes on each side, gently pushing cooked portion to center and tilting skillet to allow uncooked portion to flow underneath.

5. Stack omelets on serving plate. Pour warm soy sauce mixture over omelets.

Makes 4 servings

Shrimp La Louisiana

1 tablespoon margarine
1½ cups uncooked long-grain white rice*
1 medium onion, chopped
1 green pepper, chopped
2¾ cups beef broth
¼ teaspoon salt
¼ teaspoon ground black pepper
¼ teaspoon hot pepper sauce
1 pound medium shrimp, peeled and deveined
1 can (4 ounces) sliced mushrooms, drained
3 tablespoons snipped parsley
¼ cup sliced green onions for garnish (optional)

**Recipe based on regular-milled long-grain white rice.*

Melt margarine in 3-quart saucepan. Add rice, onion and green pepper. Cook 2 to 3 minutes. Add broth, salt, black pepper and pepper sauce; bring to a boil. Cover and simmer 15 minutes. Add shrimp, mushrooms and parsley. Cook 5 minutes longer or until shrimp turn pink. Garnish with green onions. *Makes 8 servings*

Favorite recipe from **USA Rice Federation**

Shrimp Milano

1 pound frozen cleaned shrimp, cooked, drained
2 cups mushroom slices
1 cup green or red pepper strips
1 clove garlic, minced
¼ cup (½ sticks) butter or margarine
¾ pound (12 ounces) VELVEETA® Pasteurized Prepared Cheese Product, cut up
¾ cup whipping cream
½ teaspoon dill weed
⅓ cup KRAFT® 100% Grated Parmesan Cheese
8 ounces fettuccine, cooked, drained

• In large skillet, sauté shrimp, vegetables and garlic in butter. Reduce heat to low.

• Add prepared cheese product, cream and dill. Stir until prepared cheese product is melted.

• Stir in Parmesan cheese. Add fettuccine; toss lightly.
Makes 4 to 6 servings

Prep Time: 20 minutes
Cook Time: 15 minutes

Sonora Shrimp

2 tablespoons butter
1 medium green bell pepper, chopped
½ cup chopped onion
½ cup chopped celery
1 can (14½ ounces) whole peeled tomatoes, undrained and cut up
½ cup dry white wine
½ teaspoon LAWRY'S® Seasoned Salt
½ teaspoon LAWRY'S® Seasoned Pepper
¼ teaspoon LAWRY'S® Garlic Powder with Parsley
¼ teaspoon dried thyme, crushed
1 pound medium shrimp, peeled and deveined
1 can (2¼ ounces) sliced black olives, drained

In large skillet, heat butter. Add bell pepper, onion and celery and cook over medium-high heat until onion is tender. Add remaining ingredients except shrimp and olives; mix well. Bring to a boil over medium-high heat; reduce heat to low and cook, uncovered, 15 minutes, stirring occasionally. Add shrimp and olives; cook additional 10 minutes or until shrimp turn pink.
Makes 4 to 6 servings

Serving Suggestions: Serve over hot fluffy rice.

Shrimp & Ham Jambalaya

1 onion, cut into wedges
1 large green bell pepper, chopped
2 cloves garlic, minced
¼ teaspoon ground red pepper
2 tablespoons FLEISCHMANN'S® Original Margarine
3 cups cooked rice
2 cups large shrimp, cooked and cleaned (about 1 pound)
2 cups cubed cooked ham (about 1¼ pounds)
1 (16-ounce) can peeled tomatoes, chopped (undrained)
1 teaspoon natural hickory seasoning

1. Cook and stir onion, bell pepper, garlic and red pepper in margarine in large skillet over medium heat until vegetables are tender.

2. Stir in remaining ingredients. Cook for 10 to 15 minutes or until heated through, stirring occasionally. Serve immediately. *Makes 8 servings*

Preparation Time: 30 minutes
Cook Time: 20 minutes
Total Time: 50 minutes

Helpful Hints

Shrimp may be peeled and deveined either before or after they are cooked. If cooked, peel and devein them while they are still warm. The shell is easily removed with your fingers.

Shrimp & Ham Jambalaya

Jambalaya Stir-Fry on Cajun Rice

1¾ cups water
1 cup uncooked converted rice
1 can (16 ounces) diced tomatoes, undrained
½ cup finely chopped celery
2 teaspoons chicken bouillon granules
1 bay leaf
8 ounces andouille sausage, cut into ¼-inch rounds*
1½ cups chopped onions
1 cup chopped green bell pepper
½ pound raw large shrimp, peeled and deveined
½ pound boneless chicken breasts, cut into 1-inch pieces
¾ teaspoon dried thyme leaves
¼ cup chopped fresh parsley
1 teaspoon salt
½ teaspoon ground red pepper
½ teaspoon paprika
Hot pepper sauce

**If unavailable, use kielbasa sausage.*

1. Bring water to a boil in medium saucepan. Add rice, tomatoes and their liquid, celery, bouillon granules and bay leaf. Return to a boil; reduce heat, cover tightly and simmer 20 minutes or until all liquid is absorbed. Remove and discard bay leaf.

2. Meanwhile, heat large skillet over medium-high heat 1 minute. Add sausage, onions and bell pepper; cook and stir 10 minutes.

3. Increase heat to high; add shrimp, chicken and thyme. Cook and stir 5 minutes. Add parsley, salt, ground red pepper and paprika. Stir to blend thoroughly.

4. Place rice on platter. Spoon shrimp mixture over rice and serve with pepper sauce. *Makes 4 servings*

Basil Shrimp Fettuccine

3 tablespoons butter
3 tablespoons olive oil
2 tomatoes, peeled, seeded and chopped
1 clove garlic, minced
½ cup HOLLAND HOUSE® White Cooking Wine
⅓ cup evaporated skim milk
½ cup fresh basil, chopped
½ cup shrimp, peeled and deveined
4 tablespoons Parmesan cheese, grated and divided
4 tablespoons fresh parsley, chopped and divided
1 pound fettuccine, cooked and drained

Melt butter and oil in medium saucepan over medium heat. Add tomatoes and garlic; simmer until tomatoes are softened. Add cooking wine and milk; simmer 10 minutes. Stir in basil and shrimp; simmer 3 minutes or until shrimp turn pink and are opaque. Add 2 tablespoons cheese and 2 tablespoons parsley. Serve over cooked fettuccine. Sprinkle with remaining 2 tablespoons each, cheese and parsley.
Makes 4 to 6 servings

Noodles with Baby Shrimp

1 package (3.75 ounces) bean thread noodles
3 green onions with tops
1 tablespoon vegetable oil
1 package (16 ounces) frozen mixed vegetables (such as cauliflower, broccoli and carrots)
1 cup vegetable broth
8 ounces frozen baby shrimp
1 tablespoon soy sauce
2 teaspoons Asian sesame oil
¼ teaspoon black pepper

Place noodles in large bowl. Cover with hot tap water; let stand 10 to 15 minutes or just until softened. Drain noodles and cut into 5- or 6-inch pieces; set aside.

Cut onions into 1-inch pieces.

Heat wok over high heat about 1 minute or until hot. Drizzle vegetable oil into wok and heat 30 seconds. Add onions; stir-fry 1 minute. Add mixed vegetables; stir-fry 2 minutes. Add broth; bring to a boil. Reduce heat to low; cover and cook about 5 minutes or until vegetables are crisp-tender.

Add shrimp to wok and cook just until thawed. Stir in noodles, soy sauce, sesame oil and black pepper; stir-fry until heated through. Transfer to serving dish.
Makes 4 to 6 servings

Shrimp Fried Rice

2 eggs
2 tablespoons water
2 tablespoons vegetable oil
3 green onions and tops, chopped
3 cups cold cooked rice
¼ pound cooked baby shrimp, chopped
3 tablespoons KIKKOMAN® Soy Sauce

Beat eggs with water just to blend; set aside. Heat oil in hot wok or large skillet over medium heat. Add green onions; stir-fry 30 seconds. Add eggs and scramble. Stir in rice and cook until heated, gently separating grains. Add shrimp and soy sauce; cook and stir until heated through. Serve immediately. *Makes 6 servings*

Jambalaya Stir-Fry on Cajun Rice

Crab and Rice Primavera

- **2 cups frozen broccoli, cauliflower and carrot blend**
- **¼ cup water**
- **2 cups fat-free milk**
- **1 package (8 ounces) imitation crabmeat**
- **1 tablespoon butter or margarine**
- **¼ teaspoon garlic powder**
- **1½ cups MINUTE® White Rice, uncooked**
- **½ cup KRAFT FREE® Nonfat Grated Topping**

BRING vegetables and water to boil in medium saucepan, stirring occasionally. Reduce heat; cover and simmer 3 minutes.

ADD milk, imitation crabmeat, butter and garlic powder. Bring to boil.

STIR in rice and grated topping; cover. Remove from heat. Let stand 5 minutes. Fluff with fork.

Makes 6 servings

Prep Time: 10 minutes
Cook Time: 10 minutes plus standing

Elegant Crabmeat Frittata

- **3 tablespoons butter or margarine, divided**
- **¼ pound fresh mushrooms, sliced**
- **2 green onions, cut into thin slices**
- **8 eggs, separated**
- **¼ cup milk**
- **¼ teaspoon salt**
- **½ teaspoon hot pepper sauce**
- **½ pound lump crabmeat or imitation crabmeat, flaked and picked over to remove any shells**
- **½ cup (2 ounces) shredded Swiss cheese**

1. Melt 2 tablespoons butter in large ovenproof skillet over medium-high heat. Add mushrooms and onions; cook and stir 3 to 5 minutes or until vegetables are tender. Remove from skillet; set aside.

2. Beat egg yolks with electric mixer at high speed until slightly thickened and lemon color. Stir in milk, salt and hot pepper sauce.

3. Beat egg whites in clean large bowl with electric mixer at high speed until foamy. Gradually add to egg yolk mixture, whisking just until blended.

4. Melt remaining 1 tablespoon butter in skillet. Pour egg mixture into skillet. Cook until egg is almost set. Remove from heat.

5. Preheat broiler. Broil frittata 4 to 6 inches from heat until top is set. Top with crabmeat, mushroom mixture and cheese. Return frittata to broiler; broil until cheese is melted. Garnish, if desired. Serve immediately.

Makes 4 servings

Crabmeat with Herbs and Pasta

- **1 small onion, minced**
- **1 carrot, shredded**
- **1 clove garlic, minced**
- **⅓ cup olive oil**
- **3 tablespoons butter or margarine**
- **6 ounces canned crabmeat, drained and flaked**
- **¼ cup chopped fresh basil *or* 1 teaspoon dried basil leaves, crushed**
- **2 tablespoons chopped fresh parsley**
- **1 tablespoon lemon juice**
- **½ cup chopped pine nuts (optional)**
- **½ teaspoon salt**
- **½ package (8 ounces) uncooked vermicelli, hot cooked and drained**

In large skillet over medium-high heat, cook and stir onion, carrot and garlic in hot oil and butter until vegetables are tender, but not brown. Reduce heat to medium. Stir in crabmeat, basil, parsley and lemon juice. Cook 4 minutes, stirring constantly. Stir in pine nuts and salt. Pour sauce over vermicelli in large bowl; toss gently to coat. Garnish as desired.

Makes 4 servings

Favorite recipe from **New Jersey Department of Agriculture**

Easy Crab Asparagus Pie

- **4 ounces crabmeat, shredded**
- **12 ounces fresh asparagus, cut into 1-inch pieces and cooked**
- **½ cup chopped onion, cooked**
- **1 cup (4 ounces) shredded Monterey Jack cheese**
- **¼ cup (1 ounce) grated Parmesan cheese**
- **Black pepper**
- **¾ cup all-purpose flour**
- **¾ teaspoon baking powder**
- **½ teaspoon salt**
- **2 tablespoons cold butter or margarine**
- **1½ cups milk**
- **4 eggs, slightly beaten**

1. Preheat oven to 350°F. Lightly grease 10-inch quiche dish or pie plate.

2. Layer crabmeat, asparagus and onion in prepared pie plate; top with cheeses. Season with pepper.

3. Combine flour, baking powder and salt in large bowl. With pastry blender or 2 knives, cut in butter until mixture forms coarse crumbs. Stir in milk and eggs; pour over cheese mixture.

4. Bake 30 minutes or until filling is puffed and knife inserted near center comes out clean. Serve hot.

Makes 6 servings

Elegant Crabmeat Frittata

Chesapeake Crab Strata

4 tablespoons butter or margarine
4 cups unseasoned croutons
2 cups shredded Cheddar cheese
2 cups milk
8 eggs, beaten
½ teaspoon dry mustard
½ teaspoon seafood seasoning
Salt and black pepper to taste
1 pound crabmeat, picked over to remove any shells

Preheat oven to 325°F. Place butter in 11×7-inch baking dish. Heat in oven until melted, tilting to coat dish. Remove dish from oven; spread croutons over melted butter. Top with cheese; set aside.

Combine milk, eggs, dry mustard, seafood seasoning, salt and black pepper; mix well. Pour egg mixture over cheese in dish; sprinkle with crabmeat. Bake 50 minutes or until mixture is set. Remove from oven and let stand about 10 minutes. Garnish, if desired. *Makes 6 to 8 servings*

Cajun-Style Corn with Crayfish

6 ears corn on the cob
1 tablespoon vegetable oil
1 medium onion, chopped
½ cup chopped green bell pepper
½ cup chopped red bell pepper
1 cup water
1 teaspoon salt
⅛ teaspoon black pepper
⅛ teaspoon ground red pepper
¾ pound crayfish tail meat

1. Cut corn from cobs in two or three layers so that kernels are not left whole. Scrape cobs to remove remaining juice and pulp.

2. Heat oil in large skillet over medium heat. Add onion and bell peppers; cook 5 minutes, stirring occasionally. Add corn, water, salt, black pepper and ground red pepper; bring to a boil. Reduce heat to low; simmer 10 to 15 minutes.

3. Add crayfish; return mixture to a simmer. Cook 3 to 5 minutes or just until crayfish turn opaque. Garnish, if desired. *Makes 6 servings*

Hot Crab and Cheese on Muffins

4 English muffins, split
1 tablespoon butter or margarine
3 green onions, chopped
⅓ cup chopped red bell pepper
½ pound fresh crabmeat, drained and flaked*
1 to 2 teaspoons hot pepper sauce
1 cup (4 ounces) shredded Cheddar cheese
1 cup (4 ounces) shredded Monterey Jack cheese

**Two cans (6 ounces each) fancy crabmeat, drained, can be substituted for fresh crabmeat.*

1. Preheat broiler. Place muffin halves on lightly greased baking sheet. Broil 4 inches from heat 2 minutes or until muffins are lightly toasted. Place on large microwavable plate.

2. Melt butter in medium skillet over medium heat. Add green onions and bell pepper; cook and stir 3 to 4 minutes or until tender. Remove from heat; stir in crabmeat, hot pepper sauce and cheeses. Spoon about ⅓ cup crab mixture onto muffin halves.

3. Microwave at HIGH 2 to 3 minutes, rotating platter once, or until crab mixture is heated through.
Makes 8 servings

Prep and Cook Time: 12 minutes

Linguine with Savory Clam Sauce

2 tablespoons olive oil, margarine or butter
3 cloves garlic, minced
1 can (10½ ounces) whole baby clams *or* 2 cans (6½ ounces each) minced clams in juice, undrained
1 package KNORR® Recipe Classics™ Vegetable Soup, Dip and Recipe Mix
½ cup water
½ cup milk
¼ teaspoon dried oregano
8 ounces linguine, cooked and drained

• In large skillet, heat oil over medium-high heat and cook garlic 30 seconds. Add clams with juice, recipe mix, water, milk and oregano. Bring to a boil over high heat. Reduce heat to low and simmer, stirring occasionally, 3 minutes.

• Toss with hot linguine.
Makes 4 servings

Prep Time: 20 minutes
Cook Time: 5 minutes

Chesapeake Crab Strata

Linguine with Red Clam Sauce

Nonstick cooking spray
1 onion, finely chopped
2 cloves garlic, minced
2 tablespoons finely chopped fresh parsley
2 teaspoons dried oregano leaves
1 can (14 ounces) Italian plum tomatoes, undrained and coarsely chopped
1 can (8 ounces) reduced-sodium tomato sauce
2 cans (7½ ounces each) baby clams, undrained
1 tablespoon lemon juice
Salt and black pepper
8 ounces linguine, cooked and kept warm

1. Spray large saucepan with cooking spray. Heat over medium heat until hot. Add onion and garlic; cook and stir about 3 minutes or until tender. Stir in parsley and oregano; cook 1 to 2 minutes.

2. Add tomatoes with juice and tomato sauce to saucepan; bring to a boil. Reduce heat and simmer, uncovered, about 10 minutes or until mixture is of medium sauce consistency. Stir in clams and lemon juice; cook about 3 minutes or until heated through. Season to taste with salt and pepper.

3. Spoon sauce over linguine in large bowl and toss. *Makes 4 servings*

Seafood Lasagna

1 package (16 ounces) lasagna noodles
2 tablespoons margarine or butter
1 large onion, finely chopped
1 package (8 ounces) cream cheese, cut into ½-inch pieces, at room temperature
1½ cups cream-style cottage cheese
2 teaspoons dried basil leaves
½ teaspoon salt
⅛ teaspoon black pepper
1 egg, lightly beaten
2 cans (10¾ ounces each) cream of mushroom soup
⅓ cup milk
1 clove garlic, minced
½ pound bay scallops, rinsed and patted dry
½ pound flounder fillets, rinsed, patted dry and cut into ½-inch cubes
½ pound medium raw shrimp, peeled and deveined
½ cup dry white wine
1 cup (4 ounces) shredded mozzarella cheese
2 tablespoons grated Parmesan cheese

1. Cook lasagna noodles according to package directions; drain.

2. Melt margarine in large skillet over medium heat. Cook onion in hot margarine until tender, stirring frequently. Stir in cream cheese, cottage cheese, basil, salt and pepper; mix well. Stir in egg; set aside.

3. Combine soup, milk and garlic in large bowl until well blended. Stir in scallops, fillets, shrimp and wine.

4. Preheat oven to 350°F. Grease 13×9-inch baking pan.

5. Place a layer of noodles in prepared pan, overlapping the noodles. Spread half the cheese mixture over noodles. Place a layer of noodles over cheese mixture and top with half the seafood mixture. Repeat layers. Sprinkle with mozzarella and Parmesan cheeses.

6. Bake 45 minutes or until bubbly. Let stand 10 minutes before cutting.
Makes 8 to 10 servings

Helpful Hints

Bay scallops are tiny scallops harvested mainly along the east coast of the United States; they are generally fairly expensive. Sea scallops are much larger than bay scallops and if cut into halves or quarters they make an inexpensive alternative to bay scallops.

Linguine with Red Clam Sauce

Paella

1 pound littleneck clams
8 to 10 ounces sea scallops
6 ounces raw medium shrimp
4 teaspoons olive oil, divided
3¼ cups reduced-sodium chicken broth, divided
1 medium onion, finely chopped
3 cloves garlic, chopped
2 cups long-grain white rice
1 teaspoon dried thyme leaves, crushed
½ teaspoon saffron threads, crushed
1 pint cherry tomatoes, halved
1 cup frozen petit peas, thawed
1 tablespoon chopped fresh parsley

1. Discard any clams that remain open when tapped with fingers. To clean clams, scrub with stiff brush under cold running water. Soak clams in mixture of ⅓ cup salt to 1 gallon of water 20 minutes. Drain water; repeat 2 more times. Slice sea scallops in half crosswise into rounds. Peel shrimp leaving tails on, if desired; devein.

2. Heat 1 teaspoon oil over medium-high heat in large saucepan. Add shrimp; cook, stirring occasionally, 3 minutes or until shrimp turn pink. Transfer to bowl; cover. Add scallops to saucepan and cook 2 minutes or until scallops are opaque. Transfer to bowl with shrimp. Add clams and ¼ cup broth to pan. Cover; boil 2 to 8 minutes or until clams open. Transfer clams and broth to bowl with shrimp and scallops; discard any unopened clams.

3. Heat remaining 3 teaspoons oil in same saucepan. Add onion and garlic; cook and stir 4 minutes or until tender. Add rice; cook and stir 2 minutes. Add remaining 3 cups broth, thyme and saffron; reduce heat to medium-low. Cover; simmer 15 minutes or until rice is tender. Stir in tomatoes, peas and parsley. Stir in seafood and accumulated juices. Cover; remove from heat. Let stand 3 to 5 minutes or until seafood is hot.
Makes 6 servings

Scallop Stir-Fry

6 ounces uncooked ramen noodles
1 tablespoon olive oil
1 pound asparagus, cut into 1-inch pieces
1 red bell pepper, cut into thin rings
3 green onions, chopped
1 large clove garlic, minced
1 pound sea scallops, halved crosswise
2 tablespoons soy sauce
1 teaspoon hot pepper sauce
1 teaspoon Asian sesame oil
Juice of ½ lime

1. Cook noodles in lightly salted boiling water according to package directions.

2. Meanwhile, heat olive oil in wok or large skillet over high heat. Add asparagus, red pepper, onions and garlic. Stir-fry 2 minutes.

3. Add scallops; stir-fry until scallops turn opaque.

4. Stir in soy sauce, hot pepper sauce, sesame oil and lime juice. Add noodles; heat thoroughly, stirring occasionally. *Makes 4 servings*

Tip: Substitute vermicelli for ramen noodles.

Seafood Lasagna

4 ounces lasagna noodles
1 jar (28-ounces) spaghetti, pasta sauce or favorite homemade recipe
1 package (6 ounces) frozen cooked salad shrimp, thawed and drained
4 ounces Surimi Seafood, thawed and thinly sliced
½ cup low-fat ricotta cheese
¼ cup freshly grated Parmesan cheese
1 tablespoon minced fresh parsley
⅛ teaspoon black pepper
⅔ cup shredded low-fat mozzarella cheese

Heat oven to 375°F. Prepare lasagna noodles according to package directions. Pour spaghetti sauce into saucepan and simmer for 10 minutes until thickened and reduced to about 3 cups; stir in shrimp and Surimi Seafood. Combine ricotta cheese, Parmesan cheese, parsley and pepper in small bowl.

To assemble lasagna, place half of noodles in 8×8-inch casserole. Top with half of seafood sauce and drop half of ricotta mixture by small teaspoonfuls on top. Sprinkle with half of mozzarella cheese. Repeat layers. Bake for 35 minutes or until bubbly. Let stand 10 minutes before cutting.
Makes 6 servings

Favorite recipe from **National Fisheries Institute**

Paella

Make It Meatless

Hearty Lentil Stew

- 1 cup dried lentils, rinsed and drained
- 1 package (16 ounces) frozen green beans
- 2 cups cauliflower florets
- 1 cup chopped onion
- 1 cup baby carrots, cut in half crosswise
- 3 cups fat free reduced-sodium chicken broth
- 2 teaspoons ground cumin
- ¾ teaspoon ground ginger
- 1 can (15 ounces) chunky tomato sauce with garlic and herbs
- ½ cup dry-roasted peanuts

Slow Cooker Directions

1. Place lentils in slow cooker. Top with green beans, cauliflower, onion and carrots. Combine broth, cumin and ginger in large bowl; mix well. Pour mixture over vegetables. Cover and cook on LOW 9 to 11 hours.

2. Stir in tomato sauce. Cover and cook on LOW 10 minutes. Ladle stew into bowls. Sprinkle peanuts evenly onto each serving.

Makes 6 servings

Broccoli & Cheese Strata

- 2 cups chopped broccoli florets
- 4 slices firm white bread, ½ inch thick
- 4 teaspoons butter
- 1½ cups (6 ounces) shredded Cheddar cheese
- 3 eggs
- 1½ cups low-fat (2%) milk
- ½ teaspoon salt
- ½ teaspoon hot pepper sauce
- ⅛ teaspoon black pepper

Slow Cooker Directions

1. Cook broccoli in boiling water 10 minutes or until tender. Drain. Spread one side of each bread slice with 1 teaspoon butter.

2. Arrange 2 slices bread, buttered sides up, in greased 1-quart casserole. Layer cheese, broccoli and remaining 2 bread slices, buttered sides down.

3. Beat together eggs, milk, salt, hot pepper sauce and pepper in medium bowl. Gradually pour over bread.

4. Place small wire rack in 5-quart slow cooker. Pour in 1 cup water. Place casserole on rack. Cover and cook on HIGH 3 hours.

Makes 4 servings

Baked Ziti with Walnuts

- 1 cup uncooked ziti pasta
- 1 box (10 ounces) BIRDS EYE® frozen Peas & Pearl Onions
- 1 cup tomato sauce
- ½ cup chopped walnuts
- 1 tablespoon olive oil
- 2 tablespoons grated Parmesan cheese

• Preheat oven to 350°F.

• Cook ziti according to package directions; drain and set aside.

• In large bowl, combine vegetables, tomato sauce, walnuts and oil. Add ziti; toss well.

• Place mixture in 13×9-inch baking pan. Sprinkle with cheese.

• Bake 20 minutes or until heated through.

Makes 4 servings

Prep Time: 10 minutes
Cook Time: 20 minutes

Hearty Lentil Stew

Broccoli-Stuffed Shells

1 tablespoon butter or margarine
¼ cup chopped onion
1 cup ricotta cheese
1 egg
2 cups chopped cooked broccoli *or* 1 package (10 ounces) frozen chopped broccoli, thawed and well drained
1 cup (4 ounces) shredded Monterey Jack cheese
20 jumbo pasta shells
1 can (28 ounces) crushed tomatoes with added purée
1 package (1 ounce) HIDDEN VALLEY® Milk Recipe Original Ranch® salad dressing mix
¼ cup grated Parmesan cheese

Preheat oven to 350°F. In small skillet, melt butter over medium heat. Add onion; cook until onion is tender but not browned. Remove from heat; cool. In large bowl, stir ricotta cheese and egg until well-blended. Add broccoli and Jack cheese; mix well. In large pot of boiling water, cook pasta shells 8 to 10 minutes or just until tender; drain. Rinse under cold running water; drain again. Stuff each shell with about 2 tablespoons broccoli-cheese mixture.

In medium bowl, combine tomatoes, sautéed onion and salad dressing mix; mix well. Pour one third of the tomato mixture into 13×9-inch baking dish. Arrange filled shells in dish. Spoon remaining tomato mixture over top. Sprinkle with Parmesan cheese. Bake, covered, until hot and bubbly, about 30 minutes.

Makes 4 servings

Bean and Vegetable Burritos

Slow Cooker

2 tablespoons chili powder
2 teaspoons dried oregano leaves
1½ teaspoons ground cumin
1 large sweet potato, peeled and diced
1 can black beans or pinto beans, rinsed and drained
4 cloves garlic, minced
1 medium onion, halved and thinly sliced
1 jalapeño pepper,* seeded and minced
1 green bell pepper, chopped
1 cup frozen corn, thawed and drained
3 tablespoons lime juice
1 tablespoon chopped fresh cilantro
¾ cup (3 ounces) shredded Monterey Jack cheese
4 (10-inch) flour tortillas
Sour cream (optional)

**Jalapeño peppers can sting and irritate the skin; wear rubber gloves when handling peppers and do not touch eyes. Wash hands after handling.*

Slow Cooker Directions

Combine chili powder, oregano and cumin in small bowl. Set aside.

Layer ingredients in slow cooker in the following order: sweet potato, beans, half of chili powder mix, garlic, onion, jalapeño pepper, bell pepper, remaining half of chili powder mix and corn. Cover and cook on LOW 5 hours or until sweet potato is tender. Stir in lime juice and cilantro.

Preheat oven to 350°F. Spoon 2 tablespoons cheese in center of each tortilla. Top with 1 cup filling. Fold all 4 sides to enclose filling. Place burritos seam side down on baking sheet. Cover with foil and bake 20 to 30 minutes or until heated through. Serve with sour cream, if desired.

Makes 4 servings

Classic Stuffed Shells

1 jar (26 to 28 ounces) RAGÚ® Old World Style® Pasta Sauce, divided
2 pounds part-skim ricotta cheese
2 cups part-skim shredded mozzarella cheese (about 8 ounces)
¼ cup grated Parmesan cheese
3 eggs
1 tablespoon finely chopped fresh parsley
⅛ teaspoon ground black pepper
1 box (12 ounces) jumbo shells pasta, cooked and drained

Preheat oven to 350°F. In 13×9-inch baking pan, evenly spread 1 cup Ragú® Old World Style Pasta Sauce; set aside.

In large bowl, combine cheeses, eggs, parsley and black pepper. Fill shells with cheese mixture, then arrange in baking pan. Evenly top with remaining sauce. Bake 45 minutes or until sauce is bubbling.

Makes 8 servings

Tip: For a change of shape, substitute cooked and drained cannelloni or manicotti tubes for the jumbo shells. Use a teaspoon or pastry bag to fill the tubes from end to end, being careful not to overfill them.

Classic Stuffed Shells

Eggplant and Feta Skillet

¼ cup olive oil
1 medium eggplant, cut into 1-inch pieces
1 medium zucchini, cut into ½-inch slices
1 package (16 ounces) frozen bell peppers and onions blend, thawed and drained
2 teaspoons bottled minced garlic
2 cans (14½ ounces each) Italian-style diced tomatoes, drained
1 can (2¼ ounces) sliced black olives, drained
1½ cups prepared croutons
¾ cup feta cheese with basil and tomato, crumbled

1. Heat oil in large skillet over high heat until hot.

2. Add eggplant, zucchini, peppers and onions, and garlic; cook and stir 6 minutes. Add tomatoes; simmer 3 minutes. Stir in olives.

3. Sprinkle croutons and feta cheese over top. *Makes 6 servings*

Prep and Cook Time: 20 minutes

Baked Bow-Tie Pasta in Mushroom Cream Sauce

1 teaspoon olive or vegetable oil
1 package (10 ounces) sliced mushrooms
1 large onion, thinly sliced
⅛ teaspoon ground black pepper
1 jar (16 ounces) RAGÚ® Cheese Creations!® Light Parmesan Alfredo Sauce
8 ounces bow tie pasta, cooked and drained
1 tablespoon grated Parmesan cheese
1 tablespoon plain dry bread crumbs (optional)

1. Preheat oven to 400°F. In 10-inch nonstick skillet, heat oil over medium heat and cook mushrooms, onion and pepper, stirring frequently, 10 minutes or until vegetables are golden. Stir in Ragú Cheese Creations! Sauce.

2. In 2-quart shallow baking dish, combine sauce mixture with hot pasta. Sprinkle with cheese combined with bread crumbs. Cover with aluminum foil and bake 20 minutes. Remove foil and bake an additional 5 minutes.

Makes 6 servings

Prep Time: 10 minutes
Cook Time: 35 minutes

Cannellini Parmesan Casserole

2 tablespoons olive oil
1 cup chopped onion
2 teaspoons minced garlic
1 teaspoon dried oregano leaves
¼ teaspoon black pepper
2 cans (14½ ounces each) onion- and garlic-flavored diced tomatoes, undrained
1 jar (14 ounces) roasted red peppers, drained and cut into ½-inch squares
2 cans (19 ounces each) white cannellini beans or Great Northern beans, rinsed and drained
1 teaspoon dried basil leaves *or* 1 tablespoon chopped fresh basil
¾ cup (3 ounces) grated Parmesan cheese

1. Heat oil in Dutch oven over medium heat until hot. Add onion, garlic, oregano and black pepper; cook and stir 5 minutes or until onion is tender.

2. Increase heat to high. Add tomatoes with juice and red peppers; cover and bring to a boil.

3. Reduce heat to medium. Stir in beans; cover and simmer 5 minutes, stirring occasionally. Stir in basil and sprinkle with cheese.

Makes 6 servings

Cheesy Spinach Bake

8 ounces uncooked spinach fettuccine noodles
1 tablespoon vegetable oil
1 cup fresh mushroom slices
1 green onion with top, finely chopped
1 clove garlic, minced
4 to 5 cups fresh spinach, coarsely chopped *or* 1 package (10 ounces) frozen spinach, thawed and drained
1 tablespoon water
1 container (15 ounces) ricotta cheese
¼ cup heavy cream
1 egg
½ teaspoon ground nutmeg
½ teaspoon black pepper
½ cup (2 ounces) shredded Swiss cheese

1. Preheat oven to 350°F. Cook pasta according to package directions, omitting salt. Drain; set aside.

2. Heat oil in medium skillet over medium heat. Add mushrooms, green onion and garlic. Cook and stir until mushrooms are softened. Add spinach and water. Cover; cook until spinach is wilted, about 3 minutes.

3. Combine ricotta cheese, cream, egg, nutmeg and black pepper in large bowl. Gently stir in noodles and vegetables; toss to coat evenly.

4. Grease 1½-quart casserole. Spread noodle mixture in casserole. Spinkle with Swiss cheese.

5. Bake 25 to 30 minutes or until knife inserted halfway into center comes out clean.

Makes 6 (1-cup) servings

Eggplant and Feta Skillet

Cheesy Baked Barley

- 2 cups water
- ½ cup medium pearled barley
- ½ teaspoon salt, divided
- Nonstick cooking spray
- ½ cup diced onion
- ½ cup diced zucchini
- ½ cup diced red bell pepper
- 1½ teaspoons all-purpose flour
- Seasoned pepper
- ¾ cup fat-free (skim) milk
- 1 cup (4 ounces) shredded reduced-fat Italian blend cheese, divided
- 1 tablespoon Dijon mustard

1. Bring water to a boil in 1-quart saucepan. Add barley and ¼ teaspoon salt. Cover; reduce heat and simmer 45 minutes or until tender and most water is evaporated. Let stand covered, 5 minutes.

2. Preheat oven to 375°F. Spray medium skillet with cooking spray. Cook onion, zucchini and bell pepper over medium-low heat about 10 minutes or until soft. Stir in flour, remaining ¼ teaspoon salt and seasoned pepper to taste; cook 1 to 2 minutes. Add milk, stirring constantly; cook and stir until slightly thickened. Remove from heat and add barley, ¾ cup cheese and mustard; stir until cheese is melted.

3. Spread in even layer in casserole. Sprinkle with remaining ¼ cup cheese. Bake 20 minutes or until hot. Preheat broiler. Broil casserole 1 to 2 minutes or until cheese is lightly browned. *Makes 2 servings*

Colorful Pepper Fusilli

- 2 tablespoons olive oil
- 1 onion, chopped
- 1 yellow bell pepper, diced
- 1 red bell pepper, diced
- 1 green bell pepper, diced
- 8 ounces mushrooms, sliced
- 4 green onions, chopped
- 4 cloves garlic, minced
- ¼ teaspoon red pepper flakes
- 2 cans (14½ ounces each) diced tomatoes, undrained
- ½ cup chopped fresh basil *or* 2 teaspoons dried basil leaves
- 1 teaspoon salt
- ½ teaspoon black pepper
- 1 pound fusilli, cooked and drained
- 2 tablespoons chopped fresh parsley

1. Heat olive oil in large skillet over medium-high heat until hot. Add onion and bell peppers; cook and stir 3 minutes. Add mushrooms; cook and stir 2 minutes. Add green onions, garlic and red pepper flakes; cook and stir 2 minutes. Add tomatoes; cook and stir 5 minutes. Add basil, salt and black pepper; stir well.

2. Combine sauce with fusilli in large bowl; stir gently. Sprinkle parsley over top. *Makes 6 servings*

Helpful Hints

Fusilli is a spiral shaped pasta that is generally about 2 inches long. If it is not available, substitute rotini.

Chiles Rellenos Casserole

- 3 eggs, separated
- ¾ cup milk
- ¾ cup all-purpose flour
- ½ teaspoon salt
- 1 tablespoon butter or margarine
- ½ cup chopped onion
- 2 cans (7 ounces each) whole green chilies, drained
- 8 slices (1 ounce each) Monterey Jack cheese, cut into halves
- Garnishes: sour cream, sliced green onions, pitted ripe olive slices, guacamole and salsa

1. Preheat oven to 350°F.

2. Combine egg yolks, milk, flour and salt in blender or food processor container. Cover; process until smooth. Pour into bowl; let stand until ready to use.

3. Melt butter in small skillet over medium heat. Add onion; cook and stir until tender.

4. Pat chilies dry with paper towels. Slit each chili lengthwise and carefully remove seeds. Place 2 halves of cheese and 1 tablespoon onion in each chili; reshape chilies to cover cheese. Place in single layer in greased 13×9-inch baking dish.

6. In small clean bowl, beat egg whites until soft peaks form; fold into yolk mixture. Pour over chilies.

7. Bake 20 to 25 minutes or until topping is puffed and knife inserted in center comes out clean. Broil 4 inches below heat 30 seconds or until topping is golden brown. Serve with desired garnishes. *Makes 4 servings*

Cheesy Baked Barley

Eggplant Crêpes with Roasted Tomato Sauce

Roasted Tomato Sauce (recipe follows)
2 eggplants (about 8 to 9 inches long), cut lengthwise into 18 (¼-inch-thick) slices
Nonstick olive oil cooking spray
1 package (10 ounces) frozen chopped spinach, thawed and pressed dry
1 cup ricotta cheese
½ cup grated Parmesan cheese
1¼ cups (5 ounces) shredded Gruyère* cheese
Fresh oregano leaves for garnish

**Gruyère cheese is a Swiss cheese that has been aged for 10 to 12 months. Any Swiss cheese may be substituted.*

1. Prepare Roasted Tomato Sauce. *Reduce oven temperature to 425°F.*

2. Arrange eggplant on nonstick baking sheets in single layer. Spray both sides of eggplant slices with cooking spray. Bake eggplant 10 minutes; turn and bake 5 to 10 minutes or until tender. Cool. *Reduce oven temperature to 350°F.*

3. Combine spinach, ricotta and Parmesan cheese; mix well. Spray 12×8-inch baking pan with cooking spray. Spread spinach mixture evenly on eggplant slices; roll up slices, beginning at short ends. Place rolls, seam side down, in baking dish.

4. Cover dish with foil. Bake 25 minutes. Uncover; sprinkle rolls with Gruyère cheese. Bake, uncovered, 5 minutes or until cheese is melted.

5. Serve with Roasted Tomato Sauce. Garnish, if desired.

Makes 4 to 6 servings

Roasted Tomato Sauce

20 ripe plum tomatoes (about 2⅔ pounds), cut in half and seeded
3 tablespoons olive oil, divided
½ teaspoon salt
⅓ cup minced fresh basil
½ teaspoon black pepper

Preheat oven to 450°F. Toss tomatoes with 1 tablespoon oil and salt. Place, cut sides down, on nonstick baking sheet. Bake 20 to 25 minutes or until skins are blistered. Cool. Process tomatoes, remaining 2 tablespoons oil, basil and pepper in food processor until smooth.

Makes about 1 cup

Easy Cheesy Lasagna

2 tablespoons olive oil
3 small zucchini, quartered and thinly sliced
1 package (8 ounces) mushrooms, thinly sliced
1 medium onion, chopped
5 cloves garlic, minced
2 containers (15 ounces each) reduced-fat ricotta cheese
¼ cup grated Parmesan cheese
2 eggs
½ teaspoon dried Italian seasoning
¼ teaspoon garlic salt
⅛ teaspoon black pepper
1 can (28 ounces) crushed tomatoes in purée, undrained
1 jar (26 ounces) spaghetti sauce
1 package (16 ounces) lasagna noodles, uncooked
4 cups (16 ounces) shredded mozzarella cheese, divided

Preheat oven to 375°F. Spray 13×9-inch baking dish or lasagna pan with nonstick cooking spray.

Heat oil in large skillet over medium heat until hot. Add zucchini, mushrooms, onion and garlic. Cook and stir 5 minutes or until vegetables are tender. Set aside.

Combine ricotta, Parmesan, eggs, Italian seasoning, garlic salt and pepper in medium bowl. Combine tomatoes and spaghetti sauce in another medium bowl.

Spread about ¾ cup tomato mixture in prepared dish. Place layer of noodles over tomato mixture, overlapping noodles. Spread half of vegetable mixture over noodles; top with half of ricotta mixture. Sprinkle 1 cup mozzarella over ricotta mixture. Place second layer of noodles over mozzarella. Spread about 1 cup tomato mixture over noodles. Top with remaining vegetable and ricotta cheese mixtures. Sprinkle 1 cup mozzarella over ricotta mixture. Place third layer of noodles over mozzarella. Spread remaining tomato mixture over noodles. Sprinkle remaining 2 cups mozzarella evenly over top.

Cover tightly with foil and bake 1 hour or until noodles in center are soft. Uncover; bake 5 minutes or until cheese is melted and lightly browned. Remove from oven; cover and let stand 15 minutes before serving.

Makes 6 servings

Eggplant Crêpes with Roasted Tomato Sauce

Gourmet Bean & Spinach Burritos

Avocado Relish (recipe follows)
1 pound spinach leaves, divided
2 teaspoons olive oil
1 cup finely chopped onion
2 cloves garlic, minced
2 cans (15 ounces each) black beans, drained
1 can (10 ounces) whole tomatoes with green chilies, undrained
2 teaspoons ground cumin
½ teaspoon ground oregano
8 flour tortillas (8-inch)
2 cups (8 ounces) shredded Monterey Jack cheese
Sour cream (optional)

1. Prepare Avocado Relish.

2. Wash and dry spinach. Remove and discard stems from spinach leaves. Set aside 24 to 30 large leaves. Stack remaining leaves and cut crosswise into ¼-inch-wide pieces. Set aside.

3. Heat olive oil in large nonstick skillet over medium heat until hot. Add onion and garlic; cook and stir 5 minutes or until tender. Add beans, tomatoes, cumin and oregano. Simmer, uncovered, until mixture is dry. Remove from heat; mash bean mixture with potato masher.

4. Preheat oven to 350°F. Arrange 3 to 4 whole spinach leaves on each tortilla. Spoon bean mixture onto bottom half of tortillas; sprinkle cheese evenly over bean mixture.

5. Roll up to enclose filling. Repeat with remaining tortillas, spinach and bean mixture.

6. Arrange, seam side down, in 12×8-inch baking dish. Cover with foil. Bake 20 minutes or until heated through.

7. To serve, arrange about ½ cup spinach pieces on each serving plate; top with 2 burritos. Serve with Avocado Relish. Garnish, if desired.

Makes 4 servings

Avocado Relish

1 large, firm, ripe avocado, finely diced
2 tablespoons fresh lime juice
¾ cup finely chopped seeded tomato
½ cup minced green onions
⅓ cup minced fresh cilantro
½ to 1 teaspoon hot pepper sauce

Combine avocado and lime juice in bowl; toss. Add tomato, onions, cilantro and hot sauce; toss gently. Cover and refrigerate 1 hour. Serve at room temperature.

Makes about 2¼ cups

Creamy Vegetable Casserole

1 large butternut squash, (about 2½ pounds), peeled and cut into ¼-inch-thick slices
1 teaspoon chopped fresh thyme leaves *or* ¼ teaspoon dried thyme leaves, crushed
1 package (10 ounces) frozen chopped spinach, thawed and squeezed dry
1 jar (16 ounces) RAGÚ® Cheese Creations!® Classic Alfredo Sauce
½ cup chicken broth or water
⅔ cup grated Parmesan cheese
3 tablespoons fresh bread crumbs

1. Preheat oven to 400°F. In greased 2½-quart casserole, arrange ½ of the squash. Season, if desired, with salt and ground black pepper. Sprinkle with ½ teaspoon thyme, then top with spinach and remaining squash.

2. In medium bowl, combine Ragú Cheese Creations! Sauce and broth; evenly pour over vegetables. Cover with aluminum foil and bake 40 minutes or until squash is tender.

3. Remove foil and sprinkle with cheese combined with bread crumbs. Bake an additional 15 minutes or until golden.

Makes 6 servings

Tip: Make this dish one day ahead, then reheat before serving.

Prep Time: 15 minutes
Cook Time: 55 minutes

Italian Baked Frittata

1 cup broccoli flowerettes
½ cup sliced mushrooms
½ red bell pepper, cut into rings
2 green onions, sliced into 1-inch pieces
1 tablespoon margarine
8 eggs
¼ cup GREY POUPON® Dijon or COUNTRY DIJON® Mustard
¼ cup water
½ teaspoon Italian seasoning
1 cup (4 ounces) shredded Swiss cheese

1. Cook broccoli, mushrooms, red pepper and green onions in margarine in 10-inch ovenproof skillet over medium-high heat until tender-crisp, about 5 minutes. Remove from heat.

2. Beat eggs, mustard, water and Italian seasoning in small bowl with electric mixer at medium speed until foamy; stir in cheese. Pour mixture into skillet over vegetables.

3. Bake at 375°F for 20 to 25 minutes or until set. Serve immediately.

Makes 4 servings

Gourmet Bean & Spinach Burritos

Lasagna à la Zucchini

- **8 (2-inch-wide) uncooked lasagna noodles**
- **3 medium zucchini, thinly sliced**
- **1 can (16 ounces) Italian-style sliced stewed tomatoes, drained**
- **¼ pound fresh mushrooms, cut into thin slices**
- **1 small onion, chopped**
- **2 cloves garlic, minced**
- **1 teaspoon dried Italian seasoning**
- **¼ teaspoon salt**
- **⅛ teaspoon black pepper**
- **1 can (6 ounces) tomato paste**
- **1 container (16 ounces) small curd cottage cheese**
- **6 eggs, lightly beaten**
- **¼ cup grated Parmesan cheese**
- **2 cups (8 ounces) shredded mozzarella cheese**

1. Preheat oven to 350°F.

2. Cook lasagna noodles according to package directions until tender but still firm. Drain; set aside.

3. Combine zucchini, tomatoes, mushrooms, onion, garlic, Italian seasoning, salt and pepper in large skillet. Cook over medium-high heat 5 to 7 minutes or until zucchini is tender. Stir in tomato paste; remove from heat.

4. Combine cottage cheese, eggs and Parmesan cheese in medium bowl; stir until well blended.

5. Place 4 noodles on bottom of greased 13×9-inch baking dish. Pour ½ of egg mixture evenly over noodles. Cover egg mixture with ½ of tomato mixture; sprinkle with 1½ cups mozzarella. Repeat layers with remaining ingredients, ending with ½ cup mozzarella.

6. Bake covered 30 minutes. Uncover; bake 10 minutes or until heated through. Let stand 10 minutes before serving. *Makes 8 to 10 servings*

Mushroom Frittata

- **1 teaspoon butter or margarine**
- **1 medium zucchini, shredded**
- **1 medium tomato, chopped**
- **1 can (4 ounces) sliced mushrooms, drained**
- **6 eggs, beaten**
- **2 cups (8 ounces) shredded Swiss cheese**
- **¼ cup milk**
- **2 teaspoons Dijon mustard**
- **½ teaspoon LAWRY'S® Seasoned Salt**
- **½ teaspoon LAWRY'S® Seasoned Pepper**

In large, ovenproof skillet, melt butter. Cook zucchini, tomato and mushrooms over medium-high heat

Lasagna à la Zucchini

1 minute. In large bowl, combine remaining ingredients; mix well. Pour egg mixture into skillet; cook 10 minutes over low heat. To brown top, place skillet under broiler 2 to 3 minutes. *Makes 4 servings*

Serving Suggestion: Serve directly from skillet or remove frittata to serving dish. Serve with additional Swiss cheese and fresh fruit.

Hint: Try serving frittata with prepared LAWRY'S® Spaghetti Sauce Seasoning Blend with Imported Mushrooms.

Eggplant Pasta Bake

4 ounces bow-tie pasta
1 pound eggplant, diced
1 clove garlic, minced
¼ cup olive oil
1½ cups shredded Monterey Jack cheese, divided
1 cup sliced green onions
½ cup grated Parmesan cheese
1 can (14½ ounces) DEL MONTE® Diced Tomatoes with Basil, Garlic & Oregano

1. Preheat oven to 350°F. Cook pasta according to package directions; drain.

2. Cook eggplant and garlic in oil in large skillet over medium-high heat until tender.

3. Toss eggplant with cooked pasta, 1 cup Jack cheese, green onions and Parmesan cheese.

4. Place in greased 9-inch square baking dish. Top with undrained tomatoes and remaining ½ cup Jack cheese. Bake 15 minutes or until heated through.

Makes 6 servings

Prep and Cook Time: 30 minutes

Lentil Stew over Couscous

1 cup dried lentils
2 tablespoons butter or margarine
1 medium onion, chopped
2 medium ribs celery, sliced
1 small green bell pepper, chopped
1¾ cups chicken broth
¾ cup canned tomato purée
½ cup water
½ teaspoon dried marjoram leaves
¼ teaspoon salt
⅛ teaspoon black pepper
1½ to 2 cups hot cooked couscous
½ cup shredded Swiss cheese
Celery leaves and carrot curls for garnish

1. Rinse lentils thoroughly in colander under cold water, picking out any debris or blemished lentils; set aside.

2. Heat butter in large saucepan over medium heat. Add onion; cook until tender. Add celery, bell pepper, lentils, chicken broth, tomato purée, water, marjoram, salt and pepper to onion. Bring to a boil over high heat. Reduce heat to medium-low; simmer, uncovered, about 45 minutes or until lentils are tender, stirring occasionally. Add additional water if lentils are not tender and mixture becomes dry.

3. Serve lentil mixture over couscous. Sprinkle with cheese. Garnish, if desired. *Makes 4 servings*

Pasta Roll-Ups

1 package (1.5 ounces) LAWRY'S® Original-Style Spaghetti Sauce Spices & Seasonings
1 can (6 ounces) tomato paste
2¼ cups water
2 tablespoons butter or vegetable oil
2 cups cottage cheese or ricotta cheese
1 cup (4 ounces) shredded mozzarella cheese
¼ cup grated Parmesan cheese
2 eggs, lightly beaten
½ to 1 teaspoon LAWRY'S® Garlic Salt
½ teaspoon dried basil, crushed (optional)
8 ounces lasagna noodles, cooked and drained

In medium saucepan, prepare Spaghetti Sauce Spices & Seasonings according to package directions using tomato paste, water and butter. In large bowl, combine remaining ingredients except noodles; mix well. Spread ¼ cup cheese mixture on entire length of each lasagna noodle; roll up. Place noodles, seam side down, in microwave-safe baking dish. Cover with vented plastic wrap and microwave on HIGH 6 to 7 minutes or until cheese begins to melt. Pour sauce over rolls and microwave on HIGH 1 minute longer, if necessary, to heat sauce. *Makes 6 servings*

Serving Suggestion: Sprinkle with additional grated Parmesan cheese. Garnish with fresh basil leaves.

Meatless Sloppy Joes

- Nonstick cooking spray
- 2 cups thinly sliced onions
- 2 cups chopped green bell peppers
- 2 cloves garlic, finely chopped
- 2 tablespoons ketchup
- 1 tablespoon mustard
- 1 can (about 15 ounces) kidney beans, drained and mashed
- 1 can (8 ounces) tomato sauce
- 1 teaspoon chili powder
- Cider vinegar (optional)
- 2 sandwich rolls, halved

Slow Cooker Directions

Combine all ingredients except rolls in slow cooker. Cover and cook on LOW 5 to 5½ hours or until vegetables are tender. Serve on rolls.

Makes 4 servings

Penne Puttanesca

- 3 tablespoons olive or vegetable oil
- 2 cloves garlic, finely chopped
- 1 jar (26 to 28 ounces) RAGÚ® Old World Style® Pasta Sauce
- ¼ cup chopped pitted oil-cured olives
- 1 tablespoon capers, rinsed
- ½ teaspoon dried oregano leaves, crushed
- ¼ teaspoon crushed red pepper flakes
- 1 box (16 ounces) penne pasta, cooked, drained

In 12-inch skillet, heat oil over low heat and cook garlic 30 seconds. Stir in remaining ingredients except pasta. Simmer uncovered, stirring occasionally, 15 minutes. Serve sauce over hot pasta. Garnish, if desired, with chopped fresh parsley.

Makes 8 servings

Latin-Style Pasta & Beans

- 8 ounces uncooked mostaccioli, penne or bow tie pasta
- 1 tablespoon olive oil
- 1 medium onion, chopped
- 1 yellow or red bell pepper, diced
- 4 cloves garlic, minced
- 1 can (15 ounces) red or black beans, rinsed and drained
- ¾ cup canned vegetable broth
- ¾ cup medium-hot salsa or picante sauce
- 2 teaspoons ground cumin
- ⅓ cup coarsely chopped fresh cilantro
- Lime wedges

1. Cook pasta according to package directions, omitting salt. Drain; set aside.

2. Meanwhile, heat oil in large skillet over medium heat. Add onion; cook 5 minutes, stirring occasionally. Add bell pepper and garlic; cook 3 minutes, stirring occasionally. Add beans, vegetable broth, salsa and cumin; simmer, uncovered, 5 minutes.

3. Add pasta to skillet; cook 1 minute, tossing frequently. Stir in cilantro; spoon onto 4 plates. Serve with lime wedges.

Makes 4 servings

Red, White and Black Bean Casserole

- 2 tablespoons olive oil
- 1 yellow or green bell pepper, cut into ½-inch strips
- ½ cup sliced green onions
- 1 can (14½ ounces) chunky-style salsa
- 1 can (4½ ounces) green chilies, drained
- 1 package (1½ ounces) taco seasoning mix
- 2 tablespoons chopped fresh cilantro
- ½ teaspoon salt
- 2 cups cooked white rice
- 1 can (19 ounces) white cannellini beans, rinsed and drained
- 1 can (15½ ounces) red kidney beans, rinsed and drained
- 1 can (15½ ounces) black beans, rinsed and drained
- 1 cup (4 ounces) shredded Cheddar cheese, divided
- 1 package flour tortillas (6 inches)

Heat oil in large saucepan over medium-high heat. Cook and stir pepper and green onions about 5 minutes. Add salsa, chilies, taco seasoning, cilantro and salt; cook 5 minutes, stirring occasionally. Stir in rice and beans. Remove from heat; stir in ½ cup cheese.

Spoon mixture into prepared baking dish. Sprinkle remaining ½ cup cheese evenly over top. Cover and bake 30 to 40 minutes or until heated through. Serve with warm tortillas.

Makes 6 servings

Helpful Hints

Lime juice adds a refreshing tang to both sweet and savory dishes. A sprinkle of lime juice heightens the flavor of fruits, such as melons, mangoes and papayas.

Latin-Style Pasta & Beans

Quick Skillet Quiche

4 eggs
⅓ cup 1% milk
2 teaspoons Cajun seasoning
1 cup reduced-fat Cheddar cheese, divided
1 cup UNCLE BEN'S® Instant Rice
1 cup chopped fresh asparagus
¾ cup chopped green onions
½ cup chopped red bell pepper

1. Preheat oven to 350°F. In medium bowl, whisk eggs, milk, Cajun seasoning and ½ cup cheese. Set aside.

2. Cook rice according to package directions.

3. Meanwhile, spray medium skillet with nonstick cooking spray. Heat over medium heat until hot. Add asparagus, green onions and bell pepper. Cook and stir 5 minutes. Add rice and mix well.

4. Shape rice mixture to form crust on bottom and halfway up side of skillet. Pour egg mixture over crust. Sprinkle with remaining ½ cup cheese. Cover; cook over medium-low heat 10 minutes or until eggs are nearly set. Transfer skillet to oven and bake 5 minutes or until eggs are completely set.

Makes 6 servings

Pesto Rice and Beans

1 can (15 ounces) Great Northern beans, rinsed and drained
1 can (14 ounces) chicken broth
¾ cup uncooked long-grain white rice
1½ cups frozen cut green beans, thawed and drained
½ cup prepared pesto sauce
Grated Parmesan cheese (optional)

Slow Cooker Directions
Combine Great Northern beans, chicken broth and rice in slow cooker. Cover and cook on LOW 2 hours.

Stir in green beans; cover and cook 1 hour or until rice and beans are tender. Turn off slow cooker and remove insert to heatproof surface. Stir in pesto sauce and Parmesan cheese, if desired. Let stand, covered, 5 minutes or until cheese has melted. Serve immediately.

Makes 8 servings

Pasta with Onions and Goat Cheese

2 teaspoons olive oil
4 cups thinly sliced sweet onions
¾ cup (3 ounces) goat cheese
¼ cup skim milk
6 ounces uncooked baby bow tie or other small pasta
1 clove garlic, minced
2 tablespoons dry white wine or fat-free reduced-sodium chicken broth
1½ teaspoons chopped fresh sage *or* ½ teaspoon dried sage leaves
½ teaspoon salt
¼ teaspoon black pepper
2 tablespoons chopped toasted walnuts

Heat oil in large nonstick skillet over medium heat. Add onions; cook slowly until golden and caramelized, about 20 to 25 minutes, stirring occasionally.

Combine goat cheese and milk in small bowl; stir until well blended. Set aside.

Cook pasta according to package directions, omitting salt. Drain and set aside.

Add garlic to onions in skillet; cook until softened, about 3 minutes. Add wine, sage, salt and pepper; cook until moisture is evaporated. Remove from heat; add pasta and goat cheese mixture, stirring to melt cheese. Sprinkle with walnuts.

Makes 8 (½-cup) servings

Meatless Ravioli Bake

4 cups finely chopped eggplant
½ cup chopped onion
¼ cup chopped carrots
¼ cup chopped celery
3 tablespoons olive oil
2 cans (8 ounces each) HUNT'S® No Salt Added Tomato Sauce
1 can (14.5 ounces) HUNT'S® Crushed Tomatoes
½ teaspoon sugar
⅛ teaspoon pepper
1 package (18 ounces) frozen large ravioli, prepared according to package directions

1. Preheat oven to 375°F.

2. In saucepan, sauté eggplant, onion, carrots and celery in hot oil; cook until tender.

3. Stir in Hunt's Tomato Sauce, Hunt's Tomatoes, sugar and pepper. Simmer, uncovered, 10 minutes; stirring occasionally.

4. Spoon *1½ cups* of tomato mixture into 13×9×2-inch baking dish; top with half the ravioli and *half of the remaining sauce.* Repeat layers.

5. Bake, uncovered, 30 minutes or until bubbly.

Makes 6 (7-ounce) servings

Pasta with Onions and Goat Cheese

Polenta Lasagna

1½ cups whole grain yellow cornmeal
4 teaspoons finely chopped fresh marjoram
1 teaspoon olive oil
1 pound fresh mushrooms, sliced
1 cup chopped leeks
1 clove garlic, minced
½ cup (2 ounces) shredded part-skim mozzarella cheese
2 tablespoons chopped fresh basil
1 tablespoon chopped fresh oregano
⅛ teaspoon black pepper
2 red bell peppers, chopped
¼ cup freshly grated Parmesan cheese, divided

1. Bring 4 cups water to a boil in medium saucepan over high heat. Slowly add cornmeal to water, stirring constantly with wire whisk. Reduce heat to low; stir in marjoram. Simmer 15 to 20 minutes or until polenta thickens and pulls away from side of saucepan. Spread on 13×9-inch *ungreased* baking sheet. Cover and chill about 1 hour or until firm.

2. Heat oil in medium nonstick skillet. Cook and stir mushrooms, leeks and garlic over medium heat 5 minutes or until vegetables are crisp-tender. Stir in mozzarella, basil, oregano and black pepper.

3. Place bell peppers and ¼ cup water in food processor or blender; process until smooth. Preheat oven to 350°F. Spray 11×7-inch baking dish with nonstick cooking spray.

4. Cut cold polenta into 12 (3½-inch) squares; arrange 6 squares in bottom of prepared pan. Spread with half of bell pepper mixture, half of vegetable mixture and 2 tablespoons Parmesan Place remaining 6 squares polenta over Parmesan; top with remaining bell pepper and vegetable mixtures and Parmesan. Bake 20 minutes or until cheese is melted and polenta is golden brown.

Makes 6 servings

Quick Skillet Rice Gratin

2 tablespoons olive oil
1 onion, chopped
2 cloves garlic, minced
2 medium carrots, peeled and chopped
1 teaspoon dried thyme leaves
2 cups uncooked instant white rice
2 cups water
1 can (15½ ounces) kidney beans, drained and rinsed
1 teaspoon salt
Black pepper
⅓ cup grated Parmesan cheese

1. Heat oil in large skillet over medium-high heat until hot. Add onion and garlic; cook and stir 2 minutes. Add carrots and thyme; cook and stir 4 minutes more.

2. Add rice, water, beans and salt; season to taste with black pepper. Stir well. Bring to a boil. Reduce heat to low. Sprinkle with cheese. Cover and simmer 5 minutes or until cheese has melted and all liquid has evaporated.

Makes 4 to 6 servings

Tip: Effortless to prepare, this vegetarian gratin can be served as an entrée or as a side dish.

Prep and Cook time: 15 minutes

Saucy Mediterranean Frittata

Tomato Sauce (recipe follows)
1 tablespoon olive oil
1 small onion, chopped
1 medium tomato, seeded and diced
1 tablespoon finely chopped fresh basil *or* 1 teaspoon dried basil leaves
¼ teaspoon dried oregano leaves
⅓ cup cooked orzo
⅓ cup chopped pitted black olives
8 eggs
½ teaspoon salt
⅛ teaspoon black pepper
2 tablespoons butter
½ cup (2 ounces) shredded mozzarella cheese

1. Prepare Tomato Sauce.

2. Heat oil in ovenproof 10-inch skillet over medium heat. Cook and stir onion until tender. Add tomato, basil and oregano; cook and stir 3 minutes. Stir in orzo and olives; remove from skillet.

3. Beat eggs, salt and pepper in medium bowl with electric mixer at low speed. Stir in tomato mixture.

4. Melt butter in same skillet over medium heat. Add egg mixture; top with cheese. Reduce heat to low. Cook 8 to 10 minutes or until bottom and most of middle is set.

5. Place skillet on rack 4 inches from broiler. Broil 1 to 2 minutes or until top is browned. Cut into wedges; serve with Tomato Sauce. Garnish as desired. *Makes 4 to 6 servings*

Tomato Sauce: Combine 1 (8-ounce) can tomato sauce, 1 teaspoon minced dried onion, ¼ teaspoon *each* basil and oregano leaves, and ⅛ teaspoon *each* minced dried garlic and black pepper in small saucepan. Simmer 5 minutes stirring often. Makes about 1 cup.

Polenta Lasagna

Quick Veg•All® Enchiladas

- **1 can (15 ounces) VEG•ALL® Original Mixed Vegetables, drained**
- **1 can (15 ounces) refried beans**
- **8 (6-inch) corn tortillas**
- **1 can (10 ounces) enchilada sauce**
- **1 cup shredded Cheddar cheese**
- **1 cup sour cream**
- **½ cup chopped green onions**
- **½ cup chopped ripe olives**

Preheat oven to 350°F. Combine Veg•All and beans in medium bowl. Divide mixture and place in center of each tortilla; roll up. Place rolled tortillas in baking dish. Cover tortillas with enchilada sauce and cheese. Bake for 30 minutes. Top with sour cream, green onions, and ripe olives.

Makes 4 servings

Note: If tortillas unfold as you are assembling them, turn seam side down.

Prep Time: 7 minutes
Cook Time: 30 minutes

Southwestern Tortilla Stack

- **1 (30-ounce) can vegetarian refried beans**
- **½ cup sour cream**
- **1 (4-ounce) can chopped green chilies, drained**
- **½ teaspoon ground cumin**
- **3 (10-inch) flour tortillas**
- **1 cup (4 ounces) shredded Cheddar cheese**

1. Preheat oven to 425°F. Grease 10-inch round casserole.

2. Combine beans, sour cream, chilies and cumin; set aside.

3. Place one tortilla in bottom of prepared casserole. Top with half of the bean mixture and one third of the cheese. Top with second tortilla; repeat layers of beans and cheese.

4. Cover with remaining tortilla; sprinkle with remaining cheese. Cover.

5. Bake 20 minutes or until thoroughly heated. Cut into wedges. Serve with salsa, if desired.

Makes 4 to 6 servings

Speedy Mac & Cheese

- **1 can (10¾ ounces) condensed Cheddar cheese soup**
- **1 cup milk**
- **4 cups hot cooked medium shell macaroni (3 cups uncooked)**
- **1⅓ cups *French's® Taste Toppers™* French Fried Onions, divided**
- **1 cup (4 ounces) shredded Cheddar cheese**

Combine soup and milk in 2-quart microwavable casserole. Stir in macaroni, *⅔ cup* ***Taste Toppers*** and cheese. Cover; microwave on HIGH 10 minutes* or until heated through, stirring halfway through cooking time. Top with remaining *⅔ cup* ***Taste Toppers***. Microwave 1 minute or until ***Taste Toppers*** are golden.

Makes 6 servings

*Or, bake, covered, in 350°F oven 25 to 30 minutes.

Prep Time: 10 minutes
Cook Time: 11 minutes

Southwestern Lasagna

- **1 tablespoon vegetable oil**
- **1 medium onion, thinly sliced**
- **1 clove garlic, finely chopped**
- **1 tablespoon chili powder**
- **1 tablespoon paprika**
- **¾ cup water**
- **1 can (6 ounces) tomato paste**
- **¼ cup honey**
- **¼ cup fresh lime juice**
- **1 can (15 ounces) black beans, undrained**
- **1 can (12 ounces) whole kernel corn**
- **6 medium corn tortillas, cut in quarters**
- **1 package (15 ounces) part skim ricotta cheese**
- **1 can (7 ounces) whole green chilies, cut lengthwise into ½-inch strips**
- **½ cup (2 ounces) shredded Monterey Jack cheese**

In medium saucepan, heat oil over medium-high heat until hot; cook and stir onion and garlic 3 to 5 minutes or until onion is tender. Add chili powder and paprika; cook and stir 1 minute. Stir in water, tomato paste, honey and lime juice; stir until well mixed. Stir in black beans and corn. Bring to a boil; reduce heat and simmer 5 minutes.

Spoon ⅓ of sauce into 1½-quart rectangular baking pan; arrange ½ of tortilla quarters evenly over sauce in pan. Spread with ½ of ricotta cheese and arrange ½ of green chili strips evenly over cheese. Repeat with ⅓ of sauce, remaining tortillas, ricotta cheese and green chilies. Spread remaining sauce evenly over top of lasagna; sprinkle evenly with shredded cheese. Bake at 350°F 20 to 25 minutes, or until heated through.

Makes 6 servings

Quick Veg•All® Enchiladas

Ratatouille Pot Pie

- ¼ cup olive oil
- 1 medium eggplant (about 1 pound), peeled and cut into ½-inch pieces
- 1 large onion, chopped
- 1 green or yellow bell pepper, chopped
- 1½ teaspoons minced garlic
- 1 can (14½ ounces) pasta-ready diced tomatoes with garlic and herbs or Italian stewed tomatoes, undrained
- 1 teaspoon dried basil leaves
- ½ teaspoon red pepper flakes
- ¼ teaspoon salt
- 1 tablespoon balsamic vinegar
- 2 cups (8 ounces) shredded mozzarella cheese, divided
- 1 package (10 ounces) refrigerated pizza dough

1. Preheat oven to 425°F. Heat oil in large skillet over medium heat until hot. Add eggplant, onion, bell pepper and garlic. Cook 10 minutes or until eggplant begins to brown, stirring occasionally. Stir in tomatoes with juice, basil, pepper flakes and salt. Cook, uncovered, over medium-low heat 5 minutes.

2. Remove from heat; stir in vinegar. Let stand 10 minutes; stir in 1 cup cheese. Transfer mixture to *ungreased* 11×7-inch casserole dish. Sprinkle with remaining cheese.

3. Unroll pizza dough; arrange over top of casserole. Make decorative cut-outs using small cookie cutter, if desired. Spray dough with nonstick cooking spray. Bake 15 minutes or until crust is golden brown and vegetable mixture is bubbly. Let stand 5 minutes before serving.

Makes 6 servings

Spinach Stuffed Manicotti

- 1 package (10 ounces) frozen spinach
- 8 uncooked manicotti shells
- 1½ teaspoons olive oil
- 1 teaspoon dried rosemary
- 1 teaspoon dried sage leaves
- 1 teaspoon dried oregano leaves
- 1 teaspoon dried thyme leaves
- 1 teaspoon chopped garlic
- 1½ cups chopped fresh tomatoes
- ½ cup ricotta cheese
- ½ cup fresh whole wheat bread crumbs
- 2 egg whites, lightly beaten
- Yellow pepper rings and sage sprig for garnish

1. Cook spinach according to package directions. Place in colander to drain. Let stand until cool enough to handle. Squeeze spinach with hands to remove excess moisture. Set aside.

2. Cook pasta according to package directions, drain. Rinse under cold running water until cool enough to handle; drain.

3. Preheat oven to 350°F. Heat oil in small saucepan over medium heat. Cook and stir rosemary, sage, oregano, thyme and garlic in hot oil about 1 minute. Do not let herbs turn brown. Add tomatoes; reduce heat to low. Simmer, uncovered, 10 minutes, stirring occasionally.

4. Combine spinach, cheese and crumbs in bowl. Fold in egg whites. Fill shells with spinach mixture using spoon.

5. Place one third of tomato mixture on bottom of 13×9-inch baking pan. Arrange manicotti in pan. Pour tomato mixture over top. Cover with foil.

6. Bake 30 minutes or until bubbly. Garnish, if desired.

Makes 4 servings

Spicy Ravioli and Cheese

- 1 medium red bell pepper, thinly sliced
- 1 medium green bell pepper, thinly sliced
- 1 medium yellow bell pepper, thinly sliced
- 1 tablespoon olive or vegetable oil
- ½ teaspoon LAWRY'S® Seasoned Salt
- ¼ teaspoon LAWRY'S® Garlic Powder with Parsley
- ¼ teaspoon sugar
- 1 package (8 or 9 ounces) fresh or frozen ravioli
- 1½ cups chunky salsa
- 4 ounces mozzarella cheese, thinly sliced
- 2 green onions, sliced

Place bell peppers in broilerproof baking dish; sprinkle with oil, Seasoned Salt, Garlic Powder with Parsley and sugar. Broil 15 minutes or until tender and browned, turning once. Prepare ravioli according to package directions. Pour ¾ cup salsa in bottom of 8-inch square baking dish. Alternate layers of bell peppers, ravioli, cheese and green onions. Pour remaining ¾ cup salsa over layers. Cover with foil; bake in 350°F oven 15 to 20 minutes or until heated through and cheese melts.

Makes 4 to 6 servings

Serving Suggestion: Excellent with thin, crisp bread sticks and a small green salad.

Ratatouille Pot Pie

Triple Pepper Tomato Provolone Lasagna

1 red bell pepper, chopped
1 yellow bell pepper, chopped
1 green bell pepper, chopped
1 package (8 ounces) sliced fresh mushrooms
½ cup chopped onion
1 cup thinly sliced zucchini
4 cloves garlic, minced
1½ cups vegetable juice cocktail
1 can (16 ounces) diced tomatoes, undrained
1½ to 1¾ teaspoons dried Italian seasoning
1 tablespoon olive oil
9 uncooked lasagna noodles
1 cup nonfat cottage cheese
⅓ cup grated Parmesan cheese
4 ounces sliced reduced-fat provolone cheese

1. Preheat oven to 350°F. Combine peppers, mushrooms, onion, zucchini, garlic, vegetable juice cocktail, tomatoes with juice and Italian seasoning in Dutch oven. Bring to a boil over high heat. Reduce heat to low; simmer, uncovered, 15 minutes. Remove from heat; stir in oil.

2. Spray 12×8-inch baking pan with nonstick cooking spray. Place 3 lasagna noodles on bottom of pan. Spread ⅓ of the sauce over noodles. Spread ½ cup cottage cheese evenly over sauce; sprinkle with 2 tablespoons Parmesan cheese. Repeat layers, ending with sauce.

3. Bake, uncovered, 1 hour or until bubbly. Tear provolone cheese in small pieces; place on top of lasagna. Sprinkle with remaining Parmesan cheese. Bake 5 minutes longer or until cheese is melted. Let stand 15 minutes before serving.

Makes 6 servings

Tip: For extra convenience, purchase 3 cups chopped red, green and yellow bell pepper mixture from the grocery store salad bar.

Skillet Pesto Tortellini

1¼ cups water
1¼ cups milk
1 envelope (1.2 ounces) creamy pesto sauce mix
1 package (16 ounces) frozen vegetable medley
1 package (12 ounces) frozen tortellini
Dash ground red pepper
½ cup (2 ounces) shredded mozzarella cheese

1. Blend water, milk and sauce mix in large deep skillet. Bring to a boil over high heat. Stir in vegetables, tortellini and ground red pepper; return to a boil.

2. Cook vegetables and tortellini, uncovered, over medium-high heat 8 to 10 minutes or until tortellini is tender and sauce has thickened, stirring occasionally.

3. Sprinkle with cheese just before serving. *Makes 4 servings*

Prep and Cook Time: 22 minutes

Valley Eggplant Parmigiano

2 eggplants (about 1 pound each)
⅓ cup olive or vegetable oil
1 container (15 ounces) ricotta cheese
2 packages (1 ounce each) HIDDEN VALLEY® Milk Recipe Original Ranch® Salad Dressing Mix
2 eggs
2 teaspoons dry bread crumbs
1 cup tomato sauce
½ cup shredded mozzarella cheese
1 tablespoon grated Parmesan cheese
Chopped parsley

Preheat oven to 350°F. Cut eggplants into ½-inch slices. Brush some of the oil onto two large baking sheets. Arrange eggplant slices in single layer on sheets and brush tops with additional oil. Bake until eggplant is fork-tender, about 20 minutes.

In large bowl, whisk together ricotta cheese and salad dressing mix; whisk in eggs. In 13×9×2-inch baking dish, layer half the eggplant. Sprinkle 1 teaspoon bread crumbs over eggplant; spread ricotta mixture on top. Arrange remaining eggplant in another layer. Sprinkle with remaining 1 teaspoon bread crumbs; top with tomato sauce. Sprinkle cheeses on top. Bake until cheeses begin to brown, about 30 minutes. Sprinkle with parsley.

Makes 6 to 8 servings

Vegetarian Stir-Fry

1 bag (16 ounces) BIRDS EYE® frozen Mixed Vegetables
2 tablespoons water
1 can (14 ounces) kidney beans, drained
1 jar (14 ounces) spaghetti sauce
½ teaspoon garlic powder
½ cup grated Parmesan cheese

• In large skillet, place vegetables in water. Cover; cook 7 to 10 minutes over medium heat.

• Uncover; stir in beans, spaghetti sauce and garlic powder; cook until heated through.

• Sprinkle with cheese.

Makes 4 servings

Serving Suggestion: Serve over hot cooked rice or pasta.

Prep Time: 2 minutes
Cook Time: 12 to 15 minutes

Skillet Pesto Tortellini

Spicy African Chick-Pea and Sweet Potato Stew

Spice Paste (recipe follows)
1½ pounds sweet potatoes, peeled and cubed
2 cups canned vegetable broth or water
1 can (16 ounces) plum tomatoes, undrained, chopped
1 can (16 ounces) chick-peas, drained and rinsed
1½ cups sliced fresh okra *or* 1 package (10 ounces) frozen cut okra, thawed
Yellow Couscous (recipe follows)
Hot pepper sauce
Fresh cilantro for garnish

1. Prepare Spice Paste.

2. Combine sweet potatoes, broth, tomatoes with juice, chick-peas, okra and Spice Paste in large saucepan. Bring to a boil over high heat. Reduce heat to low. Cover and simmer 15 minutes. Uncover; simmer 10 minutes or until vegetables are tender.

3. Meanwhile, prepare Yellow Couscous.

4. Serve stew with couscous and pepper sauce. Garnish, if desired.

Makes 4 servings

Spice Paste

6 cloves garlic, peeled
1 teaspoon coarse salt
2 teaspoons sweet paprika
1½ teaspoons cumin seeds
1 teaspoon cracked black pepper
½ teaspoon ground ginger
½ teaspoon ground allspice
1 tablespoon olive oil

Process garlic and salt in blender or small food processor until garlic is finely chopped. Add remaining spices. Process 15 seconds. While blender is running, pour oil through cover opening; process until mixture forms paste. *Makes 3 cups*

Yellow Couscous

1 tablespoon olive oil
5 green onions, sliced
1⅔ cups water
⅛ teaspoon saffron threads *or* ½ teaspoon ground turmeric
¼ teaspoon salt
1 cup precooked couscous*

**Check ingredient label for "precooked semolina."*

Heat oil in medium saucepan over medium heat until hot. Add onions; cook and stir 4 minutes. Add water, saffron and salt. Bring to a boil. Stir in couscous. Remove from heat. Cover; let stand 5 minutes.

Makes 3 cups

Vegetable Cheese Frittata

½ cup fresh green beans, cut into 1-inch pieces
1 small onion, chopped
3 tablespoons butter or margarine
¼ red bell pepper, chopped
¼ cup sliced fresh mushrooms
¼ cup dry bread crumbs
½ cup prepared HIDDEN VALLEY® Original Ranch® salad dressing
6 eggs, beaten
⅓ cup shredded Cheddar cheese
¼ cup grated Parmesan cheese

Preheat oven to 350°F. In medium saucepan, steam green beans over boiling water until crisp-tender, about 4 minutes. In medium skillet, sauté onion in butter until onion is softened; stir in beans, red pepper and mushrooms. Fold vegetables, bread crumbs and salad dressing into eggs. Pour into buttered quiche dish. Sprinkle with cheeses. Bake until set, about 25 minutes.

Makes 6 servings

Vegetarian Paella

1 tablespoon olive oil
1 medium onion, chopped
1 serrano pepper,* finely chopped
1 red bell pepper, diced
1 green bell pepper, diced
3 cloves garlic, minced
½ teaspoon saffron threads, crushed
½ teaspoon paprika
1 cup uncooked long-grain white rice
3 cups water
1 can (15 ounces) chick-peas, rinsed and drained
14 ounces artichoke hearts in water, drained and cut into halves
1 cup frozen green peas
1½ teaspoons grated lemon peel

**Serrano peppers can sting and irritate the skin; wear rubber gloves when handling peppers and do not touch eyes. Wash hands after handling.*

1. Preheat oven to 375°F. Heat oil in large paella pan or heavy, ovenproof skillet over medium-high heat. Add onion, serrano pepper and bell peppers; cook and stir about 7 minutes.

2. Add garlic, saffron and paprika; cook 3 minutes. Add rice; cook and stir 1 minute. Add water, chick-peas, artichoke hearts, green peas and lemon peel; mix well.

3. Cover and bake 25 minutes or until rice is tender. Garnish with fresh bay leaves and lemon slices, if desired.

Makes 6 servings

Spicy African Chick-Pea and Sweet Potato Stew

Herbed Veggie Cheese and Rice

- 1 bag (16 ounces) BIRDS EYE® frozen Farm Fresh Mixtures Broccoli, Green Beans, Pearl Onions & Red Peppers
- 2 cups cooked white rice
- 2 tablespoons grated Parmesan cheese
- 1 teaspoon dried basil
- 1 teaspoon dill weed
- ½ cup reduced-fat shredded Cheddar cheese
- ½ cup reduced-fat shredded Monterey Jack cheese

• In large saucepan, cook vegetables according to package directions; drain and return to saucepan.

• Add rice, using fork to keep rice fluffy.

• Add Parmesan cheese, basil, dill and salt and pepper to taste.

• Add Cheddar and Monterey Jack cheeses; toss together. Cook over medium heat until heated through.

Makes 4 servings

Prep Time: 6 minutes
Cook Time: 12 to 15 minutes

Spinach and Mushroom Enchiladas

- 2 packages (10 ounces each) frozen chopped spinach, thawed
- 1½ cups sliced mushrooms
- 1 can (15 ounces) pinto beans, drained and rinsed
- 3 teaspoons chili powder, divided
- ¼ teaspoon red pepper flakes
- 1 can (8 ounces) low-sodium tomato sauce
- 2 tablespoons water
- ½ teaspoon hot pepper sauce
- 8 (8-inch) corn tortillas
- 1 cup shredded Monterey Jack cheese
- Shredded lettuce (optional)
- Chopped tomatoes (optional)
- Low-fat sour cream (optional)

1. Combine spinach, mushrooms, beans, 2 teaspoons chili powder and red pepper in large skillet over medium heat. Cook and stir 5 minutes; remove from heat.

2. Combine tomato sauce, water, remaining 1 teaspoon chili powder and pepper sauce in medium skillet. Dip tortillas into tomato sauce mixture; stack tortillas on waxed paper.

3. Divide spinach filling into 8 portions. Spoon onto center of tortillas; roll up and place in 11×8-inch microwavable dish. (Secure rolls with wooden picks if desired.) Spread remaining tomato sauce mixture over enchiladas.

4. Cover with vented plastic wrap. Microwave at MEDIUM (50%) 10 minutes or until heated through. Sprinkle with cheese. Microwave at MEDIUM 3 minutes or until cheese is melted. Serve with lettuce, tomatoes and sour cream.

Makes 4 servings

Southwestern Two Bean Chili & Rice

- 1 bag (about ½ cup uncooked) boil-in-bag white rice
- 1 tablespoon vegetable oil
- 1 cup chopped onion
- 1 cup chopped green bell pepper
- 1½ teaspoons bottled minced garlic
- 1 can (15½ ounces) chili beans in spicy or mild sauce, undrained
- 1 can (15½ ounces) black or pinto beans, drained
- 1 can (10 ounces) diced tomatoes with green chilies, undrained
- 1 tablespoon chili powder
- 2 teaspoons ground cumin
- 1 cup (4 ounces) shredded Cheddar or Monterey Jack cheese

1. Cook rice according to package directions.

2. While rice is cooking, heat oil in large saucepan over medium-high heat until hot. Add onion, bell pepper and garlic. Cook 5 minutes, stirring occasionally. Stir in chili beans with sauce, black beans, tomatoes with juice, chili powder and cumin. Cover; bring to a boil over high heat. Reduce heat to medium-low. Simmer, covered, 10 minutes.

3. Transfer rice to 4 shallow bowls. Ladle bean mixture over rice; top with cheese.

Makes 4 servings

Prep and Cook Time: 20 minutes

Spinach and Mushroom Enchiladas

Vegetable & Tofu Gratin

Nonstick cooking spray
1 teaspoon olive oil
¾ cup thinly sliced fennel bulb
¾ cup thinly sliced onion
2 cloves garlic, minced
¾ cup cooked brown rice
2 tablespoons balsamic vinegar, divided
2 teaspoons dried Italian seasoning, divided
3 ounces firm tofu, crumbled
¼ cup crumbled feta cheese
6 ounces ripe plum tomatoes, sliced ¼ inch thick
6 ounces zucchini, sliced ¼ inch thick
⅛ teaspoon salt
⅛ teaspoon black pepper
¼ cup fresh bread crumbs
2 tablespoons grated fresh Parmesan cheese

1. Preheat oven to 400°F. Spray 1-quart shallow baking dish with nonstick cooking spray.

2. Spray medium skillet with cooking spray. Heat oil in skillet over medium heat. Add fennel and onion. Cook 10 minutes or until tender and lightly browned, stirring often. Add garlic; cook and stir 1 minute. Spread over bottom of prepared baking dish.

3. Combine rice, 1 tablespoon vinegar and ½ teaspoon Italian seasoning in small bowl. Spread over onion mixture.

4. Combine tofu, feta cheese, remaining 1 tablespoon vinegar and 1 teaspoon Italian seasoning in same small bowl; toss to combine. Spoon over rice.

5. Top with alternating rows of tomato and zucchini slices. Sprinkle with salt and pepper.

6. Combine bread crumbs, Parmesan cheese and remaining ½ teaspoon Italian seasoning. Sprinkle over top. Spray bread crumb topping lightly with cooking spray. Bake 30 minutes or until heated through and topping is browned. *Makes 2 servings*

Vegetable Lasagna

Tomato-Basil Sauce (recipe follows)
2 tablespoons olive oil
4 medium carrots, thinly sliced
3 medium zucchini, thinly sliced
6 ounces spinach leaves, washed, stemmed and torn in bite-size pieces
¼ teaspoon salt
¼ teaspoon black pepper
1 egg
3 cups ricotta cheese
½ cup plus 2 tablespoons grated Parmesan cheese, divided
12 uncooked lasagna noodles
1½ cups (6 ounces) shredded mozzarella cheese
1½ cups (6 ounces) shredded Monterey Jack cheese
½ cup water
Belgian endive leaves, Bibb lettuce leaves and fresh basil sprigs for garnish

1. Prepare Tomato-Basil Sauce.

2. Heat oil in large skillet over medium heat until hot. Add carrots; cook and stir 4 minutes. Add zucchini; cook and stir 8 minutes or until crisp-tender. Add spinach; cook and stir 1 minute or until spinach is wilted. Stir in salt and pepper.

3. Preheat oven to 350°F. Beat egg in medium bowl. Stir in ricotta cheese and ½ cup Parmesan cheese.

4. Spread 1 cup Tomato-Basil Sauce in bottom of 13×9-inch baking pan; top with 4 uncooked lasagna noodles. Spoon ⅓ of ricotta cheese mixture over noodles; carefully spread with spatula.

5. Spoon ⅓ of vegetable mixture over cheese. Top with 1 cup Tomato-Basil Sauce. Sprinkle with ½ cup each mozzarella and Monterey Jack cheeses. Repeat layers 2 times beginning with noodles and ending with mozzarella and Monterey Jack cheeses. Sprinkle with remaining 2 tablespoons Parmesan cheese.

6. Carefully pour water around sides of pan. Cover pan tightly with foil.

7. Bake lasagna 1 hour or until bubbly. Uncover. Let stand 10 to 15 minutes. Cut into squares. Garnish, if desired.
Makes 8 servings

Tomato-Basil Sauce

2 cans (28 ounces each) plum tomatoes
1 teaspoon olive oil
1 medium onion, chopped
3 cloves garlic, minced
1 tablespoon sugar
1 tablespoon dried basil leaves
¼ teaspoon salt
¼ teaspoon black pepper

1. Drain tomatoes, reserving ½ cup juice. Seed and chop tomatoes.

2. Heat oil in large skillet over medium heat until hot. Add onion and garlic; cook and stir 5 minutes or until tender. Stir in tomatoes, reserved juice, sugar, basil, salt and pepper.

3. Bring to a boil over high heat. Reduce heat to low. Simmer, uncovered, 25 to 30 minutes or until most of juices have evaporated.
Makes 4 cups

Vegetable Lasagna

Comforting Soups

Farmhouse Ham and Vegetable Chowder

- 2 cans (10¾ ounces each) cream of celery soup
- 2 cups diced cooked ham
- 1 package (10 ounces) frozen corn
- 1 large baking potato, cut in ½-inch pieces
- 1 medium red bell pepper, diced
- ½ teaspoon dried thyme leaves
- 2 cups small broccoli florets
- ½ cup milk

Slow Cooker Directions

1. Combine all ingredients, except broccoli and milk in slow cooker; stir to blend. Cover and cook on LOW 6 to 8 hours or on HIGH 3 to 4 hours.

2. If cooking on LOW, turn to HIGH and stir in broccoli and milk. Cover and cook 15 minutes or until broccoli is crisp tender.

Makes 6 servings

Campfire Sausage and Potato Soup

- 1 can (15½ ounces) dark kidney beans, rinsed and drained
- 1 can (14½ ounces) diced tomatoes, undrained
- 1 can (10½ ounces) condensed beef broth, undiluted
- 8 ounces kielbasa sausage, cut lengthwise into halves, then crosswise into ½-inch pieces
- 1 large baking potato, cut into ½-inch cubes
- 1 medium green bell pepper, diced
- 1 medium onion, diced
- 1 teaspoon dried oregano leaves
- ½ teaspoon sugar
- 1 to 2 teaspoons ground cumin

Slow Cooker Directions

Combine all ingredients, except cumin, in slow cooker. Cover and cook on LOW 8 hours or on HIGH 4 hours. Stir in cumin; serve.

Makes 6 to 7 servings

Ham and Navy Bean Soup

- 8 ounces dried navy beans, rinsed and drained
- 6 cups water
- 1 ham bone
- 1 medium yellow onion, chopped
- 2 stalks celery, finely chopped
- 2 bay leaves
- 1½ teaspoons dried tarragon leaves
- 1½ teaspoons salt
- ¼ teaspoon black pepper

Slow Cooker Directions

1. Place beans in large bowl; cover completely with water. Soak 6 to 8 hours or overnight. Drain beans; discard water.

2. Combine beans, water, ham bone, onion, celery, bay leaves and tarragon leaves in slow cooker. Cook on LOW 8 hours or on HIGH 4 hours. Discard ham bone and bay leaves; stir in salt and pepper.

Makes 8 servings

Farmhouse Ham and Vegetable Chowder

Garden Soup Italiano

½ pound boneless tender beef steak (sirloin, rib eye or top loin)
4 tablespoons KIKKOMAN® Soy Sauce, divided
1 teaspoon cornstarch
1 large clove garlic, minced
1 tablespoon vegetable oil
2 cups water
1½ pounds fresh Italian plum tomatoes, coarsely chopped
2 teaspoons chopped fresh oregano *or* ½ teaspoon dried oregano, crumbled
¾ teaspoon sugar
¼ pound fresh green beans, trimmed and cut into 1-inch lengths
½ cup uncooked elbow macaroni
1 can (8 ounces) kidney beans, rinsed and drained

Cut beef into ½-inch cubes. Combine 1 tablespoon soy sauce, cornstarch and garlic in small bowl; stir in beef. Heat oil in Dutch oven or large saucepan over high heat. Add beef and stir-fry 1 minute; remove. Add water, remaining 3 tablespoons soy sauce, tomatoes, oregano and sugar to Dutch oven, stirring to combine. Simmer, covered, 15 minutes. Add green beans; simmer, covered, 10 minutes. Stir in macaroni and simmer, covered, 10 minutes longer, or until macaroni is tender, yet firm. Add beef and kidney beans; cook and stir just until beans are heated.

Makes 4 to 6 servings

Ground Beef, Spinach and Barley Soup

12 ounces lean ground beef
4 cups water
1 can (14½ ounces) no-salt-added stewed tomatoes, undrained
1½ cups thinly sliced carrots
1 cup chopped onion
½ cup quick-cooking barley
1½ teaspoons beef bouillon granules
1½ teaspoons dried thyme leaves, crushed
1 teaspoon dried oregano leaves, crushed
½ teaspoon garlic powder
¼ teaspoon black pepper
⅛ teaspoon salt
3 cups torn stemmed washed spinach leaves

Cook beef in large saucepan over medium heat until no longer pink, stirring to separate. Rinse beef under warm water; drain. Return beef to saucepan; add water, stewed tomatoes with juice, carrots, onion, barley, bouillon granules, thyme, oregano, garlic powder, pepper and salt.

Bring to a boil over high heat. Reduce heat to medium-low. Cover and simmer 12 to 15 minutes or until barley and vegetables are tender, stirring occasionally. Stir in spinach; cook until spinach starts to wilt.

Makes 4 servings

Fiesta Black Bean Soup

6 cups chicken broth
¾ pound potatoes, peeled and diced
1 can (16 ounces) black beans, drained
½ pound ham, diced
½ onion, diced
1 can (4 ounces) chopped jalapeño peppers
2 cloves garlic, minced
2 teaspoons dried oregano leaves
1½ teaspoons dried thyme leaves
1 teaspoon ground cumin
Sour cream, chopped bell peppers and chopped tomatoes for garnish

Slow Cooker Directions

Combine all ingredients, except garnish, in slow cooker. Cover and cook on LOW 8 to 10 hours or on HIGH 4 to 5 hours. Garnish, if desired.

Makes 6 to 8 servings

Helpful Hints

Barley is available in several forms: hulled, grits, scotch barley and pearled. The most common form, pearled barley, has been polished to remove the bran and most of the germ. Pearled barley is also available in a quick-cooking form.

Fiesta Black Bean Soup

Navy Bean Bacon Chowder

Slow Cooker

1½ cups dried navy beans, rinsed
2 cups cold water
6 slices thick-cut bacon
1 medium carrot, cut lengthwise into halves, then cut into 1-inch pieces
1 rib celery, chopped
1 medium onion, chopped
1 small turnip, cut into 1-inch pieces
1 teaspoon dried Italian seasoning
⅛ teaspoon black pepper
1 large can (46 ounces) reduced-sodium chicken broth
1 cup milk

Slow Cooker Directions
Soak beans overnight in cold water.

Cook bacon in medium skillet over medium heat. Drain and crumble. Combine carrot, celery, onion, turnip, Italian seasoning, pepper, beans and bacon in slow cooker; mix slightly. Pour broth over top. Cover and cook on LOW 7½ to 9 hours or until beans are crisp-tender.

Ladle 2 cups of soup mixture into food processor or blender. Process until smooth; return to slow cooker. Add milk; cover and heat on HIGH 10 minutes or until heated through.

Makes 6 servings

Creamy Reuben Soup

1 cup FRANK'S® or SNOWFLOSS® Kraut, well drained
½ cup chopped onion
¼ cup chopped celery
3 tablespoons butter or margarine
¼ cup unsifted flour
3 cups water
4 teaspoons beef-flavored bouillon *or* 4 beef bouillon cubes
½ pound corned beef, shredded
3 cups half-and-half
3 cups (12 ounces) shredded Swiss cheese, divided
6 to 8 slices rye or pumpernickel bread, toasted and cut into quarters

1. In large saucepan, cook onion and celery in butter until tender.

2. Stir in flour until smooth.

3. Gradually stir in water and bouillon and bring to boil. Reduce heat and simmer uncovered 5 minutes.

4. Add corned beef, kraut, half-and-half and 1 cup cheese.

5. Cook over low heat for 30 minutes until slightly thickened, stirring frequently.

6. Ladle into 8 oven-proof bowls. Top each with toasted bread and ¼ cup cheese. Broil until cheese melts. Serve immediately.

Makes 8 servings

Prep Time: 20 minutes
Cook Time: 45 minutes

Sausage Vegetable Rotini Soup

6 ounces bulk sausage
1 cup chopped yellow onion
1 cup chopped green bell pepper
3 cups water
1 can (14½ ounces) diced tomatoes, undrained
¼ cup ketchup
2 teaspoons reduced-sodium beef bouillon granules
2 teaspoons chili powder
4 ounces uncooked tri-colored rotini
1 cup frozen corn kernels, thawed

Heat Dutch oven over medium-high heat until hot. Coat with nonstick cooking spray. Add sausage and cook 3 minutes or until no longer pink, breaking up sausage into small pieces. Add onion and pepper; cook 3 to 4 minutes or until onion is translucent.

Add water, tomatoes with juice, ketchup, bouillon granules and chili powder; bring to a boil over high heat. Stir in pasta and return to a boil. Reduce heat to medium-low; simmer, uncovered, 12 minutes or until tender. Stir in corn and cook 2 minutes.

Makes 4 servings (6½ cups)

Helpful Hints

Cooking times for rotini may vary from brand to brand. For this recipe, choose a brand with a shorter cooking time.

Navy Bean Bacon Chowder

Beef and Pasta Soup

1 tablespoon vegetable oil
½ pound round steak, cut into ½-inch cubes
1 medium onion, chopped
3 cloves garlic, minced
4 cups canned beef broth
1 can (10¾ ounces) tomato purée
2 teaspoons dried Italian seasoning
2 bay leaves
1 package (9 ounces) frozen Italian green beans
½ cup uncooked orzo or rosamarina (rice-shaped pastas)
Salt
Lemon slices and fresh oregano for garnish
Freshly grated Parmesan cheese (optional)
French bread (optional)

1. Heat oil in 5-quart Dutch oven over medium-high heat; add beef, onion and garlic. Cook and stir until meat is crusty brown and onion is slightly tender.

2. Stir in beef broth, tomato purée, Italian seasoning and bay leaves. Bring to a boil over high heat. Reduce heat to medium-low; simmer, uncovered, 45 minutes.

3. Add beans and uncooked pasta. Bring to a boil over high heat. Simmer, uncovered, 8 minutes or until beans and pasta are tender, stirring frequently. Season with salt to taste.

4. Remove bay leaves. Ladle into bowls. Garnish, if desired. Serve with freshly grated Parmesan cheese and French bread, if desired.

Makes 5 servings

Chorizo and Black Bean Soup

¾ pound chorizo,* crumbled
1 large onion, chopped
3 carrots, diced
1 cup chopped celery
½ cup diced green bell pepper
1 clove garlic, minced
1 can (15-ounce) black beans, rinsed and drained
2 tomatoes, peeled and diced
4 cups chicken broth
1 teaspoon distilled white vinegar
Sour cream

**The Spanish sausage, chorizo, is available in the meat section of the supermarket.*

Cook and stir chorizo over medium heat in Dutch oven or large saucepan. Pour off fat. Add onion, carrots, celery, bell pepper and garlic; cook and stir 2 to 3 minutes.

Add beans, tomatoes, broth, and vinegar; simmer for 30 minutes.

Serve soup in individual bowls garnished with dollop of sour cream.

Makes 4 to 6 servings

Potato-Bacon Soup

2 cans (about 14 ounces each) chicken broth
3 russet potatoes (1¾ to 2 pounds), peeled and cut into ½-inch cubes
1 medium onion, finely chopped
1 teaspoon dried thyme leaves
4 to 6 strips bacon (4 to 6 ounces), chopped
½ cup (2 ounces) shredded Cheddar cheese

1. Combine broth, potatoes, onion and thyme in Dutch oven; bring to a boil over high heat. Reduce heat to medium-high and boil 10 minutes or until potatoes are tender.

2. While potatoes are cooking, place bacon in microwavable container. Cover with paper towels and cook on HIGH 6 to 7 minutes or until bacon is crisp. Break up bacon.

3. Immediately transfer bacon to broth mixture; simmer 3 to 5 minutes. Season to taste with salt and pepper. Ladle into bowls and sprinkle with cheese.

Makes 4 servings

Prep and Cook Time: 27 minutes

Helpful Hints

Chorizo is a spicy pork sausage popular in Mexican and Spanish cuisine. It is usually seasoned with garlic and chili powder. To use chorizo remove it from its casing and crumble it.

Beef and Pasta Soup

Kansas City Steak Soup

Nonstick cooking spray
½ pound ground sirloin or ground round beef
1 cup chopped onion
3 cups frozen mixed vegetables
2 cups water
1 can (14½ ounces) stewed tomatoes, undrained
1 cup sliced celery
1 beef bouillon cube
½ to 1 teaspoon black pepper
1 can (10½ ounces) defatted beef broth
½ cup all-purpose flour

1. Spray Dutch oven with cooking spray. Heat over medium-high heat until hot. Add beef and onion. Cook and stir 5 minutes or until beef is browned.

2. Add vegetables, water, tomatoes with juice, celery, bouillon cube and pepper. Bring to a boil. Whisk together beef broth and flour until smooth; add to beef mixture, stirring constantly. Return mixture to a boil. Reduce heat to low. Cover and simmer 15 minutes, stirring frequently.

Makes 6 servings

Note: If time permits, allow the soup to simmer an additional 30 minutes—the flavors just get better and better.

Beef Soup with Noodles

2 tablespoons soy sauce
1 teaspoon minced fresh ginger
¼ teaspoon red pepper flakes
1 boneless beef top sirloin steak, cut 1 inch thick (about ¾ pound)
1 tablespoon peanut or vegetable oil
2 cups sliced fresh mushrooms
2 cans (about 14 ounces each) beef broth
3 ounces (1 cup) fresh snow peas, cut diagonally into 1-inch pieces
1½ cups hot cooked fine egg noodles (2 ounces uncooked)
1 green onion, cut diagonally into thin slices
1 teaspoon dark sesame oil (optional)
Red bell pepper strips for garnish

1. Combine soy sauce, ginger and red pepper flakes in small bowl. Spread mixture evenly over both sides of steak. Marinate at room temperature 15 minutes.

2. Heat deep skillet over medium-high heat. Add peanut oil; heat until hot. Drain steak; reserve soy sauce mixture (there will only be a small amount of mixture). Add steak to skillet; cook 4 to 5 minutes per side.* Let stand on cutting board 10 minutes.

3. Add mushrooms to skillet; stir-fry 2 minutes. Add broth, snow peas and reserved soy sauce mixture; bring to a boil, scraping up browned meat bits. Reduce heat to medium-low. Stir in noodles.

4. Cut steak across the grain into ⅛-inch slices; cut each slice into 1-inch pieces. Stir into soup; heat through. Stir in onion and sesame oil, if desired. Ladle into soup bowls. Garnish with red pepper strips.

Makes 4 main-dish or 6 appetizer servings (about 6 cups)

*Cooking time is for medium-rare doneness. Adjust time for desired doneness.

Dijon Ham and Lentil Soup

1 cup finely chopped onion
¾ cup finely chopped green bell pepper
½ cup finely chopped carrot
1 clove garlic, minced
1 bay leaf
2 (14½-fluid ounce) cans chicken broth or lower sodium chicken broth
1 (14½-ounce) can stewed tomatoes
1¼ cups water
1 cup diced ham
¾ cup dry lentils
½ cup GREY POUPON® COUNTRY DIJON® Mustard

Combine all ingredients except mustard in large saucepan. Heat to a boil over medium-high heat. Reduce heat; simmer, uncovered, for 1 hour. Stir in mustard. Serve hot.

Makes 6 servings

Kansas City Steak Soup

Turkey Vegetable Soup

- **2½ pounds TURKEY WINGS**
- **5 cups water**
- **2 onions, quartered**
- **1 carrot, cut into chunks**
- **1 bay leaf**
- **5 peppercorns**
- **2 cubes low-sodium chicken bouillon**
- **4 medium tomatoes, peeled and cut into quarters**
- **1 cup green beans**
- **1 medium zucchini, cut into ½- to ¾-inch slices**
- **1 carrot, cut into ½-inch slices**
- **1 stalk celery, cut into ½-inch slices**
- **1 leek, thinly sliced**
- **½ cup lima beans**
- **3 tablespoons pearl barley**
- **3 tablespoons chopped fresh parsley *or* 1 tablespoon dry parsley**
- **1½ teaspoons fresh oregano *or* ½ teaspoon dry oregano**
- **1 clove garlic mashed with ¼ teaspoon salt**
- **¾ teaspoon seasoned pepper**
- **½ cup peas**
- **1 ear corn, cut into ½-inch slices**
- **1 cup broccoli flowerettes**

1. In 5-quart saucepan, combine first seven ingredients. Bring to a boil over high heat. Skim off any foam. Reduce heat, cover and simmer for 1 to 1¼ hours or until turkey is tender.

2. Remove turkey from cooking liquid and allow to cool. Cut meat from bones, discard skin and bones. Cube meat.

3. Strain broth. Discard vegetables, seasonings and spices. Skim off any remaining fat. Return broth to saucepan.

4. Add tomatoes, green beans, zucchini, carrot, celery, leek, lima beans, barley and seasonings. Over high heat, bring mixture to a boil. Cover and reduce heat to a simmer. Cook 20 minutes.

5. Add turkey, peas, corn and broccoli; cook 5 minutes. Adjust seasoning to taste.

Makes 4 servings

Favorite recipe from **National Turkey Federation**

Mexican Fiesta Soup

- **3 cans (14½ ounces each) chicken broth**
- **1 can (17 ounces) whole kernel corn, undrained**
- **2 cups cubed cooked chicken**
- **1 can (12 ounces) vegetable or tomato juice**
- **1 cup cubed peeled potatoes**
- **1 cup chopped carrots**
- **1 cup chopped onions**
- **1 cup chopped celery**
- **1 cup tomato salsa**
- **½ cup HOLLAND HOUSE® Vermouth Cooking Wine**
- **1 can (4 ounces) chopped green chilies, undrained**
- **¼ cup chopped fresh cilantro (optional)**
- **Shredded Monterey Jack cheese (optional)**
- **Tortilla chips (optional)**

In large saucepan, combine chicken broth, corn, chicken, vegetable juice, potatoes, carrots, onions, celery, salsa, cooking wine, green chilies and cilantro, if desired, and place over medium-high heat. Bring to a boil; reduce heat. Simmer 20 to 30 minutes or until vegetables are tender. Serve with cheese and tortilla chips as garnishes, if desired.

Makes 8 (1½-cup) servings

Savory Pea Soup with Sausage

- **8 ounces smoked sausage, cut lengthwise into halves, then cut into ½-inch pieces**
- **2 cans (14½ ounces each) reduced-sodium chicken broth**
- **1 package (16 ounces) dried split peas, sorted and rinsed**
- **3 medium carrots, sliced**
- **2 ribs celery, sliced**
- **1 medium onion, chopped**
- **¾ teaspoon dried marjoram leaves**
- **1 bay leaf**

Slow Cooker Directions

Heat small skillet over medium heat. Add sausage; cook 5 to 8 minutes or until browned. Drain well. Combine sausage and remaining ingredients in slow cooker. Cover and cook on LOW 4 to 5 hours or until peas are tender. Turn off heat. Remove and discard bay leaf. Cover and let stand 15 minutes to thicken.

Makes 6 servings

Helpful Hints

Fresh herbs are very perisable, so purchase them in small amounts a day or two before you plan to use them.

Savory Pea Soup with Sausage

Chicken and Vegetable Chowder

Slow Cooker

1 pound boneless skinless chicken breasts, cut into 1-inch pieces
10 ounces frozen broccoli cuts
1 cup sliced carrots
1 jar (4½ ounces) sliced mushrooms, drained
½ cup chopped onion
½ cup whole kernel corn
2 cloves garlic, minced
½ teaspoon dried thyme leaves
1 can (14½ ounces) reduced-sodium chicken broth
1 can (10¾ ounces) condensed cream of potato soup
⅓ cup half-and-half

Slow Cooker Directions
Combine all ingredients except half-and-half in slow cooker. Cover and cook on LOW 5 hours or until vegetables are tender and chicken is no longer pink in center. Stir in half-and-half. Turn to HIGH. Cover and cook 15 minutes or until heated through. *Makes 6 servings*

Tortellini Vegetable Soup

1 package (14 ounces) turkey or pork breakfast sausage, crumbled
2 quarts water
6 HERB-OX® Beef Bouillon cubes*
½ teaspoon garlic powder
1 package (9 ounces) fresh tortellini cheese pasta
1 package (16 ounces) frozen vegetable combination (broccoli, cauliflower, red pepper), thawed

**1 bouillon cube = 1 teaspoon instant bouillon = 1 packet instant broth and seasoning.*

In Dutch oven over medium-high heat, cook sausage until browned; drain. Add water, bouillon and garlic powder; bring to a boil. Add pasta; boil 5 minutes. Stir in vegetables. Simmer, uncovered, 10 minutes until vegetables and pasta are tender.

Makes 8 servings

Chicken & Orzo Soup

Nonstick olive oil cooking spray
3 ounces boneless skinless chicken breast, cut into bite-size pieces
1 can (about 14 ounces) fat-free, reduced-sodium chicken broth
1 cup water
⅔ cup shredded carrot
⅓ cup sliced green onion
¼ cup uncooked orzo pasta
1 teaspoon grated fresh ginger
⅛ teaspoon ground turmeric
2 teaspoons lemon juice
Black pepper
Sliced green onions (optional)

1. Spray medium saucepan with cooking spray. Heat over medium-high heat. Add chicken. Cook and stir 2 to 3 minutes or until no longer pink. Remove from saucepan and set aside.

2. In same saucepan combine broth, water, carrot, onion, orzo, ginger and turmeric. Bring to a boil. Reduce heat and simmer, covered, 8 to 10 minutes or until orzo is tender. Stir in chicken and lemon juice; cook until hot. Season to taste with pepper.

3. Ladle into serving bowls. Sprinkle with green onions, if desired.

Makes 2 servings

Corn and Chicken Chowder

3 tablespoons butter or margarine, divided
1 pound boneless skinless chicken breasts, cut into chunks
2 medium leeks, sliced (2 cups)
2 medium potatoes, cut into bite-size chunks
1 large green bell pepper, diced
2 tablespoons paprika
2 tablespoons flour
3 cups chicken broth
2½ cups fresh corn kernels
1½ teaspoons TABASCO® brand Pepper Sauce
1 teaspoon salt
1 cup half-and-half

In 4-quart saucepan over medium-high heat, melt 1 tablespoon butter. Cook chicken until well browned on all sides, stirring frequently. With slotted spoon, remove chicken; set aside.

Add remaining 2 tablespoons butter to drippings in saucepan. Over medium heat, cook leeks, potatoes and green pepper until tender, stirring occasionally. Stir in paprika and flour until well blended; cook for 1 minute. Add chicken broth, corn kernels, TABASCO® Sauce, salt and chicken. Over high heat, heat to boiling. Reduce heat to low; cover and simmer 20 minutes. Stir in half-and-half; heat through. *Makes 8 cups*

Chicken and Vegetable Chowder

Mulligatawny Soup

2 tablespoons butter or margarine
1½ cups chopped onions
1 (10-ounce) package frozen mixed vegetables, thawed
2 tablespoons flour
2 teaspoons curry powder
1 teaspoon salt
½ teaspoon TABASCO® brand Pepper Sauce
¼ teaspoon ground cloves
1 quart water
1 (10½-ounce) can condensed chicken with rice soup
1 cup diced cooked chicken
1 cup chopped peeled apple

Melt butter in large soup pot over medium heat. Add onions and mixed vegetables; cook and stir about 5 minutes or just until onion is tender. Stir in flour, curry powder, salt, TABASCO® Sauce and cloves. Add water, soup, chicken and apple. Heat to boiling; reduce heat to low and simmer, covered, 20 minutes. Ladle into serving bowls. Serve with additional TABASCO® Sauce, if desired. *Makes 6 servings*

Country Chicken Chowder

2 tablespoons margarine or butter
1½ pounds chicken tenders, cut into ½-inch pieces
2 small onions, chopped
2 ribs celery, sliced
2 small carrots, sliced
2 cups frozen corn
2 cans (10¾ ounces each) cream of potato soup
1½ cups chicken broth
1 teaspoon dried dill weed
½ cup half-and-half

Slow Cooker Directions

Melt margarine in large skillet. Add chicken; cook until browned. Add cooked chicken, onions, celery, carrots, corn, soup, chicken broth and dill to slow cooker. Cover and cook on LOW 3 to 4 hours or until chicken is no longer pink and vegetables are tender.

Turn off heat; stir in half-and-half. Cover and let stand 5 to 10 minutes or just until heated through. *Makes 8 servings*

Note: For a special touch, garnish soup with croutons and fresh dill.

Tortilla Rice Soup

Vegetable cooking spray
⅓ cup sliced green onions
4 cups chicken broth
2 cups cooked rice
1 can (10½ ounces) diced tomatoes with green chilies, undrained
1 cup cooked chicken breast cubes
1 can (4 ounces) chopped green chilies, undrained
1 tablespoon lime juice
Salt to taste
Tortilla chips
½ cup chopped tomato
½ avocado, cut into small cubes
4 lime slices for garnish
Fresh cilantro for garnish

Heat Dutch oven or large saucepan coated with cooking spray over medium-high heat until hot. Add onions; cook and stir until tender. Add broth, rice, tomatoes with juice, chicken and chilies. Reduce heat to low; cover and simmer 20 minutes. Stir in lime juice and salt. Just before serving, pour into soup bowls; top with tortilla chips, chopped tomato and avocado. Garnish with lime slices and cilantro. *Makes 4 servings*

Favorite recipe from **USA Rice Federation**

Chicken Rotini Soup

½ pound boneless skinless chicken breasts, cut into ½-inch pieces
1 cup water
2 tablespoons butter or margarine
½ medium onion, chopped
4 ounces fresh mushrooms, sliced
4 cups chicken broth
1 teaspoon Worcestershire sauce
¼ teaspoon dried tarragon leaves
¾ cup uncooked rotini
1 small zucchini
Fresh basil for garnish

Combine chicken and water in medium saucepan. Bring to a boil over high heat. Reduce heat to medium-low; simmer 2 minutes. Drain water and rinse chicken. Melt butter in 5-quart Dutch oven or large saucepan over medium heat. Add onion and mushrooms. Cook and stir until onion is tender. Stir in chicken, chicken broth, Worcestershire and tarragon. Bring to a boil over high heat. Stir in uncooked pasta. Reduce heat to medium-low; simmer, uncovered, 5 minutes. Cut zucchini into ⅛-inch slices; halve any large slices. Add to soup; simmer, uncovered, about 5 minutes, or until pasta is tender. Ladle into bowls. Garnish, if desired.

Makes 4 servings

Chicken Rotini Soup

Oriental Chicken and Rice Soup

- 12 TYSON® Fresh Chicken Breast Tenders or Individually Fresh Frozen® Boneless, Skinless Chicken Tenderloins
- 1½ cups UNCLE BEN'S® Instant Rice
- 6 cups defatted reduced-sodium chicken broth
- 2 slices gingerroot (about ¼ inch thick)
- ½ cup chopped carrots
- 1 cup sliced pea pods
- ¼ cup chopped green onions

PREP: CLEAN**:** Wash hands. Remove protective ice glaze from frozen chicken by holding under cool running water 1 to 2 minutes. Cut into 1-inch pieces. CLEAN: Wash hands.

COOK: Heat chicken broth and gingerroot in large saucepan; add chicken. Simmer 5 minutes (8 minutes if using frozen chicken). Add carrots; simmer about 5 minutes or until internal juices of chicken run clear. (Or insert instant-read meat thermometer in thickest part of chicken. Temperature should read 170°F.) Stir in pea pods and rice. Remove from heat; cover. Let stand 5 minutes. Remove gingerroot.

SERVE: Sprinkle with green onions. Serve with herb bread and tea, if desired.

CHILL: Refrigerate leftovers immediately. *Makes 4 servings*

Prep Time: 10 minutes
Cook Time: 25 minutes

Creamy Turkey Soup

- 2 cans (10½ ounces each) cream of chicken soup
- 2 cups chopped cooked turkey breast meat
- 1 package (8 ounces) sliced mushrooms
- 1 medium yellow onion, chopped
- 1 teaspoon rubbed sage *or* ½ teaspoon dried poultry seasoning
- 1 cup frozen peas, thawed
- ½ cup milk
- 1 jar (about 4 ounces) diced pimientos

Slow Cooker Directions

1. Combine soup, turkey, mushrooms, onion and sage in slow cooker. Cook on LOW 8 hours or on HIGH 4 hours.

2. If cooking on LOW, turn to HIGH; stir in peas, milk and pimientos. Cook an additional 10 minutes or until heated through.

Makes 5 to 6 servings

Minute Minestrone Soup

- ½ pound turkey sausage, cut into small pieces
- 2 cloves garlic, crushed
- 3 cans (14½ ounces *each*) low-sodium chicken broth
- 2 cups frozen Italian blend vegetables
- 1 can (15 ounces) white kidney beans, rinsed and drained
- 1 can (14½ ounces) Italian stewed tomatoes, undrained
- 1 cup cooked ditalini or small shell pasta (½ cup uncooked)
- 3 tablespoons *French's*® Worcestershire Sauce

1. In medium saucepan, stir-fry sausage and garlic 5 minutes or until sausage is cooked; drain. Add broth, vegetables, beans and tomatoes. Heat to boiling. Simmer, uncovered, 5 minutes or until vegetables are crisp-tender.

2. Stir in pasta and Worcestershire. Cook until heated through. Serve with grated cheese and crusty bread, if desired. *Makes 6 servings*

Prep Time: 10 minutes
Cook Time: about 10 minutes

Manhattan Clam Chowder

- 2 slices bacon, diced
- 1 large red bell pepper, diced
- 1 large green bell pepper, diced
- 1 stalk celery, chopped
- 1 carrot, peeled and chopped
- 1 small onion, chopped
- 1 clove garlic, finely chopped
- 2 cups bottled clam juice
- 1 cup CLAMATO® Tomato Cocktail
- 2 medium potatoes, peeled and diced
- 1 large tomato, chopped
- 1 teaspoon dried oregano
- ½ teaspoon black pepper
- 2 cups fresh or canned clams, chopped (about 24 shucked clams)

In heavy 4-quart saucepan, sauté bacon, bell peppers, celery, carrot, onion and garlic over medium heat until tender, about 10 minutes. (Do not brown bacon.) Add clam juice, Clamato, potatoes, tomato, oregano and black pepper. Simmer 35 minutes or until potatoes are tender. Add clams; cook 5 minutes more.

Makes 8 servings

Creamy Turkey Soup

Potato-Crab Chowder

1 cup frozen hash brown potatoes
1 package (10 ounces) frozen corn
¾ cup finely chopped carrots
1 teaspoon dried thyme leaves
¾ teaspoon garlic-pepper seasoning
3 cups fat-free reduced-sodium chicken broth
½ cup water
1 cup evaporated milk
3 tablespoons cornstarch
½ cup sliced green onion
1 can (6 ounces) crabmeat, drained

Slow Cooker Directions
1. Place potatoes, corn and carrots in slow cooker. Sprinkle with thyme and garlic-pepper seasoning.

2. Add broth and water. Cover and cook on LOW for 3½ to 4½ hours.

3. Stir together evaporated milk and cornstarch in medium bowl. Stir into slow cooker. Turn temperature to HIGH. Cover and cook 1 hour. Stir in green onions and crabmeat.

Makes 5 servings

Black Bean Bisque with Crab

3 cups low sodium chicken broth, defatted
1 jar (16 ounces) GUILTLESS GOURMET® Black Bean Dip (Spicy or Mild)
1 can (6 ounces) crabmeat, drained
2 tablespoons brandy (optional)
8 tablespoons low fat sour cream
Chopped fresh chives (optional)

Microwave Directions: Combine broth and bean dip in 2-quart glass measure or microwave-safe casserole. Cover with vented plastic wrap or lid; microwave on HIGH (100% power) 6 minutes or until soup starts to bubble.

Stir in crabmeat and brandy, if desired; microwave on MEDIUM (50% power) 2 minutes or to desired serving temperature. To serve, ladle bisque into 8 individual ramekins or soup bowls, dividing evenly. Swirl 1 tablespoon sour cream into each serving. Garnish with chives, if desired. *Makes 8 servings*

Stove Top Directions: Combine broth and bean dip in 2-quart saucepan; bring to a boil over medium heat. Stir in crabmeat and brandy, if desired; cook 2 minutes or to desired serving temperature. Serve as directed.

Oyster Soup

¼ cup (½ stick) butter or margarine
½ cup thinly sliced green onions
2 tablespoons flour
2 cups half-and-half
2 cups shucked fresh oysters and their liquid
½ teaspoon TABASCO® brand Pepper Sauce
2 tablespoons chopped fresh parsley

Melt butter in 3-quart saucepan over medium heat. Add green onions and cook 5 minutes. Add flour; cook 1 minute, stirring constantly. Gradually stir in half-and-half until smooth.

Heat to boiling, stirring constantly. Add oyster liquid and TABASCO® Sauce; return to boil. Cook until soup thickens, stirring constantly. Add oysters and parsley; simmer over low heat 5 to 10 minutes, stirring frequently. (Do not boil.)

Makes 4 servings

Seafood Bisque

2 leeks, cut in half lengthwise
2 tablespoons butter or margarine
3 cups milk
2 cups chopped peeled potatoes
1 (8 ounce) package imitation crab flakes, rinsed
½ teaspoon dried thyme leaves
⅛ to ¼ teaspoon hot pepper sauce
½ pound (8 ounces) VELVEETA® Pasteurized Prepared Cheese Product, cut up
2 tablespoons dry sherry (optional)

Thinly slice white portion and 1 inch of light green portion of leeks; sauté in margarine.

Add all remaining ingredients except prepared cheese product and sherry.

Bring to boil. Reduce heat to low; cover. Simmer 15 minutes or until potatoes are tender.

Add prepared cheese product and sherry; stir until prepared cheese product is melted. Garnish with fresh chives and lemon peel.

Makes 6 servings

Microwave Directions: Reduce milk to 2½ cups. Mix together leeks, margarine and potatoes in 2-quart casserole; cover with lid. Microwave on HIGH 8 to 10 minutes or until vegetables are almost tender. Stir in milk and all remaining ingredients except prepared cheese product and sherry; cover. Microwave 8 to 14 minutes or until potatoes are tender, stirring every 4 minutes. Add prepared cheese product and sherry; stir until prepared cheese product is melted. Garnish as directed.

Prep Time: 40 minutes
Microwave Cooking Time: 24 minutes

Potato-Crab Chowder

Beer and Cheese Soup

Slow Cooker

2 to 3 slices pumpernickel or rye bread
¼ cup finely chopped onion
2 cloves garlic, minced
¾ teaspoon dried thyme leaves
1 can (about 14 ounces) chicken broth
1 cup beer
6 ounces American cheese, shredded or diced
4 to 6 ounces sharp Cheddar cheese, shredded
½ teaspoon paprika
1 cup milk

Slow Cooker Directions
Preheat oven to 425°F. Slice bread into ½-inch cubes; place on baking sheet. Bake 10 to 12 minutes, stirring once, or until crisp; set aside.

Combine onion, garlic, thyme, chicken broth and beer in slow cooker. Cover and cook on LOW 4 hours. Turn to HIGH. Stir cheeses, paprika and milk into slow cooker. Cook 45 to 60 minutes or until soup is hot and cheeses are melted. Stir soup well to blend cheeses. Ladle soup into bowls; top with croutons.

Makes 4 (1-cup) servings

Cream of Asparagus Soup

1 tablespoon margarine or butter
1 small onion, chopped
2 cans (14½ ounces each) chicken broth
1 jar (16 ounces) RAGÚ® Cheese Creations!® Classic Alfredo Sauce
2 packages (10 ounces each) frozen asparagus spears, thawed

1. In 3½-quart saucepan, melt margarine over medium heat and cook onion, stirring occasionally, 5 minutes or until tender. Stir in broth, Ragú Cheese Creations! Sauce and asparagus. Bring to a boil over medium heat, stirring frequently. Reduce heat to low and simmer 5 minutes or until asparagus is tender.

2. In blender or food processor, purée hot soup mixture until smooth. Return soup to saucepan and heat through. Season, if desired, with salt and ground black pepper.

Makes 8 servings

Variation: For a Cream of Broccoli Soup, substitute frozen broccoli spears for asparagus.

Tip: Serve soup with cheese toast croutons. Simply place Swiss cheese on sliced French bread rounds and broil until cheese is melted.

Prep Time: 5 minutes
Cook Time: 20 minutes

French Mushroom Soup

1 pound fresh mushrooms, sliced
1 large onion, thinly sliced
2 tablespoons butter
2 tablespoons all-purpose flour
4 cups beef broth
¾ cup HARVEYS® Bristol Cream®
½ cup shredded Gruyère cheese
6 slices French bread

In 4-quart saucepan, cook mushrooms and onion in butter until onion is soft. Stir in flour. Cook, stirring, 1 to 2 minutes. Add broth. Simmer, covered, 10 minutes. Stir in Harveys® Bristol Cream®. Sprinkle cheese on bread, broil until melted. Place toast on each serving of soup.

Makes 6 servings

Pasta e Fagioli

2 tablespoons olive oil
1 cup chopped onion
3 cloves garlic, minced
2 cans (14½ ounces each) Italian-style stewed tomatoes, undrained
3 cups ⅓-less-salt chicken broth
1 can (about 15 ounces) cannellini beans (white kidney beans), undrained*
¼ cup chopped fresh Italian parsley
1 teaspoon dried basil leaves
¼ teaspoon black pepper
4 ounces uncooked small shell pasta

**One can (about 15 ounces) Great Northern beans, undrained, may be substituted for cannellini beans.*

1. Heat oil in 4-quart Dutch oven over medium heat until hot; add onion and garlic. Cook and stir 5 minutes or until onion is tender.

2. Stir tomatoes with juice, chicken broth, beans with liquid, parsley, basil and pepper into Dutch oven; bring to a boil over high heat, stirring occasionally. Reduce heat to low. Simmer, covered, 10 minutes.

3. Add pasta to Dutch oven. Simmer, covered, 10 to 12 minutes or until pasta is just tender. Serve immediately. Garnish as desired.

Makes 8 servings

Pasta e Fagioli

Vegetable Medley Soup

Slow Cooker

- 3 sweet potatoes, peeled and chopped
- 3 zucchini, chopped
- 2 cups chopped broccoli
- 1 onion, chopped
- ¼ cup butter, melted
- 3 cans (about 14 ounces each) chicken broth
- 2 white potatoes, peeled and shredded
- 1 rib celery, finely chopped
- 1 tablespoon salt
- 1 teaspoon ground cumin
- 1 teaspoon black pepper
- 2 cups half-and-half or milk

Slow Cooker Directions

Combine sweet potatoes, zucchini, broccoli, onion and butter in large bowl. Add chicken broth; stir. Add white potatoes, celery, salt, cumin and pepper; stir. Pour mixture into slow cooker. Cover and cook on LOW 8 to 10 hours or on HIGH 4 to 5 hours. Add half-and-half; cook 30 minutes to 1 hour.

Makes 12 servings

Double Thick Baked Potato-Cheese Soup

Slow Cooker

- 2 pounds baking potatoes, peeled and cut into ½-inch cubes
- 2 cans (10½ ounces each) cream of mushroom soup
- 1½ cups finely chopped green onions, divided
- ¼ teaspoon garlic powder
- ⅛ teaspoon ground red pepper
- 1½ cups (6 ounces) shredded sharp Cheddar cheese
- 1 cup (8 ounces) sour cream
- 1 cup milk
- Black pepper

Slow Cooker Directions

1. Combine potatoes, soup, 1 cup green onions, garlic powder and red pepper in slow cooker. Cover and cook on HIGH 4 hours or on LOW 8 hours.

2. Add cheese, sour cream and milk; stir until cheese has completely melted. Cover and cook on HIGH an additional 10 minutes. Season to taste with black pepper. Garnish with remaining green onions.

Makes 7 servings

Easy Italian Vegetable Soup

Slow Cooker

- 1 can (14½ ounces) diced tomatoes, undrained
- 1 can (10½ ounces) condensed beef broth, undiluted
- 1 package (8 ounces) sliced mushrooms
- 1 medium zucchini, thinly sliced
- 1 medium green bell pepper, chopped
- 1 medium yellow onion, chopped
- ⅓ cup dry red wine or beef broth
- 1½ tablespoons dried basil leaves
- 2½ teaspoons sugar
- 1 tablespoon extra-virgin olive oil
- ½ teaspoon salt
- 1 cup (4 ounces) shredded Mozzarella cheese (optional)

Slow Cooker Directions

1. Combine tomatoes, broth, mushrooms, zucchini, bell pepper, onion, wine, basil and sugar in slow cooker. Cook on LOW 8 hours or on HIGH 4 hours.

2. Stir oil and salt into soup. Garnish with cheese, if desired.

Makes 5 to 6 servings

Oniony Mushroom Soup

- 2 cans (10¾ ounces each) condensed golden mushroom soup
- 1 can (13¾ ounces) reduced-sodium beef broth
- 1⅓ cups ***French's® Taste Toppers™*** French Fried Onions, divided
- ½ cup water
- ⅓ cup dry sherry wine
- 4 slices French bread, cut ½ inch thick
- 1 tablespoon olive oil
- 1 clove garlic, finely minced
- 1 cup (4 ounces) shredded Swiss cheese

Combine mushroom soup, beef broth, *1 cup* ***Taste Toppers***, water and sherry in large saucepan. Bring to a boil over medium-high heat, stirring often. Reduce heat to low. Simmer 15 minutes, stirring occasionally.

Preheat broiler. Place bread on baking sheet. Combine oil and garlic in small bowl. Brush oil over both sides of bread slices. Broil bread until toasted and crisp, turning once.

Ladle soup into 4 broiler-safe bowls. Place 1 slice of bread in each bowl. Sprinkle evenly with cheese and remaining *⅓ cup* ***Taste Toppers***. Place bowls on baking sheet. Place under broiler about 1 minute or until cheese is melted and ***Taste Toppers*** are golden.

Makes 4 servings

Prep Time: 20 minutes
Cook Time: 18 minutes

Vegetable Medley Soup

Spectacular Stews

Panama Pork Stew

- **2 small sweet potatoes, peeled and cut into 2-inch pieces (about 12 ounces total)**
- **1 package (10 ounces) frozen corn**
- **1 package (9 ounces) frozen cut green beans**
- **1 cup chopped onion**
- **1¼ pounds lean pork stew meat, cut into 1-inch cubes**
- **1 can (14½ ounces) diced tomatoes**
- **1 to 2 tablespoons chili powder**
- **½ teaspoon salt**
- **½ teaspoon ground coriander**

Slow Cooker Directions
Place potatoes, corn, green beans and onion in slow cooker. Top with pork. Stir together tomatoes, 1 cup water, chili powder, salt and coriander in large bowl. Pour over pork in slow cooker. Cover and cook on LOW 7 to 9 hours. *Makes 6 servings*

Beef Stew in Red Wine

- **1½ pounds boneless beef round, cut into 1-inch cubes**
- **1½ cups dry red wine**
- **2 teaspoons olive oil**
- **Peel of half an orange**
- **2 large cloves garlic, thinly sliced**
- **1 bay leaf**
- **½ teaspoon dried thyme leaves**
- **⅛ teaspoon black pepper**
- **8 ounces fresh mushrooms, quartered**
- **8 sun-dried tomatoes, quartered**
- **1 can (about 14 ounces) fat-free, reduced-sodium beef broth**
- **6 small potatoes, unpeeled, cut into wedges**
- **1 cup baby carrots**
- **1 cup fresh pearl onions, skins removed**
- **1 tablespoon cornstarch mixed with 2 tablespoons water**

1. Combine beef, wine, oil, orange peel, garlic, bay leaf, thyme and pepper in large glass bowl. Refrigerate, covered, at least 2 hours or overnight.

2. Place beef mixture, mushrooms and tomatoes in large nonstick skillet or Dutch oven. Add enough beef broth to just cover ingredients. Bring to a boil over high heat. Cover; reduce heat to low. Simmer 1 hour. Add potatoes, carrots and onions; cover and cook 20 to 25 minutes or until vegetables are tender and meat is no longer pink. Remove meat and vegetables from skillet with slotted spoon; cover and set aside. Discard orange peel and bay leaf.

3. Stir cornstarch mixture into skillet with sauce. Increase heat to medium; cook and stir until sauce is slightly thickened. Return meat and vegetables to sauce; heat thoroughly. *Makes 6 servings*

Note: Use a vegetable peeler to remove large pieces of the orange peel.

Panama Pork Stew

Favorite Beef Stew

3 carrots, cut lengthwise into halves, then cut into 1-inch pieces
3 ribs celery, cut into 1-inch pieces
2 large potatoes, peeled and cut into ½-inch pieces
1½ cups chopped onions
3 cloves garlic, chopped
1 bay leaf
4½ teaspoons Worcestershire sauce
¾ teaspoon dried thyme leaves
¾ teaspoon dried basil leaves
½ teaspoon black pepper
2 pounds lean beef stew meat, cut into 1-inch pieces
1 can (14½ ounces) diced tomatoes, undrained
1 can (about 14 ounces) reduced-sodium beef broth
½ cup cold water
¼ cup all-purpose flour

Slow Cooker Directions
Layer ingredients in slow cooker in the following order: carrots, celery, potatoes, onions, garlic, bay leaf, Worcestershire sauce, thyme, basil, pepper, beef, tomatoes with juice and broth. Cover and cook on LOW 8 to 9 hours.

Remove beef and vegetables to large serving bowl; cover and keep warm. Remove and discard bay leaf. Turn slow cooker to HIGH; cover. Stir water into flour in small bowl until smooth. Add ½ cup cooking liquid; mix well. Stir flour mixture into slow cooker. Cover and cook 15 minutes or until thickened. Pour sauce over meat and vegetables. Serve immediately.

Makes 6 to 8 servings

Brunswick Stew

12 ounces smoked ham or cooked chicken breast, cut into ¾- to 1-inch cubes
1 cup sliced onion
4½ teaspoons all-purpose flour
1 can (14½ ounces) stewed tomatoes, undrained
2 cups frozen mixed vegetables for soup (such as okra, lima beans, potatoes, celery, corn, carrots and green beans)
1 cup chicken broth

1. Spray large saucepan with nonstick cooking spray; heat over medium heat until hot. Add ham and onion; cook 5 minutes or until ham is browned. Stir in flour; cook over medium to medium-low heat 1 minute, stirring constantly.

2. Stir in tomatoes, mixed vegetables and broth; bring to a boil. Reduce heat to low; simmer, covered, 5 to 8 minutes or until vegetables are tender. Simmer, uncovered, 5 to 8 minutes or until slightly thickened. Season to taste with salt and pepper.

Makes 4 (1-cup) servings

Serving Suggestion: Brunswick Stew is excellent served over rice or squares of cornbread.

Prep and Cook Time: 30 minutes

French-Style Pork Stew

1 tablespoon vegetable oil
1 pork tenderloin (16 ounces), cut into ¾- to 1-inch cubes
1 medium onion, coarsely chopped
1 rib celery, sliced
½ teaspoon dried basil leaves
¼ teaspoon dried rosemary, crushed
¼ teaspoon dried oregano leaves
1 cup chicken broth
2 tablespoons all-purpose flour
½ package (16 ounces) frozen mixed vegetables (carrots, potatoes and peas)
1 jar (4½ ounces) sliced mushrooms, drained
1 package (about 6 ounces) long grain and wild rice
2 teaspoons lemon juice
⅛ teaspoon ground nutmeg

Slow Cooker Directions
Heat oil in large skillet over high heat. Add pork, onion, celery, basil, rosemary and oregano. Cook until pork is browned. Place pork mixture in slow cooker. Stir chicken broth into flour until smooth; pour into slow cooker.

Stir in frozen vegetables and mushrooms. Cover and cook on LOW 4 hours or until pork is barely pink in center. Prepare rice according to package directions, discarding spice packet, if desired.

Stir lemon juice, nutmeg and salt and pepper to taste into slow cooker. Cover and cook 15 minutes. Serve stew over rice.

Makes 4 (1-cup) servings

Favorite Beef Stew

New Orleans Pork Gumbo

- 1 pound pork loin roast
- Nonstick cooking spray
- 1 tablespoon margarine
- 2 tablespoons all-purpose flour
- 1 cup water
- 1 can (16 ounces) stewed tomatoes, undrained
- 1 package (10 ounces) frozen cut okra
- 1 package (10 ounces) frozen succotash
- 1 cube beef bouillon
- 1 teaspoon hot pepper sauce
- 1 teaspoon black pepper
- 1 bay leaf

1. Cut pork into ½-inch cubes. Spray large Dutch oven with cooking spray. Heat over medium heat until hot. Add pork; cook and stir 4 minutes or until pork is browned. Remove pork from Dutch oven.

2. Melt margarine in same Dutch oven. Stir in flour. Cook and stir until flour mixture is browned. Gradually whisk in water until smooth. Add pork and remaining ingredients. Bring to a boil. Reduce heat to low and simmer 15 minutes. Remove bay leaf.

Makes 4 servings

Prep and Cook Time: 30 minutes

Dijon Lamb Stew

- ½ pound boneless lamb, cut into small pieces*
- ½ medium onion, chopped
- ½ teaspoon dried rosemary
- 1 tablespoon olive oil
- 1 can (14½ ounces) DEL MONTE® Italian Recipe Stewed Tomatoes
- 1 carrot, julienne cut
- 1 tablespoon Dijon mustard
- 1 can (15 ounces) white beans or pinto beans, drained

**Top sirloin steak may be substituted for lamb.*

1. Brown meat with onion and rosemary in oil in large skillet over medium-high heat, stirring occasionally. Season with salt and pepper, if desired.

2. Add undrained tomatoes, carrot and mustard. Cover and cook over medium heat, 10 minutes; add beans.

3. Cook, uncovered, over medium heat 5 minutes, stirring occasionally. Garnish with sliced ripe olives and chopped parsley, if desired.

Makes 4 servings

Prep Time: 10 minutes
Cook Time: 20 minutes

Golden Harvest Stew

- 1 pound pork cutlets, cut into 1-inch pieces
- 2 tablespoons all-purpose flour, divided
- 1 tablespoon vegetable oil
- 2 medium Yukon gold potatoes, unpeeled and cut into 1-inch cubes
- 1 large sweet potato, peeled and cut into 1-inch cubes
- 1 cup chopped carrots
- 1 ear corn, broken into 4 pieces *or* ½ cup canned corn
- ½ cup chicken broth
- 1 jalapeño pepper, seeded and finely chopped*
- 1 clove garlic, minced
- 1 teaspoon salt
- ¼ teaspoon black pepper
- ¼ teaspoon dried thyme leaves

**Jalapeño peppers can sting and irritate the skin; wear rubber gloves when handling peppers and do not touch eyes. Wash handsafter handling.*

Slow Cooker Directions

1. Coat pork pieces with 1 tablespoon flour; set aside. Heat oil in large nonstick skillet over medium-high heat until hot. Brown pork 2 to 3 minutes per side; transfer to 5-quart slow cooker.

2. Add remaining ingredients, except remaining 1 tablespoon flour, to slow cooker. Cover and cook on LOW 5 to 6 hours.

3. Combine remaining 1 tablespoon flour and ¼ cup broth from stew in small bowl; stir until smooth. Pour flour mixture into stew; stir. Cover and cook on HIGH 10 minutes.

Makes 4 (2½-cup) servings

Easy Oven Beef Stew

- 2 pounds boneless beef stew meat, cut into 1½-inch cubes
- 1 can (16 ounces) tomatoes, undrained, cut up
- 1 can (10½ ounces) condensed beef broth
- 1 cup HOLLAND HOUSE® Red Cooking Wine
- 1 tablespoon Italian seasonings spice*
- 6 potatoes, peeled, quartered
- 6 carrots cut into 2-inch pieces
- 3 stalks celery cut into 1-inch pieces
- 2 medium onions, peeled, quartered
- ⅓ cup instant tapioca
- ¼ teaspoon black pepper
- Chopped fresh parsley

**You can substitute 1½ teaspoons each of basil and oregano for Italian seasonings.*

Heat oven to 325°F. Combine all ingredients except parsley in Dutch oven; cover. Bake 2½ to 3 hours or until meat and vegetables are tender. Garnish with parsley.

Makes 8 servings

New Orleans Pork Gumbo

Southwestern-Style Beef Stew

- **¼ cup all-purpose flour**
- **1 teaspoon seasoned salt**
- **¼ teaspoon ground black pepper**
- **2 pounds beef stew meat, cut into bite-size pieces**
- **2 tablespoons vegetable oil**
- **1 large onion, cut into wedges**
- **2 large cloves garlic, finely chopped**
- **1¾ cups (14½-ounce can) stewed tomatoes, undrained**
- **1¾ cups (16-ounce jar) ORTEGA® Garden Style Salsa, mild**
- **1 cup beef broth**
- **1 tablespoon ground oregano**
- **1 teaspoon ground cumin**
- **½ teaspoon salt**
- **3 large carrots, peeled, cut into 1-inch slices**
- **1¾ cups (15-ounce can) garbanzo beans, drained**
- **1 cup (8-ounce can) baby corn, drained, halved**

COMBINE flour, salt and pepper in medium bowl or large resealable plastic food-storage bag. Add meat; toss well to coat.

HEAT oil in large saucepan over medium-high heat. Add meat, onion and garlic; cook for 5 to 6 minutes or until meat is browned on outside and onion is tender. Stir in tomatoes with juice, salsa, broth, oregano, cumin and salt. Bring to a boil; cover. Reduce heat to low; cook, stirring occasionally, for 45 minutes or until meat is tender.

STIR in carrots, beans and baby corn. Increase heat to medium-low. Cook, stirring occasionally, for 30 to 40 minutes or until carrots are tender.

Makes 8 servings

Hungarian Beef Stew

- **¼ cup vegetable oil**
- **1 medium onion, chopped**
- **1 cup sliced mushrooms**
- **2 teaspoons paprika**
- **1 boneless beef sirloin steak, ½ inch thick, trimmed, cut into ½-inch pieces (about 2 pounds)**
- **½ cup beef broth**
- **½ teaspoon caraway seeds**
- **Salt and black pepper to taste**
- **2 tablespoons all-purpose flour**
- **1 cup sour cream**
- **Hot buttered noodles (optional)**
- **Chopped fresh parsley for garnish**

Heat oil in 5-quart Dutch oven over medium-high heat. Cook and stir onion and mushrooms in oil until onion is soft. Stir in paprika. Remove with slotted spoon; set aside.

Brown half of beef in Dutch oven over medium-high heat. Remove with slotted spoon; set aside. Brown remaining beef. Pour off drippings. Return beef, onion and mushrooms to Dutch oven. Stir in broth, caraway seeds, salt and pepper. Bring to a boil over high heat. Reduce heat to low. Cover and simmer 45 minutes or until beef is fork-tender.

Whisk flour into sour cream in small bowl. Whisk into stew. Stir until slightly thickened. *Do not boil.* Serve over noodles. Garnish with parsley.

Makes 6 to 8 servings

Lemon Lamb Lawry's®

- **2 teaspoons LAWRY'S® Lemon Pepper**
- **1 cup water**
- **2 pounds boneless lamb, cut into 1-inch cubes**
- **2 tablespoons vegetable oil**
- **1 large onion, sliced**
- **1 tablespoon olive oil**
- **½ cup lemon juice**
- **1 teaspoon LAWRY'S® Seasoned Salt**
- **1½ pounds fresh green beans, cut into 1-inch pieces**
- **1 teaspoon dried oregano**

In small bowl, combine Lemon Pepper and water; let stand while browning lamb. In large skillet or Dutch oven, heat vegetable oil; add lamb and onion and cook over medium-high heat until lamb is browned and onion is tender. Add olive oil and toss with lamb and onion to coat. Add water and lemon pepper mixture, lemon juice, Seasoned Salt, green beans and oregano. Bring to a boil over medium-high heat; reduce heat to low. Cover and simmer 1 hour, stirring occasionally. Add additional ¼ cup water during cooking, if necessary.

Makes 6 servings

Serving Suggestion: Serve with tossed green salad and crusty bread.

Helpful Hints

The flavor of paprika can vary from mild to hot. Mild varieties are available in supermarkets, but you may have to go to an ethnic market for hotter varieties. Always store paprika in a cool dry place and replenish your supply every six months or so.

Southwestern-Style Beef Stew

Hearty Ground Beef Stew

1 pound ground beef
3 cloves garlic, minced
1 package (16 ounces) Italian-style frozen vegetables
2 cups southern-style hash brown potatoes
1 jar (14 ounces) marinara sauce
1 can (10½ ounces) condensed beef broth
3 tablespoons *French's*® Worcestershire Sauce

1. Brown beef with garlic in large saucepan; drain. Add remaining ingredients. Heat to boiling. Cover. Reduce heat to medium-low. Cook 10 minutes or until vegetables are crisp-tender.

2. Serve in warm bowls with garlic bread, if desired.

Makes 6 servings

Prep Time: 5 minutes
Cook Time: 15 minutes

Italian Sausage and Vegetable Stew

Slow Cooker

1 pound hot or mild Italian sausage, cut into 1-inch pieces
1 package (16 ounces) frozen mixed vegetables (onions and green, red and yellow bell peppers)
1 can (14½ ounces) diced Italian-style tomatoes, undrained
2 medium zucchini, sliced
1 jar (4½ ounces) sliced mushrooms, drained
4 cloves garlic, minced
2 tablespoons Italian-style tomato paste

Slow Cooker Directions
Heat large skillet over high heat until hot. Add sausage, cook about 5 minutes or until browned. Pour off any drippings.

Combine sausage, frozen vegetables, tomatoes, zucchini, mushrooms and garlic in slow cooker. Cover and cook on LOW 4 to 4½ hours or until zucchini is tender. Stir in tomato paste. Cover and cook 30 mintues or until juices have thickened.

Makes 6 (1-cup) servings

Serving Suggestion: Serve with fresh hot garlic bread.

Kielbasa and Lentil Stew

1 pound kielbasa or smoked sausage, cut into small cubes
½ head green cabbage, shredded (8 cups)
1 large onion, chopped
4 carrots, shredded
2 cans (19 ounces *each*) lentil soup
1 can (16 ounces) crushed tomatoes in purée, undrained
3 tablespoons *Frank's*® *RedHot*® Cayenne Pepper Sauce

1. Cook and stir sausage in 5-quart saucepot over medium-high heat 3 minutes or until lightly browned. Add vegetables; cook and stir 5 minutes or until tender.

2. Stir in soup, tomatoes and ***Frank's RedHot***. Heat to boiling. Reduce heat to medium-low. Cook, partially covered, 10 minutes or until heated through and flavors are blended. Ladle stew into bowls.

Makes 8 to 10 servings

Prep Time: 10 minutes
Cook Time: 20 minutes

Milwaukee Pork Stew

2 pounds boneless pork shoulder or sirloin, cut into ½-inch cubes
⅓ cup all-purpose flour
1½ teaspoons salt
¼ teaspoon black pepper
2 tablespoons vegetable oil
4 large onions, sliced ½ inch thick
1 clove garlic, minced
1 can (14½ ounces) chicken broth
1 can (12 ounces) beer
¼ cup chopped fresh parsley
2 tablespoons red wine vinegar
1 tablespoon packed brown sugar
1 teaspoon caraway seeds
1 bay leaf

Coat pork with combined flour, salt and pepper. Heat oil in Dutch oven; brown meat over medium-high heat. Add onions and garlic. Cook and stir 5 minutes. Pour off drippings. Stir in remaining ingredients. Bring to a boil. Cover; cook over medium-low heat 1 to 1¼ hours or until meat is very tender. Stir occasionally.

Makes 8 servings

Prep Time: 10 minutes
Cook Time: 90 minutes

Favorite recipe from **National Pork Producers Council**

Helpful Hints

Traditionally, stews are economical one-dish meals that combine meat, poultry or seafood and vegetables. Long cooking allows time to tenderize tougher cuts of meat and blend flavors.

Hearty Ground Beef Stew

Stew Provençal

2 cans (about 14 ounces each) beef broth, divided
⅓ cup all-purpose flour
1½ pounds pork tenderloin, trimmed and diced
4 red potatoes, unpeeled and cut into cubes
2 cups frozen cut green beans
1 onion, chopped
2 cloves garlic, minced
1 teaspoon salt
1 teaspoon dried thyme leaves
½ teaspoon black pepper

Slow Cooker Directions
Combine ¾ cup beef broth and flour in small bowl. Set aside.

Add remaining broth, pork, potatoes, beans, onion, garlic, salt, thyme and pepper to slow cooker; stir. Cover and cook on LOW 8 to 10 hours or on HIGH 4 to 5 hours. If cooking on LOW, turn to HIGH last 30 minutes. Stir in flour mixture. Cook 30 minutes to thicken. *Makes 8 servings*

Pecos "Red" Stew

2 pounds boneless pork shoulder or sirloin, cut into 1½-inch cubes
2 tablespoons vegetable oil
2 cups chopped onions
1 cup chopped green bell pepper
¼ cup chopped fresh cilantro
3 to 4 tablespoons chili powder
2 cloves garlic, minced
2 teaspoons dried oregano leaves
1 teaspoon salt
½ teaspoon crushed red pepper
2 cans (14½ ounces each) chicken broth
3 cups cubed peeled potatoes, cut in 1-inch pieces
2 cups fresh or frozen whole kernel corn
1 can (16 ounces) garbanzo beans, drained

Heat oil in Dutch oven. Brown pork over medium-high heat. Stir in onions, bell pepper, cilantro, chili powder, garlic, oregano, salt, red pepper and chicken broth. Cover; cook over medium-low heat 45 to 55 minutes or until pork is tender. Add potatoes, corn and beans. Cover; cook 15 to 20 minutes longer.
Makes 8 servings

Prep Time: 20 minutes
Cook Time: 60 minutes

Favorite recipe from **National Pork Producers Council**

Pork and Cabbage Ragoût

1 tablespoon vegetable oil
1 pound pork tenderloin, cut into ½-inch slices
1 cup chopped onion
4 cloves garlic, minced
1½ teaspoons crushed caraway seeds
8 cups thinly sliced cabbage (1 pound) or prepared coleslaw mix
1 cup dry white wine
1 teaspoon chicken bouillon crystals
2 medium Cortland or Jonathan apples, peeled and cut into wedges
Instant potato flakes plus ingredients to prepare 4 servings mashed potatoes

1. Heat oil in large saucepan over medium heat until hot. Add pork; cook and stir about 2 minutes per side or until browned and barely pink in center. Sprinkle lightly with salt and pepper. Remove from saucepan and reserve. Add onion, garlic and caraway to saucepan; cook and stir 3 to 5 minutes or until onion is tender.

2. Add cabbage, wine and chicken bouillon to saucepan; bring to a boil. Reduce heat to low; simmer, covered, 5 minutes or until cabbage is wilted. Cook over medium heat, uncovered, 5 to 8 minutes or until excess liquid is gone.

3. Add apple wedges and reserved pork; cook, covered, 5 to 8 minutes or until apples are tender. Season to taste with salt and pepper. While ragoût is cooking, prepare potatoes according to package directions. Serve ragoût over potatoes.
Makes 4 (1-cup) servings

Tip: For a special touch, stir ⅓ cup sour cream into ragoût at end of cooking time; cook over low heat 2 to 3 minutes or until hot.

Tasty Pork Ragoût

½ pound pork loin, cubed
1 small onion, chopped
1 large clove garlic, pressed
½ teaspoon dried rosemary, crumbled
2 tablespoons margarine
Salt and pepper
1 bouillon cube, any flavor
½ cup boiling water
2 cups DOLE® Cauliflower, cut into flowerets
1 cup sliced DOLE® Carrots
1 cup hot cooked rice

• Brown pork with onion, garlic and rosemary in margarine. Season with salt and pepper to taste.

• Dissolve bouillon in water; stir into pork mixture. Cover; simmer 20 minutes.

• Add cauliflower and carrots. Cover; simmer 5 minutes longer or until vegetables are tender-crisp. Serve with rice. *Makes 2 servings*

Prep Time: 10 minutes
Cook Time: 25 minutes

Stew Provençal

Black Bean & Pork Stew

2 (15-ounce) cans cooked black beans, rinsed and drained
2 cups water
1 pound boneless ham, cut into ¾-inch cubes
¾ pound BOB EVANS® Italian Dinner Link Sausage, cut into 1-inch pieces
¾ pound BOB EVANS® Smoked Sausage, cut into 1-inch pieces
1 pint cherry tomatoes, stems removed
1 medium onion, chopped
1 teaspoon red pepper flakes
6 cloves garlic, minced
⅛ teaspoon grated orange peel
Cornbread or rolls (optional)

Preheat oven to 350°F. Combine all ingredients except cornbread in large Dutch oven. Bring to a boil over high heat, skimming foam off if necessary. Cover; transfer to oven. Bake 30 minutes; uncover and bake 30 minutes more, stirring occasionally. Serve hot with cornbread, if desired, or cool slightly, then cover and refrigerate overnight. Remove any fat from surface. Reheat over low heat. Refrigerate leftovers.
Makes 8 servings

Pepper & Pineapple Pork Stew

Slow Cooker

4 top loin pork chops, cut into 1-inch cubes
4 carrots, sliced
½ cup chicken broth
3 tablespoons teriyaki sauce
1 tablespoon cornstarch
1 (8-ounce) can pineapple chunks in juice, drained and juice reserved
1 green bell pepper, seeded and cut into 1-inch pieces

Slow Cooker Directions
Brown pork cubes in hot skillet, if desired (optional). Mix pork, carrots, broth and teriyaki in 3½-quart slow cooker; cover and cook on LOW for 7 to 8 hours. Mix cornstarch with reserved pineapple juice; stir into pork mixture. Stir in pineapple and green pepper. Cover and cook on HIGH 15 minutes or until thickened and bubbly. *Makes 4 servings*

Favorite recipe from **National Pork Producers Council**

Savory Braised Beef

4 slices bacon
2 pounds boneless beef chuck or round steak, cut into 1-inch cubes
1 large clove garlic, finely chopped
1 envelope LIPTON® RECIPE SECRETS® Beefy Mushroom Soup Mix*
1 can or bottle (12 ounces) beer *or* 1½ cups water
1 cup water
1 tablespoon red wine vinegar
Hot cooked rice

**Also terrific with LIPTON® RECIPE SECRETS® Onion, Onion-Mushroom, or Beefy Onion Soup Mix.*

1. In Dutch oven or 6-quart saucepot, brown bacon until crisp. Remove bacon, crumble and set aside; reserve 1 tablespoon drippings.

2. Brown beef in two batches in reserved drippings. Remove beef and set aside.

3. Add garlic to drippings and cook over medium heat, stirring frequently, 30 seconds. Return beef to Dutch oven. Add soup mix blended with beer and 1 cup water. Bring to a boil over high heat.

4. Reduce heat to low and simmer covered, stirring occasionally, 1 hour 15 minutes or until beef is tender. Skim fat, if necessary. Stir in vinegar and sprinkle with bacon. Serve over rice. *Makes 4 servings*

Skillet Sausage and Bean Stew

1 pound spicy Italian sausage, casing removed and sliced ½ inch thick
½ onion, chopped
2 cups frozen O'Brien-style potatoes with onions and peppers
1 can (15 ounces) pinto beans, undrained
¾ cup water
1 teaspoon beef bouillon granules *or* 1 cube beef bouillon
1 teaspoon dried oregano leaves
⅛ teaspoon ground red pepper

1. Combine sausage slices and onion in large nonstick skillet; cook and stir over medium-high heat 5 to 7 minutes or until meat is no longer pink. Drain drippings.

2. Stir in potatoes, beans, water, bouillon, oregano and red pepper; reduce heat to medium. Cover and simmer 15 minutes, stirring occasionally. *Makes 4 servings*

Prep and Cook Time: 30 minutes

Helpful Hints

You can reduce the calories and fat content of this dish by substituting turkey sausage for Italian sausage. Add hot pepper sauce to taste if you prefer a spicier stew.

Black Bean & Pork Stew

The Best Beef Stew

- **½ cup plus 2 tablespoons all-purpose flour, divided**
- **2 teaspoons salt**
- **1 teaspoon black pepper**
- **3 pounds beef stew meat, trimmed and cut into cubes**
- **1 can (16 ounces) diced tomatoes in juice, undrained**
- **½ pound smoked sausage, sliced**
- **3 potatoes, peeled and diced**
- **1 cup chopped leek**
- **1 cup chopped onion**
- **4 ribs celery, sliced**
- **½ cup chicken broth**
- **3 cloves garlic, minced**
- **1 teaspoon dried thyme leaves**
- **3 tablespoons water**

Slow Cooker Directions
Combine ½ cup flour, salt and pepper in resealable plastic food storage bag. Add beef; shake bag to coat beef. Place beef in slow cooker. Add remaining ingredients except remaining 2 tablespoons flour and water; stir well. Cover and cook on LOW 8 to 12 hours or on HIGH 4 to 6 hours.

One hour before serving, turn slow cooker to HIGH. Combine remaining 2 tablespoons flour and water in small bowl; stir until mixture becomes paste. Stir mixture into slow cooker; mix well. Cover and cook until thickened. *Makes 8 servings*

Pork Stew

- **2 tablespoons vegetable oil, divided**
- **3 pounds fresh lean boneless pork butt, cut into 1½-inch cubes**
- **2 medium white onions, thinly sliced**
- **3 cloves garlic, minced**
- **1 teaspoon salt**
- **1 teaspoon ground cumin**
- **¾ teaspoon dried oregano leaves**
- **1 can (8 ounces) tomatillos, drained and chopped *or* 1 cup husked and chopped fresh tomatillos**
- **1 can (4 ounces) chopped green chilies, drained**
- **½ cup reduced-sodium chicken broth**
- **1 large tomato, peeled and coarsely chopped**
- **¼ cup fresh cilantro, chopped *or* ½ teaspoon ground coriander**
- **2 teaspoons lime juice**
- **4 cups hot cooked white rice**
- **½ cup toasted slivered almonds (optional)**

Slow Cooker Directions
Heat 1 tablespoon oil in large skillet over medium heat. Add pork; cook 10 minutes or until browned on all sides. Remove and set aside. Heat remaining 1 tablespoon oil in skillet. Add onions, garlic, salt, cumin and oregano; cook and stir 2 minutes or until soft.

Combine pork, onion mixture and remaining ingredients except rice and almonds in slow cooker; mix well. Cover and cook on LOW 5 hours or until pork is tender and barely pink in center. Serve over rice and sprinkle with almonds, if desired. *Makes 10 servings*

Smoked Sausage Gumbo

Slow Cooker

- **1 cup chicken broth**
- **1 can (14 ½ ounces) diced tomatoes, undrained**
- **¼ cup all-purpose flour**
- **2 tablespoons olive oil**
- **¾ pound Polish sausage, cut into ½-inch pieces**
- **1 medium onion, diced**
- **1 green bell pepper, diced**
- **2 ribs celery, chopped**
- **1 carrot, peeled and chopped**
- **2 teaspoons dried oregano**
- **2 teaspoons dried thyme**
- **⅛ teaspoon ground red pepper**
- **1 cup uncooked long-grain white rice**

Slow Cooker Directions
Combine broth and tomatoes with juice in slow cooker. Sprinkle flour evenly over bottom of small skillet. Cook over high heat without stirring 3 to 4 minutes or until flour begins to brown. Reduce heat to medium; stir flour about 4 minutes. Stir in oil until smooth. Carefully whisk flour mixture into slow cooker.

Add sausage, onion, bell pepper, celery, carrot, oregano, thyme and ground red pepper to slow cooker. Stir well. Cover and cook on LOW 4½ to 5 hours or until juices are thickened.

About 30 minutes before gumbo is ready to serve, prepare rice. Cook rice in 2 cups boiling water in medium, covered, saucepan. Serve gumbo over rice
. *Makes 4 servings*

Note: For a special touch, sprinkle chopped parsley over each serving.

Note: If gumbo thickens upon standing, stir in additional broth.

The Best Beef Stew

Chicken Stew with Dumplings

Slow Cooker

2 cups sliced carrots
1 cup chopped onion
1 large green bell pepper, sliced
½ cup sliced celery
2 cans (about 14 ounces each) chicken broth
⅔ cup all-purpose flour
1 pound boneless skinless chicken breasts, cut into 1-inch pieces
1 large potato, unpeeled and cut into 1-inch pieces
6 ounces mushrooms, halved
¾ cup frozen peas
1 teaspoon dried basil
¾ teaspoon dried rosemary
¼ teaspoon dried tarragon
¾ to 1 teaspoon salt
¼ teaspoon black pepper
¼ cup heavy cream

Herb Dumplings
1 cup biscuit mix
¼ teaspoon dried basil leaves
¼ teaspoon dried rosemary
⅛ teaspoon dried tarragon leaves
⅓ cup reduced-fat (2%) milk

Slow Cooker Directions
Combine carrots, onion, bell pepper and celery in slow cooker. Stir in chicken broth, reserving 1 cup broth. Cover and cook on LOW 2 hours.

Stir flour into remaining 1 cup broth until smooth. Stir into slow cooker. Add chicken, potato, mushrooms, peas and herbs to slow cooker. Cover and cook 4 hours or until vegetables are tender and chicken is no longer pink. Stir in salt, black pepper and heavy cream.

Combine biscuit mix and herbs in small bowl. Stir in milk to form soft dough. Spoon dumpling mixture on top of stew in 4 large spoonfuls. Cook, uncovered, 30 minutes. Cover and cook 30 to 45 minutes or until dumplings are firm and toothpick inserted in center comes out clean. Serve in shallow bowls.

Makes 4 servings

Chicken Gumbo

4 TYSON® Fresh Skinless Chicken Thighs
4 TYSON® Fresh Skinless Chicken Drumsticks
¼ cup all-purpose flour
2 teaspoons Cajun or Creole seasoning blend
2 tablespoons vegetable oil
1 large onion, chopped
1 cup thinly sliced celery
3 cloves garlic, minced
1 can (14½ ounces) stewed tomatoes, undrained
1 can (14½ ounces) chicken broth
1 large green bell pepper, cut into ½-inch pieces
½ to 1 teaspoon hot pepper sauce or to taste

PREP: CLEAN: Wash hands. Combine flour and Cajun seasonings in reclosable plastic bag. Add chicken, 2 pieces at a time; shake to coat. Reserve excess flour mixture. CLEAN: Wash hands.

COOK: In large saucepan, heat oil over medium heat. Add chicken and brown on all sides; remove and set aside. Sauté onion, celery and garlic 5 minutes. Add reserved flour mixture; cook 1 minute, stirring frequently. Add tomatoes, chicken broth, bell pepper and hot sauce. Bring to a boil. Return chicken to saucepan, cover and simmer over low heat, stirring occasionally, 30 minutes or until internal juices of chicken run clear. (Or insert instant-read meat thermometer in thickest part of chicken. Temperature should read 180°F.)

SERVE: Serve in shallow bowls, topped with hot cooked rice, if desired.

CHILL: Refrigerate leftovers immediately.

Makes 6 to 8 servings

Prep Time: 10 minutes
Cook Time: 1 hour

Country Chicken Stew

2 tablespoons butter or margarine
1 pound boneless skinless chicken breasts, cut into 1-inch cubes
½ pound small red potatoes, cut into ½-inch cubes
2 tablespoons cooking sherry
2 jars (12 ounces each) golden chicken gravy
1 bag (16 ounces) BIRDS EYE® frozen Farm Fresh Mixtures Broccoli, Green Beans, Pearl Onions and Red Peppers
½ cup water

• Melt butter in large saucepan over high heat. Add chicken and potatoes; cook about 8 minutes or until browned, stirring frequently.

• Add sherry; cook until evaporated. Add gravy, vegetables and water.

• Bring to boil; reduce heat to medium-low. Cover and cook 6 to 7 minutes.

Makes 4 to 6 servings

Prep Time: 5 minutes
Cook Time: 20 minutes

Country Chicken Stew

Hearty One-Pot Chicken Stew

- 12 TYSON® Individually Fresh Frozen® Boneless, Skinless Chicken Tenderloins
- 1 box UNCLE BEN'S CHEF'S RECIPE™ Traditional Red Beans & Rice
- 1 can (14½ ounces) diced tomatoes, undrained
- 3 new red potatoes, unpeeled, cut into 1-inch pieces
- 2 carrots, sliced ½ inch thick
- 1 onion, cut into 1-inch pieces

PREP: CLEAN: Wash hands. Remove protective ice glaze from frozen chicken by holding under cool running water 1 to 2 minutes. Cut into 1-inch pieces. CLEAN: Wash hands.

COOK: In large saucepan, combine chicken, beans and rice, contents of seasoning packet, 2¼ cups water, tomatoes, potatoes, carrots and onion. Bring to a boil. Cover, reduce heat; simmer 20 minutes or until internal juices of chicken run clear. (Or insert instant-read meat thermometer in thickest part of chicken. Temperature should read 170°F.)

SERVE: Serve with hot rolls, if desired.

CHILL: Refrigerate leftovers immediately. *Makes 4 servings*

Prep Time: 10 minutes
Cook Time: 20 to 25 minutes

Easy Chicken Ragoût

- 2 tablespoons all-purpose flour
- ¼ teaspoon salt
- ½ teaspoon poultry seasoning
- ¼ teaspoon black pepper
- 4 boneless skinless chicken thighs (about 1½ pounds)
- 1 teaspoon olive oil
- 1 can (15 ounces) whole tomatoes, undrained
- 1 can (14½ ounces) chicken broth
- 2 cups quartered mushrooms
- 2 medium carrots, sliced
- 1 large onion, diced
- ½ to ¾ teaspoon dried thyme leaves
- 1 bay leaf
- 2 cups hot cooked rice

Combine flour, salt, poultry seasoning and pepper on sheet of waxed paper. Coat chicken thighs with flour mixture.

Heat oil in large saucepan over medium heat. Add chicken; cook and stir about 10 minutes or until chicken is browned on all sides. Remove chicken; drain fat from saucepan.

Return chicken to saucepan. Add tomatoes with juice, chicken broth, mushrooms, carrots, onion, thyme and bay leaf; stir to break up tomatoes. Bring to a boil; reduce heat to low. Cover and simmer 30 minutes or until vegetables are tender and chicken is no longer pink in center, stirring occasionally. Discard bay leaf. Serve over rice.

Makes about 6 cups or 4 servings

Chicken Gumbo

- 3 tablespoons vegetable oil
- 1 pound boneless skinless chicken breasts, cut into 1-inch pieces
- ½ pound smoked sausage, (see helpful hint below) cut into ¾-inch slices
- 1 bag (16 ounces) BIRDS EYE® frozen Farm Fresh Mixtures Broccoli, Corn and Red Peppers
- 1 can (14½ ounces) stewed tomatoes
- 1½ cups water

• Heat oil in large saucepan over high heat. Add chicken and sausage; cook until browned, about 8 minutes.

• Add vegetables, tomatoes and water; bring to boil. Reduce heat to medium; cover and cook 5 to 6 minutes. *Makes 4 to 6 servings*

Prep Time: 5 minutes
Cook Time: 20 minutes

Helpful Hints

Any type of Kielbasa or Polish sausage can be used in this recipe for Chicken Gumbo. For a spicier, more traditional flavor, choose andouille sausage, which is popular in Cajun cooking.

Hearty One-Pot Chicken Stew

Turkey Mushroom Stew

Slow Cooker

1 pound turkey cutlets, cut into 4×1-inch strips
1 small onion, thinly sliced
2 tablespoons minced green onions with tops
½ pound mushrooms, sliced
2 to 3 tablespoons flour
1 cup half-and-half or milk
1 teaspoon dried tarragon leaves
1 teaspoon salt
Black pepper to taste
½ cup frozen peas
½ cup sour cream (optional)
Puff pastry shells (optional)

Slow Cooker Directions

Layer turkey, onions and mushrooms in slow cooker. Cover and cook on LOW 4 hours. Remove turkey and vegetables to serving bowl. Turn slow cooker to HIGH.

Blend flour into half-and-half until smooth; pour into slow cooker. Add tarragon, salt and pepper to slow cooker. Return cooked vegetables and turkey to slow cooker. Stir in peas. Cover and cook 1 hour or until sauce has thickened and peas are heated through.

Stir in sour cream just before serving, if desired. Serve in puff pastry shells, if desired. *Makes 4 servings*

Cioppino in a Dash

1 tablespoon olive oil
½ cup green bell pepper cut into ½-inch squares
2 cans (14½ ounces each) no-salt-added diced tomatoes, undrained
1 can (8 ounces) no-salt-added tomato sauce
1½ teaspoons MRS. DASH® Classic Italiano Seasoning Blend
1 pound skinless boneless medium- or firm-flesh fish fillets (such as red snapper, cod, halibut or haddock), cut into ½-inch pieces
8 ounces deveined peeled shrimp
½ cup dry white wine

Heat oil in 3-quart saucepan over medium-high heat until hot. Cook bell pepper, stirring until tender, about 5 minutes. Add diced tomatoes, tomato sauce and seasoning. Heat to a boil; reduce heat and simmer 20 minutes. Add fish and shrimp; return to a boil. Reduce heat; cover and simmer 7 minutes or until done. Stir in wine during last minute of cooking. Serve immediately.

Makes 6 servings

Prep Time: 10 minutes
Cook Time: 32 minutes

Gumbo in a Hurry

2 cans (14½ ounces *each*) chicken broth
1 can (14½ ounces) tomatoes, cut up, undrained
½ cup *each* minced celery and onion
¼ cup *Frank's® RedHot®* Cayenne Pepper Sauce
2 bay leaves
1 teaspoon dried thyme leaves
1 pound medium shrimp, peeled and deveined
1 can (6 ounces) crabmeat, drained
1 (4-ounce) boneless skinless chicken breast or thigh, cut into small cubes
1 package (10 ounces) frozen sliced okra, thawed
Hot cooked rice

1. Combine broth, tomatoes, *½ cup water,* celery, onion, ***Frank's RedHot*** and seasonings in large saucepot or Dutch oven. Heat to boiling. Stir in shrimp, crabmeat and chicken. Reduce heat to medium-low. Cook, uncovered, 10 minutes; stirring occasionally.

2. Stir in okra. Cook over medium-low heat 5 minutes or until okra is tender. *Do not boil.* Serve gumbo over rice in soup bowls. Serve with crusty French bread or garlic bread, if desired.

Makes 6 servings

Prep Time: 5 minutes
Cook Time: 15 minutes

Helpful Hints

Cioppino, a San Francisco specialty, is a tomato based fish stew consisting of fish and shellfish. It's often flavored with wine.

Turkey Mushroom Stew

Oyster Corn Stew

1 pint shucked fresh oysters including liquor*
1 can (15 ounces) cream-style corn
1 cup milk
¼ teaspoon salt
¼ teaspoon celery seeds
Dash white pepper
4 tablespoons butter or margarine
1 rib celery, chopped
1 cup cream or half-and-half
Celery leaves and grated lemon peel for garnish

**Liquor is the term used to describe the natural juices of an oyster.*

1. Strain oysters through triple thickness of dampened cheesecloth into small bowl; set aside oysters and liquor.

2. Place corn, milk, salt, celery seeds and pepper in large saucepan. Bring to a simmer over medium heat; set aside.

3. Melt butter in medium skillet over medium-high heat. Add celery and cook 8 to 10 minutes or until tender. Add oyster liquor; cook until heated through. Add oysters; heat about 10 minutes, just until oysters begin to curl around edges.

4. Add oyster mixture and cream to milk mixture. Cook over medium-high heat until just heated through. *Do not boil.*

5. Serve in wide-rimmed soup bowls. Garnish, if desired.

Makes 6 servings

Spicy Shrimp Gumbo

½ cup vegetable oil
½ cup all-purpose flour
1 large onion, chopped
½ cup chopped fresh parsley
½ cup chopped celery
½ cup sliced green onions
6 cloves garlic, minced
4 cups chicken broth or water*
1 package (10 ounces) frozen sliced okra, thawed (optional)
1 teaspoon salt
½ teaspoon ground red pepper
2 pounds raw medium shrimp, peeled and deveined
3 cups hot cooked rice
Fresh parsley sprigs for garnish

**Traditional gumbo's thickness is like stew. If you prefer it thinner, add 1 to 2 cups additional broth.*

1. For roux, blend oil and flour in large heavy stockpot. Cook over medium heat 10 to 15 minutes or until roux is dark brown but not burned, stirring often.

2. Add chopped onion, chopped parsley, celery, green onions and garlic to roux. Cook over medium heat 5 to 10 minutes or until vegetables are tender. Add broth, okra, salt and red pepper. Cover; simmer 15 minutes.

3. Add shrimp; simmer 3 to 5 minutes or until shrimp turn pink and opaque.

4. Place about ⅓ cup rice into each wide-rimmed soup bowl; top with gumbo. Garnish, if desired.

Makes 8 servings

Shrimp Creole Stew

1½ cups raw small shrimp, shelled
1 bag (16 ounces) BIRDS EYE® frozen Farm Fresh Mixtures Broccoli, Cauliflower & Red Peppers
1 can (14½ ounces) diced tomatoes
1½ teaspoons salt
1 teaspoon hot pepper sauce
1 teaspoon vegetable oil

• In large saucepan, combine all ingredients.

• Cover; bring to boil. Reduce heat to medium-low; simmer 20 minutes or until shrimp turn opaque.

Makes 4 servings

Serving Suggestion: Serve over Spanish or white rice and with additional hot pepper sauce for added zip.

Prep Time: 5 minutes
Cook Time: 20 minutes

Mardi Gras Gumbo

1 bag SUCCESS® Rice
1 can (14½ ounces) low-sodium chicken broth
1 can (10¾ ounces) chicken gumbo soup
1 can (10¾ ounces) condensed tomato soup
1 can (6 ounces) crabmeat, drained and flaked

Prepare rice according to package directions.

Combine remaining ingredients in medium saucepan. Bring to a boil over medium-high heat. Reduce heat to low. Stir in rice; heat thoroughly, stirring occasionally.

Makes 4 servings

Oyster Corn Stew

Shrimp Étouffée

- **3 tablespoons vegetable oil**
- **¼ cup all-purpose flour**
- **1 cup chopped onion**
- **1 cup chopped green bell pepper**
- **½ cup chopped carrots**
- **½ cup chopped celery**
- **4 cloves garlic, minced**
- **1 can (14½ ounces) clear vegetable broth**
- **1 bottle (8 ounces) clam juice**
- **½ teaspoon salt**
- **2½ pounds large shrimp, peeled and deveined**
- **1 teaspoon crushed red pepper**
- **1 teaspoon hot pepper sauce**
- **4 cups hot cooked white or basmati rice**
- **½ cup chopped flat leaf parsley**

1. Heat oil in Dutch oven over medium heat. Add flour; cook and stir 10 to 15 minutes or until flour mixture is deep golden brown. Add onion, bell pepper, carrots, celery and garlic; cook and stir 5 minutes.

2. Stir in broth, clam juice and salt; bring to a boil. Simmer, uncovered, 10 minutes or until vegetables are tender. Stir in shrimp, red pepper and pepper sauce; simmer 6 to 8 minutes or until shrimp are opaque.

3. Ladle into eight shallow bowls; top each with ½ cup rice. Sprinkle with parsley. Serve with additional pepper sauce, if desired.

Makes 8 servings

Seafood Stew

- **2 tablespoons butter or margarine**
- **1 cup chopped onion**
- **1 cup green bell pepper strips**
- **1 teaspoon dried dill weed**
- **Dash ground red pepper**
- **1 can (14½ ounces) diced tomatoes, undrained**
- **½ cup white wine**
- **2 tablespoons lime juice**
- **8 ounces swordfish steak, cut into 1-inch cubes**
- **8 ounces bay or sea scallops, cut into quarters**
- **1 bottle (8 ounces) clam juice**
- **2 tablespoons cornstarch**
- **2 cups frozen diced potatoes, thawed and drained**
- **8 ounces frozen cooked medium shrimp, thawed and drained**
- **½ cup whipping cream**

1. Melt butter in Dutch oven over medium-high heat. Add onion, bell pepper, dill weed and red pepper; cook and stir 5 minutes or until vegetables are tender.

2. Reduce heat to medium. Add tomatoes with juice, wine and lime juice; bring to a boil. Add swordfish and scallops; cook and stir 2 minutes.

3. Combine clam juice and cornstarch in small bowl; stir until smooth.

4. Increase heat to high. Add potatoes, shrimp, whipping cream and clam juice mixture; bring to a boil. Season to taste with salt and black pepper.

Makes 6 servings

Serving Suggestion: For a special touch, garnish stew with fresh lemon wedges and basil leaves.

Prep and Cook Time: 20 minutes

Shrimp Gumbo

- **1 package (16 ounces) frozen cut okra**
- **1 can (16 ounces) stewed tomatoes, undrained**
- **2 cups water**
- **½ pound cooked ham or sausage, diced**
- **1 can (8 ounces) tomato sauce**
- **2 medium onions, sliced**
- **2 tablespoons oil**
- **½ teaspoon red pepper flakes**
- **1 bay leaf**
- **Salt and black pepper**
- **2 pounds frozen shelled deveined shrimp**

Combine all ingredients except shrimp in Dutch oven. Bring to a boil over high heat. Reduce heat to low. Simmer, partially covered, 30 minutes. Add shrimp; stir well. Cook, partially covered, stirring occasionally, until shrimp are cooked through, 10 to 15 minutes longer. Remove bay leaf before serving.

Makes 6 servings

Chili Stew

- **1 box (10 ounces) BIRDS EYE® frozen Sweet Corn**
- **2 cans (15 ounces each) chili**
- **1 can (14 ounces) stewed tomatoes**
- **Chili powder**

• In large saucepan, cook corn according to package directions; drain.

• Stir in chili and tomatoes; cook until heated through.

• Stir in chili powder to taste.

Makes 4 servings

Serving Suggestion: Serve with your favorite corn bread or sprinkle with shredded Cheddar cheese.

Prep Time: 2 minutes
Cook Time: 7 to 10 minutes

Shrimp Étouffée

Bean Ragoût with Cilantro-Cornmeal Dumplings

Slow Cooker

2 cans (14½ ounces each) tomatoes, chopped and juice reserved
1½ cups chopped red bell pepper
1 large onion, chopped
1 can (15½ ounces) pinto or kidney beans, rinsed and drained
1 can (15½ ounces) black beans, rinsed and drained
2 small zucchini, sliced
½ cup chopped green bell pepper
½ cup chopped celery
1 poblano chili pepper,* seeded and chopped
2 cloves garlic, minced
3 tablespoons chili powder
2 teaspoons ground cumin
1 teaspoon dried oregano leaves
½ teaspoon salt, divided
⅛ teaspoon black pepper
¼ cup all-purpose flour
¼ cup yellow cornmeal
½ teaspoon baking powder
1 tablespoon vegetable shortening
2 tablespoons shredded Cheddar cheese
2 teaspoons minced fresh cilantro
¼ cup milk

**Chili peppers can sting and irritate the skin; wear rubber gloves when handling peppers and do not touch eyes.*

Slow Cooker Directions
Combine tomatoes with juice, red bell pepper, onion, beans, zucchini, green bell pepper, celery, poblano pepper, garlic, chili powder, cumin, oregano, ¼ teaspoon salt and black pepper in slow cooker; mix well. Cover and cook on LOW 7 to 8 hours.

Prepare dumplings 1 hour before serving. Mix flour, cornmeal, baking powder and remaining ¼ teaspoon salt in medium bowl. Cut in shortening with pastry blender or two knives until mixture resembles coarse crumbs. Stir in cheese and cilantro. Pour milk into flour mixture. Blend just until dry ingredients are moistened. Turn slow cooker to HIGH. Drop dumplings by level tablespoonfuls (larger dumplings will not cook properly) on top of ragoût. Cover and cook 1 hour or until toothpick inserted in dumpling comes out clean.

Makes 6 servings

Middle Eastern Vegetable Stew

1 tablespoon olive oil
3 cups (12 ounces) sliced zucchini
2 cups (6 ounces) cubed peeled eggplant
2 cups (8 ounces) sliced quartered sweet potatoes
1½ cups cubed peeled butternut squash
1 can (28 ounces) crushed tomatoes in purée
1 cup drained garbanzo beans
½ cup raisins or currants
1½ teaspoons ground cinnamon
1 teaspoon grated orange peel
¾ to 1 teaspoon ground cumin
½ teaspoon salt
½ teaspoon paprika
¼ to ½ teaspoon ground red pepper
⅛ teaspoon ground cardamom
Hot cooked rice or couscous (optional)

Slow Cooker Directions
Combine all ingredients except rice in slow cooker. Cover and cook on LOW 5 to 5 ½ hours or until vegetables are tender. Serve over rice.

Makes 4 to 6 servings

Tuscan Vegetable Stew

2 tablespoons olive oil
2 teaspoons bottled minced garlic
2 packages (4 ounces each) sliced mixed exotic mushrooms *or* 1 package (8 ounces) sliced button mushrooms
¼ cup sliced shallots or chopped sweet onion
1 jar (7 ounces) roasted red peppers
1 can (14½ ounces) Italian-style stewed tomatoes, undrained
1 can (19 ounces) cannellini beans, rinsed and drained
1 bunch fresh basil leaves*
1 tablespoon balsamic vinegar
Salt
Black pepper
Grated Romano, Parmesan or Asiago cheese

**If fresh basil is not available, add 2 teaspoons dried basil leaves to stew with tomatoes.*

1. Heat oil and garlic in large deep skillet over medium heat. Add mushrooms and shallots; cook 5 minutes, stirring occasionally.

2. While mushroom mixture is cooking, drain and rinse red peppers; cut into 1-inch pieces. Snip tomatoes in can into small pieces with scissors.

3. Add tomatoes, red peppers and beans to skillet; bring to a boil. Reduce heat to medium-low. Cover and simmer 10 minutes, stirring once.

4. While stew is simmering, cut basil leaves into thin strips to measure ¼ cup packed. Stir basil and vinegar into stew; add salt and black pepper to taste. Sprinkle each serving with cheese. *Makes 4 servings*

Prep and Cook Time: 18 minutes

Bean Ragoût with Cilantro-Cornmeal Dumplings

Satisfying Chilis

Fast 'n Easy Chili

1½ pounds ground beef
1 envelope LIPTON® RECIPE SECRETS® Onion Soup Mix*
1 can (15 to 19 ounces) red kidney or black beans, drained
1½ cups water
1 can (8 ounces) tomato sauce
4 teaspoons chili powder

**Also terrific with LIPTON® RECIPE SECRETS® Beefy Mushroom, Onion-Mushroom or Beefy Onion Soup Mix.*

1. In 12-inch skillet, brown ground beef over medium-high heat; drain.

2. Stir in remaining ingredients. Bring to a boil over high heat. Reduce heat to low and simmer covered, stirring occasionally, 20 minutes. Serve, if desired, over hot cooked rice.

Makes 6 servings

First Alarm Chili: Add 5 teaspoons chili powder.

Second Alarm Chili: Add 2 tablespoons chili powder.

Third Alarm Chili: Add chili powder at your own risk.

Classic Texas Chili

¼ cup vegetable oil
3 pounds beef round or chuck, cut into 1-inch cubes
3 cloves garlic, minced
4 to 6 tablespoons chili powder
2 teaspoons salt
2 teaspoons dried oregano leaves
2 teaspoons ground cumin
2 teaspoons TABASCO® brand pepper sauce
1½ quarts water
⅓ cup white cornmeal
Hot cooked rice and beans

Heat oil in large saucepan or Dutch oven. Add beef and brown on all sides. Add garlic, chili powder, salt, oregano, cumin, TABASCO® Sauce and water; stir to mix well. Bring to a boil; cover and reduce heat. Simmer 1¼ hours, stirring occasionally. Add cornmeal and mix well. Simmer, uncovered, an additional 30 minutes or until beef is tender. Garnish with chopped onion if desired. Serve with rice and beans.

Makes 6 to 8 servings

Chilly Day Chili

2 medium onions, chopped
1 green bell pepper, chopped
2 tablespoons vegetable oil
2 pounds lean ground beef
2 to 3 tablespoons chili powder
1 can (14½ ounces) tomatoes, cut into bite-size pieces
1 can (15 ounces) tomato sauce
½ cup HEINZ® Tomato Ketchup
1 teaspoon salt
¼ teaspoon black pepper
2 cans (15½ ounces each) red kidney beans, partially drained

In large saucepan or Dutch oven, cook and stir onions and green pepper in oil until tender. Add beef; cook until beef is no longer pink, stirring occasionally. Drain excess fat. Stir in chili powder, then add tomatoes, tomato sauce, ketchup, salt and pepper. Simmer, uncovered, 30 minutes, stirring occasionally. Add kidney beans; simmer additional 15 minutes.

Makes 8 servings (about 8 cups)

Fast 'n Easy Chili

Chipotle Chili con Carne

- ¾ pound lean cubed beef stew meat
- 1 tablespoon chili powder
- 1 tablespoon ground cumin
- Nonstick cooking spray
- 1 can (about 14 ounces) reduced-sodium beef broth
- 1 tablespoon minced canned chipotle chilies in adobo sauce, or to taste
- 1 can (14½ ounces) diced tomatoes, undrained
- 1 large green bell pepper *or* 2 poblano chili peppers, cut into pieces
- 2 cans (16 ounces each) pinto or red beans, rinsed and drained
- Chopped fresh cilantro (optional)

1. Toss beef in combined chili powder and cumin. Coat large saucepan or Dutch oven with cooking spray; heat over medium heat. Add beef; cook 5 minutes, stirring occasionally. Add beef broth and chipotle chilies with sauce; bring to a boil. Reduce heat; cover and simmer 1 hour 15 minutes or until beef is very tender.

2. With slotted spoon, transfer beef to carving board, leaving juices in saucepan. Using two forks, shred beef. Return beef to saucepan; add tomatoes and bell pepper. Bring to a boil; stir in beans. Simmer, uncovered, 20 minutes or until bell pepper is tender. Garnish with cilantro, if desired. *Makes 6 servings*

Prep Time: 15 minutes
Cook Time: 1 hour 40 minutes

Chili with a Twist

- 2 tablespoons vegetable oil
- 2 pounds ground beef
- 2 cups finely chopped white onions
- 1 to 2 dried de arbol chilies
- 2 cloves garlic, minced
- 1 teaspoon ground cumin
- ½ to 1 teaspoon salt
- ¼ teaspoon ground cloves
- 1 can (28 ounces) whole peeled tomatoes, undrained, coarsely chopped
- ½ cup fresh orange juice
- ½ cup tequila or water
- ¼ cup tomato paste
- 1 tablespoon grated orange peel
- Lime wedges and cilantro sprigs (optional)

Heat oil in deep 12-inch skillet over medium-high heat until hot. Crumble beef into skillet. Brown 6 to 8 minutes, stirring occasionally. Pour off drippings. Reduce heat to medium. Add onions; cook and stir 5 minutes or until tender.

Crush chilies into fine flakes in mortar with pestle or with a rolling pin. Add chilies, garlic, cumin, salt and cloves to skillet. Cook and stir 30 seconds.

Stir in tomatoes with juice, orange juice, tequila, tomato paste and orange peel. Bring to a boil over high heat. Reduce heat to low. Cover and simmer 1½ hours, stirring occasionally.

Uncover skillet. Cook chili over medium-low heat 10 to 15 minutes or until thickened slightly, stirring frequently. Ladle into bowls. Garnish with lime wedges and cilantro if desired. *Makes 6 to 8 servings*

Chili Verde

- ¾ pound boneless lean pork, cut into 1-inch cubes
- 1 large onion, halved and thinly sliced
- 6 cloves garlic, chopped or sliced
- 1 pound fresh tomatillos, coarsely chopped
- 1 can (about 14 ounces) chicken broth
- 1 can (4 ounces) diced mild green chilies
- 1 teaspoon ground cumin
- 1 can (15 ounces) Great Northern beans, rinsed and drained
- ½ cup lightly packed fresh cilantro, chopped
- Sour cream

Slow Cooker Directions

Spray large skillet with nonstick cooking spray and heat over medium-high heat. Add pork; cook until browned on all sides.

Combine cooked pork and all remaining ingredients except cilantro and sour cream in slow cooker. Cover and cook on HIGH 3 to 4 hours. Season to taste with salt and pepper. Gently press meat against side of slow cooker with wooden spoon to shred. Reduce heat to LOW. Stir in cilantro and cook 10 mintes. Serve with sour cream.

Makes 4 servings

Helpful Hints

Tomatillos look like small green tomatoes with papery tan husks. They have a refreshing herbal flavor with a hint of lemon. To use them, peel away the husks, then rinse the tomatillos before chopping.

Chipotle Chili con Carne

Five-Way Cincinnati Chili

- 1 pound uncooked spaghetti, broken in half
- 1 pound ground chuck
- 2 cans (10 ounces each) tomatoes and green chilies, undrained
- 1 can (15 ounces) red kidney beans, drained
- 1 can (10½ ounces) condensed French onion soup
- 1¼ cups water
- 1 tablespoon chili powder
- 1 teaspoon sugar
- ½ teaspoon salt
- ¼ teaspoon ground cinnamon
- ½ cup (2 ounces) shredded Cheddar cheese
- ½ cup chopped onion

1. Cook pasta according to package directions; drain.

2. While pasta is cooking, cook beef in large saucepan or Dutch oven over medium-high heat until browned, stirring to separate; drain well. Add tomatoes with juice, beans, soup, water, chili powder, sugar, salt and cinnamon to saucepan; bring to a boil. Reduce heat to low. Simmer, uncovered, 10 minutes, stirring occasionally.

3. Serve chili over spaghetti; sprinkle with cheese and onion.

Makes 6 servings

Serving Suggestion: Serve this traditional chili your way or one of the ways Cincinnatians do—two-way over spaghetti, three-way with cheese, four-way with cheese and chopped onion or five-way with beans added to the chili.

Prep and Cook time: 20 minutes

Cowboy Chili

- 2 large onions, chopped
- 2 pounds boneless top round or sirloin steak, cut into ½-inch cubes
- 1 pound ground beef
- 1 can (28 ounces) whole tomatoes in purée, undrained
- 1 can (15 to 19 ounces) red kidney beans, undrained
- ⅓ cup *Frank's® RedHot®* Cayenne Pepper Sauce
- 2 packages (1¼ ounces *each*) chili seasoning mix

1. Cook and stir onions in *1 tablespoon hot oil* in large pot; transfer to bowl. Cook steak cubes and ground beef in batches in *3 tablespoons hot oil* until well-browned; drain well.

2. Add onions, *¾ cup water* and remaining ingredients to pot. Heat to boiling, stirring. Reduce heat to medium-low. Cook, partially covered, 1 hour or until meat is tender, stirring often. Garnish as desired.

Makes 10 servings

Ground Beef Variation: Substitute 3 pounds ground beef for the combination of top round and ground beef. Brown meat without oil. Proceed as in step 2. Simmer 20 minutes.

Prep Time: 15 minutes
Cook Time: 1 hour 15 minutes

Hearty Chili

- 2 pounds BOB EVANS® Original Recipe Roll Sausage
- 1½ cups chopped onions
- 1 (1¼-ounce) package chili seasoning
- 3 cups tomato sauce
- 3 cups tomato juice
- 1 (30-ounce) can chili or kidney beans
- Hot pepper sauce to taste (optional)

Crumble sausage into large Dutch oven. Add onions. Cook over medium heat until sausage is browned, stirring occasionally. Drain off any drippings; stir in seasoning, then remaining ingredients. Bring to a boil over high heat. Reduce heat to low; simmer, uncovered, 30 minutes. Serve hot. Refrigerate leftovers.

Makes 8 servings

Hearty Chili with Black Beans

- 1 tablespoon vegetable oil
- 1 pound ground chuck
- 1 can (about 14½ ounces) beef broth
- 1 large onion, minced
- 1 green bell pepper, seeded and diced
- 2 teaspoons chili powder
- ½ teaspoon ground allspice
- ¼ teaspoon cinnamon
- ¼ teaspoon paprika
- 1 can (15 ounces) black beans, rinsed and drained
- 1 can (14 ounces) crushed tomatoes in tomato purée
- 2 teaspoons apple cider vinegar

Heat oil in large skillet over medium-high heat until hot. Add ground beef, beef broth, onion and bell pepper. Cook and stir, breaking up meat. Cook until beef is no longer pink; drain excess fat.

Add chili powder, allspice, cinnamon and paprika. Reduce heat to medium-low; simmer 10 minutes. Add black beans, tomatoes and vinegar; bring to a boil.

Reduce heat to low; simmer 20 to 25 minutes or until chili is thickened to desired consistency. Garnish as desired. *Makes 4 servings*

Five-Way Cincinnati Chili

Hearty Chili

1¼ cups dried pinto beans
1 pound ground beef or turkey
1 onion, chopped
3 tablespoons Hearty Chili Seasoning Mix (recipe follows)
1 can (28 ounces) diced tomatoes, undrained
1 can (about 14 ounces) beef broth

1. Place beans and 8 cups cold water in large saucepan. Bring to a boil over high heat. Boil 1 minute. Remove saucepan from heat. Cover; let stand 1 hour.

2. Drain beans; rinse under cold running water. Return beans to saucepan. Add 8 cups cold water. Bring to a boil over high heat. Reduce heat to medium-low. Simmer 1 hour 15 minutes or until beans are just tender, stirring occasionally. Remove saucepan from heat and drain beans; set aside.

3. Combine ground beef and onion in large saucepan. Cook over medium-high heat 6 minutes or until beef is no longer pink, stirring to crumble beef. Spoon off and discard any drippings.

4. Add Seasoning Mix to saucepan. Cook 1 minute, stirring frequently. Add beans, tomatoes with juice and beef broth; bring to a boil over high heat. Reduce heat to medium-low. Cover; simmer 30 minutes, stirring occasionally. Store in airtight container in refrigerator up to 3 days or freeze up to 1 month.

Makes about 8 cups

Hearty Chili Seasoning Mix

½ cup chili powder
¼ cup ground cumin
2 tablespoons dried oregano leaves
2 tablespoons garlic salt
2 teaspoons ground coriander
½ teaspoon ground red pepper

Combine all ingredients in small bowl. Store in airtight container at room temperature up to 3 months.

Makes about 1 cup

Chunky Chili

1 pound lean ground beef
1 medium onion, chopped
1 tablespoon chili powder
1½ teaspoons ground cumin
2 cans (16 ounces each) diced tomatoes, undrained
1 can (15 ounces) pinto beans, rinsed and drained
½ cup prepared salsa
½ cup (2 ounces) shredded Cheddar cheese
3 tablespoons sour cream
4 teaspoons sliced black olives

Slow Cooking Directions
Heat large skillet over medium heat. Add beef and onion, cook until beef is browned and onion is tender. Drain fat. Place beef mixture, chili powder, cumin, tomatoes with juice, beans and salsa in slow cooker; stir. Cover and cook on LOW 5 to 6 hours or until flavors are blended and chili is bubbly. Season with salt and pepper to taste. Serve with cheese, sour cream and olives.

Makes 4 (1½-cup) servings

Serving Suggestion: Serve with tossed green salad and cornbread muffins.

Riverboat Chili

2 pounds lean ground beef
2 large onions, chopped
1 large green bell pepper, chopped
2 cans (14½ ounces each) FRANK'S® or SNOWFLOSS® Original Style Diced Tomatoes, undrained
1 can (14½ ounces) FRANK'S® or SNOWFLOSS® Stewed Tomatoes, undrained
⅓ cup MISSISSIPPI® Barbecue Sauce
2 bay leaves
3 whole cloves
2 teaspoons chili powder
½ teaspoon cayenne pepper
½ teaspoon paprika
4 cans (15½ ounces each) dark red kidney beans

1. Brown ground beef in large stock pot. Drain grease.

2. Add onions, green pepper, diced tomatoes, stewed tomatoes, barbecue sauce, bay leaves, cloves, chili powder, cayenne pepper and paprika. Stir well.

3. Add kidney beans and stir well.

4. Cover and simmer 2 hours, stirring occasionally. Remove and discard bay leaves before serving.

Makes 4 to 6 servings

Microwave Directions: Crumble beef into large casserole dish. Cook uncovered about 6 minutes stirring at least twice to break up meat. Drain grease. Add onions, green pepper, diced tomatoes, stewed tomatoes, barbecue sauce, bay leaves, cloves, chili powder, cayenne pepper and paprika. Cook 1 minute. Stir well. Add kidney beans and stir well. Cover and cook 15 to 20 minutes, stirring occasionally. Cover and let stand 5 minutes. Remove and discard bay leaves before serving.

Prep Time: 30 minutes
Cook Time: 2 hours

Hearty Chili

Winter White Chili

- ½ pound boneless pork loin *or* 2 boneless pork chops, cut into ½-inch cubes
- ½ cup chopped onion
- 1 teaspoon vegetable oil
- 1 (16-ounce) can navy beans, drained
- 1 (16-ounce) can chick-peas, drained
- 1 (16-ounce) can white kernel corn, drained
- 1 (14½-ounce) can chicken broth
- 1 cup cooked wild rice
- 1 (4-ounce) can diced green chilies, drained
- 1½ teaspoons ground cumin
- ¼ teaspoon garlic powder
- ⅛ teaspoon hot pepper sauce
- Chopped parsley and shredded cheese

In 4-quart saucepan, sauté pork and onion in oil over medium-high heat until onion is soft and pork is lightly browned, about 5 minutes. Stir in remaining ingredients except parsley and cheese. Cover and simmer for 20 minutes. Serve each portion garnished with parsley and shredded cheese. *Makes 6 servings*

Preparation Time: 10 minutes
Cooking Time: 25 minutes

Favorite recipe from **National Pork Board**

Ragú® Chili

- 2 pounds ground beef
- 1 large onion, chopped
- 2 cloves garlic, finely chopped
- 1 jar (26 to 28 ounces) RAGÚ® Hearty Robusto! Pasta Sauce
- 1 can (15 ounces) red kidney beans, rinsed and drained
- 2 tablespoons chili powder

In 12-inch skillet, brown ground beef with onion and garlic over medium-high heat; drain. Stir in remaining ingredients. Simmer uncovered, stirring occasionally, 20 minutes. Serve, if desired, with shredded Cheddar cheese.

Makes 8 servings

Suggestion: For spicier Ragú® Chili, stir in ½ teaspoon *each* ground cumin and dried oregano.

Soul City Chili

- 2 pounds ground beef
- ½ teaspoon LAWRY'S® Seasoned Salt
- ½ teaspoon LAWRY'S® Seasoned Pepper
- 1 pound hot Italian sausage or kielbasa sausage, cut into bite-size pieces
- 2 cups water
- 1 can (15¼ ounces) kidney beans, undrained
- 1 can (14½ ounces) stewed tomatoes, undrained
- 2 packages (1.48 ounces each) LAWRY'S® Spices & Seasonings for Chili
- ½ cup hickory flavored barbecue sauce
- ¾ cup red wine

In Dutch oven, cook beef until browned and crumbly; drain fat. Add Seasoned Salt and Seasoned Pepper; mix well. Stir in sausage, water, beans, tomatoes, Spices & Seasonings for Chili and barbecue sauce. Bring to a boil over medium-high heat; reduce heat to low, simmer, uncovered, 20 minutes. Stir in wine. Heat through.

Makes about 10 servings (9½ cups)

Serving Suggestion: Top with diced green, yellow and red bell peppers and chopped onion. Perfect with crackers, too!

Tex-Mex Chili

- 4 slices bacon diced
- 2 pounds beef round steak, trimmed and cut into ½-inch cubes
- 1 medium onion, chopped
- 2 cloves garlic, minced
- ¼ cup chili powder
- 1 teaspoon dried oregano
- 1 teaspoon ground cumin
- 1 teaspoon salt
- ½ to 1 teaspoon ground red pepper
- ½ teaspoon hot pepper sauce
- 4 cups water
- Chopped onion for garnish

Cook bacon in 5-quart kettle over medium-high heat until crisp. Remove with slotted spoon; drain on paper towels. Add half of the steak to bacon drippings in kettle; cook until lightly browned. Remove steak from kettle. Repeat with remaining steak. Reduce heat to medium. Cook medium onion and garlic in pan drippings until onion is tender. Reduce heat to medium. Return steak and bacon to kettle. Add chili powder, oregano, cumin, salt, ground red pepper, hot pepper sauce and water. Bring to a boil. Cover; reduce heat and simmer 1½ hours. Skim fat. Simmer, uncovered, 30 minutes or until steak is very tender and chili has thickened slightly. Serve in individual bowls. Garnish with chopped onion.

Makes 6 servings

Winter White Chili

Meaty Chili

1 pound coarsely ground beef
¼ pound ground Italian sausage
1 large onion, chopped
2 medium ribs celery, diced
2 fresh jalapeño peppers,* chopped
2 cloves garlic, minced
1 can (28 ounces) whole peeled tomatoes, undrained, cut up
1 can (15 ounces) pinto beans, drained
1 can (12 ounces) tomato juice
1 cup water
¼ cup ketchup
1 teaspoon sugar
1 teaspoon chili powder
½ teaspoon salt
½ teaspoon ground cumin
½ teaspoon dried thyme leaves
⅛ teaspoon black pepper

**Jalapeño peppers can sting and irritate the skin; wear rubber gloves when handling peppers and do not touch eyes. Wash hands after handling.*

Cook beef, sausage, onion, celery, jalapeños and garlic in 5-quart Dutch oven over medium-high heat until meat is browned and onion is tender, stirring frequently.

Stir in tomatoes with juice, beans, tomato juice, water, ketchup, sugar, chili powder, salt, cumin, thyme and black pepper. Bring to a boil over high heat. Reduce heat to medium-low; simmer, uncovered, 30 minutes, stirring occasionally.

Ladle into bowls. Garnish, if desired.
Makes 6 servings

Texas-Style Chili

1½ pounds ground beef or cubed round steak
1 green bell pepper, diced
1 onion, diced
1 can (2¼ ounces) diced green chiles, drained
1 package (1.48 ounces) LAWRY'S® Spices & Seasonings for Chili
1½ tablespoons cornmeal
1 tablespoon chili powder
1 teaspoon sugar
¼ to ½ teaspoon cayenne pepper
1 can (14½ ounces) diced tomatoes, undrained
¾ cup water
Sour cream (optional)
Shredded cheddar cheese (optional)

In Dutch oven or large saucepan, cook beef until browned and crumbly; drain beef, reserving fat. Set beef aside. In Dutch oven heat reserved fat. Add bell pepper and onion and cook over medium-high heat 5 minutes or until vegetables are crisp-tender. Return beef to Dutch oven. Add chiles, Spices & Seasonings for Chili, cornmeal, chili powder, sugar and cayenne pepper; mix well. Stir in tomatoes and water. Bring to a boil over medium-high heat; reduce heat to low, cover, simmer 30 minutes, stirring occasionally. *Makes 4½ cups*

Serving Suggestion: Serve topped with sour cream or cheddar cheese, if desired.

Hint: This recipe is perfect for leftover meat. Use 3½ cups shredded beef. If using shredded beef or cubed round steak, brown in 1 tablespoon vegetable oil.

Veg•All® Beef Chili

1 can (28 ounces) tomato sauce
1 pound ground beef, browned and drained
1 can (16 ounces) kidney beans, drained and rinsed
1 can (15 ounces) VEG•ALL® Original Mixed Vegetables, with liquid
1 can (14½ ounces) whole tomatoes, cut up
¾ cup sliced green onions
2 teaspoons chili powder
¼ teaspoon black pepper
Corn chips
Shredded cheese
Diced green onions

In 3-quart saucepan, combine all ingredients except chips, cheese and diced onions. Bring to a boil; reduce heat, cover, and simmer for 20 to 30 minutes, stirring occasionally. Serve hot with corn chips, shredded cheese and diced green onions as toppers. *Makes 6 to 8 servings*

Note: A vegetarian version can be made by eliminating the ground beef and adding 1 teaspoon dried oregano and ½ teaspoon ground cumin.

Prep Time: 7 minutes
Cook Time: 20 minutes

Helpful Hints

Chili often tastes better the day after it is made, so consider preparing a double batch. Leftover chili can be served over pasta, rice or baked potatoes. Or, try it as a filling for taco shells, burritos or over hot dogs for chili dogs.

Meaty Chili

Black and White Chili

- **Nonstick cooking spray**
- **1 pound chicken tenders, cut into ¾-inch pieces**
- **1 cup coarsely chopped onion**
- **1 can (15½ ounces) Great Northern beans, drained**
- **1 can (15 ounces) black beans, drained**
- **1 can (14½ ounces) Mexican-style stewed tomatoes, undrained**
- **2 tablespoons Texas-style chili powder seasoning mix**

Slow Cooker Directions
Spray large saucepan with cooking spray; heat over medium heat until hot. Add chicken and onion; cook and stir 5 minutes or until chicken is browned.

Combine cooked chicken, onion, beans, tomatoes with juice and chili seasoning in slow cooker. Cover and cook on LOW 4 to 4½ hours.

Makes 6 (1-cup) servings

Bandstand Chili

- **2 cups chopped cooked BUTTERBALL® Boneless Young Turkey**
- **1 tablespoon vegetable oil**
- **1½ cups chopped onions**
- **1½ cups chopped red bell peppers**
- **2 tablespoons mild Mexican seasoning***
- **1 clove garlic, minced**
- **1 can (28 ounces) tomato purée with tomato bits**
- **1 can (15½ ounces) light red kidney beans, undrained**

**To make your own Mexican seasoning, combine 1 tablespoon chili powder, 1½ teaspoons oregano and 1½ teaspoons cumin.*

Heat oil in large skillet over medium heat until hot. Add onions, bell peppers, Mexican seasoning and garlic. Cook and stir 4 to 5 minutes. Add tomato purée and beans; stir in turkey. Reduce heat to low; simmer 5 minutes.

Makes 8 servings

Preparation Time: 25 minutes

Chicken Chili

- **1 tablespoon vegetable oil**
- **1 pound ground chicken or turkey**
- **1 medium onion, chopped**
- **1 medium green bell pepper, chopped**
- **2 fresh jalapeño peppers,* chopped**
- **1 can (28 ounces) tomatoes, cut up, undrained**
- **1 can (15½ ounces) kidney beans, drained**
- **1 can (8 ounces) tomato sauce**
- **1 tablespoon chili powder**
- **1 teaspoon salt**
- **1 teaspoon dried oregano leaves**
- **1 teaspoon ground cumin**
- **¼ teaspoon ground red pepper**
- **½ cup (2 ounces) shredded Cheddar cheese**

**Jalapeño peppers can sting and irritate the skin; wear rubber gloves when handling peppers and do not touch eyes. Wash hands after handling.*

Heat oil in 5-quart Dutch oven or large saucepan over medium-high heat. Cook chicken, onion and bell pepper until chicken is no longer pink and onion is crisp-tender, stirring frequently to break up chicken. Stir in jalapeño peppers, tomatoes with juice, beans, tomato sauce, chili powder, salt, oregano, cumin and red pepper. Bring to a boil over high heat. Reduce heat to medium-low; simmer, uncovered, 45 minutes to blend flavors. To serve, spoon into 6 bowls and top with cheese.

Makes 6 servings

Confetti Chicken Chili

- **1 pound 90% fat-free ground chicken or 93% fat-free ground turkey**
- **1 large onion, chopped**
- **2 cans (about 14 ounces each) fat-free reduced-sodium chicken broth**
- **1 can (15 ounces) Great Northern beans, rinsed and drained**
- **2 carrots, chopped**
- **1 medium green bell pepper, chopped**
- **2 plum tomatoes, chopped**
- **1 jalapeño pepper,* finely chopped (optional)**
- **2 teaspoons chili powder**
- **½ teaspoon ground red pepper**

**Jalapeño peppers can sting and irritate the skin; wear rubber gloves when handling peppers and do not touch eyes. Wash hands after handling.*

1. Heat large nonstick saucepan over medium heat until hot. Add chicken and onion; cook and stir 5 minutes or until chicken is browned. Drain fat from saucepan.

2. Add remaining ingredients to saucepan. Bring to a boil. Reduce heat to low and simmer 15 minutes.

Makes 5 servings

Prep & Cook Time: 30 minutes

Confetti Chicken Chili

Santa Fe Skillet Chili

1 to 1¼ pounds ground turkey (93% lean)
1 cup chopped onion
1 teaspoon bottled minced garlic
1 tablespoon chili powder
1 tablespoon ground cumin
¼ to ½ teaspoon ground red pepper
1 can (15½ ounces) chili beans in spicy sauce, undrained
1 can (14½ ounces) Mexican- or chili-style stewed or diced tomatoes, undrained
1 can (4 ounces) chopped green chilies, undrained

1. Spray large deep skillet with nonstick cooking spray. Cook turkey, onion and garlic over medium-high heat, breaking meat apart with wooden spoon.

2. Sprinkle chili powder, cumin and red pepper evenly over turkey mixture; cook and stir 3 minutes or until turkey is no longer pink.

3. Stir in beans, tomatoes with juice and chilies with liquid. Reduce heat to medium; cover and simmer 10 minutes, stirring occasionally. Ladle chili into bowls.

Makes 4 servings

Serving Suggestion: Offer a variety of toppings with this skillet chili, such as chopped fresh cilantro, sour cream, shredded Cheddar or Monterey Jack cheese, and diced ripe avocado. Serve with warm corn tortillas or corn bread.

Prep and Cook Time: 19 minutes

Chunky Chicken Chili

1 pound boneless skinless chicken breast, cut into bite-size pieces
1 cup chopped onion
½ cup chopped celery
½ cup chopped carrot
2 cloves garlic, minced
1 tablespoon vegetable oil
1 can (15½ ounces) dark red kidney beans, drained
1 can (27 ounces) FRANK'S® or SNOWFLOSS® Original Style Diced Tomatoes
1 cup MISSISSIPPI® Barbecue Sauce
1 can (8 ounces) tomato sauce
1 tablespoon chili powder
½ teaspoon ground cumin
1 green bell pepper, chopped

1. In large stockpot sauté chicken, onion, celery, carrot and garlic in oil. Cook and stir until chicken is no longer pink.

2. Stir in kidney beans, tomatoes, barbecue sauce, tomato sauce, chili powder and cumin.

3. Bring to a boil then reduce heat. Simmer, uncovered, 30 minutes, stirring occasionally.

4. Add green pepper and heat through before serving.

Makes 4 to 6 servings

Prep Time: 25 minutes
Cook Time: 30 minutes

Green Flash Turkey Chili

3 tablespoons olive oil, divided
3 large stalks celery, diced
1 large green bell pepper, diced
2 green onions, sliced
2 large cloves garlic, minced
1 pound ground turkey
4 cups canned white kidney beans, drained and rinsed
1½ cups water
⅓ cup TABASCO® brand Green Pepper Sauce
1¼ teaspoons salt
¼ cup chopped fresh parsley

Heat 2 tablespoons oil in large saucepan over medium heat. Add celery and green bell pepper; cook about 5 minutes or until crisp-tender. Add green onions and garlic; cook 5 minutes, stirring occasionally. Remove vegetables to plate with slotted spoon. Add remaining 1 tablespoon oil to saucepan; cook turkey over medium-high heat until well browned, stirring frequently.

Add vegetable mixture, kidney beans, water, TABASCO® Green Pepper Sauce and salt to saucepan. Heat to boiling over high heat. Reduce heat to low; cover and simmer 20 minutes, stirring occasionally. Uncover saucepan and simmer 5 minutes. Stir in parsley just before serving.

Makes 6 servings

Helpful Hints

Although a traditional chili is made with beef, chilis are now just as likely to be made with ground chicken or turkey. Recipes for meatless chilis are also common.

Santa Fe Skillet Chili

Turkey Vegetable Chili Mac

Nonstick cooking spray
¾ pound ground turkey breast
½ cup chopped onion
2 cloves garlic, minced
1 can (about 15 ounces) black beans, rinsed and drained
1 can (14½ ounces) Mexican-style stewed tomatoes, undrained
1 can (14½ ounces) no-salt-added diced tomatoes, undrained
1 cup frozen corn
1 teaspoon Mexican seasoning
½ cup uncooked elbow macaroni
⅓ cup reduced-fat sour cream

1. Spray large nonstick saucepan or Dutch oven with cooking spray; heat over medium heat until hot. Add turkey, onion and garlic; cook 5 minutes or until turkey is no longer pink, stirring to crumble.

2. Stir beans, tomatoes with juice, corn and Mexican seasoning into saucepan; bring to a boil over high heat. Cover; reduce heat to low. Simmer 15 minutes, stirring occasionally.

3. Meanwhile, cook pasta according to package directions, omitting salt. Rinse and drain pasta; stir into saucepan. Simmer, uncovered, 2 to 3 minutes or until heated through.

4. Top each serving with dollop of sour cream. Garnish as desired.

Makes 6 servings

White Bean Chili

Slow Cooker

Nonstick cooking spray
1 pound ground chicken
1½ cups coarsely chopped onions
3 cups coarsely chopped celery
3 cloves garlic, minced
4 teaspoons chili powder
1½ teaspoons ground cumin
¾ teaspoon ground allspice
¾ teaspoon ground cinnamon
½ teaspoon black pepper
1 can (16 ounces) whole tomatoes, undrained, coarsely chopped
1 can (15½ ounces) Great Northern beans, drained and rinsed
1 cup chicken broth

Slow Cooker Directions
Spray large nonstick skillet with cooking spray; heat over high heat until hot. Add chicken; cook until browned, breaking into pieces with fork. Combine chicken, onions, celery, garlic, chili powder, cumin, allspice, cinnamon, pepper, tomatoes, beans and broth in slow cooker. Cover and cook on LOW 5½ to 6 hours or until chicken is no longer pink and celery is tender.

Makes 6 servings

Rice and Chick-Pea Chili

⅔ cup UNCLE BEN'S® ORIGINAL CONVERTED® Brand Rice
1 can (15 ounces) chick-peas, undrained
1 can (15 ounces) diced tomatoes, undrained
1 can (8 ounces) diced green chilies
1 cup frozen corn
¼ cup chopped fresh cilantro
1 tablespoon taco seasoning
½ cup (2 ounces) shredded reduced-fat Cheddar cheese

1. In medium saucepan, bring 1¾ cups water and rice to a boil. Cover, reduce heat and simmer 15 minutes.

2. Add remaining ingredients except cheese. Cook over low heat 10 minutes. Serve in bowls sprinkled with cheese.

Makes 4 servings

Serving Suggestion: To round out the meal, serve this hearty chili with corn bread and fresh fruit.

Vegetarian Chili

1 tablespoon vegetable oil
1 cup finely chopped onion
1 cup chopped red bell pepper
2 tablespoons minced jalapeño pepper*
1 clove garlic, minced
1 can (28-ounces) crushed tomatoes
1 can (14½ ounces) black beans, rinsed and drained
1 can (14-ounces) garbanzo beans, drained
½ cup canned corn
¼ cup tomato paste
1 teaspoon sugar
1 teaspoon ground cumin
1 teaspoon dried basil leaves
1 teaspoon chili powder
¼ teaspoon black pepper
1 cup shredded Cheddar cheese (optional)

**Jalapeño peppers can sting and irritate the skin; wear rubber gloves when handling peppers and do not touch eyes. Wash hands after handling.*

Slow Cooker Directions

1. Heat oil in large nonstick skillet over medium-high heat until hot. Add onion, bell pepper, jalapeño pepper and garlic; cook and stir 5 minutes or until vegetables are tender.

2. Spoon vegetables into slow cooker. Add remaining ingredients, except cheese, to slow cooker; mix well. Cover and cook on LOW 4 to 5 hours. Garnish with cheese, if desired.

Makes 4 servings

Turkey Vegetable Chili Mac

Chili with Beans and Corn

1 (16-ounce) can black-eyed peas or cannellini beans, rinsed and drained
1 (16-ounce) can kidney or navy beans, rinsed and drained
1 (15-ounce) can whole tomatoes, drained and chopped
1 onion, chopped
1 cup corn
1 cup water
½ cup chopped green onions
½ cup tomato paste
¼ cup diced jalapeño peppers*
1 tablespoon chili powder
1 teaspoon ground cumin
1 teaspoon mustard
½ teaspoon dried oregano leaves

**Jalapeño peppers can sting and irritate the skin; wear rubber gloves when handling peppers and do not touch eyes. Wash hands after handling.*

Slow Cooker Directions
Combine all ingredients in slow cooker. Cover and cook on LOW 8 to 10 hours or on HIGH 4 to 5 hours.
Makes 6 to 8 servings

Southwest Chili

1 large onion, chopped
1 tablespoon olive oil
2 large tomatoes, chopped
1 (4-ounce) can chopped green chilies, undrained
1 tablespoon chili powder
1 teaspoon ground cumin
1 (15-ounce) can red kidney beans, undrained
1 (15-ounce) can Great Northern beans, undrained
¼ cup cilantro leaves, chopped (optional)

Cook and stir onion in oil in large saucepan over medium heat until onion is soft. Stir in tomatoes, chilies, chili powder and cumin. Bring to a boil. Add beans with liquid. Reduce heat to low. Cover and simmer 15 minutes, stirring occasionally. Sprinkle individual servings with cilantro. *Makes 4 servings*

Vegetarian Rice & Black Bean Chili

2 cups UNCLE BEN'S® Hearty Soup Black Beans & Rice
2½ cups water
½ cup thinly sliced carrots
1 small zucchini, quartered lengthwise and sliced
⅓ cup diced red bell pepper
1 can (8 ounces) tomato sauce
½ cup (2 ounces) Cheddar cheese

1. Place water in medium saucepan. Stir in rice, beans and contents of seasoning packet. Bring to a boil. Add carrots. Cover; reduce heat and simmer 10 minutes.

2. Add zucchini and bell pepper. Cover; reduce heat and simmer 5 minutes. Stir in tomato sauce. Cover and simmer 8 to 10 minutes or until rice is tender. Top with cheese.
Makes 4 servings

Fireball Vegetarian Chili

1 onion, chopped
2 cloves garlic, minced
2 cans (15 to 19 ounces *each*) red kidney beans, rinsed and drained
1½ cups *each* coarsely chopped zucchini and carrots
1 can (15 ounces) crushed tomatoes in purée, undrained
1 can (7 ounces) whole kernel corn, drained
1 can (4½ ounces) chopped green chilies, drained
¼ cup *Frank's® RedHot®* Cayenne Pepper Sauce
1 tablespoon ground cumin

1. Heat *1 tablespoon oil* in large saucepot. Cook and stir onion and garlic 3 minutes or just until tender. Add remaining ingredients; stir until well blended.

2. Heat to boiling. Reduce heat to medium-low. Cook, partially covered, 20 minutes or until vegetables are tender and flavors are blended. Serve with hot cooked rice. Garnish with sour cream or shredded cheese, if desired. *Makes 6 servings*

Tip: Serve chili over hot baked potatoes.

Prep Time: 15 minutes
Cook Time: 25 minutes

Helpful Hints

Meatless chili gets its protein from beans—kidney beans, black beans, pinto beans, chili beans or Great Northern beans. Coupled with vegetables, meatless chili is a healthy alternative.

Chili with Beans and Corn

Tasty Vegetarian Chili

- 2 cans (15 ounces each) dark red kidney beans, drained
- 2 cans (14½ ounces each) diced tomatoes
- 1 can (6 ounces) tomato paste
- 1 small onion, chopped
- 3 tablespoons MRS. DASH® Garlic & Herb Seasoning
- 4 teaspoons sugar
- 1 tablespoon MRS. DASH® Extra Spicy Seasoning
- 1 tablespoon ground cumin
- Grated cheese (optional)

In medium saucepan, combine all ingredients except cheese. Simmer over medium heat 5 to 10 minutes. Garnish with grated cheese, if desired. *Makes 8 servings*

Olive-Bean Chili

- 3 tablespoons molasses
- 1½ teaspoons dry mustard
- 1½ teaspoons soy sauce
- 2 teaspoons olive oil
- 2 medium carrots, cut diagonally into ¼-inch slices
- 1 large onion, chopped
- 1 tablespoon chili powder
- 3 large tomatoes (1½ pounds), chopped
- 1 (15-ounce) can pinto beans, drained
- 1 (15-ounce) can kidney beans, drained
- ¾ cup California ripe olives, sliced
- ½ cup plain nonfat yogurt
- Crushed red pepper flakes

Combine molasses, mustard and soy sauce; set aside. Heat oil in large skillet; add carrots, onion, chili powder and ¼ cup water. Cook, covered, about 4 minutes or until carrots are almost tender. Uncover and cook, stirring, until liquid has evaporated. Add molasses mixture with tomatoes, pinto beans, kidney beans and olives. Cook, stirring gently, about 5 minutes or until mixture is hot and tomatoes are soft. Ladle chili into bowls; top with yogurt. Sprinkle with pepper flakes to taste. *Makes 4 servings*

Prep Time: About 15 minutes
Cook Time: About 10 minutes

Favorite recipe from **California Olive Industry**

Vegetarian Chili with Cornbread Topping

- 1 pound zucchini, halved and cut into ½-inch slices (about 4 cups)
- 1 red or green bell pepper, cut into 1-inch pieces
- 1 rib celery, thinly sliced
- 1 clove garlic, minced
- 2 cans (15 to 19 ounces *each*) kidney beans, rinsed and drained
- 1 can (28 ounces) crushed tomatoes in purée, undrained
- ¼ cup ***Frank's® RedHot®*** Cayenne Pepper Sauce
- 1 tablespoon chili powder
- 1 package (6½ ounces) cornbread mix plus ingredients to prepare mix

1. Preheat oven to 400°F. Heat *1 tablespoon oil* in 12-inch heatproof skillet* over medium-high heat. Add zucchini, bell pepper, celery and garlic. Cook and stir 5 minutes or until tender. Stir in beans, tomatoes, ***Frank's RedHot*** and chili powder. Heat to boiling, stirring.

2. Prepare cornbread mix according to package directions. Spoon batter on top of chili mixture, spreading to ½ inch from edges. Bake 30 minutes or until cornbread is golden brown and mixture is bubbly. *Makes 6 servings*

*If handle of skillet is not heatproof, wrap in foil.

Prep Time: 20 minutes
Cook Time: 35 minutes

Chunky Vegetable Chili

Slow Cooker

- 1 medium onion, chopped
- 2 ribs celery, diced
- 1 carrot, diced
- 3 cloves garlic, minced
- 2 cans (about 15 ounces each) Great Northern beans, rinsed and drained
- 1 cup water
- 1 cup frozen corn
- 1 can (6 ounces) tomato paste
- 1 can (4 ounces) diced mild green chilies, undrained
- 1 tablespoon chili powder
- 2 teaspoons dried oregano leaves
- 1 teaspoon salt

Slow Cooker Directions
Combine all ingredients in slow cooker. Cover and cook on LOW 5½ to 6 hours or until vegetables are tender. *Makes 6 servings*

Tasty Vegetarian Chili

International Fare

Lasagna Supreme

- 8 ounces lasagna noodles, uncooked
- ½ pound ground beef
- ½ pound mild Italian sausage, casings removed
- 1 medium onion, chopped
- 2 cloves garlic, minced
- 1 can (14½ ounces) whole peeled tomatoes, undrained and chopped
- 1 can (6 ounces) tomato paste
- 2 teaspoons dried basil leaves
- 1 teaspoon dried marjoram leaves
- 1 can (4 ounces) sliced mushrooms, drained
- 2 eggs
- 1 pound cream-style cottage cheese
- ¾ cup grated Parmesan cheese, divided
- 2 tablespoons dried parsley flakes
- ½ teaspoon salt
- ½ teaspoon black pepper
- 2 cups (8 ounces) shredded Cheddar cheese
- 3 cups (12 ounces) shredded mozzarella cheese

1. Cook lasagna noodles according to package directions; drain.

2. Cook meats, onion and garlic in large skillet over medium-high heat until meat is brown, stirring to separate meat. Drain.

3. Add tomatoes with juice, tomato paste, basil and marjoram. Reduce heat to low. Cover; simmer 15 minutes, stirring often. Stir in mushrooms; set aside.

4. Preheat oven to 375°F. Beat eggs in large bowl; add cottage cheese, ½ cup Parmesan cheese, parsley, salt and pepper. Mix well.

5. Place half the noodles in bottom of 13×9-inch baking pan. Spread half the cottage cheese mixture over noodles, then half the meat mixture and half the Cheddar cheese and mozzarella cheese. Repeat layers. Sprinkle with remaining ¼ cup Parmesan cheese.

6. Bake lasagna 40 to 45 minutes or until bubbly. Let stand 10 minutes before cutting.

Makes 8 to 10 servings

Note: Lasagna may be assembled, covered and refrigerated up to 2 days in advance. Bake, uncovered, in preheated 375°F oven 60 minutes or until bubbly.

Irish Stew

- 1 cup fat-free reduced-sodium chicken broth
- 1 teaspoon dried marjoram leaves
- 1 teaspoon dried parsley leaves
- ¾ teaspoon salt
- ½ teaspoon garlic powder
- ¼ teaspoon black pepper
- 1¼ pounds white potatoes, peeled and cut into 1-inch pieces
- 1 pound lean lamb stew meat, cut into 1-inch cubes
- 8 ounces frozen cut green beans
- 2 small leeks, cut lengthwise into halves then crosswise into slices
- 1½ cups coarsely chopped carrots

Slow Cooker Directions

Combine broth, marjoram, parsley, salt, garlic powder and pepper in large bowl; mix well. Pour mixture into slow cooker. Add potatoes, lamb, green beans, leeks and carrots. Cover and cook on LOW for 7 to 9 hours.

Makes 6 servings

Lasagna Supreme

Fiesta Beef Enchiladas

8 ounces lean ground beef
½ cup sliced green onions
2 teaspoons fresh minced or bottled garlic
1 cup cold cooked white or brown rice
1½ cups chopped tomato, divided
¾ cup frozen corn, thawed
1 cup (4 ounces) shredded reduced-fat Mexican cheese blend or Cheddar cheese, divided
½ cup salsa or picante sauce
12 (6- to 7-inch) corn tortillas
Nonstick cooking spray
1 can (10 ounces) mild or hot enchilada sauce
1 cup sliced romaine lettuce leaves

1. Preheat oven to 375°F. Cook ground beef in medium nonstick skillet over medium heat until no longer pink; drain. Add green onions and garlic; cook and stir 2 minutes.

2. Combine meat mixture, rice, 1 cup tomato, corn, ½ cup cheese and salsa; mix well. Spoon mixture down center of tortillas. Roll up; place seam side down in 13×9-inch baking dish that has been sprayed with cooking spray. Spoon enchilada sauce evenly over enchiladas.

3. Cover with foil; bake for 20 minutes or until hot. Sprinkle with remaining ½ cup cheese; bake 5 minutes or until cheese melts. Top with lettuce and remaining ½ cup tomato.

Makes 4 servings

Prep Time: 15 minutes
Cook Time: 35 minutes

Cordero Stew with Cornmeal Dumplings

2 pounds lean lamb stew meat with bones, cut into 2-inch pieces *or* 1½ pounds lean boneless lamb, cut into 1½-inch cubes
1 teaspoon salt
½ teaspoon black pepper
2½ tablespoons vegetable oil, divided
1 large onion, chopped
1 clove garlic, minced
2 tablespoons tomato paste
2 teaspoons chili powder
1 teaspoon ground coriander
4 cups water
3 small potatoes, cut into 1½-inch chunks
2 large carrots, cut into 1-inch pieces
1 package (10 ounces) frozen corn
⅓ cup coarsely chopped celery leaves
½ cup yellow cornmeal
½ cup all-purpose flour
1 teaspoon baking powder
¼ teaspoon salt
2½ tablespoons cold butter or margarine
½ cup milk
Whole celery leaves for garnish

Sprinkle meat with salt and pepper. Heat 2 tablespoons oil in 5-quart Dutch oven over medium-high heat. Add meat, a few pieces at a time, and cook until browned on all sides. Transfer meat to medium bowl. Heat remaining ½ tablespoon oil over medium heat in same Dutch oven. Add onion and garlic; cook until onion is tender. Stir in tomato paste, chili powder, coriander and water. Return meat to Dutch oven. Add potatoes, carrots, corn and chopped celery leaves. Bring to a boil. Cover; reduce heat and simmer 1 hour and 15 minutes or until meat is tender. During last 15 minutes of cooking, prepare Cornmeal Dumplings. Combine cornmeal, flour, baking powder and salt in medium bowl. Cut in butter with fingers, pastry blender or two knives until mixture resembles coarse crumbs. Make well in center; add milk all at once and stir with fork until mixture forms dough. Drop dough onto stew, making six dumplings. Cover and simmer an additional 18 minutes or until dumplings are firm to the touch and wooden toothpick inserted in center comes out clean. To serve, spoon stew onto individual plates; serve with dumplings. Garnish with whole celery leaves.

Makes 6 servings

Shepherd's Pie

1 pound ground beef
1 cup chopped onion
1 teaspoon LAWRY'S® Seasoned Salt
1 package (10 ounces) frozen peas and carrots, cooked and drained
1 package (0.88 ounces) LAWRY'S® Brown Gravy Mix
1 cup water
1 egg, beaten
3 cups mashed potatoes
Paprika

In large skillet, cook ground beef and onion over medium-high heat until beef is browned; drain fat. Add Seasoned Salt and peas and carrots; mix well. Prepare Brown Gravy Mix with 1 cup water according to package directions. Add some gravy to beaten egg; gradually add egg-gravy mixture to gravy, stirring constantly. Combine gravy with meat. In shallow, 2-quart casserole, place meat; arrange potatoes in mounds over meat. Sprinkle top with paprika. Bake, uncovered, in 400°F oven 15 minutes or until heated.

Makes 6 servings

Serving Suggestion: Serve with tossed green salad.

Fiesta Beef Enchiladas

Cassoulet

- Bretonne* (recipe follows)
- **5 slices bacon**
- **1 pound fully-cooked smoked sausage, such as Polish, Italian or garlic**
- **1 boneless pork loin roast (about ¾ pound)**
- **½ cup water**
- **2 tablespoons packed brown sugar**
- **1 tablespoon fresh lemon juice**
- **Fresh oregano sprigs for garnish**

**Bretonne is the classic French name for a dish of seasoned beans.*

1. Prepare Bretonne; set aside.

2. Preheat oven to 350°F. Cook bacon in large skillet over medium-high heat until crisp, turning occasionally. Drain bacon on paper towels, reserving 2 tablespoons drippings in skillet. Crumble bacon; set aside.

3. Cut sausage into ¼-inch slices. Cut pork into 1-inch cubes.

4. Heat bacon drippings over medium-high heat until hot; add ¼ of pork and sausage. Cook until browned on all sides. Remove pork and sausage to paper towels; drain well. Repeat process until all meat is browned; set aside.

5. Pour off drippings to remove grease; discard. To deglaze skillet, pour water into skillet. Cook over medium-high heat 2 minutes, scraping up browned bits and stirring constantly. Stir in sugar and lemon juice; bring to a boil. Boil 1 minute. Stir deglazed pan drippings mixture and reserved crumbled bacon into reserved Bretonne.

6. Spread ½ of Bretonne in lightly greased 2½-quart ovenproof casserole or Dutch oven. Top with browned pork and sausage. Spoon remaining Bretonne over browned meats.

7. Cover and bake 2 hours. Cool 10 minutes. Serve in 8 individual serving bowls. Garnish, if desired.

Makes 8 servings

Bretonne

- **1 pound dried Great Northern beans**
- **2 tablespoons butter or margarine**
- **2 cups chopped onions**
- **2 cloves garlic, minced**
- **1 can (14½ ounces) diced peeled tomatoes, undrained**
- **½ cup red wine**
- **2 tablespoons *each* chopped fresh parsley, basil and thyme**
- **¾ teaspoon salt**
- **½ teaspoon black pepper**
- **4 cups water**
- **1 large carrot, peeled and cut into 2-inch pieces**
- **1 large onion, peeled and halved**
- **2 large sprigs *each* fresh parsley, basil, thyme and oregano**

1. Rinse beans thoroughly in colander under cold running water, picking out debris and any blemished beans. Place beans in large bowl; add water to cover by 3 inches. Cover; let stand at room temperature overnight.

2. Melt butter in large saucepan over medium-high heat; add chopped onions and garlic. Cook 8 to 10 minutes until onion is softened, stirring frequently. Stir in tomatoes with juice, wine, chopped herbs, salt and pepper; bring to a boil. Reduce heat to low; simmer, uncovered, 20 minutes or until mixture reduces to 2¼ cups. Transfer mixture to small bowl; cover and refrigerate overnight.

3. Drain beans, discarding soaking water. Combine beans, 4 cups water, carrot, halved onion and herb sprigs in large saucepan or Dutch oven. Bring to a boil over high heat. Reduce heat to low; partially cover and simmer 1 hour or until beans are tender but firm.

4. Remove cooked beans to large bowl with slotted spoon, leaving cooking liquid in saucepan. Remove carrot, halved onion and herb sprigs; discard.

5. Bring bean cooking liquid to a boil over high heat. Reduce heat to medium; cook until bean liquid is reduced to ½ cup. Add liquid to cooked beans. Stir refrigerated tomato mixture into beans until blended.

Makes about 6 cups

Hungarian Lamb Goulash

- **1 package (16 ounces) frozen cut green beans**
- **1 cup chopped onion**
- **1¼ pounds lean lamb stew meat, cut into 1-inch pieces**
- **1 can (15 ounces) chunky tomato sauce**
- **1¾ cups reduced-sodium chicken broth**
- **1 can (6 ounces) tomato paste**
- **4 teaspoons paprika**
- **3 cups hot cooked noodles**

Slow Cooker Directions

Place green beans and onion in slow cooker. Top with lamb. Combine remaining ingredients, except noodles, in large bowl; mix well. Pour over lamb mixture. Cover and cook on LOW 6 to 8 hours. Stir. Serve over noodles.

Makes 6 servings

Cassoulet

Beef Enchiladas

Red Chili Sauce (recipe follows)
1½ pounds lean boneless beef chuck, cut into 1-inch cubes
½ teaspoon salt
2 tablespoons vegetable oil
½ cup finely chopped white onion
¾ cup beef broth
¼ cup raisins
1 clove garlic, minced
½ teaspoon ground cloves
¼ teaspoon anise seeds, crushed
12 (6-inch) corn tortillas
1 cup (4 ounces) shredded mild Cheddar cheese
¾ cup sour cream
⅓ cup sliced pitted black olives
Basil sprig and tomato wedge for garnish

1. Prepare Red Chili Sauce.

2. Sprinkle beef with salt. Brown beef in batches in hot oil in large skillet over medium-high heat 10 to 12 minutes. Remove to plate.

3. Reduce heat to medium. Add onion; cook and stir 4 minutes or until onion is soft. Return beef to skillet. Stir in broth, raisins, garlic, cloves, anise seeds and ¼ cup Red Chili Sauce. Bring to a boil over medium-high heat. Reduce heat to low. Cover and simmer 1½ to 2 hours until beef is very tender. Remove from heat. Using 2 forks, pull beef into coarse shreds in skillet.

4. Preheat oven to 375°F. Heat remaining Red Chili Sauce in medium skillet over medium heat until hot; remove from heat.

5. Dip 1 tortilla in sauce with tongs a few seconds until limp. Drain off excess sauce. Spread about 3 tablespoons meat filling down center of tortilla. Roll up; place in 13×9-inch baking dish. Repeat with remaining tortillas, sauce and meat filling. Pour remaining sauce over enchiladas.

6. Sprinkle cheese over top. Bake 25 minutes or until bubbly and cheese is melted. To serve, spoon sour cream down center of enchiladas. Sprinkle with olives. Garnish, if desired.

Makes 4 to 6 servings

Red Chili Sauce

3 ounces dried ancho chilies (about 5), seeded, deveined and rinsed
2½ cups boiling water
2 tablespoons vegetable oil
2 tablespoons tomato paste
1 clove garlic, minced
½ teaspoon salt
½ teaspoon dried oregano leaves
¼ teaspoon ground cumin
¼ teaspoon ground coriander

1. Place chilies in medium bowl; cover with boiling water. Let stand 1 hour.

2. Place chilies along with soaking water in blender; blend until smooth.

3. Whisk together chili mixture and remaining ingredients in medium saucepan. Bring to a boil. Reduce heat. Cover and simmer 10 minutes, stirring occasionally.

Makes about 2½ cups

Note: Sauce can be refrigerated, covered, up to 3 days or frozen up to 1 month.

Russian Borscht

4 cups thinly sliced green cabbage
1½ pounds fresh beets, shredded
5 small carrots, peeled, cut lengthwise into halves, then cut into 1-inch pieces
1 parsnip, peeled, cut lengthwise into halves, then cut into 1-inch pieces
1 cup chopped onion
4 cloves garlic, minced
1 pound lean beef stew meat, cut into ½-inch cubes
1 can (14½ ounces) diced tomatoes, undrained
3 cans (about 14 ounces each) reduced-sodium beef broth
¼ cup lemon juice
1 tablespoon sugar
1 teaspoon black pepper
Sour cream (optional)
Fresh parsley (optional)

Slow Cooker Directions
Layer ingredients in slow cooker in the following order: cabbage, beets, carrots, parsnip, onion, garlic, beef, tomatoes with juice, broth, lemon juice, sugar and pepper. Cover and cook on LOW 7 to 9 hours or until vegetables are crisp-tender. Season with additional lemon juice and sugar, if desired. Dollop with sour cream and garnish with parsley, if desired.

Makes 12 servings

Mama Mia Spaghetti Sauce

Slow Cooker

- 1 tablespoon olive oil
- 1 package (8 ounces) sliced mushrooms
- ½ cup finely chopped carrots
- 1 clove garlic, minced
- 1 shallot, minced
- 1 pound lean ground beef
- 2 cups canned or fresh crushed tomatoes
- ½ cup dry red wine or beef broth
- 2 tablespoons tomato paste
- 1 teaspoon salt
- 1 teaspoon dried oregano leaves
- ½ teaspoon dried basil leaves
- ¼ teaspoon black pepper
- 4 cups cooked spaghetti
- Grated Parmesan cheese (optional)

Slow Cooker Directions

1. Heat oil in large skillet over medium-high heat until hot. Add mushrooms, carrots, garlic and shallot to skillet. Cook and stir 5 minutes.

2. Place vegetable mixture in slow cooker. Stir in ground beef, crumbling it with spoon. Stir in tomatoes, wine, tomato paste, salt, oregano, basil and pepper. Cover and cook on HIGH 3 to 4 hours. Serve sauce with cooked spaghetti. Sprinkle with Parmesan cheese, if desired.

Makes 5 servings

Italian Sausage Lasagna

- 1½ pounds BOB EVANS® Italian Roll Sausage
- 2 tablespoons olive oil
- 2 green bell peppers, thinly sliced
- 1 large yellow onion, thinly sliced
- 4 cloves garlic, minced and divided
- 1 (28-ounce) can whole tomatoes, undrained
- 1 (8-ounce) can tomato sauce
- 2 teaspoons fennel seeds
- Salt and black pepper to taste
- 1 tablespoon butter or margarine
- 1 large yellow onion, chopped
- 2 (10-ounce) packages chopped frozen spinach, thawed and squeezed dry
- 1 cup grated Parmesan cheese, divided
- 3 cups (24 ounces) low-fat ricotta cheese
- 1 pound shredded mozzarella or provolone cheese
- 9 uncooked lasagna noodles

Crumble sausage in large heavy skillet. Cook over medium heat until well browned, stirring occasionally. Remove sausage to paper towels; set aside. Drain off drippings and wipe skillet clean with paper towels. Heat oil in same skillet over medium-high heat until hot. Add green peppers, sliced onion and half the garlic. Cook, covered, over medium heat about 10 minutes or until vegetables are wilted, stirring occasionally. Stir in tomatoes with juice, tomato sauce and fennel seeds, stirring well to break up tomatoes. Bring to a boil. Reduce heat to low; simmer, uncovered, 20 to 30 minutes to blend flavors. Stir in sausage. Season sauce mixture with salt and black pepper; set aside. Melt butter in small saucepan over medium-high heat; add chopped onion and remaining garlic. Cook and stir about 10 minutes or until onion is tender. Stir in spinach and ¼ cup Parmesan; set aside. Combine ricotta, mozzarella and ½ cup Parmesan in medium bowl. Season with salt and black pepper. Cook noodles according to package directions; drain.

Preheat oven to 350°F. Pour ⅓ of sauce mixture into greased 13×9-inch baking dish; spread evenly. Arrange 3 noodles over sauce mixture; spread half the spinach mixture over noodles. Spread half the cheese mixture evenly over spinach. Repeat layers once. Top with remaining 3 noodles and sauce mixture. Sprinkle with remaining ¼ cup Parmesan. Bake about 1 hour or until sauce is bubbly and cheese is browned on top. Let stand 10 to 15 minutes before slicing. Serve hot. Refrigerate leftovers.

Makes 8 servings

Helpful Hints

Fennel seeds are greenish-yellow in color and have a licorice flavor. Fennel seeds are added to many dishes but they are best known for providing the distinctive flavor of Italian sausage.

Caribbean Black Bean Casserole with Spicy Mango Salsa

2 cups chicken broth
1 cup uncooked basmati rice
2 tablespoons olive oil, divided
½ pound chorizo sausage
2 cloves garlic, minced
1 cup chopped red bell pepper
3 cups canned black beans, rinsed and drained
½ cup chopped fresh cilantro
2 small mangoes
1 cup chopped red onion
2 tablespoons honey
2 tablespoons white wine vinegar
1 teaspoon curry powder
½ teaspoon salt
½ teaspoon ground red pepper

1. Place chicken broth in medium saucepan. Bring to a boil over high heat; stir in rice. Reduce heat to low; simmer, covered, 20 minutes or until liquid is absorbed and rice is tender.

2. Heat 1 tablespoon oil in heavy, large skillet over medium heat. Add sausage; cook, turning occasionally, 8 to 10 minutes until browned and no longer pink in center. Remove from skillet to cutting surface. Cut into ½-inch slices; set aside. Drain fat from skillet.

3. Preheat oven to 350°F. Grease 1½-quart casserole; set aside. Add remaining 1 tablespoon oil to skillet; heat over medium-high heat. Add garlic; cook and stir 1 minute. Add bell pepper; cook and stir 5 minutes. Remove from heat. Stir in beans, sausage, rice and cilantro.

4. Spoon sausage mixture into prepared casserole; cover with foil. Bake 30 minutes or until heated through.

5. Peel mangoes. Chop enough flesh to measure 3 cups. Combine mango and remaining ingredients in large bowl.

6. Spoon sausage mixture onto serving plates. Serve with mango salsa. Garnish, if desired.

Makes 6 servings

Beef Bourguignon

1 boneless beef sirloin steak, ½ inch thick, trimmed and cut into ½-inch pieces (about 3 pounds)
½ cup all-purpose flour
4 slices bacon, diced
2 medium carrots, diced
8 small new red potatoes, unpeeled, cut into quarters
8 to 10 mushrooms, sliced
20 to 24 pearl onions
3 cloves garlic, minced
1 bay leaf
1 teaspoon dried marjoram leaves
½ teaspoon dried thyme leaves
½ teaspoon salt
Black pepper to taste
2½ cups Burgundy wine or beef broth

Slow Cooker Directions

Coat beef with flour, shaking off excess. Set aside.

Cook bacon in large skillet over medium heat until partially cooked. Add beef; cook until browned. Remove beef and bacon with slotted spoon.

Layer carrots, potatoes, mushrooms, onions, garlic, bay leaf, marjoram, thyme, salt, pepper, beef and bacon mixture and wine in slow cooker. Cover and cook on LOW 8 to 9 hours or until beef is tender. Remove and discard bay leaf.

Makes 10 to 12 servings

Moroccan Pork Tagine

1 pound well-trimmed pork tenderloin, cut into ¾-inch medallions
1 tablespoon all-purpose flour
1 teaspoon ground cumin
1 teaspoon paprika
¼ teaspoon powdered saffron *or* ½ teaspoon turmeric
¼ teaspoon ground red pepper
¼ teaspoon ground ginger
1 tablespoon olive oil
1 medium onion, chopped
3 cloves garlic, minced
2½ cups canned chicken broth, divided
⅓ cup golden or dark raisins
1 cup quick-cooking couscous
¼ cup chopped fresh cilantro
¼ cup sliced toasted almonds (optional)

1. Toss pork with flour, cumin, paprika, saffron, pepper and ginger in medium bowl; set aside.

2. Heat oil in large nonstick skillet over medium-high heat. Add onion; cook 5 minutes, stirring occasionally. Add pork and garlic; cook 4 to 5 minutes or until pork is no longer pink, stirring occasionally. Add ¾ cup chicken broth and raisins; bring to a boil over high heat. Reduce heat to medium; simmer, uncovered, 7 to 8 minutes or until pork is cooked through, stirring occasionally.

3. Meanwhile, bring remaining 1¾ cups chicken broth to a boil in medium saucepan. Stir in couscous. Cover; remove from heat. Let stand 5 minutes or until liquid is absorbed.

4. Spoon couscous onto 4 plates; top with pork mixture. Sprinkle with cilantro and almonds, if desired.

Makes 4 servings

Caribbean Black Bean Casserole with Spicy Mango Salsa

Spicy Manicotti

3 cups ricotta cheese
1 cup grated Parmesan cheese, divided
2 eggs, beaten lightly
2½ tablespoons chopped fresh parsley
1 teaspoon dried Italian seasoning
½ teaspoon garlic powder
½ teaspoon salt
½ teaspoon black pepper
1 pound spicy Italian sausage
1 can (28 ounces) crushed tomatoes in purée, undrained
1 jar (26 ounces) marinara or spaghetti sauce
8 ounces uncooked manicotti shells

Preheat oven to 375°F. Spray 13×9-inch baking dish with nonstick cooking spray.

Combine ricotta, ¾ cup Parmesan, eggs, parsley, Italian seasoning, garlic powder, salt and pepper in medium bowl; set aside.

Crumble sausage into large skillet; brown over medium-high heat until no longer pink, stirring to separate meat. Drain sausage on paper towels; drain fat from skillet.

Add tomatoes with juice and marinara sauce to same skillet; bring to a boil over high heat. Reduce heat to low; simmer, uncovered, 10 minutes. Pour about one third of sauce into prepared dish.

Stuff each shell with about ½ cup cheese mixture. Place in dish. Top shells with sausage; pour remaining sauce over shells.

Cover tightly with foil and bake 50 minutes to 1 hour or until noodles are cooked. Let stand 5 minutes before serving. Serve with remaining ¼ cup Parmesan.

Makes 8 servings

Pastitso

8 ounces uncooked elbow macaroni
½ cup cholesterol-free egg substitute
¼ teaspoon ground nutmeg
¾ pound lean ground lamb, beef or turkey
½ cup chopped onion
1 clove garlic, minced
1 can (8 ounces) tomato sauce
¾ teaspoon dried mint leaves
½ teaspoon dried oregano leaves
½ teaspoon black pepper
⅛ teaspoon ground cinnamon
2 teaspoons reduced-calorie margarine
3 tablespoons all-purpose flour
1½ cups fat-free (skim) milk
2 tablespoons grated Parmesan cheese

Cook pasta according to package directions, omitting salt. Drain and transfer to medium bowl; stir in egg substitute and nutmeg.

Lightly spray bottom of 9-inch square baking dish with nonstick cooking spray. Spread pasta mixture in bottom of baking dish. Set aside.

Preheat oven to 350°F. Cook lamb, onion and garlic in large nonstick skillet over medium heat until lamb is no longer pink. Stir in tomato sauce, mint, oregano, black pepper and cinnamon. Reduce heat and simmer 10 minutes; spread over pasta.

Melt margarine in small nonstick saucepan. Add flour. Stir constantly for 1 minute. Whisk in milk. Cook, stirring constantly, until thickened, about 6 minutes; spread over meat mixture. Sprinkle with Parmesan cheese. Bake 30 to 40 minutes or until set.

Makes 6 servings

Tijuana Tacos

1 teaspoon vegetable oil
½ cup chopped green bell pepper
½ cup chopped green onions
1 jalapeño pepper,* minced
1 pound lean ground beef
1 cup salsa
½ teaspoon ground cumin
½ teaspoon chili powder
8 taco shells
2 cups shredded lettuce
2 cups chopped tomato
1½ cups (6 ounces) shredded Cheddar cheese

**Jalapeño peppers can sting and irritate the skin; wear rubber gloves when handling peppers and do not touch eyes. Wash hands after handling.*

Heat oil in large nonstick skillet over medium-high heat until hot. Add bell pepper, onions and jalapeño pepper; cook and stir 5 minutes or until vegetables are tender.

Add beef to vegetable mixture. Cook until no longer pink; pour off excess fat. Add salsa, cumin and chili powder to meat mixture; stir to combine.

Spoon beef mixture into taco shells. Top with lettuce, tomato and Cheddar cheese. Garnish as desired.

Makes 8 servings

Spicy Manicotti

Beef with Bean Threads and Cabbage

- 1 package (3¾ ounces) bean threads
- 1 boneless beef sirloin steak, cut 1 inch thick (about 1 pound)
- 2 cloves garlic, minced
- 1 teaspoon minced fresh ginger
- 1 tablespoon peanut or vegetable oil
- ½ cup beef broth or chicken broth
- 2 tablespoons oyster sauce
- 2 cups coarsely chopped napa cabbage

1. Place bean threads in medium bowl; cover with warm water. Soak 15 minutes to soften; drain well. Cut into 2-inch lengths.

2. Cut beef across grain into ⅛-inch slices; cut each slice into 2-inch pieces. Toss beef with garlic and ginger in medium bowl.

3. Heat wok or large skillet over medium-high heat. Add oil; heat until hot. Add beef mixture; stir-fry 2 to 3 minutes until beef is barely pink in center. Add broth, oyster sauce and cabbage; stir-fry 1 minute. Add bean threads; stir-fry 1 to 2 minutes until liquid is absorbed.

Makes 4 servings

Sauerbraten

- 1 boneless beef sirloin tip roast (1¼ pounds)
- 3 cups baby carrots
- 1½ cups fresh or frozen pearl onions
- ¼ cup raisins
- ½ cup water
- ½ cup red wine vinegar
- 1 tablespoon honey
- ½ teaspoon salt
- ½ teaspoon dry mustard
- ½ teaspoon garlic-pepper seasoning
- ¼ teaspoon ground cloves
- ¼ cup crushed crisp gingersnap cookies (5 cookies)

Slow Cooker Directions

1. Heat large nonstick skillet over medium heat until hot. Brown roast on all sides; set aside.

2. Place roast, carrots, onions and raisins in slow cooker. Combine water, vinegar, honey, salt, mustard, garlic-pepper seasoning and cloves in large bowl; mix well. Pour mixture over meat and vegetables.

3. Cover and cook on LOW 4 to 6 hours or until internal temperature of roast reaches 145°F when tested with meat thermometer inserted into thickest part of roast. Transfer roast to cutting board; cover with foil. Let stand 10 to 15 minutes before slicing. (Internal temperature will continue to rise 5° to 10°F during stand time.)

4. Remove vegetables with slotted spoon to bowl; cover to keep warm. Stir crushed cookies into sauce mixture in slow cooker. Cover and cook on HIGH 10 to 15 minutes or until sauce thickens. Serve meat and vegetables with sauce.

Makes 5 servings

Spanish-Style Couscous

- 1 pound lean ground beef
- 1 can (about 14 ounces) beef broth
- 1 small green bell pepper, cut into ½-inch pieces
- ½ cup pimiento-stuffed green olives, sliced
- ½ medium onion, chopped
- 2 cloves garlic, minced
- 1 teaspoon ground cumin
- ½ teaspoon dried thyme leaves
- 1⅓ cups water
- 1 cup uncooked couscous

Slow Cooker Directions

Heat skillet over high heat until hot. Add beef; cook until browned. Pour off fat. Place broth, bell pepper, olives, onion, garlic, cumin, thyme and beef in slow cooker. Cover and cook on LOW 4 hours or until bell pepper is tender.

Bring water to a boil over high heat in small saucepan. Stir in couscous. Cover; remove from heat. Let stand 5 minutes; fluff with fork. Spoon couscous onto plates; top with beef mixture. *Makes 4 servings*

Serving Suggestion: Serve with carrot sticks.

Feijoada Completa

- 1½ pounds country-style ribs or pork spareribs
- 1 corned beef (1½ pounds)
- ½ pound smoked link sausage, such as Polish or andouille
- ½ pound fresh link sausage, such as bratwurst or breakfast links
- 3 cups water
- 1 can (15½ ounces) black beans, rinsed and drained
- 1 cup chopped onion
- 4 cloves garlic, minced
- 1 jalapeño pepper,* seeded and chopped
- Chili-Lemon Sauce (recipe follows)

**Jalapeño peppers can sting and irritate the skin; wear rubber gloves when handling peppers and do not touch eyes. Wash hands after handling.*

Slow Cooker Directions

Trim excess fat from ribs. Combine all ingredients except Chili-Lemon Sauce in slow cooker; stir to mix well. Cover and cook on LOW 7 to 8 hours or until meats are fork-tender. Meanwhile, prepare Chili-Lemon Sauce.

Remove meats to cutting board. Slice corned beef; place on large serving platter. Arrange remaining meat around corned beef. Cover meat and keep warm.

Drain liquid from beans, leaving just enough liquid so beans are moist. Transfer to serving bowl. Serve with Chili-Lemon Sauce.

Makes 10 to 12 servings

Chili-Lemon Sauce

- ¾ cup lemon juice
- 1 small onion, coarsely chopped
- 3 jalapeño peppers,* seeded and chopped
- 3 cloves garlic, cut into halves

**Jalapeño peppers can sting and irritate the skin; wear rubber gloves when handling peppers and do not touch eyes. Wash hands after handling.*

Place all ingredients in food processor or blender. Process until smooth. Serve at room temperature.

Makes about 1 cup

Middle Eastern Lamb Stew

- 1½ pounds lamb stew meat, cubed
- 2 tablespoons all-purpose flour
- 1 tablespoon vegetable oil
- 1½ cups beef broth
- 1 cup chopped onion
- ½ cup chopped carrots
- 1 clove garlic, minced
- 1 tablespoon tomato paste
- ½ teaspoon ground cumin
- ½ teaspoon red pepper flakes
- ¼ teaspoon ground cinnamon
- ½ cup chopped dried apricots
- 1 teaspoon salt
- ¼ teaspoon black pepper
- 3 cups hot cooked noodles

Slow Cooker Directions

1. Coat lamb cubes with flour; set aside. Heat oil in large nonstick skillet over medium-high heat until hot. Brown half of lamb and transfer to slow cooker; repeat with remaining lamb. Add broth, onion, carrots, garlic, tomato paste, cumin, red pepper and cinnamon to slow cooker. Cover and cook on LOW 3 hours.

2. Stir in apricots, salt and black pepper. Cover and cook on LOW 2 to 3 hours, or until lamb is tender and sauce is thickened. Serve lamb over noodles. *Makes 6 servings*

Mexican Delight Casserole

- 1 pound ground beef
- 1 medium onion, chopped
- 1 package (1.5 ounces) LAWRY'S® Burrito Spices & Seasonings
- 1 can (28 ounces) whole tomatoes, cut up
- 1 can (30 ounces) hominy, drained and rinsed
- 1 can (4 ounces) diced green chiles
- 4 cups tortilla chips
- 1½ cups (6 ounces) shredded Cheddar cheese
- 1 can (8 ounces) tomato sauce

In large skillet, cook ground beef and onion until beef is browned; drain fat. Add Burrito Spices & Seasonings and tomatoes; mix well. Bring to a boil over medium-high heat; reduce heat to low and simmer, uncovered, 10 minutes. Combine hominy and green chiles in separate bowl. In 2-quart rectangular casserole dish, layer half of meat mixture, tortilla chips and hominy mixture; add ½ cup cheese. Repeat layers, ending with ½ cup cheese. Top with tomato sauce and remaining ½ cup cheese. Bake, uncovered, in 350°F oven 35 minutes or until thoroughly heated.

Makes 8 servings

Serving Suggestion: Serve with a tossed green salad and fresh fruit.

Hint: Use purchased or homemade tortilla chips. To make chips, cut fresh corn tortillas into ½-inch strips. Fry in ½-inch salad oil until slightly crisp, about 30 seconds. Drain well on paper towels.

Spinach Lasagna

1 pound ground beef
¼ pound fresh mushrooms, thinly sliced
1 medium onion, chopped
1 clove garlic, minced
1 can (28 ounces) Italian plum tomatoes, undrained
1¼ teaspoons salt, divided
¾ teaspoon dried oregano leaves
¾ teaspoon dried basil leaves
¼ teaspoon black pepper, divided
9 uncooked lasagna noodles
¼ cup plus 1 tablespoon butter or margarine, divided
¼ cup all-purpose flour
⅛ teaspoon ground nutmeg
2 cups milk
1½ cups shredded mozzarella cheese (about 6 ounces), divided
½ cup freshly grated Parmesan cheese, divided
1 package (10 ounces) frozen chopped spinach, thawed and squeezed dry

1. For meat sauce, crumble ground beef into large skillet over medium-high heat. Brown 8 to 10 minutes, stirring to separate meat, until meat loses its pink color. Stir in mushrooms, onion and garlic; cook over medium heat 5 minutes or until onion is tender.

2. Press tomatoes with juice through sieve into meat mixture; discard seeds. Stir in ¾ teaspoon salt, oregano, basil and ⅛ teaspoon pepper. Bring to a boil over medium-high heat; reduce heat to low. Cover and simmer 40 minutes, stirring occasionally. Uncover and simmer 15 to 20 minutes more until sauce thickens. Set aside.

3. Add lasagna noodles to large pot of boiling salted water, 1 at a time, allowing noodles to soften and fit into pot. Cook 10 minutes or just until *al dente*. Drain noodles; rinse with cold water. Drain again; hang individually over pot rim to prevent sticking. Set aside.

4. For cheese sauce, melt ¼ cup butter in medium saucepan over medium heat. Stir in flour, remaining ½ teaspoon salt, remaining ⅛ teaspoon pepper and nutmeg; cook and stir until bubbly. Whisk in milk; cook and stir until sauce thickens and bubbles. Cook and stir 1 minute more. Remove from heat. Stir in 1 cup mozzarella and ¼ cup Parmesan cheeses. Stir until smooth. Set aside.

5. Preheat oven to 350°F. Spread remaining 1 tablespoon butter on bottom and sides of 12×8-inch baking dish. Spread noodles in single layer on clean kitchen (not paper) towel. Pat noodles dry.

6. Arrange 3 lasagna noodles in single layer, overlapping slightly, in bottom of baking dish. Top with ½ of meat sauce; spread evenly. Spread ½ of cheese sauce over meat sauce in even layer.

7. Repeat layers once, using 3 noodles, remaining meat sauce and remaining cheese sauce. Sprinkle spinach over cheese sauce in even layer; pat down lightly. Arrange remaining 3 lasagna noodles over spinach.

8. Mix remaining ½ cup mozzarella and ¼ cup Parmesan cheeses in cup. Sprinkle cheese mixture evenly on top of lasagna to completely cover lasagna noodles. Bake 40 minutes or until top is golden and edges are bubbly. Let lasagna stand 10 minutes before serving. Garnish as desired.

Makes 6 servings

Caribbean Jerk-Style Pork

¾ cup DOLE® Pineapple Juice or Pineapple Orange Juice, divided
1 tablespoon prepared yellow mustard
1 teaspoon dried thyme leaves, crushed
¼ teaspoon crushed red pepper
12 ounces boneless pork loin chops or chicken breasts, cut into strips
½ cup DOLE® Golden or Seedless Raisins
½ cup sliced green onions
2 medium firm DOLE® Bananas, cut diagonally into ¼-inch slices
Hot cooked rice or noodles (optional)

• Stir together ½ cup juice, mustard, thyme and red pepper in small bowl; set aside.

• Place pork in large, nonstick skillet sprayed with vegetable cooking spray. Cook and stir pork over medium-high heat 3 to 5 minutes or until pork is no longer pink. Remove pork from skillet.

• Add remaining ¼ cup juice to skillet; stir in raisins and green onions. Cook and stir 1 minute.

• Stir in pork and reserved mustard mixture; cover and cook 2 minutes or until heated through. Stir in bananas. Serve over hot rice.

Makes 4 servings

Prep Time: 10 minutes
Cook Time: 10 minutes

Spinach Lasagna

Szechwan Beef Lo Mein

- **1 pound well-trimmed boneless beef top sirloin steak, 1 inch thick**
- **4 cloves garlic, minced**
- **2 teaspoons minced fresh ginger**
- **¾ teaspoon red pepper flakes, divided**
- **1 tablespoon vegetable oil**
- **1 can (about 14 ounces) vegetable broth**
- **1 cup water**
- **2 tablespoons reduced-sodium soy sauce**
- **1 package (8 ounces) frozen mixed vegetables for stir-fry**
- **1 package (9 ounces) refrigerated angel hair pasta**
- **¼ cup chopped fresh cilantro (optional)**

1. Cut steak crosswise into ⅛-inch strips; cut strips into 1½-inch pieces. Toss steak with garlic, ginger and ½ teaspoon red pepper flakes.

2. Heat oil in large nonstick skillet over medium-high heat. Add half of steak to skillet; cook and stir 3 minutes or until meat is barely pink in center. Remove from skillet; set aside. Repeat with remaining steak.

3. Add vegetable broth, water, soy sauce and remaining ¼ teaspoon red pepper flakes to skillet; bring to a boil over high heat. Add vegetables; return to a boil. Reduce heat to low; simmer, covered, 3 minutes or until vegetables are crisp-tender.

4. Uncover; stir in pasta. Return to a boil over high heat. Reduce heat to medium; simmer, uncovered, 2 minutes, separating pasta with two forks. Return steak and any accumulated juices to skillet; simmer 1 minute or until pasta is tender and steak is hot. Sprinkle with cilantro, if desired. *Makes 4 servings*

Moussaka

- **1 large eggplant**
- **2½ teaspoons salt, divided**
- **2 large zucchini**
- **2 large russet potatoes, peeled**
- **½ cup olive oil, divided**
- **1½ pounds ground beef or lamb**
- **1 large onion, chopped**
- **2 cloves garlic, minced**
- **1 cup chopped tomatoes**
- **½ cup dry red or white wine**
- **¼ cup chopped fresh parsley**
- **¼ teaspoon ground cinnamon**
- **⅛ teaspoon black pepper**
- **1 cup grated Parmesan cheese, divided**
- **4 tablespoons butter or margarine, divided**
- **⅓ cup all-purpose flour**
- **¼ teaspoon ground nutmeg**
- **2 cups milk**

Cut eggplant lengthwise into ½-inch-thick slices. Place in large colander; sprinkle with 1 teaspoon salt. Drain 30 minutes. Cut zucchini lengthwise into ⅜-inch-thick slices. Cut potatoes lengthwise into ¼-inch-thick slices.

Heat ¼ cup oil in large skillet over medium heat until hot. Add potatoes in single layer. Cook 5 minutes per side or until tender and lightly browned. Remove potatoes from skillet; drain on paper towels. Add more oil to skillet, if needed. Cook zucchini 2 minutes per side or until tender. Drain on paper towels. Add more oil to skillet. Cook eggplant 5 minutes per side or until tender. Drain on paper towels. Drain oil from skillet; discard.

Heat skillet over medium-high heat just until hot. Add beef, onion and garlic; cook and stir 5 minutes or until meat is no longer pink. Pour off drippings. Stir in tomatoes, wine, parsley, 1 teaspoon salt, cinnamon and pepper. Bring to a boil over high heat. Reduce heat to low. Simmer 10 minutes or until liquid is evaporated.

Preheat oven to 325°F. Grease 13×9-inch baking dish. Arrange potatoes in bottom; sprinkle with ¼ cup cheese. Top with zucchini and ¼ cup cheese, then eggplant and ¼ cup cheese. Spoon meat mixture over top.

To prepare sauce, melt butter in medium saucepan over low heat. Blend in flour, remaining ½ teaspoon salt and nutmeg with wire whisk. Cook 1 minute, whisking constantly. Gradually whisk in milk. Cook over medium heat, until mixture boils and thickens, whisking constantly. Pour sauce evenly over meat mixture in dish; sprinkle with remaining ¼ cup cheese. Bake 30 to 40 minutes or until hot and bubbly. Garnish as desired. *Makes 6 to 8 servings*

Helpful Hints

One of the best known of all Greek dishes, Moussaka is a layered casserole that traditionally includes eggplant, beef or lamb, and a topping of a creamy white sauce.

Szechwan Beef Lo Mein

Welsh Ham and Leek Casserole

- **6 small leeks**
- **3 large tomatoes, chopped**
- **⅓ cup butter or margarine**
- **1 cup sliced celery**
- **12 thin slices deli ham**
- **2 cloves garlic, minced**
- **¼ cup all-purpose flour**
- **½ teaspoon salt**
- **¼ teaspoon white pepper**
- **⅛ teaspoon ground nutmeg**
- **2 cups milk**
- **½ cup half-and-half**
- **1 cup (4 ounces) shredded sharp white Cheddar cheese, divided**
- **¼ cup bread crumbs**

1. To prepare leeks, remove any withered outer leaves. Cut off 1 inch of leaf tops; discard. Cut off roots, then cut leeks in half crosswise. Make slit down length of each leek half, being careful not to cut through leek completely. Rinse thoroughly. Tie 2 leek halves together with kitchen string; repeat with remaining leeks. Place leeks in Dutch oven; pour in enough lightly salted water to cover. Bring to a boil over high heat. Reduce heat to low; simmer 6 to 8 minutes or until leeks are tender. Drain and pat dry. Remove strings.

2. Preheat oven to 350°F. Place tomatoes in bottom of 13×9-inch baking dish.

3. Melt butter in medium saucepan over medium heat. Add celery; cook 3 minutes or until celery is crisp-tender. Remove celery with slotted spoon, arranging evenly over tomatoes. Reserve butter in saucepan.

4. Wrap 1 ham slice around each leek half. Arrange, seam side down, in single layer in baking dish.

5. Add garlic to reserved butter in saucepan. Cook and stir over low heat 30 seconds. Stir in flour, salt, pepper and nutmeg. Cook 2 minutes, stirring constantly. Gradually whisk in milk and half-and-half until smooth. Cook until mixture boils and thickens, whisking constantly. Remove from heat. Stir in ¾ cup cheese; continue to stir until cheese melts.

6. Pour cheese sauce evenly over leeks. Sprinkle with remaining ¼ cup cheese and bread crumbs. Bake 30 minutes or until lightly browned and bubbly. *Makes 6 servings*

Traditional Spanish Chicken and Rice

- **4 TYSON® Individually Fresh Frozen® Boneless, Skinless Chicken Breasts**
- **1 box UNCLE BEN'S® COUNTRY INN® Mexican Fiesta Rice**
- **1 tablespoon olive oil**
- **2¼ cups water**
- **½ cup chopped red bell pepper**
- **½ cup frozen peas, thawed**
- **⅓ cup Spanish olives stuffed with pimientos, cut into halves**

PREP: CLEAN: Wash hands. Remove protective ice glaze from frozen chicken by holding under cool running water 1 to 2 minutes. CLEAN: Wash hands.

COOK: Heat oil in large skillet. Add chicken; cook over medium-high heat 10 to 15 minutes or until light brown. Add water, rice, contents of seasoning packet, bell pepper, peas and olives; mix well. Bring to a boil. Cover, reduce heat; simmer 10 minutes or until internal juices of chicken run clear. (Or insert instant-read meat thermometer in thickest part of chicken. Temperature should read 170°F.) Remove from heat; let stand, covered, 5 minutes or until liquid is absorbed.

SERVE: Serve with corn on the cob and wheat rolls, if desired.

CHILL: Refrigerate leftovers immediately. *Makes 4 servings*

Prep Time: 5 minutes
Cook Time: 30 minutes

Hearty Cassoulet

- **1 tablespoon olive oil**
- **1 large onion, finely chopped**
- **4 boneless skinless chicken thighs (about 1 pound), chopped**
- **¼ pound smoked turkey sausage, finely chopped**
- **3 cloves garlic, minced**
- **1 teaspoon dried thyme leaves**
- **½ teaspoon black pepper**
- **4 tablespoons tomato paste**
- **2 tablespoons water**
- **3 cans (about 15 ounces each) Great Northern beans, rinsed and drained**
- **½ cup dry bread crumbs**
- **3 tablespoons minced fresh parsley**

Slow Cooker Directions

Heat oil in large skillet over medium heat until hot. Add onion, cook and stir 5 minutes or until onion is tender. Stir in chicken, sausage, garlic, thyme and pepper. Cook 5 minutes or until chicken and sausage are browned.

Remove skillet from heat; stir in tomato paste and water until blended. Place beans and chicken mixture in slow cooker, cover and cook on LOW 4 to 4½ hours. Just before serving, combine bread crumbs and parsley in small bowl. Sprinkle top of cassoulet. *Makes 6 servings*

Welsh Ham and Leek Casserole

Chicken Marsala

- 4 cups (6 ounces) uncooked broad egg noodles
- ½ cup Italian-style dry bread crumbs
- 1 teaspoon dried basil leaves
- 1 egg
- 1 teaspoon water
- 4 boneless skinless chicken breast halves
- 3 tablespoons olive oil, divided
- ¾ cup chopped onion
- 8 ounces cremini or button mushrooms, sliced
- 3 cloves garlic, minced
- 3 tablespoons all-purpose flour
- 1 can (14½ ounces) chicken broth
- ½ cup dry marsala wine
- ¾ teaspoon salt
- ¼ teaspoon black pepper
- Chopped fresh parsley (optional)

Preheat oven to 375°F. Spray 11×7-inch baking dish with nonstick cooking spray.

Cook noodles according to package directions until *al dente*. Drain and place in prepared dish.

Meanwhile, combine bread crumbs and basil on shallow plate or pie plate. Beat egg with water on another shallow plate or pie plate. Dip chicken in egg mixture, letting excess drip off. Roll in crumb mixture, patting to coat.

Heat 2 tablespoons oil in large skillet over medium-high heat until hot. Cook chicken 3 minutes per side or until browned. Transfer to clean plate; set aside.

Heat remaining 1 tablespoon oil in same skillet over medium heat. Add onion; cook and stir 5 minutes. Add mushrooms and garlic; cook and stir 3 minutes. Sprinkle mushroom mixture with flour; cook and stir 1 minute. Add broth, wine, salt and pepper; bring to a boil over high heat. Cook and stir 5 minutes or until sauce thickens.

Reserve ½ cup sauce. Pour remaining sauce over noodles; stir until noodles are well coated. Place chicken on top of noodles. Spoon reserved sauce over chicken.

Bake, uncovered, about 20 minutes or until chicken is no longer pink in centers and sauce is hot and bubbly. Sprinkle with parsley, if desired.

Makes 4 servings

Hint: Serve with crusty Italian or French bread and tossed salad.

Helpful Hints

Cremini mushrooms look similar to the more common button mushroom, except they are darker in color and have a stronger flavor. Cremini, which are also known as brown mushrooms, are actually baby portobello mushrooms.

Greek-Style Chicken Stew

Slow Cooker

- 2 cups cubed peeled eggplant
- 2 cups sliced mushrooms
- ¾ cup coarsely chopped onion
- 2 cloves garlic, minced
- 1 teaspoon dried oregano leaves
- ½ teaspoon dried basil leaves
- ½ teaspoon dried thyme leaves
- 1¼ cups low-sodium chicken broth
- 1½ teaspoons all-purpose flour
- 6 skinless chicken breasts, about 2 pounds
- Additional all-purpose flour
- 3 tablespoons dry sherry or low-sodium chicken broth
- ¼ teaspoon salt
- ¼ teaspoon black pepper
- 1 can (14 ounces) artichoke hearts, drained
- 12 ounces uncooked wide egg noodles

Slow Cooker Directions

Combine eggplant, mushrooms, onion, garlic, oregano, basil, thyme, broth and 1½ teaspoons flour in slow cooker. Cover and cook on HIGH 1 hour.

Coat chicken very lightly with additional flour. Generously spray large nonstick skillet with cooking spray; heat over medium heat until hot. Cook chicken 10 to 15 minutes or until browned on all sides.

Remove vegetables to bowl with slotted spoon. Layer chicken in slow cooker; return vegetables to slow cooker. Add sherry, salt and pepper. Reduce heat to LOW and cover and cook 6 to 6½ hours or until chicken is no longer pink in center and vegetables are tender.

Stir in artichokes; cover and cook 45 minutes to 1 hour or until heated through. Cook noodles according to package directions. Serve chicken stew over noodles.

Makes 6 servings

Chicken Marsala

Thai Turkey & Noodles

- 1 package (about 1½ pounds) turkey tenderloins, cut into ¾-inch pieces
- 1 red bell pepper, cut into short, thin strips
- 1¼ cups reduced-sodium chicken broth, divided
- ¼ cup reduced-sodium soy sauce
- 3 cloves garlic, minced
- ¾ teaspoon red pepper flakes
- ¼ teaspoon salt
- 2 tablespoons cornstarch
- 3 green onions, cut into ½-inch pieces
- ⅓ cup creamy or chunky peanut butter (not natural-style)
- 12 ounces hot cooked vermicelli pasta
- ¾ cup peanuts or cashews, chopped
- ¾ cup cilantro, chopped

Slow Cooker Directions
Place turkey, bell pepper, 1 cup broth, soy sauce, garlic, red pepper flakes and salt in slow cooker. Cover and cook on LOW 3 hours.

Mix cornstarch with remaining ¼ cup broth in small bowl until smooth. Turn slow cooker to HIGH. Stir in green onions, peanut butter and cornstarch mixture. Cover and cook 30 minutes or until sauce is thickened and turkey is no longer pink in center. Stir well. Serve over vermicelli. Sprinkle with peanuts and cilantro.

Makes 6 servings

Hint: If you don't have vermicelli on hand, try substituting ramen noodles. Discard the flavor packet from ramen soup mix and drop the noodles into boiling water. Cook the noodles 2 to 3 minutes or until just tender. Drain and serve hot.

Classic Family Lasagna

- 1 package (1 pound) TYSON® Fresh Ground Chicken
- 9 lasagna noodles, cooked according to package directions
- 1 medium onion, chopped
- ½ cup chopped green bell pepper (optional)
- 2 cloves garlic, minced
- 1 jar (30 ounces) spaghetti sauce
- 1 container (15 ounces) ricotta cheese
- ¾ cup grated Parmesan cheese, divided
- 1 egg, beaten
- ¼ teaspoon black pepper
- 3½ cups (14 ounces) shredded mozzarella cheese

PREP: Preheat oven to 375°F. CLEAN: Wash hands. In large skillet, cook and stir chicken, onion, bell pepper and garlic over medium-high heat until chicken is no longer pink. Stir in sauce; heat through and set aside. In medium bowl, combine ricotta cheese, ½ cup Parmesan cheese, egg and black pepper; mix well. Spray 13×9-inch baking dish with nonstick cooking spray. Spread ⅓ cup sauce on bottom of dish. Top with 3 noodles, one third of sauce, one third of ricotta mixture and 1 cup mozzarella cheese. Repeat layers twice, except do not top with remaining 1½ cups mozzarella cheese. Cover tightly with foil sprayed lightly with nonstick cooking spray.

COOK: Bake 40 minutes. Remove foil. Top with remaining mozzarella cheese. Bake 15 minutes or until bubbly and cheese is melted.

SERVE: Serve with a green salad and garlic bread, if desired.

CHILL: Refrigerate leftovers immediately. *Makes 12 servings*

Prep Time: 35 minutes
Cook Time: 1 hour

Mediterranean Chicken and Rice

- 4 TYSON® Fresh or Individually Fresh Frozen® Boneless, Skinless Chicken Breasts
- 2 cups UNCLE BEN'S® Instant Brown Rice
- 1 tablespoon olive oil
- 1 teaspoon minced garlic
- 1 can (15 ounces) diced tomatoes, undrained
- 1½ cups water
- ½ teaspoon dried oregano leaves
- 16 pitted kalamata olives
- 2 ounces feta cheese, crumbled

PREP: CLEAN: Wash hands. Remove protective ice glaze from frozen chicken by holding under cool running water 1 to 2 minutes. CLEAN: Wash hands.

COOK: In large nonstick skillet, heat olive oil and garlic; add chicken. Cook over medium heat 4 to 6 minutes (5 to 7 minutes if using frozen chicken) or until chicken is browned. Stir in tomatoes, water and oregano; cover. Reduce heat to low; simmer 10 minutes. Stir in rice; cover. Cook 10 minutes or until rice is cooked and internal juices of chicken run clear. (Or insert instant-read meat thermometer in thickest part of chicken. Temperature should read 170°F.) Stir in olives and sprinkle with cheese.

SERVE: For a complete Mediterranean-style meal, serve with a green salad tossed with Italian vinaigrette.

CHILL: Refrigerate leftovers immediately. *Makes 4 Servings*

Prep Time: 5 minutes
Cook Time: 30 minutes

Thai Turkey & Noodles

Coq au Vin

Slow Cooker

- **4 slices thick-cut bacon**
- **2 cups frozen pearl onions, thawed**
- **1 cup sliced button mushrooms**
- **1 clove garlic, minced**
- **1 teaspoon dried thyme leaves**
- **⅛ teaspoon black pepper**
- **6 boneless skinless chicken breast halves (about 2 pounds)**
- **½ cup dry red wine**
- **¾ cup reduced-sodium chicken broth**
- **¼ cup tomato paste**
- **3 tablespoons all-purpose flour**
- **Hot cooked egg noodles (optional)**

Slow Cooker Directions

Cook bacon in medium skillet over medium heat. Drain and crumble. Layer ingredients in slow cooker in the following order: onions, bacon, mushrooms, garlic, thyme, pepper, chicken, wine and broth. Cover and cook on LOW 6 to 8 hours.

Remove chicken and vegetables; cover and keep warm. Ladle ½ cup cooking liquid into small bowl; allow to cool slightly. Turn slow cooker to HIGH; cover. Mix reserved liquid, tomato paste and flour until smooth. Return mixture to slow cooker; cover and cook 15 minutes or until thickened. Serve over hot noodles, if desired.

Makes 6 servings

Chicken Curry

- **2 boneless skinless chicken breast halves, cut into ¾-inch pieces**
- **1 small onion, sliced**
- **1 cup coarsely chopped apple, divided**
- **3 tablespoons raisins**
- **1 clove garlic, minced**
- **1 teaspoon curry powder**
- **¼ teaspoon ground ginger**
- **⅓ cup water**
- **1½ teaspoons chicken bouillon granules**
- **1½ teaspoons all-purpose flour**
- **¼ cup sour cream**
- **½ teaspoon cornstarch**
- **½ cup uncooked white rice**

Slow Cooker Directions

Combine chicken, onion, ¾ cup apple, raisins, garlic, curry powder and ginger in slow cooker. Sitr water into chicken bouillon granules and flour in small bowl until smooth. Add to slow cooker. Cover and cook on LOW 3½ to 4 hours or until onions are tender and chicken is no longer pink.

Combine sour cream and cornstarch in large bowl. Turn off slow cooker; remove insert to heatproof surface. Drain all cooking liquid from chicken mixture and stir into sour cream mixture. Add back to insert; stir well. Place insert back in slow cooker. Cover and let stand 5 to 10 minutes or until sauce is heated through.

Meanwhile, cook rice according to package directions. Serve chicken curry over rice; garnish with remaining ¼ cup apple.

Makes 2 servings

Note: For a special touch, sprinkle chicken with green onion slivers just before serving.

Turkey Stuffed Chiles Rellenos

- **1 package (1½ pounds) BUTTERBALL® 99% Fat Free Fresh Ground Turkey Breast**
- **1 envelope (1¼ ounces) taco seasoning mix**
- **⅓ cup water**
- **6 large poblano chilies, stems on, slit lengthwise and seeded**
- **1 cup (4 ounces) shredded reduced-fat Cheddar cheese**
- **1½ cups tomato salsa**

Spray large nonstick skillet with nonstick cooking spray; heat over medium heat until hot. Brown turkey in skillet over medium-high heat 6 to 8 minutes or until no longer pink, stirring to separate meat. Add taco seasoning and water. Bring to a boil. Reduce heat to low; simmer 5 minutes, stirring occasionally. In separate pan, cook chilies in boiling water 5 minutes; remove and drain. Combine turkey mixture and Cheddar cheese. Fill chilies with mixture. Pour salsa into 11×7-inch baking dish. Place stuffed chilies slit side up in baking dish. Bake, uncovered, in preheated 400°F oven 15 minutes. Serve hot with additional salsa and sour cream, if desired.

Makes 6 servings

Prep Time: 30 minutes

Coq au Vin

Caribbean Shrimp with Rice

Slow Cooker

1 package (12 ounces) frozen shrimp, thawed
½ cup chicken broth
1 clove garlic, minced
1 teaspoon chili powder
½ teaspoon salt
½ teaspoon dried oregano leaves
1 cup frozen peas
½ cup diced tomatoes
2 cups cooked rice

Slow Cooker Directions
Combine shrimp, broth, garlic, chili powder, salt and oregano in slow cooker. Cover and cook on LOW 2 hours. Add peas and tomatoes. Cover and cook on LOW 5 minutes. Stir in rice. Cover and cook on LOW an additional 5 minutes.
Makes 4 servings

Crab and Corn Enchilada Casserole

Spicy Tomato Sauce (recipe follows), divided
10 to 12 ounces fresh crabmeat or flaked or chopped surimi crab
1 package (10 ounces) frozen corn, thawed, drained
1½ cups (6 ounces) shredded reduced-fat Monterey Jack cheese, divided
1 can (4 ounces) diced mild green chilies
12 (6-inch) corn tortillas
1 lime, cut into 6 wedges
Sour cream (optional)

Preheat oven to 350°F. Prepare Spicy Tomato Sauce.

Combine 2 cups Spicy Tomato Sauce, crabmeat, corn, 1 cup cheese and chilies in medium bowl. Cut each tortilla into 4 wedges. Place one third of tortilla wedges in bottom of shallow 3- to 4-quart casserole, overlapping to make solid layer. Spread half of crab mixture on top. Repeat with another layer tortilla wedges, remaining crab mixture and remaining tortillas. Spread remaining 1 cup Spicy Tomato Sauce over top; cover.

Bake 30 to 40 minutes or until heated through. Sprinkle with remaining ½ cup cheese and bake uncovered 5 minutes or until cheese melts. Squeeze lime over individual servings. Serve with sour cream, if desired. *Makes 6 servings*

Spicy Tomato Sauce

2 cans (15 ounces each) no-salt-added stewed tomatoes, undrained *or* 6 medium tomatoes
2 teaspoons olive oil
1 medium onion, chopped
1 tablespoon minced garlic
2 tablespoons chili powder
2 teaspoons ground cumin
2 teaspoons dried oregano leaves
1 teaspoon ground cinnamon
¼ teaspoon crushed red pepper
¼ teaspoon ground cloves

Place tomatoes with juice in food processor or blender; process until finely chopped. Set aside.

Heat oil over medium-high heat in large saucepan or Dutch oven. Add onion and garlic. Cook and stir 5 minutes or until onion is tender. Add chili powder, cumin, oregano, cinnamon, red pepper and cloves. Cook and stir 1 minute. Add tomatoes; reduce heat to medium-low. Simmer, uncovered, 20 minutes or until sauce is reduced to 3 to 3¼ cups. *Makes about 3 cups*

Sicilian Fish and Rice Bake

3 tablespoons olive or vegetable oil
¾ cup chopped onion
½ cup chopped celery
1 clove garlic, minced
½ cup uncooked long-grain white rice
2 cans (14.5 ounces each) CONTADINA® Recipe Ready Diced Tomatoes, undrained
1 teaspoon salt
1 teaspoon ground black pepper
½ teaspoon granulated sugar
⅛ teaspoon cayenne pepper
1 pound firm white fish
¼ cup finely chopped fresh parsley

1. Heat oil in large skillet. Add onion, celery and garlic; sauté for 2 to 3 minutes or until vegetables are tender.

2. Stir in rice; sauté for 5 minutes or until rice browns slightly. Add tomatoes and juice, salt, black pepper, sugar and cayenne pepper; mix well.

3. Place fish in bottom of greased 12×7½-inch baking dish. Spoon rice mixture over fish; cover with foil.

4. Bake in preheated 400°F oven for 45 to 50 minutes or until rice is tender. Let stand for 5 minutes before serving. Sprinkle with parsley.
Makes 6 servings

Prep Time: 6 minutes
Cook Time: 58 minutes
Standing Time: 5 minutes

Caribbean Shrimp with Rice

Spicy Thai Noodles

- 1¼ cups water
- 2½ teaspoons brown sugar
- 2 teaspoons soy sauce
- 1 teaspoon LAWRY'S® Garlic Powder with Parsley
- ¾ teaspoon LAWRY'S® Seasoned Salt
- ½ teaspoon cornstarch
- ⅛ to ¼ teaspoon hot pepper flakes
- ¼ cup chunky peanut butter
- ¼ cup sliced green onion
- 1 tablespoon chopped fresh cilantro
- 8 ounces linguine, cooked, drained and kept hot
- 1½ cups shredded red cabbage

In large skillet, combine first seven ingredients. Bring to a boil over medium-high heat; reduce heat to low and cook, uncovered, 5 minutes. Cool 10 minutes. Stir in peanut butter, green onion and cilantro. Add hot linguine and cabbage; toss lightly to coat. Serve immediately.

Makes 4 servings

Serving Suggestion: Great served with a marinated cucumber salad.

Hearty Manicotti

- 8 to 10 uncooked manicotti shells
- 1 package (10 ounces) frozen chopped spinach, thawed, squeezed dry
- 1 carton (15 ounces) ricotta cheese
- 1 egg, lightly beaten
- ½ cup (2 ounces) grated Parmesan cheese
- ⅛ teaspoon ground black pepper
- 2 cans (6 ounces each) CONTADINA® Italian Paste with Italian Seasonings
- 1⅓ cups water
- ½ cup (2 ounces) shredded mozzarella cheese

1. Cook pasta according to package directions; drain.

2. Meanwhile, combine spinach, ricotta cheese, egg, Parmesan cheese and pepper in medium bowl; mix well.

3. Spoon into manicotti shells. Place in *ungreased* 12×7½-inch baking dish.

4. Combine tomato paste and water in small bowl; pour over manicotti. Sprinkle with mozzarella cheese. Bake in preheated 350°F oven for 30 to 40 minutes or until heated through.

Makes 4 to 5 servings

Prep Time: 15 minutes
Cook Time: 40 minutes

Four-Cheese Lasagna

- ½ pound ground beef
- ½ cup chopped onion
- ⅓ cup chopped celery
- 1 clove garlic, minced
- 1½ teaspoons dried basil leaves
- ¼ teaspoon dried oregano leaves
- ¼ teaspoon salt
- ⅛ teaspoon ground black pepper
- 1 package (3 ounces) cream cheese, cubed
- ⅓ cup light cream or milk
- ½ cup dry white wine
- ½ cup (2 ounces) shredded Wisconsin Cheddar or Gouda cheese
- 1 egg, slightly beaten
- 1 cup cream-style cottage cheese
- 6 ounces lasagna noodles, cooked and drained
- 6 ounces sliced Wisconsin Mozzarella cheese

In large skillet, brown meat with onion, celery and garlic; drain. Stir in basil, oregano, salt and pepper. Reduce heat to low. Add cream cheese and cream. Cook, stirring frequently, until cream cheese is melted. Stir in wine. Gradually add Cheddar cheese, stirring until Cheddar cheese is almost melted. Remove from heat. In small bowl, combine egg and cottage cheese.

Into greased 10×6-inch baking dish, layer ½ each of the noodles, meat sauce, cottage cheese mixture and Mozzarella cheese; repeat layers. Bake, uncovered, at 375°F, 30 to 35 minutes or until hot and bubbly. Let stand 10 minutes before cutting to serve.

Makes 6 servings

Prep Time: 1½ hours

Favorite recipe from **Wisconsin Milk Marketing Board**

Classic French Onion Soup

- ¼ cup butter
- 3 large yellow onions, sliced
- 1 cup dry white wine
- 3 cans (about 14 ounces each) beef broth or chicken broth
- 1 teaspoon Worcestershire sauce
- ½ teaspoon salt
- ½ teaspoon dried thyme
- 1 loaf French bread, sliced and toasted
- 4 ounces shredded Swiss cheese
- Fresh thyme for garnish

Slow Cooker Directions

Melt butter in large skillet over high heat. Add onions, cook and stir 15 minutes or until onions are soft and lightly browned. Stir in wine.

Combine onion mixture, beef broth, Worcestershire, salt and dried thyme in slow cooker. Cover and cook on LOW 4 to 4½ hours. Ladle soup into 4 individual bowls; top with bread slice and cheese. Garnish with fresh thyme, if desired.

Makes 4 servings

Spicy Thai Noodles

Torta Rustica

- 1 package active dry yeast
- 1 teaspoon sugar
- 1 cup warm water (105° to 115°F)
- 3 cups plus 2 tablespoons all-purpose flour, divided
- 1½ teaspoons salt, divided
- 3 tablespoons vegetable oil, divided
- 1½ teaspoons dried basil leaves, divided
- 1½ cups chopped onions
- 1 cup chopped carrots
- 2 cloves garlic, minced
- 2 medium zucchini, cubed
- ½ pound button mushrooms, sliced
- 1 can (16 ounces) whole tomatoes, undrained, chopped
- 1 can (15 ounces) artichoke hearts, drained, cut into halves
- 1 medium red bell pepper, seeded and cut into 1-inch squares
- ½ teaspoon dried oregano leaves
- ¼ teaspoon black pepper
- 2 cups (8 ounces) shredded provolone or mozzarella cheese

1. To proof yeast, sprinkle yeast and sugar over warm water in small bowl; stir until yeast is dissolved. Let stand 5 minutes or until mixture is bubbly.*

2. Combine 3 cups flour and 1 teaspoon salt in food processor. With food processor running, add yeast mixture, 2 tablespoons oil and ½ teaspoon basil.

3. Process until mixture forms dough that leaves side of bowl. If dough is too dry, add 1 to 2 tablespoons water. If dough is too wet, add remaining 1 to 2 tablespoons flour until dough leaves side of bowl. Dough will be sticky.

4. Place dough in large greased bowl. Turn dough over so that top is greased. Cover with towel; let rise in warm place about 1 hour or until doubled in bulk. To test if dough has risen enough, lightly press two fingertips about ½ inch into dough. Dough is ready if indentations remain when fingertips are removed.

5. Heat remaining 1 tablespoon oil in large saucepan over medium heat until hot. Add onions, carrots and garlic; cook and stir 5 minutes or until onions are tender. Stir in zucchini, mushrooms, tomatoes with juice, artichoke hearts, bell pepper, remaining 1 teaspoon basil, oregano, remaining ½ teaspoon salt and black pepper. Bring to a boil over high heat. Reduce heat to low. Cover and simmer 10 minutes.

6. Meanwhile, to punch down dough, push down on center of dough with your fist. Push edges of dough into center. Knead dough on lightly floured surface 1 minute. Cover with towel; let rest 10 minutes.

7. Preheat oven to 400°F. Grease 2-quart casserole or soufflé dish. Roll ⅔ of dough on lightly floured surface to ½-inch thickness. Ease dough into casserole, allowing dough to extend 1 inch over edge of casserole.

8. Spoon half the vegetable mixture into casserole. Sprinkle with 1 cup cheese. Repeat layers.

9. Roll remaining dough on lightly floured surface into circle 2 inches larger than top of casserole; cut decorative designs in top of dough with paring knife. Place dough over filling. Fold edges of top dough over bottom dough; pinch with fingertips to seal edges.

10. Bake 30 to 35 minutes or until crust is golden brown, covering edge of dough with foil if necessary to prevent overbrowning.

Makes 6 servings

*If yeast mixture does not bubble, it is no longer active. This may be the result of water that is too hot or yeast that is too old. (Always check expiration date on yeast package.) Discard yeast mixture and start again with new ingredients.

Italian Eggplant Parmigiana

- 1 large eggplant, sliced ¼ inch thick
- 2 eggs, beaten
- ½ cup dry bread crumbs
- 1 can (14½ ounces) DEL MONTE® Italian Recipe Stewed Tomatoes
- 1 can (15 ounces) DEL MONTE® Tomato Sauce
- 2 cloves garlic, minced
- ½ teaspoon dried basil
- 6 ounces mozzarella cheese, sliced

1. Dip eggplant slices into eggs, then bread crumbs; arrange in single layer on baking sheet. Broil 4 inches from heat until brown and tender, about 5 minutes per side.

2. Preheat oven to 350°F. Place eggplant in 13×9-inch baking dish.

3. Combine tomatoes, tomato sauce, garlic and basil; pour over eggplant and top with cheese.

4. Cover and bake at 350°F, 30 minutes or until heated through. Sprinkle with grated Parmesan cheese, if desired.

Makes 4 servings

Prep Time: 15 minutes
Cook Time: 30 minutes

Torta Rustica

Minestrone alla Milanese

2 cans (14½ ounces each) reduced-sodium beef broth
1 can (14½ ounces) diced tomatoes, undrained
1 cup diced potato
1 cup coarsely chopped green cabbage
1 cup coarsely chopped carrots
1 cup sliced zucchini
¾ cup chopped onion
¾ cup sliced fresh green beans
¾ cup coarsely chopped celery
¾ cup water
2 tablespoons olive oil
1 clove garlic, minced
½ teaspoon dried basil leaves
¼ teaspoon dried rosemary
1 bay leaf
1 can (15½ ounces) cannellini beans, rinsed and drained
Grated Parmesan cheese (optional)

Slow Cooker Directions
Combine all ingredients except cannellini beans and cheese in slow cooker; mix well. Cover and cook on LOW 5 to 6 hours. Add cannellini beans. Cover and cook on LOW 1 hour or until vegetables are crisp-tender. Remove and discard bay leaf. Garnish with cheese, if desired.

Makes 8 to 10 servings

Greek Spinach and Feta Pie

⅓ cup butter, melted
2 eggs
1 package (10 ounces) frozen chopped spinach, thawed and squeezed dry
1 container (15 ounces) ricotta cheese
1 package (4 ounces) crumbled feta cheese
¾ teaspoon finely grated lemon peel
¼ teaspoon black pepper
⅛ teaspoon ground nutmeg
1 package (16 ounces) frozen phyllo dough, thawed

Preheat oven to 350°F. Brush 13×9-inch baking dish lightly with butter.

Beat eggs in medium bowl. Stir in spinach, ricotta, feta, lemon peel, pepper and nutmeg. Set aside.

Unwrap phyllo dough; remove 8 sheets. Cut dough in half crosswise forming 16 rectangles about 13×8½ inches. Cover dough with damp cloth or plastic wrap to keep moist while assembling pie. Reserve remaining dough for another use.

Place 1 piece of dough in prepared dish; brush top lightly with butter. Top with another piece of dough and brush lightly with butter. Continue layering with 6 pieces of dough, brushing each lightly with butter. Spoon spinach mixture evenly over dough.

Top spinach mixture with piece of dough; brush lightly with butter. Repeat layering with remaining 7 pieces of dough, brushing each piece lightly with butter.

Bake, uncovered, 35 to 40 minutes or until golden brown.

Makes 6 servings

Serving Suggestion: Serve with a Greek vegetable salad made of cucumbers, tomatoes and red onions on a bed of romaine lettuce drizzled with red wine vinegar salad dressing.

Garden Vegetable Tabbouleh Stew

1 large onion, chopped
2 medium carrots, cut lengthwise into halves, then cut into 1-inch pieces
1 cup green beans, cut into 1-inch pieces
2 medium green onions, thinly sliced
1 small zucchini (4 ounces), sliced
1 can (15½ ounces) chick-peas (garbanzo beans), rinsed and drained
2 cans (14½ ounces each) diced tomatoes, undrained
¼ teaspoon salt
⅛ teaspoon black pepper
1 box (6 to 7 ounces) tabbouleh mix
1½ cups water
¼ cup olive oil
Sour cream (optional)
Fresh mint (optional)

Slow Cooker Directions
Layer ingredients in slow cooker in the following order: onion, carrots, green beans, green onions, zucchini, chick-peas, tomatoes with juice, salt and pepper. Sprinkle tabbouleh mix over vegetables. Pour water and olive oil evenly over top. Cover and cook on LOW 6 to 8 hours or until vegetables are crisp-tender. Serve in bowls and garnish with sour cream and fresh mint, if desired.

Makes 4 servings

Minestrone alla Milanese

Light & Easy Fare

Fajita Stuffed Shells

- **¼ cup fresh lime juice**
- **1 clove garlic, minced**
- **½ teaspoon dried oregano leaves**
- **¼ teaspoon ground cumin**
- **1 (6-ounce) boneless lean round or flank steak**
- **1 medium green bell pepper, halved and seeded**
- **1 medium onion, cut in half**
- **12 uncooked jumbo pasta shells (about 6 ounces)**
- **½ cup reduced-fat sour cream**
- **2 tablespoons shredded reduced-fat Cheddar cheese**
- **1 tablespoon minced fresh cilantro**
- **⅔ cup chunky salsa**
- **2 cups shredded leaf lettuce**

1. Combine lime juice, garlic, oregano and cumin in shallow nonmetallic dish. Add steak, bell pepper and onion. Cover and refrigerate 8 hours or overnight.

2. Preheat oven to 350°F. Cook pasta shells according to package directions, omitting salt. Drain and rinse well under cold water; set aside.

3. Grill steak and vegetables over medium-hot coals 3 to 4 minutes per side or until desired doneness; cool slightly. Cut steak into thin slices. Chop vegetables. Place steak slices and vegetables in medium bowl. Stir in sour cream, Cheddar cheese and cilantro. Stuff shells evenly with meat mixture, mounding slightly.

4. Arrange shells in 8-inch baking dish. Pour salsa over filled shells. Cover with foil and bake 15 minutes or until heated through. Divide lettuce evenly among 4 plates; arrange 3 shells on each plate.

Makes 4 servings

Creamy Ham and Garden Rotini

- **8 ounces uncooked rotini pasta**
- **1 bag (16 ounces) frozen vegetable blend (broccoli, cauliflower, red peppers and corn)**
- **4 ounces turkey ham, chopped**
- **1½ cups fat-free (skim) milk**
- **2 tablespoons all-purpose flour**
- **1¼ cups (5 ounces) shredded reduced-fat Monterey Jack cheese**
- **Black pepper**

1. Preheat oven to 325°F. Spray 11×8-inch baking pan with nonstick cooking spray; set aside. Cook pasta according to package directions, omitting salt; drain. Place in bottom of prepared pan; set aside.

2. Meanwhile, add ½ cup water to large nonstick skillet. Bring to a boil over high heat. Add vegetables; return to a boil. Reduce heat to low; simmer, covered, 4 minutes. Drain. Toss vegetables and ham with pasta; set aside.

3. Whisk milk into flour in small bowl until smooth. Pour milk mixture into same skillet; cook over medium-high heat, stirring constantly, until slightly thickened. Remove from heat. Pour over pasta mixture. Top with cheese; sprinkle with pepper. Cover loosely with foil. Bake 25 to 30 minutes or until heated through.

Makes 4 servings

Fajita Stuffed Shells

Baked Pasta Casserole

1½ cups (3 ounces) uncooked wagon wheel or rotelle pasta
3 ounces lean ground beef sirloin
2 tablespoons chopped onion
2 tablespoons chopped green bell pepper
1 clove garlic, minced
½ cup fat-free spaghetti sauce
Black pepper
2 tablespoons shredded Italian-style mozzarella and Parmesan cheese blend
Pepperoncini (optional)

1. Preheat oven to 350°F. Cook pasta according to package directions; drain. Return pasta to saucepan.

2. Meanwhile, heat small nonstick skillet over medium-high heat. Add beef, onion, bell pepper and garlic; cook and stir 3 to 4 minutes or until beef is browned and vegetables are crisp-tender. Drain.

3. Add beef mixture, spaghetti sauce and black pepper to pasta in saucepan; mix well. Spoon mixture into 1-quart baking dish. Sprinkle with cheese.

4. Bake 15 minutes or until heated through. Serve with pepperoncini, if desired. *Makes 2 servings*

Note: To make ahead, assemble casserole as directed above through step 3. Cover and refrigerate several hours or overnight. Bake, uncovered, in preheated 350°F oven for 30 minutes or until heated through.

Beef and Parsnip Stroganoff

Slow Cooker

1 cube beef bouillon
¾ cup boiling water
¾ pound well-trimmed boneless top round beef steak, 1 inch thick
Nonstick olive oil cooking spray
2 cups cubed peeled parsnips or potatoes*
1 medium onion, halved and thinly sliced
¾ pound mushrooms, sliced
2 teaspoons minced garlic
¼ teaspoon black pepper
¼ cup water
1 tablespoon plus 1½ teaspoons all-purpose flour
3 tablespoons reduced-fat sour cream
1½ teaspoons Dijon mustard
¼ teaspoon cornstarch
1 tablespoon chopped fresh parsley
4 ounces cholesterol-free wide noodles, cooked without salt, drained and kept hot

**If using potatoes, cut into 1-inch chunks and do not sauté.*

Slow Cooker Directions

1. Dissolve bouillon cube in ¾ cup boiling water; cool. Meanwhile, cut steak into 2×½-inch strips. Spray large nonstick skillet with cooking spray; heat over high heat. Cook and stir beef about 4 minutes or until meat begins to brown and is barely pink. Transfer beef and juices to slow cooker.

2. Spray same skillet with cooking spray; heat over high heat. Add parsnips and onion; cook and stir until browned, about 4 minutes. Add mushrooms, garlic and pepper; cook and stir until mushrooms are tender, about 5 minutes. Transfer mushroom mixture to slow cooker; mix with beef.

3. Stir ¼ cup water into flour in small bowl until smooth. Stir flour mixture into cooled bouillon. Add to slow cooker. Cook, covered, on LOW 4½ to 5 hours or until beef and parsnips are tender.

4. Turn off slow cooker. Remove beef and vegetables with slotted spoon to large bowl; reserve cooking liquid from beef. Blend sour cream, mustard and cornstarch in medium bowl. Gradually add reserved liquid to sour cream mixture; stir well to blend. Stir sour cream mixture into beef mixture. Sprinkle with parsley; serve over noodles. Garnish, if desired.
Makes 4 servings

Helpful Hints

Parsnips are a pale white root vegetable similar in shape to the carrot. However, the parsnip is broader at the top and has a smoother skin. Its distinctive nutty sweet flavor contributes to soups, stews and vegetable side dishes.

Beef and Parsnip Stroganoff

Beef Picante and Sour Cream Casserole

6 ounces uncooked wagon wheel pasta
8 ounces lean ground beef
1½ cups reduced-sodium mild picante sauce
1 cup red kidney beans, rinsed and drained
¾ cup water
1 tablespoon chili powder
1 teaspoon ground cumin
½ cup nonfat cottage cheese
½ cup nonfat sour cream
½ cup chopped green onion with tops
1 can (2¼ ounces) sliced black olives
¼ cup chopped fresh cilantro or fresh parsley

1. Preheat oven to 325°F. Spray 9-inch square baking pan with nonstick cooking spray; set aside. Cook pasta according to package directions, omitting salt. Drain. Place in bottom of prepared pan; set aside.

2. Brown beef in large nonstick skillet over medium-high heat 4 to 5 minutes or until no longer pink, stirring to separate beef; drain fat.

3. Add picante sauce, beans, water, chili powder and cumin; blend well. Bring to a boil over high heat. Reduce heat to low; simmer, covered, 20 minutes.

4. Combine cottage cheese, sour cream and green onions in food processor or blender; process until smooth. Spread cottage cheese mixture over pasta in prepared pan.

5. Spoon meat mixture over cottage cheese mixture; cover with foil. Bake 20 minutes or until heated through. Remove from oven; let stand 10 minutes to allow flavors to blend. Top with olives and cilantro.

Makes 4 servings

Southwestern Beef and Bean Lasagna

½ pound extra-lean ground beef
1 can (16 ounces) pinto beans, drained
1 teaspoon cumin seeds
1 teaspoon olive oil
1½ cups chopped onions
1 tablespoon minced seeded jalapeño pepper*
1 clove garlic, minced
4 cups no-salt-added tomato sauce
1 can (4 ounces) diced green chilies, undrained
2 teaspoons chili powder
1 teaspoon dried oregano leaves
1 container (8 ounces) nonfat cottage cheese
1½ cups (6 ounces) shredded reduced-fat Cheddar cheese, divided
1 egg white
¼ cup chopped fresh cilantro
½ teaspoon salt
¼ teaspoon black pepper
8 ounces uncooked lasagna noodles
1 cup water

**Jalapeño peppers can sting and irritate the skin; wear rubber gloves when handling peppers and do not touch eyes. Wash hands after handling peppers.*

1. Brown beef in large skillet. Drain off fat. Stir in beans; set aside. Place cumin seeds in large nonstick skillet. Cook and stir over medium heat 2 minutes or until fragrant. Remove from skillet. In same skillet, heat oil. Add onions, jalapeño pepper and garlic; cook until onions are soft. Add tomato sauce, green chilies, chili powder, oregano and cumin seeds. Bring to a boil; reduce heat. Simmer, uncovered, 20 minutes.

2. Preheat oven to 350°F. Combine cottage cheese, ½ cup Cheddar cheese, egg white, cilantro, salt and black pepper in medium bowl. Spray 13×9-inch baking pan with cooking spray. Cover bottom with ¾ cup tomato sauce mixture. Place layer of noodles on sauce. Spread half the beef mixture over noodles, then place another layer of noodles on top. Spread cheese mixture over noodles. Spread with remaining beef mixture. Layer with noodles. Pour remaining sauce mixture over all; sprinkle with remaining 1 cup Cheddar cheese. Pour water around edges. Cover tightly with foil. Bake 1 hour and 15 minutes or until pasta is tender. Cool 10 minutes before serving.

Makes 6 servings

Note: If cumin seeds are not available, you may substitute ground cumin. Just add ½ teaspoon to the tomato sauce mixture in step 1.

Stuffed Bell Peppers

3 large bell peppers, any color, cut in half lengthwise and seeded
1½ cups chopped fresh tomatoes
1 tablespoon chopped fresh cilantro
1 jalapeño pepper,* seeded and chopped
1 clove garlic, finely minced
½ teaspoon dried oregano leaves, divided
¼ teaspoon ground cumin
8 ounces lean ground round
1 cup cooked brown rice
¼ cup cholesterol-free egg substitute *or* 2 egg whites
2 tablespoons finely chopped onion
¼ teaspoon salt
⅛ teaspoon black pepper

**Jalapeño peppers can sting and irritate the skin; wear rubber gloves when handling peppers and do not touch eyes. Wash hands after handling.*

1. Preheat oven to 350°F.

2. Place steamer basket in large saucepan; add 1 inch of water, being careful not to let water touch bottom of basket. Place bell peppers in basket; cover. Bring to a boil; reduce heat to medium. Steam peppers 8 to 10 minutes or until tender, adding additional water if necessary; drain.

3. Combine tomatoes, cilantro, jalapeño pepper, garlic, ¼ teaspoon oregano and cumin in small bowl. Set aside.

4. Thoroughly combine beef, rice, egg substitute, onion, remaining ¼ teaspoon oregano, salt and black pepper in large bowl. Stir 1 cup of tomato mixture into beef mixture. Spoon filling evenly into pepper halves; place meat side up, in 13×9-inch baking dish. Cover tightly with foil.

5. Bake 45 minutes or until meat is browned and vegetables are tender. Serve with remaining tomato salsa, if desired. *Makes 6 servings*

Meatball Grinders

¼ cup chopped onion
1 can (15 ounces) diced tomatoes, drained and juices reserved
1 can (8 ounces) reduced-sodium tomato sauce
2 tablespoons tomato paste
1 teaspoon dried Italian seasoning
1 pound ground chicken breast
½ cup fresh whole wheat or white bread crumbs (1 slice bread)
1 egg white, lightly beaten
3 tablespoons finely chopped fresh parsley
2 cloves garlic, minced
¼ teaspoon salt
⅛ teaspoon black pepper
4 small hard rolls, split
2 tablespoons grated Parmesan cheese

Slow Cooker Directions
Combine onion, diced tomatoes, ½ cup reserved juice, tomato sauce, tomato paste and Italian seasoning in slow cooker. Cover and cook on LOW 3 to 4 hours or until onions are soft.

During the last 30 minutes of cooking time, prepare meatballs. Combine chicken, bread crumbs, egg white, parsley, garlic, salt and pepper in medium bowl. With wet hands form mixture into 12 to 16 meatballs. Spray medium nonstick skillet with cooking spray; heat over medium heat until hot. Add meatballs; cook about 8 to 10 minutes or until well-browned on all sides. Remove meatballs to slow cooker; cook 1 to 2 hours or until meatballs are no longer pink in centers and are heated through.

Place 3 to 4 meatballs in each roll. Divide sauce evenly; spoon over meatballs. Sprinkle with cheese.
Makes 4 servings

Helpful Hints

When buying ground chicken, check labels to determine if the product is low in fat. If skin and dark meat are included in the ingredients, the chicken will be higher in fat.

Broccoli-Filled Chicken Roulade

2 cups broccoli florets
1 tablespoon water
¼ cup fresh parsley sprigs
1 cup diced red bell pepper
4 ounces fat-free cream cheese, softened
2 tablespoons grated Parmesan cheese
2 tablespoons lemon juice
2 tablespoons olive oil
1 teaspoon paprika
¼ teaspoon salt
1 egg
½ cup skim milk
4 cups cornflakes, crushed
1 tablespoon dried basil leaves
8 boneless skinless chicken breast halves

1. Place broccoli and water in microwavable dish; cover. Microwave at HIGH 2 minutes. Let stand, covered, 2 minutes. Drain water from broccoli. Place broccoli in food processor or blender. Add parsley; process 10 seconds, scraping side of bowl if necessary. Add bell pepper, cream cheese, Parmesan cheese, lemon juice, oil, paprika and salt. Pulse 2 to 3 times or until bell pepper is minced.

2. Preheat oven to 375°F. Spray 11×7-inch baking pan with nonstick cooking spray. Lightly beat egg in small bowl. Add milk; blend well. Place cornflake crumbs in shallow bowl. Add basil; blend well.

3. Pound chicken breasts between two pieces of plastic wrap to ¼-inch thickness using flat side of meat mallet or rolling pin. Spread each chicken breast with ⅛ of the broccoli mixture, spreading to within ½ inch of edges. Roll up chicken breast from short end, tucking in sides if possible; secure with wooden picks. Dip roulades in milk mixture; roll in cornflake crumb mixture. Place in prepared baking pan. Bake 20 minutes or until chicken is no longer pink in center and juices run clear. Garnish, if desired.

Makes 8 servings

Jalapeño Chicken & Rice in a Skillet

4 TYSON® Fresh or Individually Fresh Frozen® Boneless, Skinless Chicken Breasts
2 cups UNCLE BEN'S® Instant Rice
1 tablespoon olive oil
1 teaspoon minced garlic
2 cups defatted reduced-sodium chicken broth
1 can (15 ounces) black beans, rinsed and drained
1 to 2 teaspoons minced jalapeño pepper*
½ teaspoon ground cumin
2 tablespoons chopped fresh cilantro

**Jalapeño peppers can sting and irritate the skin; wear rubber gloves when handling peppers and do not touch eyes. Wash hands after handling.*

PREP: CLEAN: Wash hands. Remove protective ice glaze from frozen chicken by holding under cool running water 1 to 2 minutes. Pat dry. CLEAN: Wash hands.

COOK: In large nonstick skillet, heat olive oil and garlic; add chicken. Cook over medium heat 4 to 6 minutes (5 to 7 minutes if using frozen chicken) or until chicken is lightly browned. Stir in chicken broth, beans, jalapeño pepper and cumin; cover. Simmer 10 to 15 minutes or until internal juices of chicken run clear. (Or insert instant-read meat thermometer in thickest part of chicken. Temperature should read 170°F.) Stir in rice; cover. Let stand 5 minutes.

SERVE: Sprinkle with cilantro. Serve with lime wedges and salsa, if desired.

CHILL: Refrigerate leftovers immediately. *Makes 4 servings*

Prep Time: 5 minutes
Cook Time: 30 minutes

Tuscan Pasta

1 pound boneless skinless chicken breasts, cut into 1-inch pieces
1 can (15½ ounces) red kidney beans, rinsed and drained
1 can (15 ounces) tomato sauce
2 cans (14½ ounces each) Italian-style stewed tomatoes
1 jar (4½ ounces) sliced mushrooms, drained
1 medium green bell pepper, chopped
½ cup chopped onion
½ cup chopped celery
4 cloves garlic, minced
1 cup water
1 teaspoon dried Italian seasoning
6 ounces uncooked thin spaghetti, broken into halves

Slow Cooker Directions
Place all ingredients except spaghetti in slow cooker. Cover and cook on LOW 4 hours or until vegetables are tender.

Turn to HIGH. Stir in spaghetti; cover. Stir again after 10 minutes. Cover and cook 45 minutes or until pasta is tender. Garnish with basil and bell pepper strips, if desired.

Makes 8 servings

Broccoli-Filled Chicken Roulade

Broccoli, Chicken and Rice Casserole

- 1 box UNCLE BEN'S CHEF'S RECIPE™ Broccoli Rice Au Gratin Supreme
- 2 cups boiling water
- 4 boneless, skinless chicken breasts (about 1 pound)
- ¼ teaspoon garlic powder
- 2 cups frozen broccoli
- 1 cup (4 ounces) reduced-fat shredded Cheddar cheese

1. Heat oven to 425°F. In 13×9-inch baking pan, combine rice and contents of seasoning packet. Add boiling water; mix well. Add chicken; sprinkle with garlic powder. Cover and bake 30 minutes.

2. Add broccoli and cheese, continue to bake, covered, 8 to 10 minutes or until chicken is no longer pink in center. *Makes 4 servings*

Sweet Jalapeño Mustard Turkey Thighs

- 3 turkey thighs, skin removed
- ¾ cup honey mustard
- ½ cup orange juice
- 1 tablespoon cider vinegar
- 1 teaspoon Worcestershire sauce
- 1 to 2 fresh jalapeño peppers,* finely chopped
- 1 clove garlic, minced
- ½ teaspoon grated orange peel

**Jalapeño peppers can sting and irritate the skin; wear rubber gloves when handling peppers and do not touch eyes. Wash hands after handling.*

Slow Cooker Directions

Place turkey thighs in single layer in slow cooker. Combine remaining ingredients in large bowl. Pour mixture over turkey thighs. Cover and cook on LOW 5 to 6 hours. *Makes 6 servings*

Southwest Turkey Tenderloin Stew

- 1 package (about 1½ pounds) turkey tenderloins, cut into ¾-inch pieces
- 1 tablespoon chili powder
- 1 teaspoon ground cumin
- ¼ teaspoon salt
- 1 red bell pepper, cut into ¾-inch pieces
- 1 green bell pepper, cut into ¾-inch pieces
- ¾ cup chopped red or yellow onion
- 3 cloves garlic, minced
- 1 can (15½ ounces) chili beans in spicy sauce, undrained
- 1 can (14½ ounces) chili-style stewed tomatoes, undrained
- ¾ cup prepared salsa or picante sauce
- Fresh cilantro (optional)

Slow Cooker Directions

Place turkey in slow cooker. Sprinkle chili powder, cumin and salt over turkey; toss to coat. Add red bell pepper, green bell pepper, onion, garlic, beans with sauce, tomatoes with juice and salsa. Mix well. Cover and cook on LOW 5 hours or until turkey is no longer pink in center and vegetables are crisp-tender. Ladle into bowls. Garnish with cilantro, if desired. *Makes 6 servings*

Chicken and Chili Pepper Stew

- 1 pound boneless skinless chicken thighs, cut into ½-inch pieces
- 1 pound small potatoes, cut lengthwise in halves and then cut crosswise into slices
- 1 cup chopped onion
- 2 poblano chili peppers, seeded and cut into ½-inch pieces
- 1 jalapeño pepper,* seeded and finely chopped
- 3 cloves garlic, minced
- 3 cups fat-free reduced-sodium chicken broth
- 1 can (14½ ounces) no-salt-added diced tomatoes
- 2 tablespoons chili powder
- 1 teaspoon dried oregano leaves

**Jalapeño peppers can sting and irritate the skin; wear rubber gloves when handling peppers and do not touch eyes. Wash hands after handling.*

Slow Cooker Directions

1. Place chicken, potatoes, onion, poblano peppers, jalapeño pepper and garlic in slow cooker.

2. Stir together broth, tomatoes, chili powder and oregano in large bowl. Pour broth mixture over chicken mixture in slow cooker. Stir. Cover and cook on LOW 8 to 9 hours. *Makes 6 servings*

Broccoli, Chicken and Rice Casserole

Chicken Pot Pie with Cornmeal Crust

- **4 tablespoons water, divided**
- **1 cup diagonally sliced carrots**
- **½ cup diagonally sliced celery**
- **2 cups sliced fresh mushrooms**
- **1 can (14½ ounces) fat-free reduced-sodium chicken broth, divided**
- **⅓ cup low-fat (1%) milk**
- **1⅓ cups unbleached flour, divided**
- **½ teaspoon dried thyme leaves**
- **¼ teaspoon plus ⅛ teaspoon salt, divided**
- **⅛ teaspoon white pepper**
- **⅓ cup yellow cornmeal**
- **1 teaspoon baking powder**
- **3 tablespoons canola and vegetable oil blend**
- **4 to 5 tablespoons cold water**
- **2 cups diced cooked chicken breasts**
- **1 cup frozen peas and pearl onions, thawed**

1. Bring 2 tablespoons water to a boil in small saucepan over medium-high heat. Add carrots and celery. Reduce heat; cover and simmer 10 minutes or until vegetables are crisp-tender.

2. Heat large nonstick skillet over high heat. Spray with nonstick cooking spray. Add mushrooms and 2 tablespoons water. Reduce heat to medium-high; cook and stir until water evaporates and mushrooms are lightly brown. Add *all but* ⅓ cup chicken broth to skillet. Pour milk and remaining ⅓ cup chicken broth into small jar with tight-fitting lid. Add ⅓ cup flour, thyme, ¼ teaspoon salt and pepper. Shake well. Slowly stir flour mixture into chicken broth and mushrooms. Bring to a boil. Continue to cook and stir 1 minute. Cover and set aside.

3. Preheat oven to 375°F. Combine remaining 1 cup flour, cornmeal, baking powder and remaining ⅛ teaspoon salt in large bowl; form a well in center. Combine oil and 4 tablespoons cold water. Pour into well; toss with fork until mixture holds together, sprinkling with additional water, if needed. Press together to form ball. Place between 2 pieces of waxed paper. Roll dough into 10-inch circle, ⅛ inch thick. Remove top piece of waxed paper. Cut air vent into crust with knife.

4. Combine chicken broth mixture, chicken, cooked vegetables, peas and onions in large saucepan; reheat thoroughly. Coat 9-inch pie plate with nonstick cooking spray. Pour hot mixture into pie plate. Carefully place top crust over filling; remove waxed paper. Flute edge of crust; brush with additional milk, if desired. Bake for 30 to 35 minutes or until golden brown. *Makes 6 servings*

Southern BBQ Chicken and Rice

- **1 cup UNCLE BEN'S® ORIGINAL CONVERTED® Brand Rice**
- **4 TYSON® Individually Fresh Frozen® Chicken Half Breasts**
- **1½ cups water**
- **1 cup barbecue sauce, divided**
- **1 package (6 half ears) frozen corn on the cob**

COOK: CLEAN: Wash hands. In large skillet, combine water, rice, ¾ cup barbecue sauce and chicken. Bring to a boil. Cover, reduce heat; simmer 25 minutes. Add corn; cook 15 to 20 minutes or until juices of chicken run clear. (Or insert instant-read meat thermometer in thickest part of chicken. Temperature should read 170°F.) Spoon remaining ¼ cup barbecue sauce over chicken. Remove from heat; let stand 5 minutes or until liquid is absorbed.

SERVE: Serve with extra barbecue sauce and corn bread, if desired.

CHILL: Refrigerate leftovers immediately. *Makes 4 servings*

Prep Time: none
Cook Time: 40 to 45 minutes

Classic Chicken Biscuit Pie

- **12 boneless, skinless chicken tenderloins, cut into 1-inch pieces**
- **4 cups water**
- **2 boxes UNCLE BEN'S® COUNTRY INN® Chicken Flavored Rice**
- **1 can (10¾ ounces) condensed cream of chicken soup**
- **1 bag (1 pound) frozen peas, potatoes and carrots**
- **1 container (12 ounces) refrigerated buttermilk biscuits**

1. Heat oven to 400°F. In large saucepan, combine chicken, water, rice, contents of seasoning packets, soup and vegetable mixture; mix well. Bring to a boil. Cover; reduce heat and simmer 10 minutes.

2. Place in 13×9-inch baking pan; top with biscuits.

3. Bake 10 to 12 minutes or until biscuits are golden brown. *Makes 8 to 10 servings*

Tip: For individual pot pies, place rice mixture in small ramekins or casseroles. Proceed with recipe as directed.

Southern BBQ Chicken and Rice

Mu Shu Turkey

- **1 can (16 ounces) plums, drained, rinsed and pitted**
- **½ cup orange juice**
- **¼ cup finely chopped onion**
- **1 tablespoon minced fresh ginger**
- **¼ teaspoon ground cinnamon**
- **1 pound boneless turkey breast, cut into thin strips**
- **6 (7-inch) flour tortillas**
- **3 cups coleslaw mix**

Slow Cooker Directions

1. Place plums in blender or food processor. Cover and blend until almost smooth. Combine plums, orange juice, onion, ginger and cinnamon in slow cooker; mix well. Place turkey strips over plum mixture. Cover and cook on LOW 3 to 4 hours.

2. Remove turkey strips from slow cooker and divide evenly among tortillas. Spoon about 2 tablespoons plum sauce over turkey. Top evenly with coleslaw mix. Fold bottom edge of tortilla over filling; fold in sides. Roll up to completely enclose filling. Repeat with remaining tortillas. Use remaining plum sauce for dipping.

Makes 6 servings

Broccoli Cheese Casserole

- **3 whole chicken breasts, skinned and halved**
- **1½ pounds fresh broccoli**
- **2 tablespoons margarine**
- **½ cup chopped onion**
- **1 clove garlic, minced**
- **3 tablespoons all-purpose flour**
- **1¼ cups skim milk**
- **2 tablespoons fresh parsley**
- **½ teaspoon salt**
- **½ teaspoon dried oregano leaves, crushed**
- **1½ cups 1% low-fat cream-style small curd cottage cheese**
- **1½ cups shredded reduced-fat Wisconsin Cheddar cheese**
- **¼ cup grated Wisconsin Romano cheese**
- **1 jar (4½ ounces) sliced mushrooms, drained**
- **6 ounces noodles, cooked and drained**

Microwave Directions: Place chicken breasts in microwavable glass baking dish. Microwave at HIGH (100% power) 7 minutes. Cool slightly and cube. Set aside. Remove flowerets from broccoli and cut larger ones in half. Cut stems into 1-inch pieces.

Place broccoli in 3-quart microwavable baking dish with ½ cup water. Cover and microwave at HIGH 7 minutes, stirring once. Let stand, covered, 2 minutes. Drain well; remove broccoli and set aside.

Place margarine, onion and garlic in same baking dish. Cover and microwave at HIGH 3 minutes. Stir in flour. Gradually add milk. Add parsley, salt and oregano. Microwave at HIGH 1 minute. Stir well; microwave 1 minute. Stir in cottage cheese. Microwave at HIGH 2 minutes. Stir; microwave at HIGH 2 minutes. Add Cheddar and Romano cheeses, stirring well. Microwave at MEDIUM-HIGH (70% power) 2 minutes. Stir in chicken, broccoli, mushrooms and noodles. Cover and microwave at MEDIUM (50% power) 5 minutes or until heated through.

Makes 6 to 8 servings

Favorite recipe from **Wisconsin Milk Marketing Board**

Helpful Hints

Fresh turkey parts are readily available at most supermarkets. Turkey breasts are sold whole or as halves with bone in or boned and rolled to form boneless halves. Breast cutlets are also available.

Mu Shu Turkey

Chicken Primavera Buffet

- **12 ounces uncooked thin spaghetti**
- **¼ cup prepared pesto**
- **¼ cup prepared fat-free Italian salad dressing**
- **½ teaspoon red pepper flakes**
- **2 cups water**
- **1 cup thinly sliced carrots**
- **1 cup broccoli flowerets**
- **1 cup snow peas**
- **1 can (4 ounces) sliced water chestnuts, drained**
- **Nonstick cooking spray**
- **8 boneless skinless chicken breast halves**

1. Preheat oven to 350°F. Cook pasta according to package directions, omitting salt. Drain and rinse well under cold water until pasta is cool; drain well. Place in large bowl; set aside.

2. Combine pesto, Italian dressing and red pepper flakes in small bowl. Reserve 1 tablespoon pesto mixture. Add remaining pesto mixture to pasta; toss to coat well.

3. In large saucepan, bring water to a boil over high heat. Add carrots, broccoli and snow peas; cook 3 minutes. Drain vegetables. Add water chestnuts and vegetables to pasta; toss to blend well. Spray 13×9-inch baking pan with nonstick cooking spray. Transfer pasta and vegetables to baking pan.

4. Spray large nonstick skillet with cooking spray; heat over medium heat until hot. Add chicken; cook until browned on both sides. Place chicken on pasta and vegetables. Pour juices from skillet over chicken. Spread reserved pesto mixture over chicken. Bake 30 minutes or until chicken is no longer pink in center.

Makes 8 servings

Garlic Herb Chicken and Rice Skillet

- **4 TYSON® Individually Fresh Frozen® Boneless, Skinless Chicken Breasts**
- **1 box UNCLE BEN'S® COUNTRY INN® Chicken Flavored Rice**
- **1¾ cups water**
- **2 cups frozen broccoli, carrots and cauliflower mixture**
- **¼ cup garlic and herb soft spreadable cheese**

COOK: CLEAN: Wash hands. In large skillet, combine chicken, water and contents of seasoning packet. Bring to a boil. Cover, reduce heat; simmer 10 minutes. Add rice, vegetables and cheese. Cook, covered, 10 to 15 minutes or until internal juices of chicken run clear. (Or insert instant-read meat thermometer in thickest part of chicken. Temperature should read 170°F.) Remove from heat; let stand 5 minutes or until liquid is absorbed.

SERVE: Dish out chicken to individual plates and serve while hot.

CHILL: Refrigerate leftovers immediately. *Makes 4 servings*

Prep Time: none
Cook Time: 25 to 30 minutes

Sweet Chicken Curry

Slow Cooker

- **1 pound boneless skinless chicken breast, cut into 1-inch pieces**
- **1 large green or red bell pepper, cut into 1-inch pieces**
- **1 large onion, sliced**
- **1 large tomato, seeded and chopped**
- **½ cup mango chutney**
- **2 tablespoons cornstarch**
- **1½ teaspoons curry powder**
- **1⅓ cups hot cooked rice**

Slow Cooker Directions

1. Place chicken, bell pepper and onion in slow cooker. Top with tomato. Mix chutney, ¼ cup water, cornstarch and curry powder in large bowl.

2. Pour chutney mixture over chicken mixture in slow cooker. Cover and cook on LOW 3½ to 4½ hours. Serve over rice. *Makes 4 servings*

Helpful Hints

Boneless skinless chicken breasts are lower in fat than other chicken cuts and therfore a good choice for light cooking. However, boneless chicken breasts are expensive. Look for sales and stock up or think about deboning chicken breasts at home—it's a good way to save money.

Chicken Primavera Buffet

Turkey Vegetable Crescent Pie

2 cans (about 14 ounces each) fat-free reduced-sodium chicken broth
1 medium onion, diced
1¼ pounds turkey tenderloins, cut into ¾-inch pieces
3 cups diced red potatoes
1 teaspoon chopped fresh rosemary *or* ½ teaspoon dried rosemary
¼ teaspoon salt
⅛ teaspoon black pepper
1 bag (16 ounces) frozen mixed vegetables
1 bag (10 ounces) frozen mixed vegetables
⅓ cup fat-free (skim) milk plus additional if necessary
3 tablespoons cornstarch
1 package (8 ounces) refrigerated reduced-fat crescent rolls

1. Bring broth to a boil in large saucepan. Add onion; reduce heat and simmer 3 minutes. Add turkey; return to a boil. Reduce heat, cover and simmer 7 to 9 minutes or until turkey is no longer pink. Remove turkey from saucepan with slotted spoon; place in 13×9-inch baking dish.

2. Return broth to a boil. Add potatoes, rosemary, salt and pepper; simmer 2 minutes. Return to a boil and stir in mixed vegetables. Simmer, covered, 7 to 8 minutes or until potatoes are tender. Remove vegetables with slotted spoon. Drain in colander set over bowl; reserve broth. Transfer vegetables to baking dish with turkey.

3. Preheat oven to 375°F. Blend ⅓ cup milk with cornstarch in small bowl until smooth. Add enough milk to reserved broth to equal 3 cups. Heat in large saucepan over medium-high heat; whisk in cornstarch mixture, stirring constantly until mixture comes to a boil. Boil 1 minute; remove from heat. Pour over turkey-vegetable mixture in baking dish.

4. Roll out crescent roll dough and separate at perforations; arrange dough pieces decoratively over top of turkey-vegetable mixture. Bake 13 to 15 minutes or until crust is golden brown. *Makes 8 servings*

Barbecue Chicken with Cornbread Topper

1½ pounds boneless skinless chicken breasts and thighs
1 can (15 ounces) red beans, drained and rinsed
1 can (8 ounces) tomato sauce
1 cup chopped green bell pepper
½ cup barbecue sauce
1 envelope (6.5 ounces) cornbread mix
Ingredients for cornbread mix

1. Cut chicken into ¾-inch cubes. Heat nonstick skillet over medium heat. Add chicken; cook and stir 5 minutes or until cooked through.

2. Combine chicken, beans, tomato sauce, bell pepper and barbecue sauce in 8-inch microwavable ovenproof dish.

3. Preheat oven to 375°F. Loosely cover chicken mixture with plastic wrap or waxed paper. Microwave on MEDIUM-HIGH (70% power) 8 minutes or until heated through, stirring after 4 minutes.

4. While chicken mixture is heating, prepare cornbread mix according to package directions. Spoon batter over chicken mixture. Bake 15 to 18 minutes or until toothpick inserted in center of cornbread layer comes out clean. *Makes 8 servings*

Skillet Chicken and Rice

1 teaspoon olive oil
2 boneless skinless chicken breast halves, 2 skinless thighs and 2 skinless legs *or* any combination of 6 pieces (about 1½ pounds)
1 large onion, chopped
1 green bell pepper, seeded and chopped
1 clove garlic, minced
½ teaspoon cumin seeds
1 can (14 ounces) no-salt-added whole tomatoes, undrained
1½ cups fat-free reduced-sodium chicken broth
¾ cup uncooked rice
2 ounces (2 slices) turkey-ham, sliced into 2-inch pieces
¼ teaspoon salt
⅛ to ¼ teaspoon ground red pepper
8 ounces frozen cut green beans, thawed

1. Heat oil in 12-inch nonstick skillet over medium-high heat. Add chicken; cook 3 minutes on each side or until browned. Remove chicken from skillet.

2. Add onion, bell pepper, garlic and cumin seeds to skillet; cook and stir 5 minutes. Stir in tomatoes, chicken broth, rice, turkey-ham, salt and red pepper; bring to a boil.

3. Return chicken to skillet, meaty side down. Cover; reduce heat. Simmer 15 minutes. Turn chicken pieces over; place green beans over chicken. Cover; simmer 20 to 30 minutes or until chicken is no longer pink in center, rice and green beans are tender and all liquid is absorbed. Garnish as desired. *Makes 6 servings*

Turkey Vegetable Crescent Pie

Spicy Turkey Casserole

1 tablespoon olive oil
1 pound turkey breast cutlets, cut into ½-inch pieces
2 (3-ounce) spicy chicken or turkey sausages, sliced ½-inch thick
1 cup diced green bell pepper
½ cup sliced mushrooms
½ cup diced onion
1 jalapeño pepper,* seeded and minced (optional)
½ cup fat-free reduced-sodium chicken broth or water
1 can (14 ounces) reduced-sodium diced tomatoes, undrained
1 teaspoon Italian seasoning
¼ teaspoon black pepper
½ teaspoon paprika
1 cup cooked egg yolk-free egg noodles
6 tablespoons grated Parmesan cheese
2 tablespoons coarse bread crumbs

**Jalapeño peppers can sting and irritate the skin; wear rubber gloves when handling peppers and do not touch eyes. Wash hands after handling.*

1. Preheat oven to 350°F. Heat oil in large nonstick skillet. Add turkey and sausages; cook and stir over meduim heat 2 minutes. Add bell pepper, mushrooms, onion and jalapeño pepper, if desired. Cook and stir 5 minutes. Add chicken broth; cook 1 minute, scraping any browned bits off bottom of skillet. Add tomatoes with juice, seasonings and noodles.

2. Spoon turkey mixture into shallow 10-inch round casserole. Sprinkle with cheese and bread crumbs. Bake 15 to 20 minutes or until mixture is hot and bread crumbs are brown.

Makes 6 (1-cup) servings

Roast Turkey Breast with Apple-Cornbread Stuffing

Nonstick cooking spray
1 medium onion, chopped
1¼ cups canned reduced-sodium chicken broth
1 package (8 ounces) prepared cornbread stuffing mix
1 Granny Smith apple, diced
¾ teaspoon dried sage, divided
¾ teaspoon dried thyme leaves, divided
1 (1½-pound) boneless turkey breast
1 teaspoon paprika
¼ teaspoon black pepper
1 cup canned whole berry cranberry sauce (optional)

1. Preheat oven to 450°F. Coat 1½ quart casserole with cooking spray; set aside. Coat large saucepan with cooking spray; heat over medium heat. Add onion; cook and stir 5 minutes. Add broth; bring to a simmer. Stir in stuffing mix, apple, ¼ teaspoon sage and ¼ teaspoon thyme. Transfer mixture to prepared casserole; set aside.

2. Coat a shallow roasting pan with cooking spray. Place turkey breast in pan, skin side up; coat with cooking spray. Mix paprika, remaining ½ teaspoon sage, ½ teaspoon thyme and pepper in small bowl; sprinkle over turkey. Spray lightly with cooking spray.

3. Place turkey in preheated oven; roast 15 minutes. *Reduce oven temperature to 350°F.* Place stuffing in oven alongside turkey; continue to roast 35 minutes or until internal temperature of turkey reaches 170°F when tested with meat thermometer inserted into the thickest part of breast. Transfer turkey to cutting board; cover with foil and let stand 10 to 15 minutes before carving. (Internal temperature will rise 5°F to 10°F during stand time.) Remove stuffing from oven; cover to keep warm. Carve turkey into thin slices; serve with stuffing and cranberry sauce, if desired.

Makes 6 servings

Stir-Fried Pasta with Chicken 'n' Vegetables

6 ounces angel hair pasta, broken in thirds (about 3 cups)
¼ cup *Frank's® RedHot®* Cayenne Pepper Sauce
3 tablespoons soy sauce
2 teaspoons cornstarch
1 tablespoon sugar
½ teaspoon garlic powder
1 pound boneless skinless chicken, cut in ¾-inch cubes
1 package (16 ounces) frozen stir-fry vegetables

1. Cook pasta in boiling water until just tender. Drain. Combine ***Frank's RedHot***, *¼ cup water,* soy sauce, cornstarch, sugar and garlic powder in small bowl; set aside.

2. Heat 1 tablespoon oil in large nonstick skillet over high heat. Stir-fry chicken 3 minutes. Add vegetables; stir-fry 3 minutes or until crisp-tender. Add ***Frank's RedHot*** mixture. Heat to boiling. Reduce heat to medium-low. Cook, stirring, 1 to 2 minutes or until sauce is thickened.

3. Stir pasta into skillet; toss to coat evenly. Serve hot.

Makes 4 servings

Prep Time: 5 minutes
Cook Time: 15 minutes

Spicy Turkey Casserole

Creole Shrimp and Rice

2 tablespoons olive oil
1 cup uncooked white rice
1 can (15 ounces) diced tomatoes with garlic, undrained
1 teaspoon Creole or Cajun seasoning blend
1 pound peeled cooked medium shrimp
1 package (10 ounces) frozen okra *or* 1½ cups frozen sugar snap peas, thawed

1. Heat oil in large skillet over medium heat until hot. Add rice; cook and stir 2 to 3 minutes or until opaque.

2. Add tomatoes with juice, 1½ cups water and seasoning blend; bring to a boil over high heat. Reduce heat to low. Cover; simmer 15 minutes.

3. Add shrimp and okra. Cook, covered, 3 minutes or until heated through. *Makes 4 servings*

Note: Okra are oblong green pods. When cooked, it gives off a viscous substance that acts as a good thickener.

Prep and Cook Time: 20 minutes

Scallop and Artichoke Heart Casserole

1 package (9 ounces) frozen artichoke hearts, cooked and drained
1 pound scallops
1 teaspoon canola or vegetable oil
¼ cup chopped red bell pepper
¼ cup sliced green onion tops
¼ cup all-purpose flour
2 cups low-fat (1%) milk
1 teaspoon dried tarragon leaves, crushed
¼ teaspoon salt
¼ teaspoon white pepper
1 tablespoon chopped fresh parsley
Dash paprika

Cut large artichoke hearts lengthwise into halves. Arrange artichoke hearts in even layer in 8-inch square baking dish.

Rinse scallops; pat dry with paper towel. If scallops are large, cut into halves. Arrange scallops evenly over artichokes.

Preheat oven to 350°F. Heat oil in medium saucepan over medium-low heat. Add bell pepper and green onions; cook and stir 5 minutes or until tender. Stir in flour. Gradually stir in milk until smooth. Add tarragon, salt and white pepper; cook and stir over medium heat 10 minutes or until sauce boils and thickens.

Pour hot sauce over scallops. Bake, uncovered, 25 minutes or until bubbling and scallops are opaque. Sprinkle with chopped parsley and paprika before serving.
Makes 4 servings

Impossibly Easy Salmon Pie

1 can (7½ ounces) salmon packed in water, drained and deboned
½ cup grated Parmesan cheese
¼ cup sliced green onions
1 jar (2 ounces) chopped pimiento, drained
½ cup 1% low-fat cottage cheese
1 tablespoon lemon juice
1½ cups low-fat (1%) milk
¾ cup reduced-fat baking and pancake mix
2 whole eggs
2 egg whites *or* ¼ cup egg substitute
¼ teaspoon dried dill weed
¼ teaspoon salt
¼ teaspoon paprika (optional)

1. Preheat oven to 375°F. Spray 9-inch pie plate with nonstick cooking spray. Combine salmon, Parmesan cheese, onions and pimiento in prepared pie plate; set aside.

2. Combine cottage cheese and lemon juice in blender or food processor; blend until smooth. Add milk, baking mix, whole eggs, egg whites, dill and salt. Blend 15 seconds. Pour over salmon mixture. Sprinkle with paprika, if desired.

3. Bake 35 to 40 minutes or until lightly golden and knife inserted halfway between center and edge comes out clean. Cool 5 minutes before serving. Garnish as desired.
Makes 8 servings

Creole Shrimp and Rice

Creamy Shrimp & Vegetable Casserole

1 can (10¾ ounces) reduced-fat cream of celery soup
1 pound fresh or thawed frozen shrimp, peeled and deveined
½ cup fresh asparagus *or* thawed frozen asparagus, cut diagonally into 1-inch pieces
½ cup sliced mushrooms
¼ cup sliced green onions
¼ cup diced red bell pepper
1 clove garlic, minced
¾ teaspoon dried thyme leaves
¼ teaspoon black pepper
Hot cooked rice or orzo

1. Preheat oven to 375°F. Coat 2-quart baking dish with nonstick cooking spray.

2. Combine soup, shrimp, asparagus, mushrooms, green onions, bell pepper, garlic, thyme and black pepper in large bowl; mix well. Place in prepared baking dish.

3. Cover and bake 30 minutes. Serve over rice, if desired.

Makes 4 servings

Shrimp Curry

1¼ pounds raw large shrimp
1 large onion, chopped
½ cup canned light coconut milk
3 cloves garlic, minced
2 tablespoons finely chopped fresh ginger
2 to 3 teaspoons hot curry powder
¼ teaspoon salt
1 can (14½ ounces) diced tomatoes
1 teaspoon cornstarch
2 tablespoons chopped fresh cilantro
3 cups hot cooked rice

1. Peel shrimp, leaving tails attached and reserving shells. Place shells in large saucepan; cover with water. Bring to a boil over high heat. Reduce heat to low; simmer 15 to 20 minutes. Strain shrimp stock and set aside. Discard shells.

2. Spray large skillet with nonstick cooking spray; heat over medium heat. Add onion; cover and cook 5 minutes. Add coconut milk, garlic, ginger, curry powder, salt and ½ cup shrimp stock; bring to a boil. Reduce heat to low and simmer 10 to 15 minutes or until onion is tender.

3. Add shrimp and tomatoes to skillet; return mixture to a simmer. Cook 3 minutes.

4. Stir cornstarch into 1 tablespoon cooled shrimp stock until dissolved. Add mixture to skillet with cilantro; simmer 1 to 2 minutes or just until slightly thickened, stirring occasionally. Serve over rice. Garnish with carrot and lime slices, if desired.

Makes 6 servings

Mediterranean Stew

1 medium butternut or acorn squash, peeled, seeded and cut into 1-inch cubes
2 cups unpeeled eggplant cut into 1-inch cubes
2 cups sliced zucchini
1 can (15½ ounces) chick-peas, rinsed and drained
1 package (10 ounces) frozen cut okra
1 can (8 ounces) tomato sauce
1 cup chopped onion
1 medium tomato, chopped
1 medium carrot, thinly sliced
½ cup reduced-sodium vegetable broth
⅓ cup raisins
1 clove garlic, minced
½ teaspoon ground cumin
½ teaspoon ground turmeric
¼ to ½ teaspoon ground red pepper
¼ teaspoon ground cinnamon
¼ teaspoon paprika
6 to 8 cups hot cooked couscous or rice
Fresh parsley (optional)

Slow Cooker Directions
Combine all ingredients except couscous and parsley in slow cooker; mix well. Cover and cook on LOW 8 to 10 hours or until vegetables are crisp-tender. Serve over couscous. Garnish with parsley, if desired.

Makes 6 servings

Mediterranean Stew

Ravioli with Homemade Tomato Sauce

- 3 cloves garlic, peeled
- ½ cup fresh basil leaves
- 3 cups seeded, peeled tomatoes, cut into quarters
- 2 tablespoons tomato paste
- 2 tablespoons fat-free Italian salad dressing
- 1 tablespoon balsamic vinegar
- ¼ teaspoon black pepper
- 1 package (9 ounces) refrigerated reduced-fat cheese ravioli
- 2 cups shredded spinach leaves
- 1 cup (4 ounces) shredded part-skim mozzarella cheese

Microwave Directions

1. To prepare tomato sauce, process garlic in food processor until coarsely chopped. Add basil; process until coarsely chopped. Add tomatoes, tomato paste, salad dressing, vinegar and pepper; process using on/off pulsing action until tomatoes are chopped.

2. Spray 9-inch square microwavable dish with nonstick cooking spray. Spread 1 cup tomato sauce in dish. Layer half of ravioli and spinach over tomato sauce. Repeat layers with 1 cup tomato sauce and remaining ravioli and spinach. Top with remaining 1 cup tomato sauce.

3. Cover with plastic wrap; refrigerate 1 to 8 hours. Vent plastic wrap. Microwave at MEDIUM (50%) 20 minutes or until pasta is tender and hot. Sprinkle with cheese. Microwave at HIGH 3 minutes or just until cheese melts. Let stand, covered, 5 minutes before serving.

Makes 6 servings

Black Bean & Rice Burritos

- ½ cup nonfat cottage cheese
- 2 tablespoons soft fresh goat cheese
- 1½ cups cooked brown rice or long-grain rice, kept warm
- 3 tablespoons minced red onion
- 3 tablespoons chopped fresh cilantro
- ¼ teaspoon ground cumin
- ¼ cup low-sodium chicken broth, defatted
- 8 whole wheat tortillas (6 inches each)
- ¾ cup GUILTLESS GOURMET® Spicy Black Bean Dip
- ½ cup (2 ounces) shredded low-fat Monterey Jack cheese
- 3 cups finely shredded lettuce
- ½ cup GUILTLESS GOURMET® Southwestern Grill Salsa
- Fresh cilantro sprigs (optional)

Preheat oven to 350°F. Place cottage and goat cheeses in medium bowl; blend with fork until smooth. Add rice, onion, chopped cilantro and cumin. Mix well; set aside.

Place broth in shallow bowl. Working with 1 tortilla at a time, dip tortilla in broth to moisten each side. Spread 1 heaping tablespoonful bean dip on tortilla, then top with 1 heaping tablespoonful rice mixture. Roll up tortilla and place in 12×8-inch baking dish, seam side down. Repeat with remaining tortillas, bean dip and rice mixture. Cover with foil.

Bake about 25 to 30 minutes or until heated through. Remove foil; top with shredded cheese. Return to oven until cheese melts. To serve, arrange burritos on plate. Top with lettuce and salsa. Garnish with cilantro sprigs, if desired.

Makes 8 burritos

Baked Provençal Ziti Provolone

- 10 ounces uncooked ziti
- 1 cup evaporated skimmed milk
- ½ cup skim milk
- 4 egg whites
- 1 tablespoon Dijon mustard
- ½ teaspoon salt
- ½ cup finely chopped green onions, with tops
- Black pepper
- 4 ounces sliced provolone cheese
- 2 tablespoons grated Parmesan cheese

1. Preheat oven to 325°F. Spray 9-inch square baking pan with nonstick cooking spray; set aside. Cook pasta according to package directions, omitting salt; drain. Place in bottom of prepared pan.

2. Meanwhile, combine evaporated milk, skim milk, egg whites, mustard and salt in food processor or blender; process until smooth.

3. Sprinkle green onions over pasta. Pour egg mixture over green onions. Sprinkle with pepper and top with provolone cheese.

4. Bake 35 minutes or until heated through. Remove from oven. Sprinkle with Parmesan cheese. Let stand 5 minutes before serving.

Makes 4 servings

Ravioli with Homemade Tomato Sauce

Cannelloni with Tomato-Eggplant Sauce

1 package (10 ounces) fresh spinach
1 cup fat-free ricotta cheese
4 egg whites, beaten
¼ cup (1 ounce) grated Parmesan cheese
2 tablespoons finely chopped fresh parsley
½ teaspoon salt (optional)
8 manicotti (about 4 ounces), cooked and cooled
Tomato-Eggplant Sauce (recipe follows)
1 cup (4 ounces) shredded reduced-fat mozzarella cheese

1. Preheat oven to 350°F.

2. Wash spinach; do not dry. Place spinach in saucepan; cook, covered, over medium heat 3 to 5 minutes or until spinach is wilted. Cool slightly and drain; chop finely.

3. Combine ricotta cheese, spinach, egg whites, Parmesan cheese, parsley and salt in large bowl; mix well. Spoon mixture into manicotti shells; arrange in 13×9-inch baking pan. Spoon Tomato-Eggplant Sauce over manicotti; sprinkle with mozzarella cheese.

4. Bake manicotti, uncovered, 25 to 30 minutes or until hot and bubbly.

Makes 4 servings (2 manicotti each)

Tomato-Eggplant Sauce

Olive oil-flavored nonstick cooking spray
1 small eggplant, coarsely chopped
½ cup chopped onion
2 cloves garlic, minced
½ teaspoon dried tarragon leaves
¼ teaspoon dried thyme leaves
1 can (16 ounces) no-salt-added whole tomatoes, undrained and coarsely chopped
Salt and black pepper

1. Spray large skillet with cooking spray; heat over medium heat until hot. Add eggplant, onion, garlic, tarragon and thyme; cook and stir about 5 minutes or until vegetables are tender.

2. Stir in tomatoes with juice; bring to a boil. Reduce heat and simmer, uncovered, 3 to 4 minutes. Season to taste with salt and pepper.

Makes about 2½ cups

Helpful Hints

Fat-free ricotta cheese is a good choice for this recipe. Although fat-free cheeses like Cheddar and mozzarella are available, they generally lack the flavor and melting properties of regular cheese. Consequently, reduced-fat Cheddar and mozzarella cheeses are a better option for light cooking.

Stacked Burrito Pie

½ cup GUILTLESS GOURMET® Mild Black Bean Dip
2 teaspoons water
5 low-fat flour tortillas (6 inches each)
½ cup nonfat sour cream or plain yogurt
½ cup GUILTLESS GOURMET® Roasted Red Pepper Salsa
1¼ cups (5 ounces) shredded low-fat Monterey Jack cheese
4 cups shredded iceberg or romaine lettuce
½ cup GUILTLESS GOURMET® Salsa (Roasted Red Pepper or Southwestern Grill)
Lime slices and chili pepper (optional)

Preheat oven to 350°F. Combine bean dip and 2 teaspoons water in small bowl; mix well. Line 7½-inch springform pan with 1 tortilla. Spread 2 tablespoons bean dip mixture over tortilla, then spread with 2 tablespoons sour cream and 2 tablespoons red pepper salsa. Sprinkle with ¼ cup cheese. Repeat layers 3 more times. Place remaining tortilla on top and sprinkle with remaining ¼ cup cheese.

Bake 40 minutes or until heated through. (Place sheet of foil under springform pan to catch any juices that may seep through the bottom.) Cool slightly before unmolding. To serve, cut into 4 quarters. Place 1 cup lettuce on each of 4 serving plates. Top each serving with 1 quarter burrito pie and 2 tablespoons salsa. Garnish with lime slices and pepper, if desired.

Makes 4 servings

Cannelloni with Tomato-Eggplant Sauce

Fresh Vegetable Lasagna

8 ounces uncooked lasagna noodles
1 package (10 ounces) frozen chopped spinach, thawed, well drained
1 cup shredded carrots
½ cup sliced green onions
½ cup sliced red bell pepper
¼ cup chopped fresh parsley
½ teaspoon black pepper
1½ cups low-fat cottage cheese
1 cup buttermilk
½ cup plain nonfat yogurt
2 egg whites
1 cup sliced mushrooms
1 can (14 ounces) artichoke hearts, drained and chopped
2 cups (8 ounces) shredded part-skim mozzarella cheese
¼ cup freshly grated Parmesan cheese

1. Cook pasta according to package directions, omitting salt. Drain. Rinse under cold water; drain well. Set aside.

2. Preheat oven to 375°F. Pat spinach with paper towels to remove excess moisture. Combine spinach, carrots, green onions, bell pepper, parsley and black pepper in large bowl. Set aside.

3. Combine cottage cheese, buttermilk, yogurt and egg whites in food processor or blender; process until smooth.

4. Spray 13×9-inch baking pan with nonstick cooking spray. Arrange a third of lasagna noodles in bottom of pan. Spread with half each of cottage cheese mixture, vegetable mixture, mushrooms, artichokes and mozzarella. Repeat layers, ending with noodles. Sprinkle with Parmesan.

5. Cover and bake 30 minutes. Remove cover; continue baking 20 minutes or until bubbly and heated through. Let stand 10 minutes before serving. *Makes 8 servings*

Three-Cheese Penne

2 cups uncooked penne pasta
Nonstick cooking spray
2 slices whole wheat bread, cut into cubes
2 cups nonfat cottage cheese
2 cups (8 ounces) shredded reduced-fat Cheddar cheese
1 cup chopped Roma tomatoes, divided
⅓ cup sliced green onions
¼ cup grated Parmesan cheese
¼ cup reduced-fat (2%) milk

1. Cook pasta according to package directions, omitting salt. Drain and rinse well under cold water until pasta is cool; drain well.

2. Spray large nonstick skillet with cooking spray; heat over medium heat until hot. Place bread cubes in skillet; spray bread cubes lightly with cooking spray. Cook and stir 5 minutes or until bread cubes are browned and crisp.

3. Preheat oven to 350°F. Combine pasta, cottage cheese, Cheddar cheese, ¾ cup tomatoes, green onions, Parmesan cheese and milk in medium bowl. Spray 2-quart casserole with nonstick cooking spray. Place pasta mixture in casserole. Top with remaining ¼ cup tomatoes and cooled bread cubes.

4. Bake 20 minutes or until heated through. Garnish, if desired.
Makes 6 servings

Double Spinach Bake

8 ounces uncooked spinach fettuccine noodles
1 cup fresh mushroom slices
1 green onion with top, finely chopped
1 clove garlic, minced
4 to 5 cups fresh spinach, coarsely chopped *or* 1 package (10 ounces) frozen spinach, thawed and drained
1 tablespoon water
1 container (15 ounces) nonfat ricotta cheese
¼ cup skim milk
1 egg
½ teaspoon ground nutmeg
½ teaspoon black pepper
¼ cup (1 ounce) shredded reduced-fat Swiss cheese

1. Preheat oven to 350°F. Cook noodles according to package directions, omitting salt. Drain; set aside.

2. Spray medium skillet with nonstick cooking spray. Add mushrooms, green onion and garlic. Cook and stir over medium heat until mushrooms are softened. Add spinach and water. Cover; cook until spinach is wilted, about 3 minutes.

3. Combine ricotta cheese, milk, egg, nutmeg and black pepper in large bowl. Gently stir in noodles and vegetables; toss to coat evenly.

4. Lightly coat shallow 1½-quart casserole with nonstick cooking spray. Spread noodle mixture in casserole. Sprinkle with Swiss cheese.

5. Bake 25 to 30 minutes or until knife inserted halfway into center comes out clean.
Makes 6 (1-cup) servings

Three-Cheese Penne

Bountiful Brunches

Breakfast Hash

1 pound BOB EVANS® Special Seasonings or Sage Roll Sausage
2 cups chopped potatoes
¼ cup chopped red and/or green bell pepper
2 tablespoons chopped onion
6 eggs
2 tablespoons milk

Crumble sausage into large skillet. Add potatoes, peppers and onion. Cook over low heat until sausage is browned and potatoes are fork-tender, stirring occasionally. Drain off any drippings. Whisk eggs and milk in small bowl until blended. Add to sausage mixture; scramble until eggs are set but not dry. Serve hot. Refrigerate leftovers.

Makes 6 to 8 servings

Serving Suggestion: Serve with fresh fruit.

Apple Brunch Strata

½ pound sausage, casing removed
4 cups cubed French bread
2 cups diced peeled Michigan Apples
¼ cup sliced green onions
⅓ cup sliced black olives
1½ cups (6 ounces) shredded sharp Cheddar cheese
2 cups reduced-fat milk
8 eggs
2 teaspoons spicy brown mustard
½ teaspoon salt
¼ teaspoon black pepper
Paprika

1. Brown sausage in skillet over medium-high heat. Drain on paper towels; set aside.

2. Spray 13×9×2-inch baking dish with nonstick cooking spray. Layer half of bread cubes in bottom of dish. Crumble sausage over bread. Top with Michigan Apples, green onions, olives and cheese. Place remaining bread on top.

3. Mix milk, eggs, mustard, salt and pepper in medium bowl; pour over bread. Cover with foil and refrigerate 4 hours or overnight.

4. Preheat oven to 350°F. Bake, covered, 45 minutes. Remove foil and bake 15 minutes or until center is set. Let stand 15 minutes before serving. Sprinkle with paprika, if desired.

Makes 8 servings

Tip: Suggested Michigan Apple varieties to use include Empire, Gala, Golden Delicious, Ida Red, Jonagold, Jonathan, McIntosh or Rome.

Variation: Substitute 1 can (20 ounces) sliced Michigan Apples, drained and chopped for fresh Apples.

Favorite recipe from **Michigan Apple Committee**

Breakfast Hash

Ham and Cheese Bread Pudding

- **1 small loaf (8 ounces) sourdough, country French or Italian bread, cut into 1-inch-thick slices**
- **3 tablespoons butter or margarine, softened**
- **8 ounces ham or smoked ham, cubed**
- **2 cups (8 ounces) shredded mild or sharp Cheddar cheese**
- **3 eggs**
- **2 cups milk**
- **1 teaspoon dry mustard**
- **½ teaspoon salt**
- **⅛ teaspoon white pepper**

1. Grease 11×7-inch baking dish. Spread 1 side of each bread slice with butter. Cut into 1-inch cubes; place on bottom of prepared dish. Top with ham; sprinkle with cheese.

2. Beat eggs in medium bowl. Whisk in milk, mustard, salt and pepper. Pour egg mixture evenly over bread mixture. Cover; refrigerate at least 6 hours or overnight.

3. Preheat oven to 350°F.

4. Bake bread pudding uncovered 45 to 50 minutes or until puffed and golden brown and knife inserted in center comes out clean. Garnish, if desired. Cut into squares. Serve immediately. *Makes 8 servings*

Acapulco Eggs

- **3 corn tortillas, cut into 2-inch strips**
- **3 tablespoons butter or margarine**
- **½ cup chopped onion**
- **1 can (14½ ounces) DEL MONTE® Mexican Recipe Stewed Tomatoes**
- **1 cup cooked ham, cut into thin strips, or shredded turkey**
- **½ cup green pepper strips**
- **6 eggs, beaten**
- **¾ cup shredded Monterey Jack cheese**

1. Cook tortilla strips in butter in large skillet until golden. Remove and set aside.

2. Cook onion in same skillet until tender. Drain tomatoes reserving liquid. Add reserved liquid to skillet; cook over high heat 3 minutes, stirring frequently.

3. Stir in tomatoes, ham and green pepper; heat through. Reduce heat to low; add tortillas and eggs.

4. Cover and cook 4 to 6 minutes or until eggs are set. Sprinkle with cheese; cover and cook 1 minute or until cheese is melted. Garnish with chopped cilantro or parsley, if desired. *Makes 4 to 6 servings*

Prep Time: 10 minutes
Cook Time: 15 minutes

Brunch Frittata

- **2 tablespoons vegetable oil**
- **2½ cups (12 ounces) frozen hash brown potatoes with onions and peppers (O'Brien style), thawed**
- **1 cup frozen broccoli florets, thawed**
- **6 eggs**
- **2 tablespoons half-and-half**
- **¾ teaspoon salt**
- **¼ teaspoon black pepper**
- **1 cup (4 ounces) shredded Cheddar cheese**
- **½ cup sour cream**

1. Preheat oven to 450°F. Heat oil in medium nonstick ovenproof skillet over medium heat until hot. Add potatoes; cook and stir 5 minutes. Add broccoli; cook and stir 1 minute.

2. Beat together eggs, half-and-half, salt and pepper in small bowl; pour over potato mixture. Cook 5 minutes or until edges are set (center will still be wet).

3. Transfer skillet to oven; bake 6 minutes or until center is set. Sprinkle with cheese; let stand 2 to 3 minutes or until cheese is melted.

4. Cut into wedges; serve with sour cream. *Makes 6 servings*

Helpful Hints

A frittata is an Italian omelet in which the eggs are combined with ingredients such as meat, vegetables, cheese and herbs and cooked in a skillet over low heat. The top of the frittata is finished by placing it under the broiler for a few minutes.

Ham and Cheese Bread Pudding

Sausage Vegetable Frittata

5 eggs
¼ cup milk
2 tablespoons grated Parmesan cheese
½ teaspoon dried oregano leaves
½ teaspoon black pepper
1 (10-ounce) package BOB EVANS® Skinless Link Sausage
2 tablespoons butter or margarine
1 small zucchini, sliced (about 1 cup)
½ cup shredded carrots
⅓ cup sliced green onions with tops
¾ cup (3 ounces) shredded Swiss cheese
Carrot curls (optional)

Whisk eggs in medium bowl; stir in milk, Parmesan cheese, oregano and pepper. Set aside. Cook sausage in large skillet over medium heat until browned, turning occasionally. Drain off any drippings. Remove sausage from skillet and cut into ½-inch lengths. Melt butter in same skillet. Add zucchini, shredded carrots and onions; cook and stir over medium heat until tender. Top with sausage, then Swiss cheese. Pour egg mixture over vegetable mixture. Stir gently to combine. Cook, without stirring, over low heat 8 to 10 minutes or until center is almost set. Remove from heat. Let stand 5 minutes before cutting into wedges; serve hot. Garnish with carrot curls, if desired. Refrigerate leftovers.

Makes 4 to 6 servings

Feta Brunch Bake

1 medium red bell pepper
2 bags (10 ounces each) fresh spinach, washed and stemmed
6 eggs
6 ounces crumbled feta cheese
⅓ cup chopped onion
2 tablespoons chopped fresh parsley
¼ teaspoon dried dill weed
Dash black pepper

Preheat broiler. Place bell pepper on foil-lined broiler pan. Broil, 4 inches from heat, 15 to 20 minutes or until blackened on all sides, turning every 5 minutes with tongs. Place in paper bag; close bag and set aside to cool about 15 to 20 minutes. To peel pepper, cut around core, twist and remove. Cut in half and peel off skin with paring knife; rinse under cold water to remove seeds. Cut into ½-inch pieces.

To blanch spinach, heat 1 quart water in 2-quart saucepan over high heat to a boil. Add spinach. Return to a boil; boil 2 to 3 minutes until crisp-tender. Drain and immediately plunge into cold water. Drain; let stand until cool enough to handle. Squeeze spinach to remove excess water. Finely chop.

Preheat oven to 400°F. Grease 1-quart baking dish. Beat eggs in large bowl with electric mixer at medium speed until foamy. Stir in bell pepper, spinach, cheese, onion, parsley, dill weed and black pepper. Pour egg mixture into prepared dish. Bake 20 minutes or until set. Let stand 5 minutes before serving. Garnish as desired.

Makes 4 servings

Garden Potato Casserole

1¼ pounds baking potatoes, unpeeled and sliced
1 small green or red bell pepper, thinly sliced
¼ cup finely chopped yellow onion
½ teaspoon salt
½ teaspoon dried thyme leaves
Black pepper to taste
2 tablespoons butter, cut into ⅛-inch pieces, divided
1 small yellow squash, thinly sliced
1 cup (4 ounces) shredded sharp Cheddar cheese

Slow Cooker Directions

1. Place potatoes, bell pepper, onion, salt, thyme, pepper and 1 tablespoon butter in slow cooker; mix well. Layer squash evenly over all and sprinkle with remaining 1 tablespoon butter. Cover and cook on LOW 7 hours or on HIGH 4 hours.

2. Remove potato mixture to serving platter. Sprinkle with cheese and let stand 2 to 3 minutes or until cheese melts.

Makes 5 servings

Sausage Vegetable Frittata

Egg & Sausage Casserole

- ½ pound pork sausage
- 3 tablespoons margarine or butter, divided
- 2 tablespoons all-purpose flour
- ¼ teaspoon salt
- ¼ teaspoon black pepper
- 1¼ cups milk
- 2 cups frozen hash brown potatoes
- 4 eggs, hard-boiled and sliced
- ½ cup cornflake crumbs
- ¼ cup sliced green onions

Preheat oven to 350°F. Spray 2-quart oval baking dish with nonstick cooking spray.

Crumble sausage into large skillet; brown over medium-high heat until no longer pink, stirring to separate meat. Drain sausage on paper towels. Discard fat and wipe skillet with paper towel.

Melt 2 tablespoons margarine in same skillet over medium heat. Stir in flour, salt and pepper until smooth. Gradually stir in milk; cook and stir until thickened. Add sausage, potatoes and eggs; stir to combine. Pour into prepared dish.

Melt remaining 1 tablespoon margarine. Combine cornflake crumbs and melted margarine in small bowl; sprinkle evenly over casserole.

Bake, uncovered, 30 minutes or until hot and bubbly. Sprinkle with onions.

Makes 6 servings

Make-Ahead Brunch Bake

- 1 pound bulk pork sausage
- 6 eggs, beaten
- 2 cups light cream or half-and-half
- ½ teaspoon salt
- 1 teaspoon ground mustard
- 1 cup (4 ounces) shredded Cheddar cheese
- 1⅓ cups *French's® Taste Toppers™* French Fried Onions

Crumble sausage into large skillet. Cook over medium-high heat until browned; drain well. Stir in eggs, cream, salt, mustard, *½ cup* cheese and ½ cup ***Taste Toppers***; mix well. Pour into greased 8×12-inch baking dish. Refrigerate, covered, 8 hours or overnight. Bake, uncovered, at 350°F for 45 minutes or until knife inserted in center comes out clean. Top with remaining cheese and ***Taste Toppers***; bake, uncovered, 5 minutes or until ***Taste Toppers*** are golden brown. Let stand 15 minutes before serving.

Makes 6 servings

Microwave Directions: Crumble sausage into 12×8-inch microwave-safe dish. Cook, covered, on HIGH 4 to 6 minutes or until sausage is cooked. Stir sausage halfway through cooking time. Drain well. Stir in ingredients and refrigerate as above. Cook, covered, 10 to 15 minutes or until center is firm. Stir egg mixture halfway through cooking time. Top with remaining cheese and ***Taste Toppers***; cook, uncovered, 1 minute or until cheese melts. Let stand 5 minutes.

Italian Vegetable Strata

- 1 loaf Italian bread
- 1⅓ cups *French's® Taste Toppers™* French Fried Onions, divided
- 1 cup (4 ounces) shredded mozzarella cheese, divided
- 1 small zucchini, thinly sliced
- 1 red bell pepper, sliced
- 5 eggs
- 2½ cups milk
- ⅓ cup (1½ ounces) grated Parmesan cheese
- ½ teaspoon *each* dried oregano and basil leaves

1. Preheat oven to 350°F. Grease 3-quart shallow baking dish. Cut enough slices of bread, ½ inch thick, to arrange single layer in bottom of dish, overlapping slices if necessary. Layer *⅔ cup* ***Taste Toppers***, *⅔ cup* mozzarella cheese, zucchini and bell pepper over bread.

2. Beat eggs, milk, Parmesan cheese, oregano, basil, *½ teaspoon salt* and *¼ teaspoon black pepper* in medium bowl. Pour over layers. Sprinkle with remaining *⅓ cup* mozzarella cheese. Let stand 10 minutes.

3. Bake 45 minutes or until knife inserted in center comes out clean. Sprinkle with remaining *⅔ cup* ***Taste Toppers***. Bake 5 minutes or until ***Taste Toppers*** are golden. Cool on wire rack 10 minutes. Cut into squares to serve.

Makes 8 servings

Prep Time: 10 minutes
Cook Time: 50 minutes

Egg & Sausage Casserole

Spicy Sausage Skillet Breakfast

2 bags SUCCESS® Rice
Vegetable cooking spray
1 pound bulk turkey sausage
½ cup chopped onion
1 can (10 ounces) tomatoes with green chilies, undrained
1 tablespoon chili powder
1 cup (4 ounces) shredded reduced-fat Monterey Jack cheese

Prepare rice according to package directions.

Lightly spray large skillet with cooking spray. Crumble sausage into prepared skillet. Cook over medium heat until lightly browned, stirring occasionally. Add onion; cook until tender. Stir in tomatoes, chili powder and rice; simmer 2 minutes. Reduce heat to low. Simmer until no liquid remains, about 8 minutes, stirring occasionally. Sprinkle with cheese.

Makes 6 to 8 servings

Mexican Omelet Roll-Ups with Avocado Sauce

8 eggs
2 tablespoons milk
1 tablespoon margarine or butter
1½ cups (6 ounces) shredded Monterey Jack cheese
1 large tomato, seeded and chopped
¼ cup chopped fresh cilantro
8 (7-inch) corn tortillas
1½ cups salsa
2 medium avocados, chopped
¼ cup reduced-calorie sour cream
2 tablespoons diced green chiles
1 tablespoon fresh lemon juice
1 teaspoon hot pepper sauce
¼ teaspoon salt

Preheat oven to 350°F. Spray 13×9-inch baking dish with nonstick cooking spray.

Whisk eggs and milk in medium bowl until blended. Melt margarine in large skillet over medium heat; add egg mixture to skillet. Cook and stir 5 minutes or until eggs are set, but still soft. Remove from heat. Stir in cheese, tomato and cilantro.

Spoon about ⅓ cup egg mixture evenly down center of each tortilla. Roll up tortillas and place seam side down in prepared dish. Pour salsa evenly over tortillas.

Cover tightly with foil and bake 20 minutes or until heated through. Meanwhile, process avocados, sour cream, chiles, lemon juice, hot pepper sauce and salt in food processor or blender until smooth. Serve tortillas with avocado sauce.

Makes 8 servings

Mom's Favorite Brunch Casserole

6 eggs
1 cup plain yogurt
1 cup (4 ounces) shredded Cheddar cheese
½ teaspoon black pepper
1 cup finely chopped ham
½ can (8 ounces) aerosol pasteurized process cheese

1. Preheat oven to 350°F. Lightly grease 12×8-inch baking dish.

2. Combine eggs and yogurt in medium bowl; beat with wire whisk until well blended. Stir in Cheddar cheese and pepper.

3. Place ham in prepared baking dish; pour egg mixture over ham. Bake 25 to 30 minutes or until egg mixture is set. Use process cheese to write "MOM" or other desired message to Mom on top of casserole; let stand 2 to 3 minutes or until cheese is slightly melted.

Makes 10 servings

Variation: Substitue 1 pound bulk pork sausage, browned and drained, for ham.

Helpful Hints

When planning a brunch, build the menu around an egg dish such as a strata, frittata or omelets. Choose fruit, muffins or quick breads, and fruit-based beverages to round out the menu.

Spicy Sausage Skillet Breakfast

French Toast Strata

4 ounces day-old French or Italian bread, cut into ¾-inch cubes (4 cups)
⅓ cup golden raisins
1 package (3 ounces) cream cheese, cut into ¼-inch cubes
3 eggs
1½ cups milk
½ cup maple-flavored pancake syrup
1 teaspoon vanilla
2 tablespoons sugar
1 teaspoon ground cinnamon
Additional maple-flavored pancake syrup (optional)

Spray 11×7-inch baking dish with nonstick cooking spray.

Place bread cubes in even layer in prepared dish; sprinkle raisins and cream cheese evenly over bread.

Beat eggs in medium bowl with electric mixer at medium speed until blended. Add milk, ½ cup pancake syrup and vanilla; mix well. Pour egg mixture evenly over bread mixture. Cover; refrigerate at least 4 hours or overnight.

Preheat oven to 350°F. Combine sugar and cinnamon in small bowl; sprinkle evenly over strata.

Bake, uncovered, 40 to 45 minutes or until puffed, golden brown and knife inserted in center comes out clean. Cut into squares and serve with additional pancake syrup, if desired.

Makes 6 servings

Serving Suggestion: Serve with fresh fruit compote.

Chiles Rellenos en Casserole

3 eggs, separated
¾ cup milk
¾ cup all-purpose flour
½ teaspoon salt
1 tablespoon butter or margarine
½ cup chopped onion
8 peeled roasted whole chilies *or* 2 cans (7 ounces each) whole green chilies, drained
8 ounces Monterey Jack cheese, cut into 8 slices

Condiments
Sour cream
Sliced green onions
Pitted black olive slices
Guacamole
Salsa

Preheat oven to 350°F. Place egg yolks, milk, flour and salt in blender or food processor container fitted with metal blade; process until smooth. Pour into bowl and let stand. Melt butter in small skillet over medium heat. Add onion; cook until tender. If using canned chilies, pat dry with paper towels. Slit each chili lengthwise and carefully remove seeds. Place 1 strip cheese and 1 tablespoon onion in each chili; reshape chilies to cover cheese. Place 2 chilies in each of 4 greased 1½-cup gratin dishes or place in single layer in 13×9-inch baking dish. Beat egg whites until soft peaks form; fold into yolk mixture. Dividing mixture evenly, pour over chilies in gratin dishes (or pour entire mixture over casserole). Bake 20 to 25 minutes or until topping is puffed and knife inserted in center comes out clean. Broil 4 inches below heat 30 seconds or until topping is golden brown. Serve with condiments.

Makes 4 servings

Corned Beef Hash

2 large russet potatoes, peeled and cut into ½-inch cubes
½ teaspoon salt
¼ teaspoon black pepper
¼ cup butter or margarine
1 large onion, chopped
8 ounces cooked corned beef, finely chopped
1 tablespoon prepared horseradish, drained
¼ cup whipping cream (optional)
4 poached or fried eggs

1. Place potatoes in 10-inch skillet. Cover potatoes with water. Bring to a boil over high heat. Reduce heat to low; simmer 6 minutes. (Potatoes will be firm.) Drain potatoes in colander; sprinkle with salt and pepper.

2. Wipe out skillet with paper towel. Add butter and onion; cook and stir over medium-high heat 5 minutes. Stir in corned beef, horseradish and potatoes; mix well. Press down mixture with spatula to flatten into compact layer.

3. Reduce heat to low. Drizzle cream evenly over mixture. Cook 10 to 15 minutes. Turn mixture with spatula; pat down and continue cooking 10 to 15 minutes or until bottom is well browned. Top each serving with poached egg. Serve immediately. Garnish, if desired.

Makes 4 servings

French Toast Strata

Easy Brunch Frittata

Nonstick cooking spray
1 cup small broccoli florets
2½ cups (12 ounces) frozen hash brown potatoes with onions and peppers (O'Brien style), thawed
1½ cups cholesterol-free egg substitute, thawed
2 tablespoons reduced-fat (2%) milk
¾ teaspoon salt
¼ teaspoon black pepper
½ cup (2 ounces) shredded reduced-fat Cheddar cheese

1. Preheat oven to 450°F. Coat medium nonstick ovenproof skillet with nonstick cooking spray. Heat skillet over medium heat until hot. Add broccoli; cook and stir 2 minutes. Add potatoes; cook and stir 5 minutes.

2. Beat together egg substitute, milk, salt and pepper in small bowl; pour over potato mixture. Cook 5 minutes or until edges are set (center will still be wet).

3. Transfer skillet to oven; bake 6 minutes or until center is set. Sprinkle with cheese; let stand 2 to 3 minutes or until cheese is melted.

4. Cut into wedges; serve with sour cream, if desired.

Makes 6 servings

Parmesan and Roasted Red Pepper Strata

1 loaf (16 ounces) French bread, cut into ½-inch-thick slices
2 jars (7½ ounces each) roasted red peppers, drained and cut into ½-inch pieces
1 cup grated Parmesan cheese
1 cup sliced green onions
3 cups (12 ounces) shredded mozzarella cheese
8 eggs
¾ cup reduced-fat (2%) milk
1 container (7 ounces) prepared pesto
2 teaspoons minced garlic
¾ teaspoon salt

1. Grease 13×9-inch baking dish. Arrange half of bread slices in single layer on bottom of prepared baking dish. Top bread with half of red peppers, ½ cup Parmesan, ½ cup green onions and 1½ cups mozzarella. Repeat layers with remaining bread, red peppers, Parmesan, green onions and mozzarella.

2. Combine eggs, milk, pesto, garlic and salt in medium bowl; whisk to combine. Pour egg mixture evenly over strata. Cover and refrigerate overnight.

3. Preheat oven to 375°F. Bake, uncovered, 30 minutes or until hot and bubbly. *Makes 6 servings*

Note: If time allows, you may want to let strata stand at room temperature about 15 minutes before baking.

Mushroom & Onion Egg Bake

1 tablespoon vegetable oil
4 green onions, chopped
4 ounces mushrooms, sliced
1 cup low-fat cottage cheese
1 cup sour cream
6 eggs
2 tablespoons all-purpose flour
¼ teaspoon salt
⅛ teaspoon black pepper
Dash hot pepper sauce

1. Preheat oven to 350°F. Grease shallow 1-quart baking dish.

2. Heat oil in medium skillet over medium heat. Add onions and mushrooms; cook until tender. Set aside.

3. In blender or food processor, process cottage cheese until almost smooth. Add sour cream, eggs, flour, salt, pepper and hot pepper sauce; process until combined. Stir in onions and mushrooms. Pour into greased dish. Bake about 40 minutes or until knife inserted near center comes out clean. *Makes about 6 servings*

Easy Brunch Frittata

Potato and Egg Pie

1 package (20 ounces) frozen O'Brien hash brown potatoes, thawed
⅓ cup WESSON® Vegetable Oil
1½ tablespoons chopped fresh parsley, divided
¾ cup shredded pepper-Jack cheese
¾ cup shredded Swiss cheese
1 package (12 ounces) bulk breakfast sausage, cooked, crumbled and drained
1 can (4 ounces) sliced mushrooms, drained
½ cup milk
4 eggs, beaten
1 teaspoon garlic salt
¼ teaspoon pepper
4 to 6 thin tomato slices

Preheat oven to 425°F. In medium bowl, combine potatoes and Wesson® Oil; blend to coat. Press mixture into a 10-inch pie dish. Bake for 30 minutes or until golden brown; remove from oven. *Reduce oven temperature to 350°F.* Meanwhile, in large bowl, combine 1 tablespoon parsley and *remaining* ingredients *except* tomato slices; blend well. Pour into potato crust. Bake for 25 minutes or until eggs are set. Place tomato slices over pie and top with *remaining* parsley. Bake 5 to 7 minutes longer.

Makes 6 servings

Sausage & Apple Quiche

1 (9-inch) unbaked pastry shell, 1½ inches deep
½ pound bulk spicy pork sausage
½ cup chopped onion
¾ cup shredded peeled tart apple
1 tablespoon lemon juice
1 tablespoon sugar
⅛ teaspoon red pepper flakes
1 cup (4 ounces) shredded Cheddar cheese
3 eggs
1½ cups half-and-half
¼ teaspoon salt
Dash black pepper

Preheat oven to 450°F. Line pastry shell with foil; partially fill with uncooked beans or rice to weight shell. Bake 10 minutes. Remove foil and beans; continue baking pastry 5 minutes or until lightly browned. Let cool. *Reduce oven temperature to 375°F.*

Crumble sausage into large skillet; add onion. Cook and stir over medium heat until sausage is browned and onion is tender. Spoon off and discard pan drippings. Add apple, lemon juice, sugar and red pepper flakes. Cook over medium-high heat 4 minutes or until apple is barely tender and all liquid is evaporated, stirring constantly. Let cool. Spoon sausage mixture into pastry shell; top with cheese. Whisk eggs, half-and-half, salt and black pepper in medium bowl. Pour over sausage mixture. Bake 35 to 45 minutes or until filling is puffed and knife inserted in center comes out clean. Let stand 10 minutes before cutting to serve.

Makes 6 servings

Oven Breakfast Hash

2 pounds baking potatoes, unpeeled (5 or 6 medium)
1 pound BOB EVANS® Original Recipe Roll Sausage
1 (12-ounce can) evaporated milk
⅓ cup chopped green onions
1 tablespoon Worcestershire sauce
½ teaspoon salt
¼ teaspoon black pepper
¼ cup dried bread crumbs
1 tablespoon melted butter or margarine
½ teaspoon paprika

Cook potatoes in boiling water until fork-tender. Drain and coarsely chop or mash. Preheat oven to 350°F. Crumble and cook sausage in medium skillet until browned. Drain and transfer to large bowl. Stir in potatoes, milk, green onions, Worcestershire sauce, salt and pepper. Pour into greased 2½- or 3-quart casserole dish. Sprinkle with bread crumbs; drizzle with melted butter. Sprinkle with paprika. Bake, uncovered, 30 to 35 minutes or until casserole bubbles and top is browned. Refrigerate leftovers.

Makes 6 to 8 servings

Potato and Egg Pie

Brunch Eggs Olé

- **8 eggs**
- **½ cup all-purpose flour**
- **1 teaspoon baking powder**
- **¾ teaspoon salt**
- **2 cups (8 ounces) shredded Monterey Jack cheese with jalapeño peppers**
- **1½ cups (12 ounces) small curd cottage cheese**
- **1 cup (4 ounces) shredded sharp Cheddar cheese**
- **1 jalapeño pepper,* seeded and chopped**
- **½ teaspoon hot pepper sauce**
- **Fresh Salsa (recipe follows)**

**Jalapeño peppers can sting and irritate the skin; wear rubber gloves when handling peppers and do not touch eyes. Wash hands after handling.*

1. Preheat oven to 350°F. Grease 9-inch square baking pan.

2. Beat eggs in large bowl at high speed with electric mixer 4 to 5 minutes or until slightly thickened and lemon colored.

3. Combine flour, baking powder and salt in small bowl. Stir flour mixture into eggs until blended.

4. Combine Monterey Jack cheese, cottage cheese, Cheddar cheese, jalapeño pepper and hot pepper sauce in medium bowl; mix well. Fold into egg mixture until well blended. Pour into prepared pan.

5. Bake 45 to 50 minutes or until golden brown and firm in center. Let stand 10 minutes before cutting into squares to serve. Serve with Fresh Salsa. Garnish as desired.

Makes 8 servings

Fresh Salsa

- **3 medium plum tomatoes, seeded and chopped**
- **2 tablespoons chopped onion**
- **1 small jalapeño pepper,* stemmed, seeded and minced**
- **1 tablespoon chopped fresh cilantro**
- **1 tablespoon lime juice**
- **¼ teaspoon salt**
- **⅛ teaspoon black pepper**

**Jalapeño peppers can sting and irritate the skin; wear rubber gloves when handling peppers and do not touch eyes. Wash hands after handling.*

Stir together tomatoes, onion, jalapeño pepper, cilantro, lime juice, salt and black pepper in small bowl. Refrigerate until ready to serve.

Makes 1 cup

Roasted Pepper and Sourdough Brunch Casserole

- **3 cups sourdough bread cubes**
- **1 jar (12 ounces) roasted pepper strips, drained**
- **1 cup (4 ounces) shredded reduced-fat sharp Cheddar cheese**
- **1 cup (4 ounces) shredded reduced-fat Monterey Jack cheese**
- **1 cup nonfat cottage cheese**
- **12 ounces cholesterol-free egg substitute**
- **1 cup fat-free (skim) milk**
- **¼ cup chopped fresh cilantro**
- **¼ teaspoon black pepper**

1. Spray 11×9-inch baking pan with nonstick cooking spray. Place bread cubes in pan. Arrange roasted peppers evenly over bread cubes. Sprinkle Cheddar and Monterey Jack cheeses over peppers.

2. Place cottage cheese in food processor or blender; process until smooth. Add egg substitute; process 10 seconds. Combine cottage cheese mixture and milk in small bowl; pour over ingredients in baking pan. Sprinkle with cilantro and black pepper. Cover with plastic wrap; refrigerate 4 to 12 hours.

3. Preheat oven to 375°F. Bake, uncovered, 40 minutes or until hot and bubbly and golden brown on top.

Makes 8 servings

Sausage and Cheese Potato Casserole

- **1 pound BOB EVANS® Italian Roll Sausage**
- **4 cups cubed unpeeled red skin potatoes**
- **1 cup (4 ounces) shredded Monterey Jack cheese**
- **¼ cup chopped green onions**
- **1 (4-ounce) can chopped green chiles, drained**
- **6 eggs**
- **¾ cup milk**
- **¼ teaspoon salt**
- **⅛ teaspoon black pepper**
- **½ cup grated Parmesan cheese**

Preheat oven to 350°F. Crumble and cook sausage in medium skillet until browned. Drain off any drippings. Spread potatoes in greased 13×9-inch baking pan. Top with cooked sausage, Monterey Jack cheese, green onions and chiles. Whisk eggs, milk, salt and pepper in medium bowl until frothy. Pour egg mixture over sausage layer; bake 30 minutes. Remove from oven. Sprinkle with Parmesan cheese; bake 15 minutes more or until eggs are set. Refrigerate leftovers.

Makes 6 to 8 servings

Brunch Eggs Olé

Bacon & Potato Frittata

2 cups frozen O'Brien-style potatoes with onions and peppers
3 tablespoons butter or margarine
5 eggs
½ cup canned real bacon pieces
¼ cup half-and-half or milk
⅛ teaspoon salt
⅛ teaspoon black pepper

1. Preheat broiler. Place potatoes in microwavable medium bowl; microwave at HIGH 1 minute.

2. Melt butter in large ovenproof skillet over medium-high heat. Swirl butter up side of pan to prevent eggs from sticking. Add potatoes; cook 3 minutes, stirring occasionally.

3. Beat eggs in medium bowl. Add bacon, half-and-half, salt and black pepper; mix well.

4. Pour egg mixture into skillet; reduce heat to medium. Stir gently to incorporate potatoes. Cover and cook 6 minutes or until eggs are set at edges (top will still be wet).

5. Transfer skillet to broiler. Broil 4 inches from heat about 1 to 2 minutes or until center is set and frittata is golden brown. Cut into wedges. *Makes 4 servings*

Serving Suggestion: Garnish frittata with red bell pepper strips, chopped chives and salsa.

Prep and Cook Time: 20 minutes

Spinach and Cheese Brunch Squares

1 box (11 ounces) pie crust mix
⅓ cup cold water
1 package (10 ounces) frozen chopped spinach, thawed and well drained
1⅓ cups *French's® Taste Toppers™* French Fried Onions
1 cup (4 ounces) shredded Swiss cheese
1 container (8 ounces) low-fat sour cream
5 eggs
1 cup milk
1 tablespoon *French's®* Hearty Deli Brown Mustard
½ teaspoon salt
⅛ teaspoon ground black pepper

Preheat oven to 450°F. Line 13×9×2-inch baking pan with foil; spray with nonstick cooking spray. Combine pie crust mix and water in large bowl until moistened and crumbly. Using floured bottom of measuring cup, press mixture firmly into bottom of prepared pan. Prick with fork. Bake 20 minutes or until golden. *Reduce oven temperature to 350°F.*

Layer spinach, ***Taste Toppers*** and cheese over crust. Combine sour cream, eggs, milk, mustard, salt and pepper in medium bowl; mix until well blended. Pour over vegetable and cheese layers. Bake 30 minutes or until knife inserted in center comes out clean. Let stand 10 minutes. Cut into squares* to serve.
Makes 8 main-course servings

*To serve as appetizers, cut into 2-inch squares.

Prep Time: 20 minutes
Cook Time: 50 minutes
Stand Time: 10 minutes

Spiced Apple & Cranberry Compote

Slow Cooker

2½ cups cranberry juice cocktail
1 package (6 ounces) dried apples
½ cup (2 ounces) dried cranberries
½ cup Rhine wine or apple juice
½ cup honey
2 cinnamon sticks, broken into halves
Frozen yogurt or ice cream (optional)
Additional cinnamon sticks (optional)

Slow Cooker Directions
Mix juice, apples, cranberries, wine, honey and cinnamon stick halves in slow cooker. Cover and cook on LOW 4 to 5 hours or until liquid is absorbed and fruit is tender. Remove and discard cinnamon stick halves. Ladle compote into bowls. Serve warm, at room temperature or chilled with scoop of frozen yogurt or ice cream and garnish with additional cinnamon sticks, if desired.
Makes 6 servings

Bacon & Potato Frittata

Cheddar and Leek Strata

8 eggs, lightly beaten
2 cups milk
½ cup ale or beer
2 cloves garlic, minced
¼ teaspoon salt
¼ teaspoon black pepper
1 loaf (16 ounces) sourdough bread, cut into ½-inch cubes
2 small leeks, coarsely chopped
1 red bell pepper, chopped
1½ cups (6 ounces) shredded Swiss cheese
1½ cups (6 ounces) shredded sharp Cheddar cheese

1. Combine eggs, milk, ale, garlic, salt and black pepper in large bowl. Beat until well blended.

2. Place ½ of bread cubes on bottom of greased 13×9-inch baking dish. Sprinkle ½ of leeks and ½ of bell pepper over bread cubes. Top with ¾ cup Swiss cheese and ¾ cup Cheddar cheese. Repeat layers with remaining ingredients, ending with Cheddar cheese.

3. Pour egg mixture evenly over top. Cover tightly with plastic wrap or foil. Weight top of strata down with slightly smaller baking dish. Refrigerate strata at least 2 hours or overnight.

4. Preheat oven to 350°F. Bake uncovered 40 to 45 minutes or until center is set. Garnish with fresh sage, if desired. Serve immediately.

Makes 12 servings

Skillet Sausage with Potatoes and Rosemary

1 tablespoon vegetable oil
3 cups diced red skin potatoes
1 cup diced onion
1 pound BOB EVANS® Original Recipe Roll Sausage
½ teaspoon dried rosemary
¼ teaspoon rubbed sage
Salt and black pepper to taste
2 tablespoons chopped fresh parsley

Heat oil in large skillet over medium-high heat 1 minute. Add potatoes; cook 5 to 10 minutes or until slightly brown, stirring occasionally. Add onion; cook until tender. Add crumbled sausage; cook until browned. Add rosemary, sage, salt and pepper; cook and stir until well blended. Transfer to serving platter and garnish with parsley. Refrigerate leftovers. *Makes 4 to 6 servings*

Spinach Cheese Strata

6 slices whole wheat bread
2 tablespoons butter or margarine, softened
1 cup (4 ounces) shredded Cheddar cheese
½ cup (2 ounces) shredded Monterey Jack cheese
1¼ cups milk
6 eggs, lightly beaten
1 package (10 ounces) frozen spinach, thawed and well drained
¼ teaspoon salt
⅛ teaspoon black pepper

1. Spread bread with butter. Arrange buttered slices in single layer in greased 13×9-inch baking dish. Sprinkle with cheeses.

2. Combine milk, eggs, spinach, salt and pepper in large bowl; stir well. Pour over bread and cheese.

3. Cover; refrigerate at least 6 hours or overnight.

4. Bake, uncovered, at 350°F about 1 hour or until puffy and lightly golden. *Makes 4 to 6 servings*

Helpful Hints

A strata is a cross between custard and French toast. It consists of bread, cheese and often meat and/or vegetables. A mixture of eggs and milk is poured over the other ingredients and the dish is allowed to stand in the refrigerator overnight before baking.

Cheddar and Leek Strata

Boston Brown Bread

3 (16-ounce) cleaned and emptied vegetable cans
½ cup rye flour
½ cup yellow cornmeal
½ cup whole wheat flour
3 tablespoons sugar
1 teaspoon baking soda
¾ teaspoon salt
½ cup chopped walnuts
½ cup raisins
1 cup buttermilk*
⅓ cup molasses

**Soured fresh milk may be substituted. To sour, place 1 tablespoon lemon juice plus enough milk to equal 1 cup in 2-cup measure. Stir; let stand 5 minutes before using.*

Slow Cooker Directions
Spray vegetable cans and 1 side of three 6-inch-square pieces of foil with nonstick cooking spray; set aside. Combine rye flour, cornmeal, whole wheat flour, sugar, baking soda and salt in large bowl. Stir in walnuts and raisins. Whisk buttermilk and molasses in medium bowl until blended. Add buttermilk mixture to dry ingredients; stir until well mixed. Spoon mixture evenly into prepared cans. Place 1 piece of foil, greased side down, on top of each can. Secure foil with rubber bands or cotton string.

Place filled cans in slow cooker. Pour boiling water into slow cooker to come halfway up sides of cans. (Make sure foil tops do not touch boiling water.) Cover and cook on LOW 4 hours or until skewer inserted in centers comes out clean. To remove bread, lay cans on side; roll and tap gently on all sides until bread releases. Cool completely on wire racks. *Makes 3 loaves*

Spinach Pie

1 tablespoon olive oil
1 pound fresh spinach, washed, drained and stems removed
1 medium potato, cooked and mashed
2 eggs, beaten
¼ cup cottage cheese
¼ cup grated BELGIOIOSO® Romano Cheese
Salt

Preheat oven to 350°F. Grease 8-inch round cake pan with olive oil. Tear spinach into bite-sized pieces. Combine spinach, potato, eggs, cottage cheese and BelGioioso Romano Cheese in large bowl. Spoon mixture into prepared pan. Bake 15 to 20 minutes or until set. Season to taste with salt.

Makes 6 servings

Helpful Hints

When choosing loose spinach, look for leaves with a crisp texture and fresh aroma. When purchasing prepackaged spinach, squeeze the bag to check if the contents are resilient and thus fresh and crisp.

Spinach Sensation

½ pound bacon slices
1 cup (8 ounces) sour cream
3 eggs, separated
2 tablespoons all-purpose flour
⅛ teaspoon black pepper
1 package (10 ounces) frozen chopped spinach, thawed and squeezed dry
½ cup (2 ounces) shredded sharp Cheddar cheese
½ cup dry bread crumbs
1 tablespoon margarine or butter, melted

Preheat oven to 350°F. Spray 2-quart round baking dish with nonstick cooking spray.

Place bacon in single layer in large skillet; cook over medium heat until crisp. Remove from skillet; drain on paper towels. Crumble and set aside.

Combine sour cream, egg yolks, flour and pepper in large bowl; set aside. Beat egg whites in medium bowl with electric mixer at high speed until stiff peaks form. Stir ¼ of egg whites into sour cream mixture; fold in remaining egg whites.

Arrange half of spinach in prepared dish. Top with half of sour cream mixture. Sprinkle ¼ cup cheese over sour cream mixture. Sprinkle bacon over cheese. Repeat layers, ending with remaining ¼ cup cheese.

Combine bread crumbs and margarine in small bowl; sprinkle evenly over cheese.

Bake, uncovered, 30 to 35 minutes or until egg mixture is set. Let stand 5 minutes before serving.

Makes 6 servings

Boston Brown Bread

Ham and Egg Enchiladas

2 tablespoons butter or margarine
1 small red bell pepper, chopped
3 green onions with tops, sliced
½ cup diced ham
8 eggs
8 (7- to 8-inch) flour tortillas
2 cups (8 ounces) shredded Colby-Jack cheese or Monterey Jack cheese with jalapeño peppers, divided
1 can (10 ounces) enchilada sauce
½ cup prepared salsa
Sliced avocado, fresh cilantro and red pepper slices for garnish

1. Preheat oven to 350°F.

2. Melt butter in large nonstick skillet over medium heat. Add bell pepper and onions; cook and stir 2 minutes. Add ham; cook and stir 1 minute.

3. Lightly beat eggs with wire whisk in medium bowl. Add eggs to skillet; cook until eggs are set, but still soft, stirring occasionally.

4. Spoon about ⅓ cup egg mixture evenly down center of each tortilla; top with 1 tablespoon cheese. Roll tortillas up and place seam side down in shallow 11×7-inch baking dish.

5. Combine enchilada sauce and salsa in small bowl; pour evenly over enchiladas.

6. Cover enchiladas with foil; bake 20 minutes. Uncover; sprinkle with remaining cheese. Continue baking 10 minutes or until enchiladas are hot and cheese is melted. Garnish, if desired. Serve immediately.

Makes 4 servings

Sunrise Squares

1 pound BOB EVANS® Original Recipe Roll Sausage
2 slices bread, cut into ½-inch cubes (about 2 cups)
1 cup (4 ounces) shredded sharp Cheddar cheese
6 eggs
2 cups milk
½ teaspoon salt
½ teaspoon dry mustard

Preheat oven to 350°F. Crumble sausage into medium skillet. Cook over medium heat until browned, stirring occasionally. Drain off any drippings. Spread bread cubes in greased 11×7-inch baking dish; top with sausage and cheese. Whisk eggs, milk, salt and mustard until well blended; pour over cheese. Bake 30 to 40 minutes or until set. Let stand 5 minutes before cutting into squares; serve hot. Refrigerate leftovers. *Makes 6 servings*

Tip: You can make this tasty meal ahead and refrigerate overnight before baking.

Serving Suggestion: Serve squares between toasted English muffins.

Weekend Brunch Casserole

1 pound BOB EVANS® Original Recipe Roll Sausage
1 (8-ounce) can refrigerated crescent dinner rolls
2 cups (8 ounces) shredded mozzarella cheese
4 eggs, beaten
¾ cup milk
¼ teaspoon salt
⅛ teaspoon black pepper

Preheat oven to 425°F. Crumble sausage into medium skillet. Cook over medium heat until browned, stirring occasionally. Drain off any drippings. Line bottom of greased 13×9-inch baking dish with crescent roll dough, firmly pressing perforations to seal. Sprinkle with sausage and cheese. Combine remaining ingredients in medium bowl until blended; pour over sausage. Bake 15 minutes or until set. Let stand 5 minutes before cutting into squares; serve hot. Refrigerate leftovers. *Makes 6 to 8 servings*

Serving Suggestion: Serve with fresh fruit or sliced tomatoes.

Helpful Hints

For a practical and beautiful centerpiece on your brunch table, fill a straight-side glass dish with a fresh fruit compote. Choose fruits of different colors. Fruit is an ideal accompaniment for brunch dishes like those above.

Ham and Egg Enchiladas

The publisher would like to thank the companies and organizations listed below for the use of their recipes and photographs in this publication.

A.1.® Steak Sauce

American Italian Pasta Company—Pasta LaBella

BelGioioso® Cheese, Inc.

Birds Eye®

Bob Evans®

Butterball® Turkey Company

California Olive Industry

Clamato® is a registered trademark of Mott's, Inc.

ConAgra Grocery Products Company

Del Monte Corporation

Dole Food Company, Inc.

Fleischmann's® Original Spread

The Fremont Company, Makers of Frank's & SnowFloss Kraut and Tomato Products

Grey Poupon® Dijon Mustard

Guiltless Gourmet®

Harveys® Bristol Cream®

Heinz U.S.A.

Hormel Foods, LLC

The HV Company

Kikkoman International Inc.

Kraft Foods Holdings

Lawry's® Foods, Inc.

McIlhenny Company (TABASCO® brand Pepper Sauce)

Michigan Apple Committee

Minnesota Cultivated Wild Rice Council

Holland House® is a registered trademark of Mott's, Inc.

Mrs. Dash®

National Fisheries Institute

National Honey Board

National Pork Board

National Turkey Federation

Nestlé USA

New Jersey Department of Agriculture

Norseland, Inc. / Lucini Italia Co.

The Procter & Gamble Company

Reckitt Benckiser

Riviana Foods Inc.

The J.M. Smucker Company

StarKist® Seafood Company

Tyson Foods, Inc.

Uncle Ben's Inc.

Unilever Bestfoods North America

USA Rice Federation

Veg-All®

Washington Apple Commission

Wisconsin Milk Marketing Board

METRIC CONVERSION CHART

VOLUME MEASUREMENTS (dry)

1/8 teaspoon = 0.5 mL
1/4 teaspoon = 1 mL
1/2 teaspoon = 2 mL
3/4 teaspoon = 4 mL
1 teaspoon = 5 mL
1 tablespoon = 15 mL
2 tablespoons = 30 mL
1/4 cup = 60 mL
1/3 cup = 75 mL
1/2 cup = 125 mL
2/3 cup = 150 mL
3/4 cup = 175 mL
1 cup = 250 mL
2 cups = 1 pint = 500 mL
3 cups = 750 mL
4 cups = 1 quart = 1 L

VOLUME MEASUREMENTS (fluid)

1 fluid ounce (2 tablespoons) = 30 mL
4 fluid ounces (1/2 cup) = 125 mL
8 fluid ounces (1 cup) = 250 mL
12 fluid ounces (1 1/2 cups) = 375 mL
16 fluid ounces (2 cups) = 500 mL

WEIGHTS (mass)

1/2 ounce = 15 g
1 ounce = 30 g
3 ounces = 90 g
4 ounces = 120 g
8 ounces = 225 g
10 ounces = 285 g
12 ounces = 360 g
16 ounces = 1 pound = 450 g

DIMENSIONS

1/16 inch = 2 mm
1/8 inch = 3 mm
1/4 inch = 6 mm
1/2 inch = 1.5 cm
3/4 inch = 2 cm
1 inch = 2.5 cm

OVEN TEMPERATURES

250°F = 120°C
275°F = 140°C
300°F = 150°C
325°F = 160°C
350°F = 180°C
375°F = 190°C
400°F = 200°C
425°F = 220°C
450°F = 230°C

BAKING PAN SIZES

Utensil	Size in Inches/Quarts	Metric Volume	Size in Centimeters
Baking or Cake Pan (square or rectangular)	8×8×2	2 L	20×20×5
	9×9×2	2.5 L	23×23×5
	12×8×2	3 L	30×20×5
	13×9×2	3.5 L	33×23×5
Loaf Pan	8×4×3	1.5 L	20×10×7
	9×5×3	2 L	23×13×7
Round Layer Cake Pan	8×1½	1.2 L	20×4
	9×1½	1.5 L	23×4
Pie Plate	8×1¼	750 mL	20×3
	9×1¼	1 L	23×3
Baking Dish or Casserole	1 quart	1 L	—
	1½ quart	1.5 L	—
	2 quart	2 L	—